Attacks on the Press
in 1996

330 Seventh Avenue, 12th Floor
New York, New York 10001
Phone: (212) 465-1004
Fax: (212) 465-9568
E-Mail: info@cpj.org
Web site: http://www.cpj.org

Begun in 1981, the Committee to Protect Journalists responds to attacks on the press everywhere in the world. CPJ investigates more than 2,000 cases every year and takes action on behalf of journalists and their news organizations without regard to political ideology. Join CPJ and help promote press freedom by defending the people who report the news. To maintain its independence, CPJ accepts no government funding. We depend entirely on your support.

Agence France-Presse, The Associated Press, IDT, LEXIS•NEXIS, and Reuters provided electronic news and Internet services that were used to conduct research for this report.

 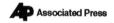 

Cover Photo: Israeli border police and soldiers detain a Palestinian journalist trying to film in Hebron at the border between Palestinian areas and the Jewish settlement, late 1996.

Editor: Alice Chasan
Deputy Editor: Julianne Slovak
Editorial Assistant: Ariana Speyer
Design and Layout Artist: James Bucknell
Special thanks to: Jeanne Sahadi

Attacks on the Press in 1996: A Worldwide Survey by the Committee to Protect Journalists
ISSN: 1078-3334
ISBN: 0-944823-16-5

CPJ Board of Directors

Preface

by Kati Marton

Subconsciously, I suppose, I have been preparing for my role as chair of the Committee to Protect Journalists since the day that I witnessed the arrest of my parents, Hungarian journalists, during the chilliest days of the Cold War. They were wire-service reporters guilty only of recounting the grim events of the 1950s in Eastern Europe. I did not see my mother for a year and my father for close to two years after their arrest in early 1955. I was a small child, but the experience of seeing my parents led away by Hungarian secret policemen while the world stood by passively left a permanent mark.

In the past two and a half years, as chair of CPJ, I have worked hard to spare other small children from a similar feeling of anger and helplessness. As this report makes all too clear, we at CPJ cannot assure the safety of our colleagues working under circumstances similar to those of my parents during the Cold War. What we can do is call attention to the obscenity of leading innocents away from their families for the crime of doing their jobs.

Twenty-six journalists were assassinated in 1996. That number is down by 25 from the previous year—cause for celebration, some might argue. But I am a journalist, not a statistician, and the assassination of 26 colleagues in the line of duty is unacceptable to me. Each killing reminds me that, although CPJ does much to ensure that our counterparts around the world enjoy the freedom to do their job, we do not always succeed. In 1996, we failed 26 times to shield our colleagues from lethal violence. We did not keep 185 reporters and editors out of prison: 36 African, 37 Asian, 4 Latin American, and 108 North African and Middle Eastern journalists were locked up at the end of 1996. (See "Journalists in Jail, p. 315.)

When thugs shot Irish crime reporter Veronica Guerin dead last June as she sat in her car at a red light, the blow was personal. She was a friend; I remember her feisty speech in 1995 when she accepted the International Press Freedom Award. The image of her little boy rushing up to the stage to claim not the reporter, but his mom, is not one I will soon forget.

Veronica stood for the best and bravest in all of us. In an effort to circumvent Ireland's onerous libel laws while reporting on organized crime, she directly

Kati Marton, *an author and journalist, is chair of the board of directors of the Committee to Protect Journalists. She is host of "America and the World," a weekly international affairs program on National Public Radio, produced by the Council on Foreign Relations.*

confronted underworld figures—a technique that led to repeated threats on her life, an attack in her home during which she was beaten and shot, and finally to her murder. While her daring methods astonished many of her colleagues and those who followed her story, we at CPJ loved and honored Veronica for her refusal to cede ground to the enemies of truth.

Ultimately, we cannot protect the men and women who practice this dangerous profession, who by the nature of their work earn the ire of those with something to hide. What we can do is to stigmatize the crimes committed against them—one of the objectives of this volume.

The Committee to Protect Journalists—the only American organization whose sole reason for being is to monitor abuses against our colleagues beyond our borders and to advocate on their behalf—also speaks truth to power at the highest levels. This year, when CPJ published its Top Ten list of "Enemies of the Press," it included the leaders of China, Nigeria, the Armed Islamic Group of Algeria, Turkey, and Slovakia, among others, as the most egregious oppressors of a free media. We have reason to believe that none of the 10 particularly enjoyed this distinction, especially because we urged U.S. officials to make note of our enemies list in their official dealings.

The Balkan cauldron continued to seethe in 1996. The region's long-muffled independent media emerged as key players in the region's tenuous democratization process. This region plays a role well beyond its size for obvious reasons. It is here that two world wars began, and here, during the past five years' warfare, that one quarter of a million people died and more than three million were left homeless. The state-controlled media in Belgrade, Zagreb, and, to a much lesser degree, Sarajevo, fueled the ethnic passion which unleashed that war. It is now essential for the security of Europe and ultimately the United States that we nurture the growth of free media in Bosnia and Herzegovina, Yugoslavia, and Croatia.

In two separate trips to the Balkans last year, I met with Serbian President Slobodan Milosevic and Croatian President Franjo Tudjman. I had a single agenda: to bring to bear the full force of the American media on these post-Communist dictators' attempts to suppress independent journalists. The mask of benevolence slipped momentarily from President Tudjman's face when I asked him point-blank why he was suing an independent—and thus critical of Tudjman—provincial newspaper for a ruinous sum. "Would any other head of state put up with this sort of coverage?" he erupted, jabbing his finger at the cover of the satirical weekly *Feral Tribune*. My answer, "All the democratically elected ones," elicited from him not the slightest sign of comprehension.

Toward the year's end, a surge of grass-roots pro-democracy, pro-free press energy came from an unexpected place: Serbia, a region many observers had written off as hopelessly mired in the most atavistic nationalism. When I learned that Radio B92, Belgrade's only independent radio station, was cut from the air, I traveled to Belgrade to voice CPJ's solidarity with independent media and express our outrage at their oppressors. This show of CPJ's support, which provoked international attention to their plight, was a tremendous morale booster to the beleaguered and isolated independent media.

By the time I held my second set of meetings with President Milosevic in late December, he was no longer the cocksure, all-powerful dictator who had greeted me last spring. Daily pro-democracy demonstrations on the icy streets of Belgrade had stunned him—as they did the rest of the world. During a two-and-a-half-hour meeting, I presented Milosevic with a document that declared his support of "a free press...and the right to publish and broadcast freely" in Serbia. He signed it. While this was primarily a symbolic document, it was an important reminder both to the Serb dictator and to the world of American journalists' commitment to a free press in the former Yugoslavia.

The tiny, vulnerable independent Serb media outfoxed Milosevic. When he pulled the plug on B92, it re-emerged unscathed on Radio Free Europe and on the Voice of America. Pro-democracy Serb students and journalists have made brilliant use of the Internet, reaching a small but influential global audience. CNN and the World Wide Web are proving that the most fortified borders are meaningless against technology's onslaught.

Ironically, the more Milosevic tried to silence the voices of dissent, the stronger they became. *Nasa Borba*, the Serb paper that has faced the harshest repression, has seen its circulation soar by 60 percent. The pro-Milosevic daily *Politika*, which used to boast a circulation of 300,000, has, since the demonstrations, plunged to a humiliating 45,000. Hunger for the truth after a long diet of lies and distortions drives this remarkable shift. Through ongoing contact with Serb journalists, and direct appeals to their oppressors, we at CPJ continue to encourage Serbia's long-delayed democratization.

The events in Serbia are nothing short of revolutionary. They are a reminder that the time when autocrats could absolutely control the flow of information to their people is past. That was the single most encouraging development for our profession in 1996.

Table of Contents

Introduction
by William A. Orme, Jr.

In late 1996, editor Ocak Işik Yurtçu sent a letter to the Committee to Protect Journalists from what he called "the deep darkness" of his Istanbul prison cell. Writing in formal, elegant Turkish, he explained that he wanted to thank us for mounting an international campaign for his release.

We should be thanking him. Journalists like Yurtçu take most of the risks for the rest of us. To work in his defense is a matter of moral and collegial obligation.

But fighting to keep good journalists out of jail is also a practical necessity in today's news business. In an increasingly interdependent world, we all need the best local reporters and editors to keep us informed about countries like Turkey—and Indonesia and Russia and Mexico and Nigeria and scores of other strategically critical places around the world.

Technology is fast making traditional means of censorship obsolete. The news today almost always gets out, and gets back to the places it matters most, whether via fax or satellite or e-mail or old-fashioned newsprint. And it is for this very reason that journalists are increasingly at risk. While electronic information is hard to control, the individual newsgatherer is visible and vulnerable. Silencing a journalist by imprisonment or assassination usually has the intended chilling effect on other reporters and news organizations. That is why an organization like CPJ is more necessary than ever: The ranks of independent journalists in dangerous and repressive countries are growing daily, and each is a potential target.

When Yurtçu was sentenced to a 15-year jail term in 1995, few outside Turkey paid much notice. The prosecution of Turkish journalists had long since become depressingly routine, and no Turkish newspaper had suffered more systematic harassment than Yurtçu's *Ozgur Gundem*, the largest-circulation daily aimed at the country's Kurdish minority. As he noted in his letter, he was punished—like so many of his colleagues—because "I tried to learn the truth and relay this truth to inform the public: in other words, to do my job."

Our job at CPJ is to inform the public about stories like Yurtçu's—and to do whatever we can to get him and others like him out of jail. In 1996 we brought

William A. Orme, Jr. *is the executive director of the Committee to Protect Journalists. Before joining CPJ in 1993, he covered Latin America for 15 years as a magazine editor and correspondent for* The Washington Post, The Economist, *and other publications. He is the author of* Understanding NAFTA: Mexico, Free Trade and the New North America *(University of Texas Press, 1996), and the editor of* A Culture of Collusion: An Inside Look at the Mexican Press *(University of Miami North-South Center Press, 1997).*

attention to his case by honoring Yurtçu with an International Press Freedom Award, presented in absentia at our annual New York awards ceremony by CPJ board member Terry Anderson. We asked scores of America's most prominent journalists to sign personal appeals to Prime Minister Necmettin Erbakan calling for Yurtçu's release. This campaign on Yurtçu's behalf received wide coverage not just in the international press, but in the daily papers of Istanbul and Ankara. And we began a series of meetings with Turkish officials to underline our continuing concern about Yurtçu's imprisonment.

Yurtçu was chosen for the International Press Freedom Award because of his outstanding professional accomplishments, his courage, and his sacrifices. He was also selected because his case is emblematic of the accelerating legal harassment of all independent Turkish journalists. At the close of 1996, as confirmed by information compiled by CPJ and published here for the first time, Turkey was holding a record 78 journalists in jail—more than four times as many as any other country, and up from what was then a record 51 confirmed cases at the end of 1995 (see "Journalists in Jail," p. 315).

The aim of this book—the main goal of CPJ—is to document and direct a harsh media spotlight at such gross abuses of press freedom. Although Yurtçu's is an especially troubling case, his imprisonment is broadly representative of the hundreds of abuses of journalists and press freedoms that we chronicle here. Verifying and responding to these incidents are the staples of CPJ's daily work.

Every week, each of CPJ's five regional programs receives dozens of reports of serious press freedom violations. These typically range from violent assaults and even homicides to criminal libel actions and the introduction of restrictive new press laws. Some of our sources are in the public domain: wire services, the local press, government announcements. Most, however, are not. Around the clock, through faxes and phone calls and the Internet, a global network of journalists' associations and human rights groups circulates confidential queries and details about such cases. We depend greatly on these organizations, as many depend in turn on CPJ's sources and documentation.

Increasingly, however, journalists in trouble contact us directly. Reporters in repressive and dangerous places are more willing to turn to the outside world for support, because they have learned that they can count on effective international response. And they are now gaining the tools to do so, as the telecommunications revolution ends what had been for so many a genuine isolation.

For CPJ, as in any journalistic enterprise, tips and sources are just a start. We must corroborate independently—and quickly—the basic facts of a case. We then examine these facts through the exacting policy optic of a press freedom organization. It is not enough to establish that a photographer was jailed, an editor sued, or a reporter beaten. We have to be able to demonstrate that these abuses were a direct consequence of their profession. Before we register a public complaint, we must also have cause to believe that the intent was to obstruct or suppress their reporting. This can be very hard to prove. As a result, we invariably exclude from this annual report scores if not hundreds of attacks on journalists that may also be legitimate examples of deliberate press freedom violations. Often, though, we are also omitting incidents that were at first assumed or reported to have been press freedom violations, but which subsequent CPJ staff investigation revealed to have had other causes.

There are other deliberate omissions in this annual survey. We do not cover the advanced industrial democracies, with one partial exception: the United States. This does not signal some naive misconception that journalists do not confront serious press freedom conflicts in France or Japan or the British Isles. Yet the local press in those countries is well-equipped to fight its own battles; we direct our finite resources toward countries where journalists are most in need of international support.

In our own country we focus on a few carefully delimited areas, including the murders of American journalists—fortunately, there were none in 1996—and government policies that affect the freedom and safety of journalists abroad. We were especially alarmed by the recent legal sanctioning of recruitment by the CIA of reporters as covert intelligence agents—and intend to fight for the policy's reversal (see "Subverting Journalism: Reporters and the CIA," p. 141). But CPJ has gladly ceded to domestically oriented journalists' groups the demanding and complex task of responding to the multiple legal challenges and other problems faced by the news business at home.

An awareness of our priorities and our limitations shapes CPJ's reporting on the rest of the world. We concentrate on places where our efforts are likely to have some constructive impact, and where we can work with local counterparts—journalists who have enough freedom to at least strive to be independent. This calculus varies from country to country and from year to year. But it also means that we consistently give rather short shrift to some of the world's worst offenders: xenophobic police states like North Korea and Iraq, and neo-feudal monarchies like Saudi Arabia and Bhutan. Ultimately, there is little for us to report in countries where reporting is a capital crime.

Even in the places where we focus our efforts, the demands of sound journalistic method circumscribe the scope of our work.

In the case of Turkey, for example, it was a major investigative undertaking simply to establish basic facts about the prosecutions and professional histories of the 78 imprisoned journalists. Assembling this list required many weeks of research by our Middle East program coordinator, Joel Campagna, and the Turkish journalists who assisted him in New York, Istanbul, and Ankara.

Similarly, it would have been impossible to track the fate and the purported legal offenses of the many journalists jailed in Ethiopia—18 by the end of 1996, 31 at the year's beginning—without on-the-ground investigations in Addis by Africa program coordinator Kakuna Kerina and CPJ board member Josh Friedman of *Newsday* (see "Clampdown in Addis," p.81). As is not uncommon in Africa, many of the Ethiopian writers and reporters were jailed without charges or any public record of their imprisonment, further complicating Kerina and Friedman's assignment.

In the course of 1996, CPJ staff experts and board members traveled to several other countries where journalists have been unjustly prosecuted. Board members Peter Arnett of CNN and Rick MacArthur of *Harper's* magazine joined Asia program coordinator Vikram Parekh for high-level discussions in Vietnam regarding, among other press freedom issues, the continuing imprisonment of five dissident political pamphleteers, including 1993 International Press Freedom Award recipient Doan Viet Hoat. (Vietnamese officials did not indicate any softening of their position, though the CPJ mission was their first open exchange of views on these issues with American press freedom advocates.) In Croatia, CPJ board chair Kati Marton met in Zagreb with President Franjo Tudjman to ask him to drop criminal charges against the muckraking weekly *Feral Tribune*, and former board chair Jim Goodale presented the newspaper's defense team a friend of the court brief challenging the seditious libel laws under which they were being tried. (Thanks to international pressure, the case was eventually dropped.) And Latin America program coordinator Suzanne Bilello traveled to Cuba to demonstrate CPJ's support for a small group of independent journalists who are routinely jailed for days and weeks in a sustained official campaign of intimidation. (None of these Cuban reporters, thankfully, is on our year-end 1996 list; the last journalist serving a long prison term was released in 1995 following a CPJ campaign on his behalf.)

There are many other journalists who had been detained for weeks or months during 1996 whose cases do not appear in our year-end tabulation of imprisoned journalists. The purpose of the annual Dec. 31 list is, first, to offer a consistent comparative snapshot of the imprisonment of journalists around the world, a portrait which includes all the profession's known long-term prisoners, and, second, to provide a documented point of departure for campaigns by CPJ and others on these prisoners' behalf. There are undoubtedly some journalists in jail about whom we are unaware, as there are others whose detention we have been unable to verify.

The same disclaimer applies to other categories of press freedom abuse charted in this volume: censorship, legal harassment, physical assault, even assassinations. Not every case is verifiable: this volume is meant to chronicle what CPJ was able to do and to document between January and December.

This book is not intended, then, to be an encyclopedic compendium of all major press freedom violations in the world in 1996. It should be read instead as a record of CPJ's work throughout that year. As such, it is deliberately and necessarily an understatement of the magnitude of the problem.

Lacunae and caveats notwithstanding, we believe—we proudly assert—that this is still the most thorough and carefully researched report of its kind. CPJ's staff investigated and documented every one of the incidents chronicled here. In most of these cases, CPJ took some immediate action in response, ranging from the mass distribution of formal letters of condemnation to orchestrating international protest campaigns to sending emissaries to raise these issues directly with government officials. Such on-site investigations further strengthen CPJ's working relationship with local reporters, and thus our knowledge of local journalism issues, while putting us in direct contact with the officials responsible for investigating abuses or for imposing troublesome press policies. It is this trademark combination of hands-on research and advocacy work that informs CPJ's brief but authoritative reports on each of the more than one hundred countries we regularly cover. We are a case-driven organization, responding to press freedom problems not in the abstract, but on behalf of individual journalists facing specific threats to their livelihood, their freedom, or their safety.

The Yurtçu case illuminates other issues we grapple with daily—issues of priorities, strategies, and responsibilities. On which countries should CPJ concentrate its finite energies—totalitarian states that are objectively the worst offenders, or the emerging democracies that veer uneasily between openness and authoritarianism? Which abuses deserve our closest attention, or our severest condemnation: assassinations by insurgents or criminals who live in defiance of the rule of law, or persecution by governments that are sworn to uphold legal guarantees of basic human rights?

The imprisonment of journalists is one objective indicator of a government's commitment to press freedom. By that particular measure, Turkey was the worst persecutor of journalists in the world last year. Yet even journalists sympathetic to CPJ's work might question whether it is fair to single out Turkey for such severe criticism. After all, Turkey's immediate neighbors—Syria, Iraq, Iran, Azerbaijan— are hardly paragons of press freedom. But Turkey, as a self-described democracy, asks to be held to a higher standard. This is the legitimate expectation of Turkey's best journalists. As an organization of independent journalists defending other independent journalists, we are most effective—and most needed—in countries where there are real working reporters and news organizations trying to do their jobs. In Iraq, by contrast, there is almost nobody for CPJ to defend.

Think Locally, Act Globally

There is another relevant consideration. Despite Turkey's status as the principal jailer of journalists, it remains a leading U.S. ally and aid recipient. In fact, two of the three countries that follow Turkey in the list of imprisoned journalists— Ethiopia, with 18 in jail, and Kuwait with 15—are also seen as solid U.S. allies. This should be a point of shame, but it is also potentially CPJ's most important point of pressure.

We have hundreds of members on all continents, and a diverse and well-traveled staff with friends and relatives around the globe. But as an organization financed largely by U.S. news organizations and directed by a board of leading U.S. journalists, CPJ is a fundamentally American institution with an international brief.

Our self-assigned mandate exposes us to charges of cultural imperialism, of acting on the arrogant supposition that American journalistic standards and practices are appropriate for the rest of the world. We are accused of imposing alien "Western" or even peculiarly "Anglo-Saxon" values on societies that purportedly do not share our views of free speech and individual liberties. Yet the loudest and bitterest complaints about the imprisonment of Ocak Işık Yurtçu came from Yurtçu's own Turkish colleagues, and we responded to their request for support. It is not CPJ's board of directors but the brave and vibrant community of reporters and editors in Hong Kong that has been most vociferous in calling upon Beijing to respect their local tradition of freedom of the press when China assumes sovereignty in the summer of 1997. And in Cuba, where the government has long contended that independent journalism is inherently subversive if not treasonous, it is not visiting American correspondents who risk jail and worse by daring to report uncensored news, but the local reporters who have refused as a matter of principle to work further for state-owned media.

Our formal letters of protest to foreign governments cite not the First Amendment, but the marvelously inclusive Article 19 of the Universal Declaration of Human Rights, which guarantees all citizens of all founding members of the United Nations the right "to seek, receive and impart information and ideas through any media and regardless of frontiers." Drafted a half-century ago, Article 19 even anticipated the Internet.

But we are ultimately guided by the ethos of American journalism, which, in its strict and constitutionally protected separation from government, is seen as a model by news professionals around the world. There are certain principles we uphold as universal goals which may be implicit in the sweeping promise of Article 19, but which have become explicit in U.S. law. Among them, to choose one important example, is the idea that elected officials should have no more protection from critical press coverage—and ideally much less—than that of any other citizen. Yet in many new self-described democracies it is a criminal act to "insult" the integrity or capacity of the president or prime minister. Another peculiarly American notion we seek to export is that the truth—the unchallenged facts of the matter—should be an ironclad defense against libel. Like most American journalists, we believe the best press law is no press law: The Jeffersonian principle that the government which governs least governs best strikes us as universally applicable at least in the arena of official regulation of the news media.

And, finally, in an era when U.S. power is again an incontrovertible fact, CPJ's ability to influence American opinion, and ultimately American policy, may be our biggest contribution to our colleagues abroad.

As an organization, CPJ is something of a hybrid. We are journalists acting on behalf of other journalists. As journalists, we must be careful with the facts, and careful to distance ourselves from political factions and ideologies. (That is one reason we refuse to accept government funds—a position seen as another aspect of CPJ's peculiarly American character.) But we are also an advocacy organization—taking positions forcefully and publicly in a way that most journalists ordinarily would not and often should not. On matters of philosophy, we make no pretense at objectivity: We oppose all forms of censorship, all attempts to harass or coerce or co-opt journalists in an attempt to control the news. And we reflexively prefer private media to state-run news organizations, NPR and the BBC notwithstanding. All this is also seen as a quintessentially American bias.

We are very much part of the human rights community in the United States as well as internationally. Freedom of expression is among the most fundamental of human rights: We take seriously our responsibility to defend not just journalists, but the public at large. And of the journalists we defend many are in trouble precisely because of their reporting about human rights violations. But what distinguishes us from the human rights world is that we are ultimately a professional organization, colleagues defending colleagues.

Killing the Messenger
The hard news generated by this annual report in past years has too often been that more journalists than ever had been killed in the line of duty. There were 72 documented cases in 1994, up from 64 in 1993 and exceeding the previous record toll of 66 in 1991. In 1995, however, with 57 documented cases (51 murders; six

accidental deaths), the death toll dropped significantly. In 1996 this downward trend continued, with 26 documented murders, the lowest number CPJ has recorded in a decade, and just one accidental death.

Still, it can hardly be a source of comfort that we were able to document 26 cases of journalists who were murdered last year simply because of their work as journalists. In another eight homicides in 1996 we suspect but cannot clearly establish that causal link (see p. 349).

Woven into these statistics are two disturbing patterns: the continuing targeting of journalists by warring factions in Algeria and Chechnya and Tajikistan, and the increasing willingness of criminal gangs from East Asia to South America and even Western Europe to dispatch hit men to silence troublesome reporters. The contract murder in June of Irish crime reporter Veronica Guerin, just six months after she received a CPJ International Press Freedom Award, had an especially profound personal impact on our board and staff, as well as on the many other American journalists who met her at our December 1995 awards ceremony.

But the sharp drop in the total number of documented homicides of journalists is a welcome and not coincidental development. In the 1990s the most dangerous countries in the world for journalists have been Algeria, Bosnia, Croatia, and Tajikistan—all places where warring factions deliberately targeted reporters for assassination under the cover of vicious civil wars.

Algeria, where seven journalists were killed, remains a horrific and dangerous place, with reporters working and living in bunker-like isolation, in many cases under the vigilance of military guards, who are themselves no friends of the press. But tightened security for the mainstream press has saved lives; in addition, many journalists who could not arrange or tolerate high-security quarters have fled into exile. Nevertheless, the number of deaths to date remains shocking: at least 59 murdered in four years, mostly by Islamist rebels, the largest death toll for journalists in any country since the so-called dirty war of Argentina in the late 1970s.

For the past two years, no journalists have been killed in Bosnia and Croatia, where at least 45 were murdered or killed in crossfire earlier in the decade. The Dayton Peace Accords, while usually honored only in the breach in respect to their press freedom guarantees, have succeeded in stopping the bloodshed. In Tajikistan, where there was one death last year but 29 since the outbreak of civil war in 1992, there are few real journalists left for either side to persecute: most have fled, and all local media is under direct state control.

It would be foolhardy to predict any permanence to the peace in the former Yugoslavia, or to evince confidence in the prospects for détente in Tajikistan. But what could conceivably prove a lasting trend is the relative rarity of official death-squad targeting of reporters, of the kind that was endemic in Central America in the 1980s and adopted by Tajiks and Croats and Bosnian Serbs in the 1990s. The slow strengthening of democracy in the developing world, coupled with pressure for the punishment of war crimes, may be putting some of these clandestine assassination teams out of business.

Despite the drop in the homicide rate, one disturbing fact remains unchanged: Those who kill journalists act in most instances with utter impunity. Murderers of journalists in Moscow or Bogota can safely assume they will never be pursued, much less arrested. And when journalists and everyone else are inured to the corruption or incompetence of local criminal justice systems, there is rarely much pressure for official accountability.

The popular outcry following the Guerin murder was an extraordinary exception to this rule. There was no precedent for such an assassination in the Republic of Ireland, and outraged citizens saw it as a direct and dangerous attack on their own right to be informed. They forced the government to go after Guerin's killers with all the resources at its disposal. They demanded legal reforms making it easier to nail criminal bosses for conspiracy and tax fraud. And Irish newspapers found the courage to name names: No longer could these accused killers and their drug-running associates hide behind the anonymity of nicknames and other elliptical references that had been used to forestall possible libel action (see special report by Michael Foley, p. 26).

"Veronica's murder brought about changes in the country," her mother, Bernadette Guerin, noted in a letter to CPJ. "I wonder if these changes will last."

They may, because her daughter's murder was anomalous in another important respect: There was no doubt about how or why she died. Most journalists are assassinated in places where violence is commonplace, investigations are cursory, and prosecutions are rare. And motive is often unclear: Journalists are by no means the only civilians who have been targeted by warlords in Algeria or Bosnia or Tajikistan.

Fundamentally, though, the murder of Veronica Guerin was like all assassinations of journalists: It was yet another example of the most brutal and final form of censorship. In the case of Ocak Işik Yurtçu, we can hold out hope for his release from prison. To honor Veronica Guerin's memory, we can only hope that her killers did not succeed in deterring other reporters from pursuing stories that need to be told.

"Veronica has been silenced," Bernadette Guerin wrote, underlining the words in her careful hand. "I pray that her silence will give voice, good and loud to all other good men and women who continue to expose evil and corruption in our world."

—February 1997

17

CPJ's 15th Anniversary: 1981-1996

THE COMMITTEE TO PROTECT JOURNALISTS marked its 15th anniversary in 1996. The American journalists who filed CPJ's papers of incorporation in 1981 dedicated the organization to the defense of the "human and professional rights of journalists around the world." Their goal was to use the power of the U.S. media on behalf of colleagues abroad threatened by authoritarian governments and other enemies of independent journalism. They were compelled by a sense of urgency. Death-squad killings of journalists were rampant in Central and South America, and violent attacks on the press were on the rise elsewhere.

The incorporating documents laid out clearly CPJ's basic mandate: the protection of journalists through "the compilation and verification of the actual or threatened violations of the professional rights of journalists; the mobilization of public opinion throughout the world for the prevention of...such violations; and the dissemination of information concerning the status and treatment of journalists throughout the world."

It was an ambitious but realistic agenda. Since 1981, CPJ has documented, protested, and publicized thousands of violations of press freedom and has grown into a vitally important institution to journalists and news organizations worldwide. It is the only U.S. organization with a full-time staff devoted solely to this important work.

Rapid-fire requests for CPJ's help can come during crises ranging from crackdowns on independent newspapers to political assassination campaigns against editors and reporters. On average, over the past decade, at least one journalist has been killed every week somewhere in the world. Scores of journalists are imprisoned every year because of what they have reported. Hundreds more are routinely subjected to physical attack, illegal detention, spurious legal action, and threats against themselves or their families. And even in the United States, where the press enjoys great power and legal protection, journalists have been murdered with impunity.

CPJ turns the spotlight of public attention on these acts. It can intervene anytime a reporter is in trouble. A professional staff of highly experienced regional specialists tracks press conditions through an extensive network of sources, reports from the field, and on-site fact-finding missions. Volunteers from its board of media leaders and its international membership are ready to assist. CPJ notifies news organizations, government officials, and human rights groups of press freedom violations. In many cases, its protest campaigns have been responsible for getting journalists out of jail or preventing their imprisonment. This year, with the establishment of CPJ's Web site (www.cpj.org), journalists everywhere have access to the latest news about press freedom conditions around the world and a vast database of information about past violations.

Paradoxically, the expansion of press freedom since the end of the Cold War has made CPJ more important than ever. Jailings and murders of journalists increase virtually every year. So do the calls for CPJ's help. Last year alone, CPJ responded directly to more than 250 press freedom violations and documented 500 other such incidents.

We are proud of what the Committee to Protect Journalists has accomplished in its first 15 years. But we are asked to do much more, and with your support, we can do more. CPJ is entirely dependent on donations from journalists, news organizations, and private foundations. It is nonpartisan, nonprofit, and nonstop.

Journalists Receive
1996 Press Freedom Awards

THE INTERNATIONAL PRESS FREEDOM AWARDS are given annually by CPJ to journalists around the world who have courageously provided independent news coverage and viewpoints under difficult circumstances. To defend press freedom, award winners have risked arrest, imprisonment, violence against themselves and their families, and even death.

The following five journalists received awards on Nov. 26 in New York City:

Kashmiri journalist **Yusuf Jameel**, one of the leading reporters on the civil war in Indian-held Kashmir, has led a career marked by violent reprisals—beatings, grenade attacks, and, last fall, a letter bomb addressed to him that killed a colleague.

Formerly a correspondent for the BBC and a stringer for Reuters and *Time* magazine, Jameel currently works as a reporter in Delhi for the newspaper *Asian Age*. He returned to Kashmir in September to report on the first state-assembly elections there since the civil war began in 1989. But getting the story was not the only purpose of Jameel's trip. He returned to attend a memorial service for Mushtaq Ali, a cameraman with Asian News International and Agence France-Presse. Ali was fatally injured in September 1995 when he opened a letter bomb addressed to Jameel, who sustained only minor injuries. Soon after, Jameel relocated to London, where he worked for the BBC for several months more before returning to India.

Jameel has had to withstand pressure and attacks from all parties to the Kashmiri conflict, which pits Indian security forces and government-backed militias against an array of guerrilla groups fighting for the state's independence or its merger with Pakistan. The combatants view the local press as biased in favor of their adversaries, and retaliate through violence and intimidation.

As a reporter for the BBC and Reuters—news organizations widely respected in Kashmir for their nonpartisan coverage of the war—Jameel was a conspicuous target for intimidation. In 1990, Indian security officers seized him, took him blindfolded to a remote location and held him incommunicado for interrogation about a colleague's alleged contacts with militants. Unlike most cases involving attacks on Kashmiri journalists, Jameel's abduction resulted in disciplinary action for three of the officers involved.

On two separate occasions in 1992, unidentified assailants threw grenades at Jameel's home and office in Srinagar. Later that year, security officers severely beat him on the head as he attempted to cover a protest march by a Kashmiri women's organization; Jameel was hospitalized for four days following the assault.

In addition to the violent reprisals, Jameel has periodically faced threats from militant separatists displeased with his coverage of the war.

Jameel has said he is "keen to return to Srinagar to resume work, but many well-wishers, concerned for my safety, insist that I should not do so." But, he added, "I believe that such risks are part of my profession."

J. Jesús Blancornelas and longtime colleague Hector Félix Miranda founded *Zeta*, a feisty weekly newspaper in Tijuana, in 1980 and set a bold agenda for Mexican journalism. In a country where the news media had historically kow-towed to government interests and where bribe-taking among journalists was so commonplace that it spawned a litany of catchphrases, *Zeta* dared to provide what few other Mexican newspapers had: hard-hitting stories on Mexico's most vexing problems—official corruption and drug trafficking.

The cost of *Zeta*'s independence has been high: Félix, a popular columnist known as "Félix the Cat," whose writing frequently targeted the wealthy and pow-erful, was murdered in 1988. The year before, unidentified assailants riddled the *Zeta* office with bullets. And over the years, the newspaper has suffered waves of harassment ranging from confiscation of its issues to outright threats to advertisers.

Zeta's drama has played out in one of the most contentious and volatile regions of Mexico. Tijuana has become one of the bloodiest battlegrounds in Mexico's ongoing internecine drug war, and in 1989, Baja California was the first state in Mexico to elect an opposition governor, ending the political monopoly of the ruling Institutional Revolutionary Party, the PRI. Blancornelas and *Zeta* played a pivotal role in this historic political turning point by providing a forum for opposition viewpoints and subjecting previous governments to close investiga-tive scrutiny.

Despite the risks, Blancornelas has not been deterred. In the wake of Félix's murder—which remains unsolved despite unprecedented public outcry—he con-tinued to print his colleague's name on the masthead of *Zeta* and in each edition reproduced one of Félix's columns opposite a black page that asked, "Who killed me?"

As late as 1989, it was still common practice for journalists to take money from elected officials, government bureaucrats, and businessmen. From *Zeta*'s founding, however, Blancornelas made the paper's policy clear: the slightest suspicion of bribe-taking is cause for dismissal.

In 1990, Baja California Gov. Ernesto Ruffo Appel prohibited state officials from offering government bribes to journalists. And former Mexican President Carlos Salinas de Gortari enacted a similar policy among his cabinet. As a result, says Blancornelas, "the tradition-bound daily newspapers have no other recourse but to change their tainted politics, speak the truth, and learn to survive through advertising and circulation sales—or die."

Blancornelas' refusal to abide by the status quo, which has shackled and silenced Mexico's press, has helped myriad publishers, editors, and reporters find the courage to build a free and independent press there. Throughout Mexico, he has been recognized as a pioneer, a rare example of courage and independence in the provincial press for more than two decades.

Daoud Kuttab has long challenged the censorship practices of both the Israeli government and the Palestinian Authority.

In the 1980s, Kuttab worked as a reporter and later managing editor of the now-defunct English-language weekly *Al-Fajr*, as a reporter and columnist for the Arabic-language East Jerusalem daily *Al-Quds*, and as a contributor to other papers, including the *Jerusalem Post*. During that time, he was arrested, searched, and fingerprinted on several occasions for activities that included participating in public demonstrations against Israeli press censorship and writing about an armed attack by Jewish extremists at the Palestinian University in Hebron.

After leaving *Al-Fajr* in 1987, Kuttab went to work for *Al-Quds*, where he broke many stories on the peace process and was the first Palestinian to conduct exclusive interviews with Israeli leaders Yitzhak Rabin and Shimon Peres.

Since implementation of the 1993 Oslo Accords, Kuttab has been a vocal critic of the anti-democratic treatment of the press by Yasser Arafat, the Palestinian Authority president. Arafat's government has dealt despotically with critical reporting and legitimate political dissent, jailing dozens of journalists.

In August 1994, Arafat ordered *Al-Quds* to stop publishing Kuttab's columns after Kuttab led independent journalists in a protest against the banning of *Al-Nahar*, Jerusalem's only other Arabic-language daily at the time. *Al-Quds* capitulated and fired Kuttab. But he refused to be silenced. He continues to write op-eds for several prominent newspapers, including *The New York Times*, *The Washington Post*, *The Los Angeles Times*, and *The International Herald Tribune*. And, as president of the Palestinian Audio-Visual Union, he has been active in protesting censorship and access violations by the Israelis and the Palestinians.

Kuttab also serves as co-director of Internews Middle East—a nonprofit, nongovernmental organization that aims to facilitate the free flow of information by supporting independent journalists and media. In April 1996, in honor of that mission, he created the censorship-free Arabic Media Internet Network on the World Wide Web (http://www.amin.org). The site features a magazine to which Palestinian journalists contribute stories that news publications will not carry for fear of official retaliation. In June, Kuttab used the site to mobilize support for Dr. Eyad Sarraj, a human rights activist arrested by the Palestinian Authority for his criticism of Arafat. Kuttab posted an open letter from Sarraj to Arafat that no newspaper had been willing to publish.

Throughout his career, Kuttab's initiatives to educate, empower, and mobilize an independent Palestinian press have been driving forces behind efforts to foster independent journalism in the Middle East.

Ocak Işik Yurtçu had little to celebrate last July 24, Journalists Day in Turkey. "Nobody in the world has been sentenced to so many years in prison for articles others have written," he said from his jail cell in an interview with the daily *Yeni Yuzyil*.

Yurtçu, former editor in chief of the now-defunct daily *Özgür Gündem*, is serving a 15-year sentence for disseminating "separatist propaganda." The case against him was based on articles about the Kurdish conflict published in *Özgür Gündem* in 1991 and 1992. Tried and convicted in 1993, he began serving jail time in December 1994, when an appeals court upheld his sentence.

For three years running, Turkey has held more journalists in prison than any other country. Yurtçu's case is emblematic of the types of charges used by the government to imprison dozens of reporters, editors, and columnists. Yurtçu was convicted of violating Articles 6, 7, and 8 of the Anti-Terror Law and Article 312 of the Penal Code. These articles in effect classify all reports on the Kurdish rebellion other than the government's as either "incitement to racial hatred" or propaganda for the insurgent Kurdistan Workers' Party, the PKK.

During Yurtçu's tenure, which began in 1991, *Özgür Gündem* was widely read and respected as an unbiased newspaper that offered readers an alternative to the inadequate coverage of the Kurdish issue by the mainstream, pro-government media. And it also broke new ground with its hard-hitting reporting on the fighting between the military and the PKK guerrillas in the country's Southeast.

Yurtçu's case was only one of many against *Özgür Gündem*. The government led a concerted campaign of arrests, bans, and trials against the paper, eventually forcing it to close in April 1994. In addition to the legal harassment, journalists at the paper were frequent targets of violent reprisal by unidentified assailants. In 1992 alone, four journalists with the paper were assassinated. The murderers were never brought to justice.

In an interview with the daily *Millyet*, Yurtçu was blunt about the impossible bind Turkish journalists are put in: "They can use laws to put you in prison just for mentioning the word 'PKK' in your news story. They take this as 'praising the terrorist organization.' How can you write about the Southeast without mentioning the PKK?"

Since Yurtçu's imprisonment, several more sentences have been handed down from other cases against him, and he says he is no longer sure how many more years he will be incarcerated.

According to a colleague, Yurtçu refused an offer of self-imposed exile when faced with prison. "He decided to stay in his country to fight against the injustice," Huseyin Akyol wrote in a successor paper to *Özgür Gündem*. "He believes that being a journalist cannot be a crime."

Arthur Ochs Sulzberger was honored with CPJ's Burton Benjamin Memorial Award for his lifelong dedication to press freedom. Twenty-five years ago, as publisher of *The New York Times*, he made a decision that profoundly strengthened the free American press. He decided that the *Times* should publish portions of the Pentagon Papers, the secret Defense Department history of U.S. involvement in Vietnam. The series of articles that followed changed the public's perception of its government—and, just as important, changed the press's view of its role in a democratic society.

The pressures on Sulzberger as publisher of the *Times* were great. The paper's longtime lawyers told him that he risked criminal prosecution. The Vietnam War was going on, with American soldiers coming back in body bags, and he was an intensely patriotic person. But he decided that the interest of telling Americans the truth about an issue that was dividing the country must prevail: that it was the public's right to know and the press's duty to report.

After the third installment of the series appeared in the *Times*, the Nixon administration won a restraining order from a judge: the first prior restraint against newspaper publication ever granted to the federal government. The Supreme Court overturned that restraint in a landmark decision. Justice Hugo L. Black, in his concurring opinion, said that "in revealing the workings of government that led to the Vietnam War," the *Times* and other newspapers that followed it "nobly did" what the framers of the Constitution had hoped and expected.

The New York Times was later awarded the Pulitzer Prize for public service.

International Press Freedom Award Winners 1991–1995

1991
Pius Njawe, *Le Messager*, Cameroon
Wang Juntao and Chen Ziming,
  Economics Weekly, China
Bill Foley and Cary Vaughan,
  United States
Tatyana Mitkova, TSN,
former Soviet Union
Byron Barrera, *La Epoca*, Guatemala

1992
David Kaplan, ABC News, United States
Muhammad Al-Saqr, *Al-Qabas*, Kuwait
Sony Esteus, Radio Tropic FM, Haiti
Gwendolyn Lister, *The Namibian*,
  Namibia
Thepchai Yong, *The Nation*, Thailand

1993
Omar Belhouchet, *El Watan*, Algeria
Doan Viet Hoat, *Freedom Forum*,
  Vietnam

Nosa Igiebor, *Tell* magazine, Nigeria
Veran Matic, Radio B92, Yugoslavia
Ricardo Uceda, *Si*, Peru
1994
Iqbal Athas, *The Sunday Leader*,
  Sri Lanka
Aziz Nesin, Turkey
Yndamiro Restano, Cuba
Daisy Li Yuet-wah, Hong Kong
  Journalists Association, Hong Kong
In memory of staff journalists, *Navidi
  Vakhsh*, Tajikistan

1995
Yevgeny Kiselyov, NTV, Russia
José Rubén Zamora Marroquín, *Siglo
  Veintiuno*, Guatemala
Fred M'membe, *The Post*, Zambia
Ahmad Taufik, Alliance of Independent
  Journalists (AJI), Indonesia
Veronica Guerin, *Sunday Independent*,
  Ireland

Burton Benjamin Memorial Award

1991
Walter Cronkite
CBS News

1992
Katharine Graham
The Washington Post Company

1993
R.E. Turner
Turner Broadcasting System Inc.

1994
George Soros
The Soros Foundations

1995
Benjamin C. Bradlee
The Washington Post

Gag Reflex: Ireland's Libel Laws Muzzle A Free Press

by Michael Foley

AFTER VERONICA GUERIN'S MURDER, the millions worldwide who read the accounts of her crusading reporting in the face of great danger undoubtedly admired her courage and persistence in getting her stories about the Irish underworld into print, but puzzled over her technique. Why had this young woman repeatedly provoked face-to-face confrontations with mobsters, even after she'd been threatened, beaten, and shot?

What seemed like inexplicable risk-taking to the outside world, however, was part of a deliberate strategy to circumvent Ireland's Byzantine libel laws. Those laws, so stifling to journalistic freedom in Ireland, led Guerin to put herself in harm's way. Lawyers had warned Guerin that published allegations of racketeering and drug-peddling could expose newspapers to libel suits, or provide legal grounds for the dismissal of future criminal charges against the subjects of her articles—unless, of course, these accused mobsters could be persuaded to respond to the charges on the record. These did not tend to be the type of people who returned phone calls. And Guerin was determined to get her stories in the paper.

When Guerin received the 1995 International Press Freedom Award from the Committee to Protect Journalists, she spoke of the need to reform her country's libel laws, expressing the views of most Irish journalists and publishers. She thought it was absurd that reporters were forced to take such risks and that criminal bosses could so easily deflect media scrutiny. She was outraged that one of her fellow crime reporters, Liz Allen of the *Irish Independent*, should be found guilty under Ireland's Official Secrets Act for publishing a document, available to police nationwide, which contained details of a bank robbery.

In Ireland, press freedom suffers primarily not because of the Official Secrets Act, or other forms of state control, as onerous as

---

Michael Foley *is media correspondent for* The Irish Times *of Dublin.*

they may be. The principal impediment to vibrant and exciting media is the constant and daily threat of libel action. There is no definition of defamation in Irish law. Lawyers rely on judicial dicta that provide a working definition of defamation as a wrongful publication of a false statement about a person, which tends to lower that person in the estimation of right-thinking members of society, or to hold a person up to hatred, ridicule, or contempt, or causes a person to be shunned or avoided.

While the truth of a statement offers the best defense, there is a presumption in favor of the plaintiff, who merely has to show that the words referred to him or her and were published by the defendant. The onus is on the defendant to prove that the statement is true. For media organizations, this means demonstrating that the statement is true according to the legal rather than the journalistic standard: The words that are the subject of the libel action must be substantially true in themselves, irrespective of any context. In practical terms, such a standard creates a conflict for journalists seeking to protect the confidentiality of their sources, who may be unwilling to appear in court and offer proof.

Irish juries tend to give very large awards to plaintiffs in libel suits against the media, without any regard to a newspaper's circulation, a radio station's listenership, or the viewing figures for particular stations or programs. Despite a nine-year-long campaign for reform of the defamation laws by newspaper proprietors and the National Union of Journalists, the situation is getting worse. The number of cases is increasing, and damage awards are getting larger.

There was hope among reporters that in the outcry over Guerin's murder the stalled effort to reform libel laws would finally move forward. But straightforward law-and-order issues took precedence in the public's imagination, and the Irish news media seemed reluctant to plead the case for its own reform agenda.

For the Irish media, the legal minefield extends from news pages to court reports, the editorial page, opinion pieces on the op-ed page, even restaurant reviews and letters to the editor. It is not as if Irish journalists are particularly cavalier. The cost to the media is simply too high for them to act irresponsibly. Awards and legal costs come to well over $50 million a year for the national newspapers alone. For modest print media in a country of 3.5 million people, that is a huge sum; and it does not take into account similar expenditures by provincial publishers and broadcast news organizations or weekly local newspapers. Small errors bring the full weight of the law down on the media. Even understandable mistakes are paid for dearly.

The chilling effect of Ireland's defamation laws reach into all forms of written expression, even into ancillary industries. Publishers have books fully "lawyered." Distribution systems and major news agents and newspaper and magazine shops have refused to stock some publications for fear of libel, because in a defamation case a plaintiff can go after the writer, the editor, the publisher, printer, distributor and seller of the offending material.

All political parties in the Republic of Ireland are now officially committed to freedom of information, despite their past support of official censorship against members of Irish Republican organizations. For 25 years, Ireland's broadcasting law contained a provision, Section 31, allowing governments to ban from the public airwaves anyone or any organization. In 1994, Michael D. Higgins, the minister responsible for broadcasting, did not renew Section 31, although it remained on the statute books. Proposals for new broadcasting legislation currently under government consideration, if adopted, will in all likelihood repeal Section 31.

The commitment to freedom of information means that the Official Secrets Act, which effectively says that all government documents are secret unless specifically stated otherwise, will be amended in the coming year. That means that the presumption of secretiveness will be turned on its head, so that all documents are public unless specifically exempted. The Official Secrets Act will then no longer be a threat to the media.

Such broad public consensus on the importance of the free flow of information might seem to presage the onset of policies fostering openness and support for Irish media to perform their watchdog role with confidence. Instead, Ireland is experiencing a de facto privatization of control of the press: The rich and powerful understand that the country's sweeping defamation laws protect them much more efficiently than anything so crude as state control.

Go through the clippings library of any Irish newspaper and search the files marked "libel" or "defamation." There you will find a virtual who's who of business people, politicians, prominent religious leaders, lawyers—even the president. Under those names are the stories of threats, suits, settlements—usually out of court—and writs. You will find few names of people belonging to the lower middle classes, the working classes, or the unemployed, because in Ireland suing the media for defamation is an establishment pursuit.

Business people and professionals comprise the largest category of those who sue the media. Within that group, lawyers are the largest single category. Politicians, who used to represent about 10 to 11 percent of plaintiffs, now constitute 23 percent. There are also many repeat plaintiffs. Journalists themselves account for about 10 percent of those taking action against the media.

Is it reasonable to regard defamation law, as it is applied in Ireland, as a tool of the establishment? Yes, I would argue: Just consider the case of civil and public servants, those at the heart of the establishment. They have a special arrangement to facilitate access to the defamation courts. The state funds public officials' and civil servants' defamation actions; they are the only groups to receive such support. If they win, they get to keep the court-ordered award; if they lose, the state absorbs their legal costs. In other words, there is a strong incentive for public officials and civil servants to sue—effectively, they cannot lose.

In contrast, there is no legal aid available to ordinary citizens for defamation cases. Irish society clearly does not value the good name of those at the bottom of society's ladder as it does those higher up.

Although regrettable, the timidity of the Irish press is understandable, considering the potentially devastating effect of large libel judgments. This institutional reticence leads journalists to adopt the adage, "If in doubt, leave out." Lawyers frequently advise news organizations that a person who has successfully sued before is likely to sue again. Thus, individuals who've gained a reputation within journalists' circles for litigiousness effectively shield themselves against press scrutiny in Ireland. This was a battle that Guerin fought constantly, and valiantly.

One of her trademark techniques was to identify crime bosses only by their underground nicknames—"The Monk," "The Warehouseman"—and to omit other crucial identifiers, such as the incorporated names of their front businesses. If the subjects of these stories were contemplating libel action, they first had to prove that they were the allegedly nefarious individuals in question. Guerin's method was usually effective, but frustrating. While her readers still did not know with certainty who these people were, reporters for U.S. newspapers covering Ireland could publish the names and other details about Dublin's crime lords in stories that they based on Guerin's own reporting.

When libel cases go to court—which is not often, because media organizations prefer to lessen the cost and settle rather than fight—the most common defense for journalists is that of "fair comment," intended to protect expressions of opinion on matters of public interest. The journalist has to prove that the comment was fair, the expression of honestly held opinion, and based upon facts that were true to the extent necessary to support the comment. Although this defense is used in over 40 percent of cases, it succeeds in only 5 percent. Even though these are not very good odds, the success rate for fair comment defenses is higher than for those defendants claiming justification or other defenses. The defendant must convincingly argue that the offending words constitute "comment"—i.e., opinion—rather than "verifiable fact." The distinction can be blurry, and the law is unhelpfully vague. If a man of meager declared income is reported to live in opulence, is this to be taken as subjective commentary, or as empirical fact?

Consequently, arguments about the nature of language and close examinations of phrases to determine which rubric they fall under dominate most libel cases. In one instance, an editorial in the *Irish Press* stated that a particular "slip up" in a diplomatic immunity case was difficult to understand. A lawyer employed by the state who had been handling the case sued for defamation, even though he was not named in the article. The offending words had appeared in a context normally accepted as "comment," but the judge ruled that whether or not there had been a "slip up" was verifiable, and therefore constituted a question of fact.

How has Ireland, a modern European democracy, retained laws so antithetical to press freedom, and how is it that juries feel compelled to punish the media with such high awards? The answers to these questions involve an understanding of the two principles at play: the right to one's good name, and the right to freedom of expression, including the freedom to communicate thoughts, opinions and criticism, to receive and impart information and to engage in public debate. We do need libel laws, but as David Gwynn Morgan, a professor of law at University College Cork, said in *The Irish Times*: "What we do not need is this remarkable relic which comes down to us from the days of the Court of the Star Chamber."

Morgan traces a direct line from present-day Ireland's laws to those of the 17th-century court whose function was to suppress any word or deed in opposition to the king. When the Star Chamber was abolished after the English Civil War, the common-law courts took over its jurisprudence in the field of libel. Morgan finds several features in contemporary Irish libel law that have come down to us virtually unreformed since the 17th century. First, the plaintiff has to prove neither negligence nor failure to exercise reasonable care on the part of the defendant. Second, a plaintiff can initiate action against material that is already in the public domain. Thus, if in researching a story a reporter relates statements made in an earlier article that the subject deems libelous, the restatement is actionable, despite the fact that the words went unchallenged when they first appeared in print. At no time does information become safe for journalists to report. Finally, according to Morgan, "Alone among legal causes for action," the plaintiff in an Irish libel suit does not have to show that he or she suffered any loss or damage: "The law obligingly presumes that to be so."

The statement in the Irish Constitution on freedom of the press has always been considered too weak to have any real impact on the common-law approach to defamation, says Marie McGonagle, Ireland's foremost expert on media law and author of the authoritative work on the subject, *A Text Book on Media Law*. In direct contrast, she argues, the United States Constitution, with its strong First Amendment commitment to freedom of the press, has dominated and reshaped the American tort of defamation. "In Ireland, as a consequence of following developments in Britain, which has no such guarantees, the tort of defamation has continued to operate along common law lines as [if] the Constitution did not exist," McGonagle says.

The contrast with the United States is manifest in the landmark 1964 case, *New York Times Co. v. Sullivan*. That judgment by the U.S. Supreme Court held that if the plaintiff is a public figure, he or she must establish malice. The Court's 1974 decision in *Gertz v. Welch* made it more difficult for private figures involved in matters of public interest to maintain libel actions. Unfortunately for freedom of the press in Ireland, the Irish Supreme Court in a 1980 decision chose not to use the constitution to import the principles of *New York Times Co. v. Sullivan* into Irish law.

Thus, for defendants in Irish libel suits, a public-interest defense is generally as ineffectual as a fair-comment defense. And public figures, far from having to establish malice in order to succeed, often receive larger judgments than do private citizens from Irish juries—who not only decide defendants' culpability but also determine the size of awards. McGonagle has argued that given Ireland's history of dispossession and poverty, it is understandable that human dignity—and with it the importance of a good name—should occupy a special place in the value system. "This may go some way to explaining why a jury made up of twelve citizens will sometimes award higher damages for reputation than they would for physical injuries," McGonagle theorizes.

"It is also a fact of life that the higher a person's material wealth and standing in the community, the higher the amount of damages likely to be awarded. The more ordinary the person, the lower the damages—if the person can afford to bring an action in the first place," she maintains.

Since the early 1990s—especially since the long and expensive judicial inquiry into abuses in the beef industry and its links to powerful political interests—all political parties have promised more openness, insisting that they favor the abolition of the culture of secrecy that has pervaded Ireland since the founding of the state. The Law Reform Commission, a government-funded body that examines laws and recommends change, in 1991 published a report recommending libel law reform. The commission's recommendations became the basis of a bill drafted by the publishers' lobbying organization, the National Newspapers of Ireland. Nothing has been heard of the proposed legislation since. The political parties that came together to form the present coalition promised that they would look at defamation laws and reform them. But more recently the Minister for Equality and Law Reform, Mervyn Taylor, has stated that libel law reform is not a priority. It is unlikely that any government will make reform of the libel statute a priority—the status quo is just too lucrative and useful.

Civil libertarians and journalists' organizations are now beginning to look seriously outside the state, especially to the European Court of Human Rights in Strasbourg, as the only viable route to challenge the defamation laws. The Strasbourg court hears cases brought under the European Convention of Human Rights, which Ireland has signed. Article 10 of the convention, a strong statement in favor of freedom of expression, has been used throughout Europe to protect and extend press freedom. So significant has Article 10 become that there is now support from journalists and civil libertarians for its inclusion in the Irish Constitution in place of the existing Article 40, which has so many exceptions and caveats that it is nearly useless as a guarantor of press freedom.

The Strasbourg court has a growing body of jurisprudence which has sought to balance an individual's rights, such as the right to one's good name, against freedom of expression, where the two collide. Its judges have demonstrated understanding of the complex role of the media in modern democracies. In a 1989 ruling in the case of *Tolstoy v. United Kingdom*, the court found that a large libel award had the effect of limiting freedom of expression.

If a government loses a case in the Strasbourg court, it is obliged to change its laws to ensure that they conform to the ruling. Moreover, the rulings also exert a moral pressure throughout the region that can influence the application of law in other countries. A case in point in Ireland was that of Barry O'Kelly, a reporter for the *Star*, who faced jail for refusing to name his sources in a 1996 civil case in the Dublin Circuit Court. O'Kelly's lawyers cited *Goodwin v. United Kingdom*, in which the Strasbourg court overturned a British court's contempt of court ruling against Bill Goodwin, a British journalist, for refusing to name his sources. Just as Goodwin, with the support of Britain's National Union of Journalists, had taken his case all the way to Strasbourg, O'Kelly's attorneys argued, so would their client and his newspaper if the Dublin court found him in contempt. In response, the judge decided that O'Kelly did not have to name his sources.

The changes that Veronica Guerin advocated are likely to come to Ireland only when a newspaper, radio station, or television company has the will to challenge a libel case to the Supreme Court and if necessary, to continue on to the Strasbourg court. Unfortunately, that might not happen, so inured are Irish media organizations to out-of-court settlements as relatively inexpensive and quick fixes to the problem. If inertia prevails over a more visionary approach to the libel dilemma, the Irish media will remain a sort of lottery in which many of the players win. Freedom of the press will continue to be the big loser.

Veronica Guerin 1959-1996

Veronica Guerin, Ireland's leading investigative reporter, was killed on June 26, 1996, by two unidentified gunmen on the outskirts of Dublin. Guerin, who worked for the *Sunday Independent*, was in her car, stopped at a traffic light, when two men on a motorcycle drove by and shot her in the neck and chest at least five times. She died almost instantly. CPJ issued a public statement expressing outrage at her killers, and calling for the Irish government to launch an immediate investigation into the murder and to prosecute those responsible. In early 1997, Irish authorities announced that they had arrested a known Dublin drug trafficker and charged him with Guerin's murder.

Guerin, who was awarded CPJ's 1995 International Press Freedom Award, had been the target of several attacks and death threats since 1994 for her reporting on Ireland's criminal underworld. In October 1994, shots were fired at her house after she wrote about the slaying of gangster Martin Cahill. Despite an investigation by the Department of Justice, no suspects were ever arrested. Three months later, in January 1995, a masked intruder broke into her home and shot her in the thigh. The shooting occurred a day after the *Independent* ran her profile of the suspected mastermind behind the biggest robbery in Irish history. In September 1995, an Irish businessman, with whom Guerin was seeking an interview, slammed her head against her car and threatened to kill her if she wrote about him or his family.

Enemies of the Press:
The Ten Worst Offenders

E ach year on May 3, World Press Freedom Day, CPJ announces
its list of the ten worst enemies of the press—individuals whose
actions aim to eradicate the independent press in their countries.
Heading the list for the second straight year is Abu Abdul Rahman
Amin, the head of Algeria's rebel Armed Islamic Group, who claims
responsibility for many of the 59 assassinations of journalists in
Algeria since 1993. All of this year's top ten are responsible for brutal campaigns against journalists and press freedom, as documented
by CPJ in its monitoring of press freedom violations worldwide.

1. Abu Abdul Rahman Amin, Leader of the Armed Islamic Group of Algeria
His insurgent faction has claimed responsibility for many of the 59
assassinations of journalists in Algeria over the past three years. Rahman Amin has threatened all secular journalists with death. "Those
who fight with the pen," he proclaimed, "shall die by the sword."

2. Deng Xiaoping, China
Deng, China's nonagenarian strongman, no longer ran his government on a daily basis, but his ruling philosophy—"socialism with
Chinese characteristics"—continued to serve as a pretext for the
complete suppression of independent reporting. When China
resumes sovereignty over Hong Kong in June 1997, it is expected to
muzzle one of the most vibrant and pluralistic news centers in all of
Asia. As the man who ordered the June 1989 crackdown in Tiananen-
men Square, which included the imprisonment of China's leading
journalists, Deng was directly responsible for restricting the press
freedom rights of more than one-fifth of the world's population.

3. President Sani Abacha, Nigeria
Abacha persecutes independent journalists by ordering or encouraging editorial office bombings, seizures of periodicals and equipment,
and the arbitrary detention of journalists, often without charges.

One result is a steady stream into exile of the profession's best and brightest. For those who stay, the risks are great: In 1995, four journalists were sentenced by a secret military tribunal to 15 years in prison for reporting on dissident army officers accused of plotting the overthrow the regime.

3. Prime Minister Mesut Yilmaz, Turkey

Yilmaz runs a government that at any given moment holds more journalists in jail than any other in the world. Yilmaz has done nothing to improve on his predecessor Tansu Ciller's dismal press freedom record. At the end of 1995, CPJ documented 51 cases of Turkish journalists who were then in jail simply for engaging in their profession. Most were imprisoned for reporting that was allegedly sympathetic to the Kurdish cause. Despite international criticism, Yilmaz has so far chosen to retain and enforce the notorious Articles 7 and 8 of the Anti-Terror Law and Article 312 of the penal code, which effectively criminalize independent news reporting about separatist movements, army counterinsurgency tactics, Islamic fundamentalism, and other topics central to the country's political life.

5. President Emomali Rakhmonov, Tajikistan

President Rakhmonov has overseen the systematic elimination of independent Tajik news media. The paramilitary forces he commanded during the recent civil war were responsible for many of the 29 death-squad killings of journalists since 1992. All independent local news organizations have been forced to close, and hundreds of Tajik journalists are in hiding or in exile. The repressive Rakhmanov regime is wholly dependent on Russian military and economic aid.

6. President Suharto, Indonesia

President Suharto has orchestrated a two-year-long crackdown on the country's independent press. After banning three leading newsweeklies in June 1994, his regime brutally suppressed demonstrations by journalists and others against the closures. Last September, the leader of the only independent journalists union, Ahmad Taufik, and his colleague Eko Maryadi were sentenced to three years in prison for publishing an unlicensed magazine and supposedly subjecting the government to "hostility, hatred, and contempt." At least 80 members of Taufik's union, the Alliance of Independent Journalists, have been fired from their jobs due to government pressure.

7. President Fidel Castro, Cuba
Cuba remains the only country in the Americas without any independent publications or broadcasters. Reporters not employed by state media are not allowed to own or operate a computer or a fax machine. Independent local journalists who attempt to send news dispatches to clients abroad face such retaliatory measures as internal travel bans, overnight detentions, the harassment of friends and relatives, seizures of equipment, and threats of prolonged imprisonment.

8. King Fahd bin Abdulaziz Ibn Saud, Saudi Arabia
King Fahd uses his enormous financial and diplomatic clout to silence dissenting voices not just in Ryadh but throughout the Arab world. The Saudi press, though privately owned, is one of the most restricted in the world. King Fahd must approve the hiring of editors; he also can (and does) dismiss them at will. More disturbing still, the Saudi royal family has acquired the most important international Arab periodicals and broadcast outlets and uses its influence to suppress all criticism—indeed, all serious examination—of its business interests and diplomatic entanglements.

9. President Daniel arap Moi, Kenya
President Moi has declared war on the independent press and widened his net to include foreign correspondents. Critical coverage of Moi has been decreed a criminal offense, while newspapers and printers have been arbitrarily closed for publishing opposing viewpoints. Journalists covering the trial of human rights activist Koigi wa Wamwere were physically attacked by pro-government thugs. The government last year introduced a restrictive new press law, including government-mandated "codes of conduct" for journalists, only to withdraw the initiative in the face of fierce international condemnation.

10. Prime Minister Vladimir Meciar, Slovakia
In his latest assault on press freedom, the thin-skinned prime minister pushed through parliament an amendment to the criminal code that would imprison journalists and others found guilty of "spreading false information abroad." Since Meciar dismissed all but one of the 18 members of the state radio and television supervising councils

in November 1994, the Slovakian broadcasters have become mouth-pieces and apologists for the prime minister's increasingly autocratic rule. This backslide into repression bodes ill not only for Slovakia but for all of post-communist Central Europe.

How CPJ Investigates and Classifies Attacks on the Press

CPJ's research staff investigated and verified the cases of press freedom violations described in this volume. Each account was corroborated by more than one source for factual accuracy, confirmation that the victims were journalists or news organizations, and verification that intimidation was the probable motive. CPJ defines journalists as people who cover news or write commentary on a regular basis. For additional information on individual cases, contact CPJ at (212) 465-1004. CPJ classifies the cases in this report according to the following definitions:

Killed
Murdered, or missing and presumed dead, with evidence that the motive was retribution for news coverage or commentary. Includes accidental deaths of journalists in the line of duty.

Missing
No group or government agency takes responsibility for the journalist's disappearance; in some instances, feared dead.

Imprisoned
Arrested or held against one's will; kidnapped for no less than 48 hours.

Attacked
In the case of journalists, wounded or assaulted; in the case of news facilities, damaged, raided, or searched; non-journalist employees attacked because of news coverage or commentary.

Threatened
Menaced with physical harm or some other type of retribution.

Harassed
Access denied or limited; materials confiscated or damaged; entry or exit denied; family members attacked or threatened; dismissed or demoted (when it is clearly the result of political or outside pressure); freedom of movement impeded.

Legal Action
Credentials denied or suspended; fined; sentenced to prison; visas denied or canceled; passage of a restrictive law; libel suit intended to inhibit coverage.

Expelled
Forced to leave a country because of news coverage or commentary.

Censored
Officially suppressed or banned; editions confiscated; news outlet closed.

Africa

OVERVIEW
OF **Africa**

by Kakuna Kerina

NATIONAL AND LOCAL ELECTIONS throughout the region
brought an increase in attacks against journalists, both physical and legal.
The tactics of intimidation against journalists by first-time candidates,
such as Gambian former military ruler, and now president, Yahya Jammeh, were
remarkably similar to those of their more experienced colleagues facing their second elections, such as Zambian president Frederick Chiluba. Both severely
restricted, and at times banned, the participation of opposition political candidates, and used strong-arm methods to silence the press or prevent its coverage of
the electoral process.

In Nigeria, Gen. Sani Abacha—the most recent in a long line of African military dictators who are reinventing themselves as democratically elected heads of
state—has implemented a "transition process" slated for completion in 1998 that
includes the destruction of the independent press. Abacha has given Nigerian
journalists vivid examples of their fate should they continue their criticism of the
current military junta: the assassination in broad daylight of Mrs. Kudirat Abiola,
wife of publisher and president-elect Moshood Abiola, who remains under incommunicado detention; the attempted assassination of *The Guardian* publisher Alex
Ibru; and the incommunicado detention without charge of *Tell* editor Nosa Igiebor, *TheNEWS* editor Bayo Onanuga, media attorney Gani Fawehinmi, and
numerous other media professionals and their legal representatives. CPJ's international campaign, "Nigeria: The Press Under Siege," worked closely with Lagos-
based journalists to secure the June release of Igiebor, and the subsequent release
of Onanuga and Fawehinmi, and continues to spotlight world attention on the
crisis facing Nigeria's independent press.

Kakuna Kerina *is the program coordinator for Africa. An editor, author, and award-winning documentary filmmaker, she has lived in Ghana and Botswana and traveled throughout Africa.*

Special thanks to **Selam Demeke,** *CPJ research assistant for Africa, contributed significantly to this report.* **Joel Campagna,** *CPJ's program coordinator for the Middle East and North Africa, wrote the Sudan section of the report. Special thanks to* **Thomas R. Lasner.**

Seditious libel is the legal charge that governments throughout the region use most often against journalists. A compromised and complicit judiciary in partnership with the government and its officials leaves journalists little recourse to challenge this now-routine form of harassment. The excessive fines and court costs growing out of seditious libel convictions are efficient methods to financially cripple or censor the private press, and many of the new multi-party democracies have switched from more thuggish methods of intimidation of journalists to this relatively subtle technique, hoping in the process to improve their international image. CPJ is collaborating with African journalists and their attorneys to strengthen their defense against seditious libel charges and to bring this trend to the attention of the international community.

Parliamentary officials throughout Africa are also targeting journalists with charges of "contempt of parliament" for perceived unfavorable coverage. These contempt charges are rarely heard in courts of law. Instead, parliamentarians serve as prosecutors, jury, and judge, forcing journalists to face charges and receive sentencing, ranging from fines to imprisonment, from their accusers.

The implementation of new restrictive press laws is a major threat to press freedom in the region. CPJ delegates visited Ethiopia this year to investigate the country's press freedom violations, and found an institutionalized system of judicial harassment of journalists, based upon vague and contradictory press laws combined with an antiquated penal code. (See "Clampdown in Addis: Ethiopia's Journalists at Risk," p. 81.) Parliaments throughout Africa are currently drafting and passing, often secretly, media bills and constitutional amendments with the sole purpose of facilitating prosecution of journalists for critical reporting.

Angola, Rwanda, Burundi, and Nigeria continue to be among the most dangerous places in the region for journalists to work. In many countries, self-censorship is the only protection for journalists who face attacks from governments as well as police and fellow citizens. For the second time in two years, an Angolan journalist who had criticized government officials was murdered, and the government failed to launch an official investigation to identify the journalist's killers.

Broadcast media, the most effective means for reaching the majority of citizens outside urban areas, remained under state control throughout most of Africa. Few governments appear willing to sacrifice their broadcast monopolies, especially since the restriction of private press and opposition political parties from ownership of broadcast media denies the majority of the population access to information that could threaten current governments' future success at the ballot box.

Economic obstacles and direct or de facto state telecommunications monopo-

Economic obstacles and direct or de facto state telecommunications monopolies limit the access of most African journalists to the Internet, although some enterprising newspapers—notably in Zambia—have been able to use E-mail and the World Wide Web to circumvent cross-border censorship efforts.

Africa's independent press must buck a daunting set of obstacles, including competition with subsidized state-owned media for advertising, the escalating costs of production, government harassment in the form of court fees and fines, and the steady erosion of the population's already limited or non-existent disposable income. Despite these impediments, the region's independent journalists persevere with great conviction. Professional competitors are forming alliances, and some independent journalists are reaching out to former enemies—journalists employed by the state have begun to join with their independent colleagues to strengthen media professionals' defense against autocratic and intolerant governments.

Angola

The October murder of Antonio Casemero, a journalist with the state-run Angolan Popular Television, by four unidentified gunmen was a chilling reminder of the crisis facing Angola's press. Journalists are skeptical that the government is actively investigating Casemero's murder because it took place in Cabinda, a province where there is no international community to pressure the powerful local governors who consider themselves above criticism or the law.

Confronted routinely with death threats, attacks, and warnings from anonymous sources, state security agents and government officials, both independent and state journalists in Angola are working in one of the most dangerous environments in the region and practice self-censorship as a defense against harassment. Last year's unsolved murder of Ricardo de Melo, director of *Imparcial Fax*, remains fresh in journalists' minds as a politically motivated act with the goal of silencing the media.

Limited national distribution outlets restrict the print media primarily to the capital, Luanda. In previous years, the government controlled the only fully functional printing press in the country, granting priority to state publications and imposing strict editorial guidelines on independent newspapers. The recent launch of Agora, a privately owned printing company, is an indication that the state has loosened its grip on the printing industry, but it remains to be seen if Agora will be targeted for harassment if it produces newspapers that publish critical or opposing views. Weekly newsletters, such as *A4* and *Actual Fax*, sell extremely well and offer readers access to news that is rarely covered in the state media. *Jornal de Angola*, the government daily newspaper, continues to enjoy state subsidies.

Television broadcasting remains under state monopoly. Radio is the most effective medium in Angola in the aftermath of the decades-long civil war, which took its toll on both the technical infrastructure and the population's literacy. The government has now given official sanction to private ownership of radio stations. Affiliations exist between local independent radio stations and international radio networks such as the Voice of America, and two new private radio broadcasters are expected to become fully functional in early 1997, bringing the total of independent broadcasters to six.

October 30

Antonio Casemero, Angolan Popular Television, KILLED

Casemero, a reporter working for the state-run Angolan Popular Television, was murdered by four unidentified gunmen at his home in Cabinda. The motive behind the murder has not yet been established, but informed sources in Angola report that Casemero had quarreled with a government official two weeks before he was murdered. CPJ asked President Jose Eduardo Dos Santos to conduct an immediate and thorough investigation into the circumstances of Casemero's death.

Botswana

Botswana's small and vibrant independent press is increasingly becoming the target for legal actions based on repressive colonial-era press laws, further eroding the country's reputation as a model democracy.

Journalists have been arrested and charged in contravention of the National Security Act for reporting on classified or confidential information, the Alarming Publication Act, which prohibits the publication of material that "may create panic or disturb public peace," and the Directorate on Corruption and Economic Crime Act, which bars the publication of information relating to an ongoing criminal investigation. Government officials, eager to insulate themselves from unfavorable press coverage, brought sedition and defamation charges against independent journalists and their publications. Foreign journalists can be subject to deportation if it is determined that they have violated Botswana's media laws. Confrontational public statements by government officials, accusing the press of irresponsibility and a lack of professionalism, indicate that this trend toward repression will continue in the coming year.

A 10-percent tax on newspaper sales became effective in March, threatening the financial viability of privately owned newspapers which already pay significant taxes for printing requisites.

Although the government passed a mass media communications bill to pave the way for private broadcasting in Botswana, radio and television broadcasting remains under government control.

August 14
Professor Malema, *Botswana Guardian,*
LEGAL ACTION
Tshimologo Boitumelo, *Botswana Guardian,*
LEGAL ACTION
Joel Sebonego, *Botswana Guardian,*
LEGAL ACTION
Horace Somanje, *Botswana Guardian,*
LEGAL ACTION
Botswana Guardian, LEGAL ACTION
The attorney general's office served *Botswana Guardian* editors Malema, Boitumelo, Sebonego, and Somanje with summonses to appear before the Gaborone Magistrate Court on Oct. 1. The four journalists were accused of publishing information on the identity of a person still under investigation by the Office of the

Directorate on Corruption and Economic Crime (DCEC) in the *Botswana Guardian's* July 28, 1995, and Aug. 4, 1995, issues. On Oct. 1, Malema appeared in court on charges of contravening Section 44 of the Corruption and Economic Crime Act of 1994, which prohibits disclosure of information relating to an ongoing investigation by the DCEC. On Nov. 1, Chief Magistrate Leonard Sechele repealed all of the state's charges against Malema for lack of evidence. The state eventually withdrew the charges against Boitumelo, Sebonego, and Somanje.

Cameroon

Despite his recent election to the high-profile position as head of the Organization of African Unity, President Paul Biya has escalated his iron-fisted assault on the media, publicly proclaiming his intolerance for free speech in Cameroon. Sweeping opposition victories in the Jan. 21 local elections spurred Biya's crackdown on the independent press for its critical coverage of his ruling party, the Cameroon People's Democratic Movement (CPDM).

The Organization for Freedom of the Press in Cameroon (OCALIP) was unsuccessful in its efforts to block parliament's passage of a harsh amendment to the country's already repressive media law. The amendment contains restrictive and complex licensing procedures, grants the CPDM indiscriminate authority to withdraw media licenses and impose post-publication censorship by seizing entire runs of "offending" editions, and expands its authority to ban newspapers. Newspapers that carry articles deemed to conflict with principles of public policy, endanger public order, or violate "acceptable" standards of good behavior are routinely banned and ordered to pay prohibitive fines intended to render them financially insolvent.

Cameroon remains one of the few countries in the world practicing pre-publication censorship. Official preventive censorship laws require all newspapers to submit their material to the Territorial Administration Service (TAS), the state censor, four hours prior to publication. Newspapers containing offending articles routinely appear on the newsstands with blank spaces, or not at all.

Journalists and their publications face a growing incidence of prosecution on libel charges such as defamation of the president, members of the National Assembly and other government officials in what appear to be little more than attempts to muzzle criticism of ruling party members. The severely compromised judiciary continues to allow serious legal irregularities in the prosecution of journalists—for example, the public prosecutor's office has filed libel charges against journalists prior to receiving the plaintiff's requisite written complaint.

Fearing police and government reprisals, many journalists practice self-censorship or go into hiding to avoid imprisonment. Police have assaulted news vendors, and authorities harass citizens caught reading banned publications.

Radio and television broadcasting remains under state control, and it is highly unlikely that President Biya will allow private ownership of the broadcast media in the coming year.

August
Paddy Mbawa, *Cameroon Post*, LEGAL ACTION
Mbawa, publisher of the independent *Cameroon Post*, was released from prison during the last week of August after serving 11 months of two consecutive six-month sentences. Mbawa was sentenced on July 13, 1995, for libeling an insurance company executive. The *Cameroon Post* alleged that the executive had embezzled money from the company.

August 8
Gaston Ekawalla, *La Détente*, LEGAL ACTION
La Détente, CENSORED
Ekawalla, a journalist with the newspaper *La Détente*, was sentenced to five months in prison and fined 1,000 CFA (US$200) for defaming a member of Parliament, Albert Dzongang. The newspaper was suspended from publishing for six months. The verdict was in connection with an article in the Aug. 18, 1993, edition of *La Détente*, which said that Dzongang had been involved in an illegal network that was issuing false diplomatic passports. At year's end, Ekawalla had not started serving his sentence.

August 14
Pierre Essamba Essomba, *Cameroon Tribune*,
   HARASSED
Essomba, editorial director of the state-run daily *Cameroon Tribune*, was arrested in connection with an Aug. 12 article that was critical of Justice Minister Douala Moutome and Transportation Minister Issa Tchiroma. Essomba was released the same day.

August 20
Vianney Ombe Ndzana, *Generation*, ATTACKED
Ndzana, director of the privately owned newspaper *Generation*, was shot in Yaounde by several armed individuals who opened fire on his vehicle as he was leaving the newspaper's editorial offices. Ndzana was hospitalized for his injuries. He had escaped a similar attack on July 29 when a bystander saw the would-be assailants and warned Ndzana to get out of the way.

October 3
Pius Njawe, *Le Messager Popoli*, IMPRISONED,
   LEGAL ACTION
Eyoum Ngangue, *Le Messager Popoli*,
   LEGAL ACTION
An appeals court for the Littoral region upheld the libel conviction of Njawe, publisher for the newspaper *Le Messager Popoli*, and Ngangue, a journalist with the paper. The two had been

charged with insulting the president and members of the National Assembly and disseminating "false news." Their conviction was in connection with a satirical article in the December 1995 issue of *Le Messager Popoli*.

Njawe was sentenced to six months' imprisonment and a 100,000 CFA (US$200) fine, and Ngangue to one year in prison and a 300,000 CFA (US$600) fine. The sentences invalidated a Feb. 27 verdict from the Court of First Instance in Douala, under which the two had only been fined. Njawe was arrested on Oct. 29 by judicial police for the Littoral region and taken to judicial police headquarters, then transferred to New Bell prison in Douala. The court issued a warrant for Ngangue's arrest, but he has not been detained.

In early November, Cameroon authorities refused to issue a visa to a representative of the World Association of Newspapers, who had been scheduled to visit Cameroon on Nov. 12-13 to meet with Njawe in prison and with government officials to discuss Njawe's case.

Njawe was granted bail on Nov. 14 and released the next day. His Supreme Court appeal should be heard within a few months.

November 27
Evarisite Menouga, *Le Nouvel Indépendant,*
IMPRISONED
Menouga, a reporter for *Le Nouvel Indépendant*, was detained for questioning at Yaounde police headquarters and later remanded into custody at the Yaounde gendarmerie. Authorities prohibited Menouga from meeting with his attorney and denied him visits from his family until Dec. 5. Menouga's interrogators pressured him to reveal his sources for various articles.

December 4
Peter William Mandio, *Le Nouvel Indépendant,*
Le Front Indépendant, IMPRISONED
Military authorities arrested Mandio in connection with his Oct. 3 article in the weekly *Le Nouvel Indépendant*, which was critical of Minister of Public Works Jean Baptiste Bokam.

Authorities placed Mandio in isolation at the Yaoude gendarmerie before transferring him Dec. 9 to a military center. Security forces questioned Mandio about information he had published in the weekly *Le Front Indépendant*, a newspaper Mandio founded on Oct. 8 during a temporary shutdown of *Le Nouvel Indépendant*. Mandio was released on Dec. 16.

December 10
Daniel Atangana, *Le Front Indépendant,*
IMPRISONED
Police arrested Atangana, a journalist for the weekly *Le Front Indépendant*, in Douala. They took him to the gendarmerie in Yaounde and then to a detention center. The arrest was in connection with a Dec. 2 article in the newspaper that was critical of presidential guard commander Titus Ebogo.

Central African Republic

Against the backdrop of three army mutinies within the year, more than a dozen independent newspapers were in circulation in the Central African Republic at varying intervals. The private press continued to publish, despite the threat of lawsuits routinely brought by government officials who managed to charge journalists with defamation for reporting on government corruption whenever clashes between mutineers, security force loyalists, and French troops died down.

In May, French troops based in Bangui intervened on President Ange-Felix Patasse's behalf after the first mutiny in April, sparked by demands that Patasse resign for bankrupting the country. In late

48

December, a truce was negotiated after Patasse managed to maintain his control over central Bangui and refused to accede to mutineers' demands on the grounds that they were unconstitutional.

Government officials repeatedly sued *Le Novateur* journalist Marcel Mokwapi and convicted him of defamation, a charge that is punishable by prison sentences of up to two years and prohibitive fines, for articles critical of government officials and their activities.

The state controls one newspaper, which publishes sporadically, a wire service news bulletin, and a radio and television station. A Christian radio broadcaster runs the only independent radio station currently in operation in the country, which airs strictly religious programming. The government refused to allow the establishment of other privately owned radio stations, claiming they would become voices for the opposition.

September 11
Marcel Mokwapi, *Le Novateur,* IMPRISONED, LEGAL ACTION
Mokwapi, managing editor of the weekly *Le Novateur,* was arrested for defamation in connection with articles published in the June and August issues of *Le Novateur* criticizing the slowness of the country's judicial system. He was detained until Sept. 18, when he was convicted, fined 500,000 CFA (US$975), and ordered to pay damages to the plaintiff, Judge Alain Gbaziale, in the symbolic amount of one CFA.

October 24
Marcel Mokwapi, *Le Novateur,* IMPRISONED
Mokwapi, managing editor of the daily *Le Novateur,* appeared before the Bangui Court of High Instance and was placed in preventive custody pending proceedings in a defamation lawsuit filed on behalf of the prime minister. The lawsuit was in connection with an article in the Aug. 27 issue of *Le Novateur,* which alleged that the prime minister had not given Hydro-Congo, a Congolese hydroelectric company, the full amount of a payment that the government had collected for it from the Petroca company, one of Hydro-Congo's customers in the Central African Republic. The article was based on an Aug. 19 letter from Hydro-Congo to Petroca.

Congo

In July, concurrent with the passage of a new press law defining the rights and responsibilities of journalists, requiring the independent press to obtain commercial licenses, and outlining procedures to establish private ownership of radio and television, the government of President Pascal Lissouba issued a decree reiterating the provisions of the new law. The purpose of the decree was to force the private press to submit the required documentation for obtaining commercial licenses. Journalists had vigorously but unsuccessfully protested the law's provisions and were involved in discussions with the Senate prior to the law's passage.

On July 5, Minister of Communication and Democratic Culture Albertine Lipou-Massala granted the private press fifteen days to comply with the law, charging that some of the private press neglected to provide the required information and warning them that "nothing will be tolerated" during the Aug. 15 visit to Congo by French President Jacques Chirac.

In August, the government enforced the new law by banning all 15 independent newspapers and magazines and ordering the seizure of all copies of the publications from newsstands, vendors, and printers. Publishers reacted strongly to the ban and it was lifted in September. By the following month, most of the private press had complied with the press law and were again publishing and distributing for sale.

The government currently retains a monopoly over the broadcast media pending the launch of privately owned radio and television stations. Inadequate financing has crippled Rural Radio, a station that has been in opeation since 1976 and has been an important source of news and information for the majority of the rural population.

August

The Private Press, THREATENED, CENSORED

In mid-August, the government issued a decree banning all of Congo's 15 private newspapers and magazines and ordered the seizure of all existing copies. The government accused media owners of violating a new press law that requires the private press to obtain commercial licenses. Minister for Communication and Democratic Culture Albertine Lipou-Massala ordered members of the private press to comply within 15 days, and warned them to conduct themselves "properly" during a scheduled visit by French President Jacques Chirac and an upcoming pan-African Music Festival, and on the upcoming holiday, National Day.

November 4

Ben Ossete Obelas, *Le Choc,* IMPRISONED, LEGAL ACTION

Obelas, director of the independent biweekly *Le Choc,* was sentenced to eight months in prison for "spreading false news and defamation," fined 250,000 CFA (US$500), and ordered to pay 2 million CFA (US$3,887) in damages to William Desire Dibas, head of the National Social Security Office (CNSS). Obelas was arrested in connection with an article in the Oct. 1-15 edition of *Le Choc,* accusing CNSS management of embezzlement. Four months of the prison sentence were subsequently suspended, and Obelas is serving the remainder at the central prison in Brazzaville.

CPJ wrote a letter to President Pascal Lissouba urging him to do everything in his power to secure Obelas' immediate and unconditional release.

Ethiopia

As a result of Prime Minister Meles Zenawi's government's deliberate campaign to restrict press freedom, Ethiopia succeeded, for the fourth consecutive year, in imprisoning more journalists than any other country in sub-Sahara Africa. The state targeted the print media, and by year's end four editors of the Amharic daily newspaper and weekly magazine *Tobia* had suffered arrest and detention without charge. The judicial system was complicit in press freedom violations, granting the state the right to detain journalists without charge while investigating them.

Using a barrage of charges including defamation, incitement of ethnic conflict, and publishing and distributing false or potentially dangerous information, journalists are regularly harassed, censored, arrested, and illegally detained for weeks, or months, without charge or trial. Those who were tried and convicted under the country's often-contradictory press laws faced exorbitant fines and prison sentences of up to two years. Several independent newspapers have folded under the weight of excessive fines, and journalists have gone into hiding or fled the country to avoid persecution. Despite government efforts to silence the print media, 74 private newspapers and magazines continue to publish, although some appear irregularly.

In March 1996, CPJ delegates went to Ethiopia to research press freedom issues and meet with government officials and members of the press. (For a more comprehensive discussion of CPJ's findings in Ethiopia, see "Clampdown in Addis: Ethiopia's Journalists at Risk," p.81.) Despite indications that the Parliament would review the country's repressive press law, press freedom violations have not abated. Promises to open the airwaves to private investors have not materialized and the broadcast media remain under government control.

January 10
Binyam Tadesse, *Agere,* IMPRISONED
Binyam, publisher and manager of *Agere,* was arrested and detained in connection with a Jan. 6 jailbreak from the Addis Ababa Central Prison. He was released on unspecified bail on July 8.

January 14
Kumsa Burayu, *Meda Walabu,* MISSING
Kumsa, a journalist for the now-defunct Oromo-language weekly newspaper *Meda Walabu,* has been missing since Jan. 14. According to Kumsa's family members, he was forcibly taken by armed men to an unknown destination and has not been seen or heard from since.

February
Terefe Mengesha, *Roha,* IMPRISONED,
LEGAL ACTION
In early February, Terefe, the former editor in chief of the Amharic-language weekly *Roha,* was sentenced by the Central High Court to an additional one-year prison term just as he completed a one-year sentence for "publishing and distributing false information" and for "inciting the public to anxiety and insecurity." Terefe was leaving the prison grounds when policemen re-arrested him and transported him to Ma'ekelawi Central Prison in Addis Abba. Terefe's original conviction cited two articles, published in the October and December 1994 issues of *Roha,* entitled "Colonel Mengistu on the Offensive in Gambella" and "Woyane Combatants Suffered Heavy Defeats in South, West, and East Ethiopia."

March 1
Iskinder Nega, *Habesha,* IMPRISONED
Iskinder, the editor in chief of the popular independent English-language weekly *Habesha,* was abducted. Iskinder's mother reported that armed plainclothes police broke into their home in Addis Ababa, apprehended him and pushed him into a police van. He is reportedly being kept incommunicado. Police have denied

arresting him, although his mother recorded the licence plate number of the van, which was also marked "police." On March 26, Iskinder appeared in court. He was charged with "writing derogatory statements against the government and government officials" and with "depicting officials erroneously in a manner that could abuse their very person." The charges brought against Iskinder cite a cartoon published in *Habesha* in late 1995, which depicted someone under President Bill Clinton's foot. Government officials claimed the person under Clinton's foot was Ethiopian Prime Minister Meles Zanawi. Iskinder was initially denied bail, even though he was legally entitled to produce a guarantor or surety, and was remanded into custody at Ma'ekelawi. On March 28, Iskinder appeared before court and was granted bail of 5,000 birr (US$ 1,000).

March 4
Aklilu Tadesse, *Andebet,* IMPRISONED
Aklilu, owner and editor in chief of *Andebet* and former editor in chief of *Maebel,* was detained for failing to appear in court. He was released during the first week of April.

March 7
Solomon Lemma, *Wolafen,* IMPRISONED,
LEGAL ACTION
Solomon, editor of the independent Amharic-language weekly newspaper *Wolafen,* was sentenced to an 18-month prison term for "publishing false reports in order to incite war and unrest." The reports in question, a series of articles published in 1995, were about an insurgency group fighting in three provinces in western Ethiopia. Solomon had just completed a one-year sentence without parole.

March 25
Tesfaye Tegen, *Beza,* IMPRISONED
Tesfaye, the editor in chief of the Amharic weekly *Beza,* was summoned to appear at Ma'ekelawi Central Prison in Addis Ababa where he was asked to present a personal guar-

antor for 10,000 birr (US$2,000). When Tesfaye failed to do so, he was transported to Central State Prison where he is currently being held incommunicado. The summons cited a cartoon, published in *Beza* in late 1995, portraying Prime Minister Meles Zenawi and other government officials as members of a soccer team. Meles was depicted as much larger than his colleagues.

March 26
Dereje Haile, *Ethiop*, IMPRISONED
Five editors, reporters and clerical workers,
   Tekwami and *Ethiop*, HARASSED
Tekwami and Ethiop, CENSORED
State Security police arrested Dereje, a journalist with the newspaper *Ethiop*, and five other editors, reporters and clerical employees with *Ethiop* and the newspaper *Tekwami*. The arrests were made as the papers were being printed in the city of Bole. Police seized the newspapers' galleys and transported the journalists and clerical workers to Ma'ekelawi Central Prison. Everyone was released later that day except Dereje, who was released on April 5. The newspapers' galleys were not returned.

April
Bekele Dissassa, IMPRISONED
Bekele, a distributor of publications, including the newspaper *Urji* and a magazine of the same name, in the Welega Province town of Nekemte, was detained. He was released from prison during the first week of June.

April 3
Alemayehu Kifle, *Genanaw*, IMPRISONED,
   LEGAL ACTION
Alemayehu, the editor in chief of the newspaper *Genanaw*, was arrested without charge as he was leaving a court in Nazareth, about 100 kilometers east of Addis Ababa, the capital. Just prior to his arrest, Alemayehu had been released from prison, where he had served time in connection with an article comparing Nazareth prisons to Nazi death camps. Cpl. Kassa Wayessa, director

of prisons in Nazareth, ordered Alemayehu's rearrest. The editor was transferred to a prison in Addis Ababa and then released on May 6 on bail of 5,000 birr (US$800).

April 17
Tamrat Gemeda, *Seife Nebelbal*, IMPRISONED
Tamrat, acting editor in chief of the independent Amharic weekly newspaper *Seife Nebelbal*, was detained at the Central Criminal Investigation Office prison. He was released on June 5 on bail of an unspecified amount.

July 9
Mulugeta Lule, *Tobia*, LEGAL ACTION
Tobia, LEGAL ACTION
Mulugeta, manager of the independent monthly magazine *Tobia* and a weekly newspaper of the same name, was summoned to the Central Criminal Investigation Department at Ma'ekelawi Prison for questioning. Both he and *Tobia* were charged with violating Ethiopia's press law by not having a deputy editor in chief on staff. Mulugeta was also informed that he was under investigation in connection with an article published in December 1995, about a doctor who had unsuccessfully performed surgery on Maj. Admassie Zeleke, the former head of parliament. No charge has yet been filed in relation to that article.

Mulugeta had to produce a surety bond of 10,000 birr (US$1,600) for each accusation. He has now given the authorities a total of 16 surety bonds, at 10,000 birr each, in connection with all the cases launched against him to date.

Mulugeta, who is also vice chairman of the Ethiopian Free Journalists Association (EFJA), was released after four hours and is awaiting notification of a court date for a hearing.

November 22
Taye Belachew, *Tobia* , IMPRISONED
Taye, editor in chief of the privately owned weekly magazine *Tobia* and the monthly magazine of the same name, was arrested without charge by plainclothes security police officers at

the publication's editorial offices. He is being detained at Ma'ekelawi Central Criminal Investigation Office. Police interrogated Taye about an article titled "A Strategy to Reunite Eritrea With Ethiopia," written by University of California at Davis Professor Tilahun Yilma and published in the November issue of *Tobia*. On Dec. 9, Taye appeared in Addis Ababa District Court, where Ma'ekelawi police, claiming they had lost their files, requested that Taye be detained for an additional 14 days. The court granted the request.

November 25
Anteneh Merid, *Tobia,* IMPRISONED
Anteneh, the deputy editor in chief of the weekly magazine *Tobia* and the monthly magazine of the same name, was arrested without charge and detained at Ma'ekelawi Central Criminal Investigation Office. Police interrogated Anteneh about an article published in the November issue of *Tobia* titled "A Strategy to Reunite Eritrea With Ethiopia." On Dec. 9, Anteneh appeared in the Addis Ababa District Court. The court granted a police request to detain him for an additional 14 days because they had lost their files. He remains in prison.

December 5
Sintayehu Abate, *Remet,* IMPRISONED
Sintayehu, editor in chief of the privately owned Amharic weekly magazine *Remet*, was rearrested on the day he should have been released after completing a one-year sentence. The new arrest came after his magazine published articles and a photograph that the public prosecutor deemed pornographic. Sintayehu remains in Addis Ababa Central Prison.

December 8
Tefera Kitila, *Tikuret,* IMPRISONED
During the week of Dec. 8, Tefera, editor in chief of the privately owned Ahmaric weekly *Tikuret*, was arrested and detained without charge. Authorities have not provided any reasons for his detention.

December 11
Aklilu Tadesse, *Ma'ebel,* IMPRISONED
Aklilu, editor in chief of the Amharic weekly *Ma'ebel*, was arrested and detained without charge at Ma'ekelawi Central Criminal Investigation Office. Officials gave no reason for the arrest.

December 11
Dawit Kebede, *Fyameta,* IMPRISONED
Dawit, publisher of the Amharic weekly *Fyameta*, was arrested and detained in the Woreta Ten police station, in the district of Woreta. Observers believe his arrest is in connection with *Fyameta*'s Dec. 4 story titled "Police College Has Trained a Thief."

December 11
Daniel Dershe, *Kitab,* IMPRISONED, LEGAL ACTION
The High Court found Daniel, editor in chief of the now-defunct Amharic-language weekly *Kitab*, guilty of an unspecified charge and immediately remanded him into police custody. Officials have not released information about the length of his sentence.

December 12
Goshu Moges, AKPAC, IMPRISONED
Security officers arrested Goshu, acting manager of AKPAC, which publishes the weekly magazine *Tobia* and the monthly magazine of the same name, without charge. The arrest was in connection with an article about the November hijacking of Ethiopian Airlines Flight 961. Goshu is being held at Ma'ekelawi Central Criminal Investigation Office.

December 12
Wesson Seged Mersha, *Kitab,* IMPRISONED, LEGAL ACTION
Wesson, publisher of the Amharic weekly *Kitab*, was sentenced to a six-month prison term and immediately jailed. Officials have not provided any reasons for his incarceration.

December 13

Kassahun Seboqa, *Amharic,* HARASSED
Kassahun, editor in chief of the independent weekly *Amharic,* fled to Kenya after being harassed and interrogated by Ethiopian security personnel. The interrogation, ordered by the attorney general, focused on Kassahun's interview with a relative of the late emperor, Haile Selassie. The article covered repressive laws, harassment of opposition leaders, and the eviction of citizens from their houses.

December 18

Tilahun Bekele, *Ruhama,* IMPRISONED
Tilahun, editor in chief of the privately owned Amharic weekly *Ruhama,* was arrested and detained without charge. Authorities refused to provide reasons for his detention.

The Gambia

On Sept. 24, Captain Yahya Yammeh, leader of the Alliance for Patriotic Reorientation and Construction Party, transformed himself from military strongman to president in flawed and unfair elections which excluded The Gambia's main opposition politicians. Yammeh's monopoly of the state broadcast media denied his few challengers access to radio and television to air their platforms. And the independent press suffered routine harassment for publishing opposing or critical views during the period leading up to the election.

In February, Yammeh's Armed Forces Provisional Ruling Council (AFPRC) issued Decrees 70 and 71, which modify the 1944 Newspaper Act and require all independent newspapers to pay an increased registration bond of 100,000 dalasis (US$10,000) and provide property as collateral. State-owned publications are not subject to these decrees, whose clear intent is to cripple the independent press financially and eliminate the competition. CPJ protested the imposition of the decrees to the Gambian government and urged that they be revoked.

Journalists who report on government corruption, or criticize the government or its officials, are frequently charged with violation of Article 212 of The Gambia's draft constitution, which places restrictions on the media for "reasons of national security, public order, public morality and for the purpose of protecting the reputation, rights and freedoms of others." In March, for the first time in the history of The Gambia's press, four independent publishers were charged with violating Section 5 of the Newspaper Act for failing to submit their newspapers' annual registration documents after the AFPRC deemed failure to register a criminal offense.

Since the elections, the government's harassment of the private press has taken many forms: bans on state-run printing presses' production of independent newspapers; unprecedented charges against editors and publishers for violations of the Newspaper Act; routine detention of journalists who refuse to name their sources, causing others to flee the country rather than divulge this information; and threats of deportation against immigrant employees of the private press.

February 22

Boubacar Sankanu, Free-lancer, IMPRISONED, HARASSED
Sankanu, a free-lancer for the biweekly newspaper *The Point*, Voice of America (VOA), Radio Deutsche Welle, and the British Broadcasting Corp. (BBC), was detained incommunicado for one week and interrogated about his reports for VOA. He was released on bail, without charge, and directed to report daily to the police for one week. Sankanu was also "strongly encouraged" by state security agents to cease filing radio reports for broadcast on international networks.

February 26
All independent newspapers, LEGAL ACTION,
CENSORED
The Armed Forces Provisional Ruling Council
(AFPRC) introduced Decree 71, which
required all independent newspapers to pay a
registration bond of 100,000 dalasis
(US$10,000) and provide property as collateral,
or face closure. Decree 71 extended Decree 70
(passed by the AFPRC on Feb. 14), which
required only new independent newspapers to
pay 100,000 dalasis to register. State-owned
publications are not subject to either decree.

All seven Gambian independent newspapers
managed to meet the requirements of Decree
71 but were prohibited from publishing for the
two weeks during which their affidavits were
being reviewed. CPJ protested the imposition
of the decrees to the Gambian government and
urged that they be revoked.

March
The independent press, CENSORED
The Gambian Ministry of Justice ordered the
state-run printing press to stop printing independent newspapers. Five of the six newspapers,
*The Point, New Citizen, The Gambian, Gambia
News* and *Monthly Report* and *Toiler* were forced
to print their editions in Senegal or pay higher
prices to print on the private presses of other
independent newspapers.
The Point acquired its own printing press, but
the *New Citizen, The Gambian, Gambian News*
and *Monthy Report* and *Toiler* have gone out of
business. CPJ protested the measure to the
Gambian government, and demanded that it be
lifted immediately.

March 8
Ebrima Ceesay, *The Daily Observer,*
LEGAL ACTION
Theophilus George, *The Daily Observer,*
LEGAL ACTION
Deyda Hydara, *The Point,* LEGAL ACTION
Pap Seine, *The Point,* LEGAL ACTION
Sam Sarr, *Foroyaa,* LEGAL ACTION

Halifah Sallah, *Foroyaa,* LEGAL ACTION
Sidia Jatta, *Foroyaa,* LEGAL ACTION
Boubacarr Gaye, *New Citizen,* LEGAL ACTION
The editors and publishers of four independent
newspapers were summoned to appear before
the Banjul Magistrate Court to answer charges
of violating Section 5 of the 1944 Newspaper
Act by failing to submit their papers' annual
registration documents. Into the first years of
Yahya Jammeh's rule, no newspaper was
charged for violating this provision in the act.
Newspapers have been allowed to simply provide publishing information on their back
pages. Now, Jammeh's armed forces provisional
ruling council has made failure to register a
criminal offense, and is prosecuting those who
do not comply.

Those summoned on March 8 were: Ebrima
Ceesay, editor of the *Daily Observer*, and
Theophilus George, the paper's publisher; Sam
Sarr, Halifa Sallah and Sidia Jatta, editors of
Foroyaa; Boubacarr Gaye, editor and publisher
of the *New Citizen*; and Deyda Hydara and Pap
Saine, editors of *The Point*. The eight publishers
and editors pleaded not guilty and were released
on bond of 1,000 dalasis (US$100) each. The
case is pending.

May 6
Alieu Badara Sowe, *The Point,* IMPRISONED
Bruce Asemota, *Daily Observer,* IMPRISONED
Sowe, a reporter for the weekly newspaper *The
Point*, and the Nigerian-born Asemota, a
reporter for the independent *Daily Observer*,
were arrested by plainclothes police officers
from the criminal investigations unit and held
incommunicado. The officers ordered the journalists to disclose their sources for articles they
had written about the National Police, allegedly
to determine if those sources were associated in
any way with the police force. Both men refused
to cooperate. In the April 29 issue of *The Point*,
Sowe reported on the fraud division chief's
involvement in the theft of recovered stolen
money at the police station. In the May 6 issue
of the *Daily Observer*, Asemota reported on the

reshuffling of top officials in the National Police as a result of the theft involving the fraud division chief. He made reference to Sowe's article and quoted an anonymous source who revealed the names of the reassigned officials. On May 9, CPJ wrote a letter to the Gambian leader Capt. Yahya Jammeh and the inspector-general of police urging them to release Asemota and Sowe immediately. Sowe was released that same day after paying a fine of US$250. On May 22, Asemota was released on bail but was not charged with an offense. He has been prohibited by the police from working as a journalist under threat of expulsion from The Gambia.

Sowe was forced to flee The Gambia on June 2 after receiving daily death threats and a beating on May 25. One of his attackers yelled, "As long as you don't stop your negative reports about security agents, we will continue to deal with you." He is now in hiding in a neighboring country.

June 13
Ansumana Badjie, *The Point*, THREATENED, HARASSED
Badjie, a senior reporter for the independent newspaper *The Point*, was arrested on June 13 by the National Intelligence Agency (NIA) and detained for an hour in the police station of the rural town of Soma. Badjie was in Soma to cover a June 3-15 tour by the Armed Forces Provisional Ruling Council (AFPRC) of its rural infrastructure projects. The NIA accused him of referring to the tour in print as a "political tour" and of writing other unspecified "negative reports."

The NIA agents seized his documents and manuscripts before releasing him, but said they were "not finished" with him yet. When Badjie returned to *The Point's* head office in Fajara at the end of the tour, he reported the arrest in the newspaper's June 17 issue. On June 18, *The Point's* bureau in the capital of Banjul informed him that two officers from the "serious crimes unit" had been looking for him there. Badjie has since gone into hiding.

June 28
Boubacar Sankanu, Free-lancer, HARASSED
Sankanu, the Banjul stringer for the Voice of America, was stopped by immigration officials at a checkpoint and prohibited from leaving The Gambia. Sankanu was on his way to Senegal to cover stories there. Police claimed that he has been under surveillance since he was released from detention Feb. 29, and must obtain police clearance to cross borders.

July 22
Boubacar Sankanu, Free-lancer, THREATENED, HARASSED
Sankanu, a stringer for the Voice of America, was interviewing spectators at a Banjul celebration when three intelligence officers detained him and drove him from the event to a distant road. They confiscated his script for a VOA story that quoted sources as calling for interim elections, and demanded he identify his sources or "pay the consequences." He was released the same day.

Ghana

President Jerry Rawlings' National Democratic Congress (NDC) government targeted the independent press with legal actions aimed at repressing unfavorable reporting on the state and its officials. Using the Supreme Court's July ruling that all citizens are subject to provisions under seditious libel laws and a 1960 law prohibiting defamation of the state, among other restrictive laws, the state charged journalists who wrote articles deemed "unacceptable" with seditious libel and contempt of court. Despite the government's intolerance for "false reporting," the NDC engaged in smear campaigns against its critics, using newspapers, such as the *Ghanaian Palaver*, as weapons through which to carry out its vendetta.

The government-owned daily newspa-

pers, the *Ghanaian Times* and the *Daily Graphic*, rarely publish articles critical of government policy or state officials. Reporters working for the state media who are accused of unfavorable reporting are vulnerable to disciplinary action or dismissal. Consequently, many state journalists practice self-censorship to avoid government reprisals.

The government controls the principal radio and television stations, which broadcast throughout the country. Despite the Ghana Frequency Registration and Control Board's (GFRB) non-refundable "commitment fees" of US$20,000 and US$40,000 for radio and television respectively, six independent radio stations and a private television station began operations by year's end.

February 9
Nana Kofi Coomson, *The Ghanaian Chronicle,* IMPRISONED, HARASSED
Eben Quarcoo, *The Free Press,* IMPRISONED, HARASSED
Tommy Thompson,
    Tommy Thompson Books, Ltd.,
    IMPRISONED, ATTACKED, HARASSED
On Feb. 9, police arrested and questioned Coomson, the editor in chief of the independent daily *Ghanaian Chronicle,* and later released him on bail of 10 million cedis (US$6,700). Quarcoo, the editor of *The Free Press,* and Thompson, its publisher, had been away from their offices when police delivered a summons ordering them to report to police headquarters for questioning the same day. Instead, they reported to police headquarters Feb. 12 and each was released on bail of 10 million cedis after interrogation.

On Feb. 14, Circuit Court Judge Nuhu Bila revoked the bail without explanation, and the three were immediately remanded into custody. Counsel for the journalists filed an appeal with the High Court.

Coomson, Quarcoo, and Thompson were charged with "publishing false news with the intent of injuring the reputation of the State," a violation of Section 185 of the Criminal Code of 1960, an ordinance from the colonial era. If convicted, they could face a maximum sentence of 10 years in prison.

The Free Press and the *Ghanaian Chronicle* reprinted in their January 31 and February 1 editions, respectively, a story published in the New York-based biweekly *The African Observer,* which reported that the Ghanaian diplomat Frank Benneh, of the Ghanaian Permanent Mission to the United Nations in Geneva, had been arrested in Switzerland for selling drugs. The article also alleged that President Jerry Rawlings of Ghana had used proceeds from illegal drug sales to buy arms.

On Feb. 15, CPJ sent a letter of protest to President Rawlings, calling for the immediate release of the three journalists and the repeal of Section 185 of the antiquated Criminal Code.

On Feb. 23, Judge Bila granted bail in the amount of 6 million cedis (US$4,000) for the journalists, who were then released. Judge Bila also referred the constitutional issues of the case to the Supreme Court. The criminal case has been adjourned until the Supreme Court renders a decision.

April 17
Eben Quarcoo, *The Free Press,* HARASSED, LEGAL ACTION
Tommy Thompson,
    Tommy Thompson Books, Ltd., HARASSED, LEGAL ACTION
Quarcoo, editor of the weekly *The Free Press,* and Thompson, owner of Tommy Thompson Books, the newspaper's publisher, were summoned by the police to answer accusations that they violated Section 185 of the 1960 Criminal Code, which forbids "publishing falsehoods with the intent of injuring the reputation of the state." They were detained for five hours, interrogated, then released without charge on bail of 10 million cedis (US$6,700) each.

The detention was in connection with an April 10 article in *The Free Press.* The story, based on an article originally published in the March 14-27 issue of the New York biweekly *The African Observer*, alleged that Ghanaian President Jerry Rawlings had impregnated the daughter of former Togolese head of state Nicholas Yao Grunitzky. CPJ condemned the detention of Quarcoo and Thompson in a letter to President Rawlings.

August 9
Cofie Ammuako-Annan, *Ghanaian Chronicle,*
    IMPRISONED, LEGAL ACTION
General Portfolio, LEGAL ACTION
Kofi Coomson, *Ghanaian Chronicle,*
    LEGAL ACTION
Darkwa, *Ghanaian Chronicle*, LEGAL ACTION
Ammuako-Annan, acting editor of the independent daily *Ghanaian Chronicle*, was convicted of contempt of court, sentenced to 30 days' imprisonment, and incarcerated, and the newspaper's publishing company, General Portfolio, was fined 1 million cedis (US$700). Ammuako-Annan was released on Aug. 30. *Ghanaian Chronicle* directors Coomson and Darkwa, who had also been charged with contempt, were acquitted. The charges stemmed from the newspaper's criticism of a high court judge's courtroom behavior during a murder trial. The judge had ordered a news blackout of the murder-trial proceedings.

November 25
Opiesie Nkansa-Daaduam, *The Free Press,*
    HARASSED
Nkansa-Daaduam, a columnist with the independent weekly *The Free Press*, was arrested in his office by agents of the military police, who then drove him to the Bureau of National Investigation. Nkansa-Daaduam was accused of publishing "subversive and treasonable" material in a Nov. 20 article about the televised speech of a military officer. In a letter to President Jerry Rawlings, CPJ denounced Nkansa-Daaduam's arrest and requested his immediate and unconditional release. Nkansa-Daaduam was released approximately 24 hours after his arrest.

Ivory Coast

Despite significant restrictions on press freedom, and the threat of seditious libel charges, the Ivoirien independent press continues to publish articles critical of President Konan Bédié and his government's policies. President Bédié has little tolerance for what he considers "insults or attacks on the honor of the country's highest officials," and he is strictly enforcing the penalty for the "crime" of critical reporting: a three-month -to-two-year prison term for offending the president, the prime minister, foreign chiefs of state, or their diplomatic representatives, or defaming state institutions.

Opposition newspapers such as *La Voie* are routinely hauled into court to face defamation charges. In December, *La Voie* publisher Abou Drahamane Sangaré, deputy editor Freedom Neruda, and reporter Emmanuel Koré completed the first year of their two-year prison terms for insulting the president. In August, Bédié had offered the journalists a presidential pardon, which they refused, choosing instead to challenge the outstanding charges against them in the Supreme Court. With a severely compromised judiciary on his side, Bédié has succeeded in keeping the case out of the courts and, to date, the journalists have been refused a court date to file their appeal.

The state owns both television channels and two major radio stations, which are used to promote government policies; only the primary government radio and television stations are broadcast nationwide. Currently, four independent radio stations and a private television subscription service, Canal Horizon, broadcast primarily in the Abidjan metropolitan area.

January 2
Freedom Neruda, *La Voie*, IMPRISONED
Neruda, deputy editor of the independent

opposition daily *La Voie*, was taken into custody for questioning. Police had been searching for him since the December 1995 arrest of his colleagues Abou Drahamane Sangaré, the publications director of the Nouvel Horizon group, which owns *La Voie*, and Emmanuel Koré, a *La Voie* reporter. On Jan. 3, Neruda was charged with insulting the head of state in connection with a satirical article published in *La Voie* suggesting that President Henri Konan Bédié's presence at the African Champions Cup final brought bad luck to the Ivorian soccer team, which lost to South Africa's Orlando Pirates. On Jan. 11, Neruda was sentenced to two years in prison and fined CFA 6 million (US$12,000). CPJ wrote to President Bédié on two occasions: first, to protest Neruda's arrest, and second, to condemn his sentencing and urge the president to revoke it along with the other two-year prison sentences handed down to Sangaré and Koré for "offending the chief of state."

On June 12, an appeals court confirmed the sentences and Neruda and his colleagues filed an appeal with the Supreme Court. CPJ again wrote to Bédié and called for the reversal of the convictions and the immediate release of Neruda, Sangaré, and Koré. They were released on Jan. 1, 1997.

January 2
La Voie, CENSORED
Police seized copies of the independent opposition daily *La Voie* from newsstands when it reappeared in defiance of a three-month suspension otder issued in December 1995. The paper was suspended for allegedly defaming President Henri Konan Bédié. Defense attorneys for *La Voie* justified the paper's premature return on the grounds that neither the newspaper nor its printers had been served with a formal court order. CPJ wrote to President Bédié and urged him to lift the ban on *La Voie*. On Jan. 3, the newspaper, which is an organ of the opposition Ivorian Popular Front (FPI), began publishing under a new name, *L'Alternative*. In April 1996, when the ban was lifted, it resumed publishing

under its original name.

Kenya

President Daniel arap Moi's Kenya African National Union (KANU) government has escalated its war against the independent press, refusing to tolerate any criticism of government officials or its policies. Journalists routinely face intimidation, harassment, attacks, imprisonment without charge, fines, charges of seditious libel or defamation, and pressure to reveal their sources. The government rarely launches investigations following the frequent acts of violence against the press or media houses.

In January, after protests from the international community and foreign diplomats based in Nairobi, President Moi ordered proposed draft media bills shelved indefinitely. The proposed media regulations included licensing of local and foreign journalists, the establishment of a government-mandated code of press conduct, and the creation of a council to regulate media operations. Possession of the proposed media bills by Kenyan journalists was deemed a criminal offense to discourage the information from becoming public until after it had secretly been passed by Parliament. Kenyan authorities subsequently submitted written requests to foreign diplomats calling for recommendations of press laws that would be appropriate for Kenya.

The proposed legislation provided for a comprehensive licensing process for journalists, and the print and broadcast media. It would establish a press council for the purpose of registering and monitoring the conduct of journalists, including foreign correspondents based in Kenya. The council would have the authority to review news content on the basis of prescribed standards, and ban journalists and the news media.

With elections scheduled for 1997, and confrontations escalating between the government and the political opposition, the independent press expects to be the target of increased government harassment during the period leading up to the elections.

May 14
Njehu Gatabaki, *Finance*, IMPRISONED
Gatabaki, editor in chief of the independent monthly magazine *Finance* and a member of parliament, was arrested at his home in the Lavington district of Nairobi. He was taken to the headquarters of the Criminal Investigation Department (CID), then to Parklands police station, where he made a statement denying police accusations that he was involved in the May 1995 murder of police superintendent Bernard Kahumbi. He was released without charge on May 22.

July 15
Waite Mwangi, *East African Standard*, HARASSED
The Nyeri District Criminal Investigation Department (CID), located 150 kilometers northeast of Nairobi, demanded that *East African Standard* reporter Mwangi reveal his sources for a July 14 story about criminals in downtown Nyeri. Mwangi refused to cooperate.

July 27
Journalists, *Nation*, ATTACKED
Journalists, *East African Standard*, ATTACKED
Several journalists from the newspapers *Nation* and *East African Standard* were assaulted by security guards at the British High Commission in Nairobi. The journalists were investigating claims by visa applicants that there were excessive delays in obtaining visas.

August 27
Fotoform Printers, ATTACKED
The production facilities of Fotoform Printers in Westlands, Nairobi, were firebombed. The gasoline used in the bombing was contained in two plastic cans that were placed near a gate

leading to the basement, where the printing presses were located. No one was arrested or charged in the bombing. In a letter to President Daniel arap Moi, CPJ condemned the bombing as an act of intimidation against the press.

November 1
Peter Kamau, *Nation*, ATTACKED, HARASSED
Kamau, a correspondent for the *Nation*, was arrested when he sought clarification over remarks made by Vice President George Saitoti during a speech at a National Youth Development fund-raising event in Lodwar. On Saitoti's orders, security guards punched and kicked Kamau as they arrested him. Saitoti later apologized for the incident.

November 21
Finance, LEGAL ACTION
Using a seditious libel statute, the High Court in Nairobi ordered *Finance* magazine to discontinue publishing articles concerning Kuria Kanyingi, chairman of the Kenya African National Union for the Kiambu District. The order remains in effect until Jan. 22, 1997, when court proceedings begin against the magazine on charges of contempt. The ban was prompted by an article in the Oct. 15, 1996, issue of *Finance*, which claimed that "the self-imposed chairman of the ruling party in Kiambu District is behind and involved in criminal activities in the district." In a letter to President Daniel arap Moi, CPJ condemned the use of seditious libel statutes and called for the immediate revocation of the ban.

November 22
Nation Newspapers Ltd., LEGAL ACTION
Wangethi Mwangi, Nation Group, LEGAL ACTION
Emman Omari, *Nation*, LEGAL ACTION
Comptroller of State Houses Franklin Bett filed a lawsuit against publishing company Nation Newspapers Ltd.; Mwangi, managing editor of the Nation Group, a division of the company; and Omari, chief parliamentary reporter for the

Nation, a daily published by the Nation Group. Bett brought the suit because of a Nov. 13 *Nation* article called "Kanu (Kenya African National Union Party) Faction Demands Poll," which contained what Bett claimed was a reference to him as a member of the Kanu faction.

Liberia

During April's factional fighting, both sides in the conflict—Charles Taylor's National Patriotic Front of Liberia (NPFL) and Roosevelt Johnson's United Liberation Movement (ULIMO)—menaced Liberia's private press. Intent on preventing critical reporting about their activities, factional partisans chased local journalists—especially those working as stringers for international news organizations—into hiding or exile, and conducted a reign of abductions, threats and assaults.

In an effort to silence the local press, arsonists looted and torched the editorial offices of all the independent newspapers, including the *Inquirer, Daily News, New Democrat, Daily Observer* , and *The News*. Intruders ransacked the offices and burned the transmitters of all of the independent radio stations, including those operated by religious organizations. The offices of the outspoken Press Union of Liberia were looted, riddled with bullets and littered with shell casings. An arson attack on the privately owned Sabanoh Printing Press, the largest and most viable printer in the country, sent its owner into exile and halted production of publications for months.

The only media spared in the fighting were the NPFL's KISS-FM radio station and *The Patriot* newspaper. Equipment looted from privately owned media resurfaced, shortly after the fighting died down, fully operational at KISS-FM and *The Patriot*.

In early August, the *Inquirer* became the first independent newspaper to resume publication under extremely challenging conditions; the newspaper is currently being produced by candlelight on two used typewriters. All of Liberia's newspapers are now back in circulation, and journalists have again become targets for harassment.

January 9
James Seitua, *Daily Observer,* IMPRISONED
Seitua, the editor in chief of the *Daily Observer*, was arrested following a meeting with the Director of the National Police, Joseph Tate. Although no official reason was given for the arrest, it was reportedly in connection with an article published in the Dec. 29, 1995 edition of the *Daily Observer* that alleged there were links between rebels in Sierra Leone and the main Liberian faction, the National Patriotic Front of Liberia. On Jan. 11, Seitua was charged with "criminal malevolence" and released on bail of L\$25,000 (US\$350). Under the conditions of his release, Seitua cannot travel outside Monrovia, and must report daily to the police.

January 10
Stanton Peabody, *Daily Observer,* IMPRISONED
Peabody, the acting managing director of the *Daily Observer*, went to police headquarters to intervene on behalf of the newspaper's detained editor in chief, James Seitua. Upon arrival, Peabody was summoned to the office of the Director of National Police, Joseph Tate, where he was immediately arrested. On Jan. 12, Peabody was charged with "criminal malevolence" and released on bail of L\$20,000 (US\$400).

On Jan. 17, the case against Peabody was dismissed. As he was leaving the courtroom, Peabody was handed another arrest warrant on the same charge of criminal malevolence, and he was remanded to prison. Peabody was released two hours later on a bond of L\$20,000 (US\$400).

January 11

Jacob Doe, *Inquirer,* THREATENED

Liberian police stormed the offices of the independent *Inquirer* newspaper, demanding the arrest of the production manager Jacob Doe. Passersby and staff succeeded in preventing police officers from seizing Doe. The attempted arrest was in response to a front-page article in the Jan. 11 edition of the *Inquirer*, entitled "Jungle Justice at Police Station." The article criticized the Jan. 9 arrest of James Seitua, the editor-in-chief of the *Daily Observer*, and the Jan. 10 arrest of Stanton Peabody, the acting managing director of the *Daily Observer*.

January 13

D. Sompon Weah II, *The News,* ATTACKED

Pewee S. Flomoku, *The News,* ATTACKED, HARASSED

Shortly after their arrival in Po River, in northern Liberia, *The News* reporter Weah and photographer Flomoku were attacked as they covered skirmishes between West African peacekeeping forces (ECOMOG) and warring factions of the United Liberation Movement (ULIMO-J). The journalists were beaten by order of the executive director of the Liberia Refugees Repatriation & Resettlement Commission, Weade Kobbah Wreh. During the beating, administered by Wreh's personal bodyguards and some ECOMOG soldiers, Flomoku's camera was destroyed.

February 28

Sandoo Moore, *The National,* ATTACKED, HARASSED

Moore, the publisher of the weekly newspaper *The National*, was arrested by Minister of Justice Francis Garlawulo in Garlawulo's office. Garlawulo summoned Moore and Kortu Kerbeh, the editor in chief of *The National*, to answer questions about an article, published in the paper's Feb. 27 edition, entitled "Hit Squad Reported in Town." The article, written by an anonymous reporter, alleged that a Monrovia-based group received orders from the National

Patriotic Front of Liberia (NPFL) to assassinate government officials. The hit squad was allegedly headed by a soldier known as "Lt.-Gen. Jack-the-Rebel." Upon the orders of Garlawulo, Moore was severely beaten by six police officers and detained in a prison cell. No charges were filed against Moore, and he was released on parole later that day and ordered to appear in Circuit Court the next morning where his case was adjourned.

April 1

Stanley Seaklo, *The News,* ATTACKED, LEGAL ACTION

Nyekeh Forkpa, *The News,* ATTACKED, LEGAL ACTION

The Council of State, Liberia's transitional ruling council, ordered the closure of the independent biweekly newspaper *The News* and initiated court proceedings against the publication for referring to two council members, Charles Taylor and Alhaji Kromah, as "warlords." On March 27, Taylor summoned *The News*'s editor, Seaklo, and its publisher, Forkpa, to the executive mansion, where they were detained and beaten during interrogation. Proceedings against *The News* were halted when fighting erupted on April 6 between Taylor's forces and those of Roosevelt Johnson.

April

ELCM Radio, ATTACKED

Ducor Radio, ATTACKED

Radio Monrovia, ATTACKED

The Inquirer, ATTACKED

New Democrat, ATTACKED

Sabanoh Printing Press, ATTACKED

Several news outlets that had been critical of the Liberian Council of State, a recently formed coalition group, were attacked in April during factional fighting between the National Patriotic Front of Liberia (NPFL), whose leader Charles Taylor is a vice-chairman of the Council, and the United Liberation Movement (ULIMO), led by Roosevelt Johnson.

The editorial offices of the independent newspapers *The Inquirer* and *New Democrat* and the transmitter of ELCM, an FM radio station operated by the Catholic Church, were destroyed by arson in separate attacks in the capital of Monrovia. In a third arson attack, Sabanoh Printing Press, a privately owned printer that services all of Liberia's state and independent newspapers, was partially destroyed. In another incident, the offices of the privately owned Ducor Radio and Radio Monrovia were ransacked.

All of the news outlets have been targeted in the past by fighting factions loyal to the NPLF and ULIMO. However, it is suspected by many that the NPLF is responsible for the attacks. The Press Union of Liberia condemned the destructive acts and told CPJ that it believes they were calculated attempts on the parts of some members of warring factions to silence the press.

April 7
Nyenati Allison, Associated Press (AP),
  British Broadcasting Corporation (BBC),
  THREATENED
Allison, a correspondent covering the outbreak of fighting in Monrovia for AP and the BBC's "Focus on Africa," was chased into hiding by fighters belinging to the United Liberation Movement (ULIMO), the warring faction led by Roosevelt Johnson, on April 7. Johnson accused Allison of reporting lies about ULIMO's role in the fighting that erupted in Monrovia the previous day. Allison fled to safety in the U.N. compound for two nights, during which ULIMO fighters returned, circled the compound, and fired their guns. On April 9, because his presence was putting the lives of others in the compound at risk, Allison left in disguise. He sought refuge at the headquarters of ECOMOG, the West African peacekeeping force. Allison returned to covering the conflict on April 11.

April 19
Nyenati Allison, Associated Press (AP),
  British Broadcasting Corporation (BBC),
  HARASSED
Allison, a reporter for AP and the BBC'S "Focus on Africa", was detained up by soldiers from Charles Taylor's National Patriotic Front of Liberia. The fighters cited Allison's critical reports on fighting in Monrovia and the neighboring suburbs as the reason for his detention. Allison was released on April 21.

May 3
Nyenati Allison, Associated Press (AP), and
  British Broadcasting Corporation (BBC),
  HARASSED
Allison, the Liberian correspondent for AP and the BBC, fled the country with his two children after being threatened by soldiers for the third time. On May 3, a commander of the National Patriotic Forces of Liberia (NPFL) ordered Allison to go with him to NPFL headquarters to answer questions about a story the correspondent had filed in which he reported that no armed faction had the upper hand in the fighting. Before reaching the headquarters, however, Allison managed to escape. He picked up his two children, and together they boarded a fishing boat that took them to the Ivorian capital of Abidjan. But immediately after learning that several NPFL agents were in the city, they left by bus for Ghana.

Namibia

An increase in government intolerance for media coverage of critical views compromised Namibia's reputation as a model democracy. On numerous occasions, the media have accused President Sam Nujoma and other senior government officials of restricting free speech and abuse of public broadcasting facilities in their use of the state-owned Namibian Broadcasting Corpora-

tion (NBC) Television to promote government policies or air the opinions of public officials. Incidences of censorship, effected by NBC management's refusal to release or air footage of interviews with government officials that contain sensitive issues or attacks on individuals or organizations that criticized government officials and their policies, have also increased in frequency.

Journalists are facing new legal threats. Provisions of the Privileges and Immunities of Parliament Law, passed in April, define the publication of "false information" about Parliament or its proceedings as an offense, and a National Assembly amendment defines the intentional or negligent publication or disclosure of information placed before a parliamentary committee as an offense. Both are punishable by a maximum fine of N$20,000 (U$5,000) and/or five years' imprisonment.

The year ended with the publication of an interview with President Nujoma in the state-funded newspaper *New Era*, in which he accused the country's press of being an "enemy," "reactionary," not "Namibian," and run by foreigners. None of Namibia's private press operates under foreign ownership.

September 25
Alfred Oxurub, *New Era*, HARASSED
Two security guards confiscated Oxurub's film outside the home of the chief of parliament. They accused Oxurub of falsely representing himself as a journalist and of taking pictures without permission.

September 30
Hannes Smith, *The Windhoek Advertiser,*
  LEGAL ACTION
Esther Smith, *The Windhoek Advertiser,*
  LEGAL ACTION
Elizabeth Haase, *The Windhoek Advertiser,*
  LEGAL ACTION
Judge Theo Frank dropped charges against Hannes Smith, former editor of *The Windhoek Advertiser*, and the paper's directors, Esther

Smith and Haase. The three had been charged in July 1995 with contravening the 1991 Racial Discrimination Prohibition Act after running an advertisement in the paper's Aug. 17, 1994, edition commemorating the seventh anniversary of the death of Rudolf Hess, Adolf Hitler's deputy. The ad referred to Hess as a "martyr of peace" and the "last representative of a better Germany."

Niger

General Ibrahim Bare Mainassara, who led the overthrow of former president Mahamane Ousmane in January, claimed an outright victory in the July elections, which were widely viewed as fraudulent. Gen. Mainassara had placed his opponents under house arrest and the army commandeered the ballot boxes in many areas of the country. Mainassara declared himself the winner shortly after he dissolved the Independent National Electoral Commission, imposing a nationwide ban on demonstrations and public gatherings, and cutting international telephone lines. He reversed the ban and the telephone restrictions on Oct. 4, in preparation for November legislative elections which opposition parties boycotted. Voter turnout was low, and the ruling party swept to victory, thereby creating a new parliament.

Press freedom was imperiled following the presidential elections as the new government attempted to maintain tight control over the media. Soldiers stormed and occupied independent radio stations and harassed, arrested, and detained both local and foreign journalists. The government blocked the media's access to certain regions of the country, and the director general of Niger's radio and television broadcasting agency, Maitourare Abdou Saleye, canceled opposition parties', unions', and associations' access to the national radio and television network.

May 5
Ibrahim Hamidou, *Tribune du Peuple,*
IMPRISONED
Hamidou, managing director of the independent weekly *Tribune du Peuple,* was arrested without charge in connection with the May 3 publication of an article critical of Col. Ibrahim Barre Mainassara. Hamidou was released on May 13.

July 6
Radio Anfani, CENSORED
Soldiers took over the offices of Radio Anfani (FM100 MHZ), a privately owned radio station and Voice of America affiliate in Niamey. The military's actions were believed to be in retaliation for the station's coverage of the political opposition during the run-up to presidential elections, held July 7-8. Radio Anfani resumed broadcasting on Aug. 4.

July 30
Abdoulaye Senyi, *Haske,* British Broadcasting
Corp. (BBC), IMPRISONED
Senyi, a reporter for the independent newspaper *Haske* and a correspondent for the BBC, was arrested, apparently because of a BBC broadcast in which Senyi quoted a U.S. State Department communiqué that said the U.S. government intended to cut aid to Niger. Senyi was not charged. He was released on Aug. 3.

Nigeria

Gen. Sani Abacha escalated his brutal tactics aimed at decimating the independent press and driving journalists out of their profession or into exile. The incommunicado detention without charge of *Tell* editor Nosa Igiebor, *TheNEWS* editor Bayo Onanuga, media attorney Gani Fawehinmi, and numerous other media professionals and their legal representatives paled in comparison with the assassination in broad daylight of Kudirat Abiola, wife of publisher and President-elect Moshood Abiola, and the attempted assassination of Alex Ibru, publisher of *The Guardian.*

The year saw a rash of detentions of independent journalists—all without charge—in connection with articles that were critical of the military regime and its officials. Journalists were under constant pressure to name their sources, but chose to face indefinite prison stays rather than provide information to State Security Service (SSS) agents or their interrogators.

A number of purportedly privately owned publications came into existence, under the leadership of individuals with no previous media experience who are unknown to the country's media professionals. The financing for many of these publications is believed to come from individuals connected to Gen. Abacha's regime.

The year ended with a number of arrests of editors and correspondents employed by the independent press and the announcement of the establishment of a press court, a separate court with a mandate to function solely for the purpose of prosecuting journalists and media professionals. Additional restrictions in the form of a media council, a body of six presidential appointees who manage the annual printed press registration process, was instituted by Decree 43. Among the list of requirements for registration are a pre-registration deposit of 250,000 naira (US$3,100) and a non-refundable fee of 100,000 naira (US$1,240), and evidence concerning the good character, competence, and integrity of the directors and of other persons responsible for or in charge of the publication of newspapers or magazines. License renewal is contingent upon the media council's satisfaction with the publication's performance.

CPJ, through its international campaign,

"Nigeria: The Press Under Siege," worked closely with Lagos-based journalists to secure the June release of Igiebor, and the subsequent release of Onanuga and Fawehinmi, and continues to spotlight attention on the crisis facing Nigeria's independent press.

January 4

Paul Adams, *Financial Times*, IMPRISONED

Adams, a correspondent for the London-based *Financial Times*, was arrested by State Security Service agents in Bori, a major town in southeast Nigeria's Ogoniland. Adams was covering local protests against pollution caused by oil firms and local demands for a greater share in oil revenues. He was transferred to Port Harcourt, where he remained in detention until his release on Jan. 11. Adams was charged with "possession of seditious literature" in connection with a leaflet about Ogoni issues that was in his possession at the time of his arrest.

February 2

Alex Ibru, *The Guardian*, ATTACKED

Ibru, publisher of the independent daily newspaper *The Guardian* and a former Internal Affairs Minister in Gen. Sani Abacha's government, was shot and wounded by unknown assailants in the evening, while driving from his office to his home in Lagos. Ibru, who sustained gunshot wounds to his face and left hand, was transported to London for emergency medical care. Police have classified the attempted murder of Ibru as attempted armed robbery, and arrested nine men in connection with the crime, despite the fact that nothing was stolen from Ibru's car or from his person. In a letter to Gen. Abacha, CPJ condemned the attack and called for an investigation into the attempted murder of Ibru.

February 15

Hillary Anderson, British Broadcasting Corp. (BBC), HARASSED

Anderson, a correspondent for the BBC, was arrested by State Security Service (SSS) agents as she was leaving the Reuter office in Lagos. Anderson was transported to SSS headquarters and detained without charge. She was released on Feb. 16. Anderson had arrived in Lagos just days before her arrest to begin her work for the BBC.

March

Jude Sinnee, newspaper vendor, IMPRISONED

Armed agents of the Rivers State Internal Security Task Force arrested Sinnee, a newspaper vendor in Bori, an Ogoni settlement in Rivers State, at his newsstand. The agents also seized 500 copies of various publications and the vendor's accumulated sales of the day. They then transported Sinnee to the Internal Security Task Force's office at Kpor, near Bori, where he is being held incommunicado. Sinnee, a disabled person, went on a hunger strike to protest his detention.

Early March

Baguda Kaltho, *TheNEWS*, KILLED

Kaltho, the Kaduna-based senior correspondent for *TheNEWS*, has been missing since the first week of March. Kaltho left the newspaper's editorial office alone one evening and has not been seen since. *TheNEWS* management and Kaltho's family have been unable to ascertain his whereabouts, and he is presumed dead.

May

Chinedu Offoaro, *The Guardian*, KILLED

Offoaro, a reporter for *The Guardian*, has been missing since the third week of May. Offoaro failed to return to *The Guardian's* editorial offices on May 26 as expected from a reporting assignment in Owerri, in Imo State. His family has been unsuccessful in their attempts to locate him and fear he is dead. State Security Service officials have refused to cooperate with the family, and have not answered questions about whether they detained Offoaro.

May 15

George Onah, *Vanguard*, IMPRISONED

Onah, defense correspondent for the independent newspaper *Vanguard*, was arrested without charge and is being held in incommunicado detention. Onah is being pressured to reveal his sources for an article he wrote about promotions and other changes in rank among Nigerian military officers. On Dec. 31, Chief of Defense Staff Maj. Gen. Abdul Salaam Abubakar told reporters that he would look into Onah's case, but to date officials have not released any information on Onah's status or location.

May 28
Alphonsus Agborh, *Punch*, IMPRISONED
Police arrested Agborh, a reporter for the independent daily *Punch*, at the newspaper's editorial office in Port Harcourt. Although authorities gave no official reason for the arrest, observers believe it is related to a May 26 article in *Punch* about Nigeria's importation of weapons from a South African company. On May 31, Agborh was released on bail.

June 24
Hassan Anwar, Middle East News Agency,
    IMPRISONED, EXPELLED
Anwar was detained by Nigerian security authorities when he applied for a residence permit to begin his assignment as correspondent in Abuja for the Middle East News Agency. Anwar had been officially welcomed by the minister of information, but the security authorities accused him of coming to Nigeria to carry out a mission. They were not specific about what kind of mission or what organization he was thought to be representing. Anwar was released after one week and ordered to leave Nigeria immediately; he arrived in Egypt on July 1.

July 31
Okina Deesor, Radio Rivers, IMPRISONED
Deesor, a producer with Radio Rivers in the state of Rivers, was arrested and detained at the Government House Cell prison, reportedly without food or water. On Aug. 3, he was trans-

ferred to the Mobile Police Headquarters in Port Harcourt. According to Maj. Obi Umabi, who ordered the arrest, Deesor's detention was in connection with the July 18 Radio Rivers broadcast of the national anthem of the Ogoni people. As of Dec. 18, Deesor remained in prison. In a letter to President Sani Abacha, CPJ denounced Deesor's continued detention and asked for his immediate and unconditional release.

August 11
Bayo Onanuga, *TheNEWS*, IMPRISONED
Babafemi Ojudu, *TheNEWS*, IMPRISONED
Onanuga and Ojudu, editors of the independent weekly magazine *TheNEWS*, were arrested by State Security Service (SSS) agents in connection with the newspaper's reports about Dan Etete, the oil minister, and Mariam Abacha, the wife of Gen. Sani Abacha. The two editors were taken to Shagisha prison on the outskirts of Lagos. Ojudu was released on Aug. 13. Onanuga was transferred to the Lagos State Federal Intelligence Office at Alagbon Close and released on Aug. 17.

October 13
Dele Alake, *National Concord*, ATTACKED
Alake, editor of the *National Concord*, escaped an attack by gunmen in Lagos as he drove toward the Murtala Muhammed Airport. He managed to drive to a police station, where he reported the incident. Witnesses said that the assailants' car had been spotted before the incident near the editorial offices of the *National Concord*.

October 13
Richard Akinnola, *National Concord*,
    IMPRISONED, HARASSED
Akinnola, the judicial correspondent for the independent daily *National Concord*, was arrested without charge by State Security Service (SSS) agents and detained at the SSS office on Awolowo Road in Lagos. He was released without explanation on Nov. 20.

December 18

Godwin Agbroko, *The Week*, IMPRISONED

Three men who said they were security agents arrested Agbroko, editor in chief of the privately owned weekly magazine *The Week*, at his office. Observers believe the arrest is in connection with an article in the Dec. 16-23 edition of *The Week* titled "A Deadly Power Play," about a dispute between Army Chief of Staff Ishaya Bamaiyi and Guard Brigade Commander Yakubu Mu'azu.

Rwanda

The alarming numbers of killings and other acts of violence against unarmed civilians perpetrated by the Rwandan Patriotic Front have sabotaged Rwandans' efforts to rebuild their country. Citizens and returnees have fallen victim to arbitrary detention, gross abuse, or murder, and the overstretched, at times non-existent, judicial system leaves little recourse for these victims.

Although Rwandan Fundamental Law provides for freedom of the press, security forces continue to assault, kidnap, and detain members of the independent press. Journalists practice self-censorship to avoid being arrested for their reporting and to protect themselves against accusations of perpetrating the genocide. Some journalists have gone undercover in fear for their lives. Privately owned newspapers that practice critical reporting have been subject to seizures and outright government bans.

Broadcast media are state controlled. And, given the role that hate radio has played in stirring up the antagonisms that contributed to the 1994 genocide, it is unlikely that the government will grant licenses to private radio stations in the foreseeable future.

July 30

Appolos Hakizimana, *Intego*, IMPRISONED

Intego , CENSORED

Hakizimana, a journalist with the privately owned newspaper *Intego*, was detained by police and accused of being an "interahamwe," a term used to describe Hutu accomplices to genocide. He was held at the Muhima Brigade in Kigali. The arrest occurred after authorities seized the July issue of *Intego* and banned publication of future issues until further notice.

It is believed the ban was prompted by an article in the seized issue that was critical of certain government authorities and a government campaign to raise awareness about security risks posed by armed opposition groups. The article implied that these awareness-raising efforts resembled a terror campaign. Hakizimana was released during the week of Aug. 19.

August 6

Amiel Nkuliza, *Intego* and *Le Partisan*, IMPRISONED

Intego, CENSORED

Nkuliza, director of the privately owned newspaper *Intego* and editor of the independent newspaper *Le Partisan*, was arrested without charge by officers of the Rwanda security forces. The arrest occurred after authorities seized the July issue of *Intego* and banned publication of future issues until further notice.

It is believed the ban was prompted by an article in the seized issue that was critical of certain government authorities and a government campaign to raise awareness about security risks posed by armed opposition groups. The article implied that these awareness-raising efforts resembled a terror campaign. Nkuliza was released on Aug. 13.

Senegal

Many observers regard Senegal under the government of President Abdou Diouf as respectful of freedom of expression and the

press. A broad spectrum of opinion is available to the public through regularly published magazines and newspapers, including foreign publications, and numerous independent radio stations. A government monopoly controls local television, an important source of news. French-owned pay television is available, but offers no local news.

Publishers must gain government approval through a registration process prior to starting publication. While the government routinely approves such registrations, laws prohibiting the press from the expression of views that "discredit" the state, incite the population to disorder, or disseminate "false news" do exist.

According to Senegalese law, the burden of proof rests with the accused in a defamation suit. This places the media in a quagmire, because building their case amounts to disclosing their sources. Journalists are convicted if they decline to provide the necessary documentation, as was the case with the defamation case against the independent daily newspaper *Sud Quotidien* stemming from an article published in the Oct. 13 edition, which claimed that the Mimran Corporation used fraudulent practices in its importation of sugar from Brazil.

May 14
Babacar Toure, Sud Communication,
    LEGAL ACTION
Abdoulaye Ndiaga Sylla, Sud Communication,
    Sud Quotidien, LEGAL ACTION
Sidy Gaye, *Sud Quotidien*, LEGAL ACTION
Bocar Niang, *Sud Quotidien*, LEGAL ACTION
Mame Oll Faye, *Sud Quotidien*, LEGAL ACTION
Ibrahim Sarr, *Sud Quotidien*, LEGAL ACTION
Toure, chairperson and president of Sud Communication, a private Senegalese media company which owns the independent newspaper *Sud Quotidien* and radio station Sud FM; Sylla, first vice president of Sud Communication and director of *Sud Quotidien*; Gaye, editor in chief of *Sud Quotidien*; and Niang, Faye, and Sarr,

reporters for the newspaper, went to trial for public defamation in a suit brought by the Mimran Group, a foreign-owned sugar producer. An article in the Oct. 13, 1995, edition of Sud Quotidien claimed that Mimran used fraudulent practices in its importation of sugar from Brazil.

On June 27, Sud Communication and *Sud Quotidien* were found liable and were ordered to pay Mimran 500 million CFA (US$1 million). Journalists Sylla, Gaye, Niang, Faye, and Sarr were convicted of libel, and each was sentenced to one month in prison. So far, they have not been arrested. Toure was acquitted. CPJ protested the fine and jail sentences in a letter to Senegalese President Abdou Diouf.

Sierra Leone

Despite the transfer of power from military ruler Gen. Julius Maada Bio to newly elected President Ahmed Tejan Kabbah in March, the government and its officials continue to threaten press freedom in Sierra Leone. Independent journalists routinely face harassment, detention without charge, and charges of sedition, libel, or contempt of parliament for their coverage of government corruption, the civil war, and human rights issues.

During the election campaign and in its aftermath, the promise of a democratic society encouraged the launch of a number of newspapers. Yet contrary to expectations, the government of President Kabbah has shown intolerance toward criticism of its policies or officials by banning newspapers that publish uncomplimentary articles and detaining journalists. The frequent use of criminal libel and sedition charges against independent journalists has encouraged self-censorship, and the imposition of heavy fines is financially crippling the private press.

In May, the parliament passed a set of guidelines restricting journalists from reporting on committee decisions and secret sessions. These guidelines also defined the charge of "contempt of parliament," the basis for the arrest of Sheka Parawali, editor of *Torchlight* and editor Gibril Koroma and reporter Max Jimmy of *Expo Times*. The parliament sentenced some of the journalists charged with contempt without the benefit of trial or even a court appearance.

In October, the Sierra Leone Association of Journalists (SLAJ) submitted a revised code of conduct and a 20-point media proposal to the Ministry of Information that called for the removal of all government licensing procedures of the press, the establishment of state corporations to guarantee the independence of Sierra Leone Broadcasting Services (SLBS), and the creation of a press council to arbitrate public complaints against the media.

In February 1997, Minister of Information Abdul-Thorlu Bangura is scheduled to present Parliament with a bill promulgating further press-freedom restrictions. The bill is expected to require, as a condition of permission to publish, that publications obtain insurance policies covering future libel charges and maintain collateral assets for use in defending such suits. Parliament is also slated to take up the issue of proposed qualifications for editors and publishers that would restrict entry into the journalism profession.

While some private radio stations have received licenses, the registration process has favored politically well-connected entrepreneurs. Currently, five private radio stations are fully operational; three of them air programming produced by the British Broadcasting Corporation, Voice of America, and Radio France Internationale.

July 19
Edison Yongai, *The Point*, IMPRISONED, LEGAL ACTION
Yongai, editor of the independent newspaper

The Point, was arrested by five plainclothes Criminal Investigations Department (CID) agents at the newspaper's editorial office, which the agents searched. The arrest was in connection with a story titled "Corrupt Ministers" in the July 18 issue.

Yongai was taken to CID headquarters, where he was interrogated. On July 23, he was charged with seditious libel. He was released the following day after paying bail in the amount of 10 million leones (US$11,000). On Aug. 8, however, Yongai was arrested again, by order of the High Court. The Court set new terms for his case, demanding a higher bail. Yongai was unable to pay the additional bail and spent the night in Pademba Road Prison before being released on Aug. 9. Charges against Yongai were unofficially dropped before his scheduled hearing date of Oct. 10.

August 28
Ibrahim Seaga Shaw, *Expo Times*, IMPRISONED, HARASSED
Gibril Koroma, *Expo Times*, HARASSED
Ten Central Investigation Department (CID) officers searched the editorial offices of the *Expo Times* for "subversive documents" and arrested publisher and editor in chief Shaw and news editor Koroma. The search and arrests were in connection with an Aug. 28 story about the Sierra Leone government's interception of a message from rebel leader Foday Sankoh of the Revolutionary United Front. The message contained instructions to his forces to begin fighting, which would effectively put an end to a cease-fire in Sierra Leone's civil war. CID agents failed to uncover any documents related to the article.

Koroma was released from CID custody one hour later. Shaw continues to be detained without charge at CID headquarters. In a letter to President Ahmed Tejan Kabbah, CPJ asked for Shaw's unconditional release and the cessation of CID harassment of journalists.

September 6
Torchlight, CENSORED
Minister of Information George Banda Thomas banned *Torchlight*, a new independent newspaper that was to come out twice a week, on the same day the first issue was published. The newspaper, sponsored by the opposition United National People's Party (UNPP), was banned on the grounds that its first issue contained uncomplimentary articles about President Ahmed Tejan Kabbah. Thomas retracted the ban the same day and gave *Torchlight* permission to publish until after an upcoming government review of proposed changes to the press law.

October 9
Max Jimmy, *Expo Times,* ATTACKED
Jimmy, a staff writer for *Expo Times*, was assaulted by Special Security Department (SSD) officers in front of Vice President Joe Demby's office as he was leaving the premises. Jimmy had gone to Demby's office to confirm information alleging that a deputy minister, Theresa Koroma, had granted a nongovernment employee the use of an official government vehicle. SSD officers refused to allow him to speak with Koroma but referred him to Permanent Secretary Aiah Ngongor to get the necessary permission. Ngongor refused to speak to Jimmy about the alleged case.

October 11
Sheka Parawali, *Torchlight,* IMPRISONED,
 LEGAL ACTION
Parawali, editor of the independent newspaper *Torchlight*, was sentenced to one month in prison after appearing before Parliament to answer charges of contempt of Parliament. The charges were in connection with an Oct. 8 article titled "Kabbah Bribes MPs," referring to President Ahmed Tejan Kabbah. In a letter to Kabbah, CPJ denounced Parawali's conviction without trial. Parawali was released on Nov. 11.

October 12
Hilton Fyle, *1 2 3,* LEGAL ACTION

Fyle, editor of the weekly newspaper *1 2 3* and a former announcer for the BBC's Africa Service, was charged with "seditious publication." The charge was in connection with a story published in the newspaper's Oct. 7 issue that alleged that justice officials had accepted bribes to drop a fraud case against a former foreign minister and a businessman. Fyle pleaded not guilty, and was freed on bail of 10 million leones (US$10,000).

In a letter to President Ahmed Tejan Kabbah, CPJ condemned the use of seditious libel statutes because they silence critical reporting of the government.

November 5
Gibril Koroma, *Expo Times,* LEGAL ACTION
Max Jimmy, *Expo Times,* LEGAL ACTION
Expo Times acting editor Koroma and reporter Jimmy pleaded not guilty to charges of contempt of Parliament before the Parliament Privileges Committee. The charge was in connection with an Oct. 29 article alleging that commercial banks had been pressured by the government to loan members of Parliament 320 million leones (US$34,042,550) to buy Mercedes Benz automobiles for their personal use. The members of Parliament maintain that the loans were personal, but parliamentarians have a history of failing to pay off their own loans, allowing the government to assume responsibility for the debts. Koroma and Jimmy's case, which had been scheduled to be heard by the full Parliament on Nov. 18, was postponed indefinitely.

December 18
Ibrahim Seaga Shaw, *Expo Times,* IMPRISONED
Charles Roberts, *Expo Times,* IMPRISONED
Expo Times publisher and editor in chief Shaw, and acting editor Roberts, were arrested and detained at the Criminal Investigations Department (CID). They were released on Dec. 23 and ordered to report regularly to CID.

The arrests were in connection with an article in the Dec. 18 issue of *Expo Times* about an alleged coup attempt, which had been announced by government radio. *Expo Times* reported that police were seeking to arrest a number of army officers and Steven Bio, a local businessman and older brother of former head of state Julius Maada Bio.

Sudan

Since the 1989 coup that brought the Islamist-backed regime of Lt. General Omar Hassan al-Bashir to power, the press has remained under constant threat. The new military regime abruptly closed newspapers that had flourished during the brief period of multi-party government (1986-89) and imprisoned dozens of journalists for their links with the opposition press.

Authorities continue to keep a watchful eye on independent-minded journalists. They invoked the restrictive 1993 Press and Publications Law when they deemed the reporting to be too critical. In January, for example, the government used the law to revoke the license of the privately owned daily *Akhar Khabar* for what it described as the newspaper's repeated "exaggerations" and violations of public morality. Another private paper, the outspoken independent *Al-Rai al-Akher*, closed after the government revoked the license of its publisher, Dar al-Ahlah, in July. The newspaper had been hit with a two-week publication suspension in May after publishing an article on a prison riot south of the capital, Khartoum.

In December, the Sudanese parliament passed a revised press law that imposed further constraints on the press. In addition to the existing ban on coverage of the army and national security issues, the new law also prohibits reporting on the national police. Newspapers in violation of the new law risk a two-month closure or even the permanent cancellation of their operating licenses.

Some positive features of the law, on the other hand, include provisions that guarantee journalists the right to protect the confidentiality of their sources and require the authorities to notify the Journalists Syndicate in cases of journalists' arrest. Given the Sudanese government's disregard for the rule of law, however, observers voice skepticism about how rigorously authorities will enforce these protective provisions.

January 19
Akhar Khabar, CENSORED
The privately owned newspaper *Akhar Khabar* was permanently closed down by the government's Press and Publications Council for allegedly violating professional ethics. The paper was accused of having published articles that exacerbated tensions between Sunni and Shi'ite Muslims. *Akhar Khabar* was temporarily closed by the government in July 1995 for publishing an article that criticized Sudan's press law.

February
Osama Ghandi, Sudanese Television,
    IMPRISONED, LEGAL ACTION
Hassan Saleh, Sudanese Television,
    IMPRISONED, LEGAL ACTION
Ghandi and Saleh, a cameraman and a technician for state-owned Sudanese Television, were detained in February for their alleged involvement in a coup attempt by Sudanese army officers earlier in the year. Both men were prosecuted as part of a secret military court trial that convened on Aug. 21. In a Sept. 18 session, Ghandi said that his confession of involvement in the coup attempt had been coerced under torture by military intelligence agents. During the proceeding, he removed his shirt to reveal scars that he said were the result of his torture. CPJ Oct. 3 criticized the government's use of a military court to prosecute Ghandi and Saleh, who are civilians. CPJ also called on the Sudanese government to transfer their cases to a civilian court and to discard any evidence

extracted under torture.

May 19
Al Rai al-Akhar, ATTACKED, CENSORED
A group of armed men stormed the offices of the privately owned daily *Al-Rai al-Akhar* and confiscated all 20,000 copies of that day's edition. The attack took place one day after the newspaper reported on a prison revolt south of Khartoum that was carried out by 95 soldiers suspected of taking part in a coup d'etat. On May 20, authorities banned the paper for a two-week period.

July 12
Al-Rai al-Akhar, CENSORED
Al-Majalis, CENSORED
The National Press and Publications Council effectively shut down the privately owned daily *Al-Rai al-Akhar* and the triweekly newspaper *Al-Majalis* by revoking the license of their publishing house, Dar al-Ahila. The government accused *Al-Rai al-Akhar* of threatening security and social harmony.

September 4
Babakr Othaman, *Al-Watan,* IMPRISONED, MISSING
Othaman, a reporter for the Qatari daily *Al-Watan,* was arrested by Sudanese authorities. Othaman's colleagues believe he was arrested in relation to articles he had written about the Sudanese government. Sudanese officials maintained that Othaman's arrest and detention were unrelated to his writing and were undertaken for security reasons. On Sept. 26, CPJ wrote to Sudanese President Omar Hassan al-Bashir, urging him to ascertain Othaman's whereabouts and to make public the official charges, if any, against him. Othaman was released on Nov. 28.

Uganda

The April presidential election and June's

parliamentary balloting unleashed a wave of government repression of the press. And journalists' attempts to cover the country's civil war also tested the limits of press freedom in Uganda. In each instance, journalists faced intimidation, harassment, and physical attack. Members of the ruling and opposition parties and rebel groups accused reporters of biased or false reporting, and misrepresentation. President Yoweri Museveni issued a warning that authorities will arrest journalists for "irresponsible reporting" that endangers national security.

Despite the fact that existing sedition laws directly contradict provisions contained in Uganda's constitution, the Supreme Court legally upheld the controversial 1995 conviction of Haruna Kanaabi, editor of *The Shariat.* The government used its right of censorship, as well as charges of public alarm and civil defamation carrying exorbitant fines, to silence its critics.

Parliament passed an electronic media bill that defines the terms for setting up private radio and television stations. The legislation also calls for the creation of a broadcasting council, comprised of government officials, to monitor programs aired by private broadcasters and censor those that are deemed unacceptable. Parliament is reportedly considering revising the journalists and press statute of 1995, a draconian body of law that monitors the licensing and conduct of journalists and media houses, but there is as yet no indication of the nature of the changes under consideration.

November 13
Haruna Kanaabi, *The Shariat,* LEGAL ACTION
The Uganda High Court rejected Kanaabi's appeal of a sedition conviction. Kanaabi, editor in chief of the weekly Muslim newsletter *The Shariat,* was arrested on Aug. 25, 1995, for publishing an article called "Rwanda is Now a Ugandan Province," and on Dec. 19, 1995, he was found guilty of sedition and publishing false

news. He was released on Dec. 27, 1995, after international pressure. In a 1996 letter to President Yoweri Museveni, CPJ requested that the conviction be overturned.

December 4
Peter Busiku, *The Uganda Express,*
LEGAL ACTION
Busiku, editor of the Kampala weekly *The Uganda Express,* was arrested and charged with publishing "false statements or reports which are likely to cause fear and alarm to the public." The newspaper had published an article called "Uganda, Burundi, Rwanda Plan Assault on Tanzania" in the Nov. 27-Dec. 4 issue. Busiku was remanded to Luzira prison and later released on US$500 bail. He was scheduled to appear in court on Dec. 19.

Zaire

Despite guarantees for freedom of expression in Zaire's constitution and the 1993 Transition Act, agents of President Mobutu Sese Seko's Special Presidential Division (DSP) and the Military Action and Intelligence Service (SARM) continue to intimidate, harass, detain, torture, and inflict grave human rights abuses on journalists and media officials. Harassment of the press has escalated, and the lack of protections for journalists combined with a weak, ineffectual judiciary provides journalists accused of press law violations with little legal recourse.

The government has used charges of sedition, disseminating false information, and jeopardizing national security to silence the press. Newspaper publishers are required to deposit copies of each issue with the ministry of information prior to publication, effectively promoting self-censorship among reporters and facilitating government censorship of unfavorable coverage. Foreign journalists who investigated charges that Zairean troops were pillaging Rwandan refugees camps were either deported or barred from leaving the country.

Newspaper circulation is limited to Kinshasa and a few other large cities, the result of a severely dilapidated infrastructure and a failing economy. Radio is the most effective means of communicating with the citizenry. Private radio stations, most of which carry Christian programs, have started broadcasting since the transition. The state has promised to fix non-functioning transmitters and increase the transmission power of government-owned radio and television in preparation for the national elections, but it remains to be seen whether opposition parties will be granted access to the state-owned media stations. A second state television station, Tele Zaire 2, was installed to broadcast cultural programs.

A constitutional referendum has been postponed to Feb. 1997, and elections that were originally scheduled for July 1995 have again been postponed, to May 1997. Despite plans to move toward a democratically elected government in the coming year, the outlook for local journalists remains bleak without an independent judiciary and an accountable internal security and police force.

Februaury 15
Jane Standley, BBC, EXPELLED
BBC crew, HARASSED
Nairobi-based correspondent Standley was expelled from Zaire at the border town of Goma because of her coverage of relief workers' charges that Zairean troops were pillaging the Kibumba camp for Rwandan refugees. The expulsion was ordered by Zairean Interior Minister Gustave Malumba Mbangula, who claimed the workers' charges were "full of lies and damaged the dignity and security of the Zairean State."

In a related incident, a BBC television crew

in Goma was blocked from leaving the country by Zairean intelligence officials, who confiscated their passports.

May 23
Adrien de Mun, Free-lancer, HARASSED, EXPELLED
De Mun, a French free-lance journalist based in Rwanda and working for Radio France Internationale and several other international radio networks, was detained on unspecified charges in the Goma region of Zaire, then transferred to Kinshasa. The arrest followed the Zairean government's ban on journalists crossing into Zaire from neighboring countries. De Mun was accused of working illegally in Zaire and expelled on May 29.

September 17
Michel Luya, *Le Palmares,* IMPRISONED
Le Palmares, CENSORED
Luya, publisher of the opposition newspaper *Le Palmares,* was arrested at his home in connection with an article published by his newspaper. The article cited a Swiss source who claimed President Mobutu Sese Seko, who had gone to Europe for medical treatment, would be "operated on for throat cancer after undergoing a surgery on his prostate." Minister of Information and the Press Boguo Makeli said that revealing information about Mobutu's health was an affront to the president of the republic, whose inviolability is constitutionally guaranteed. Luya faces up to 12 months' imprisonment. On Sept. 18, Makeli ordered *Le Palmares* suspended indefinitely.

Zambia

President Frederick Chiluba's Movement for Multiparty Democracy (MMD) was relentless in its escalating efforts to silence critical reporting during this election year. Under a barrage of charges including criminal libel,

contempt of parliament, and possession of "secret documents," many of the country's journalists faced state intimidation tactics. The situation further deteriorated in the months approaching the Nov. 18 elections, when the media attempted to cover the banning of opposition leaders from participating in the election process and numerous other electoral irregularities.

In the first act of censorship on the Internet in Africa, Chiluba banned the Feb. 5 edition of the independent daily *The Post* and ordered, by decree, its removal from the publication's World Wide Web site. *The Post* managing editor Fred M'membe and editors Masautso Phiri and Bright Mwape, who were arrested the following day and charged with possession of the banned publication and state secrets, faced numerous legal actions during the year, all of which were postponed until after the elections.

Members of Parliament (MPs) also targeted journalists for their critical reporting on the MPs' use of the Public Order Act requiring citizens to obtain police permits for demonstrations and other public gatherings. After charging journalists with contempt of parliament, the National Assembly Standing Orders Committee sentenced them to indefinite detention without court trials.

In November, press freedom was further circumscribed when media workers were banned from covering the upcoming elections and related issues. Government officials attacked, threatened, and suspended journalists who either aired programs funded by the opposition or presented views considered "threatening" by the state.

The state monopoly on the broadcast media appears unchallenged. President Chiluba, who recently declared Zambia a Christian nation, granted a limited number of broadcast licenses to private radio owners, most of whom are Christian religious organizations.

February 5
The Post, CENSORED
Fred M'membe, *The Post,* IMPRISONED
Bright Mwape, *The Post,* IMPRISONED
Masautso Phiri, *The Post,* IMPRISONED
President Frederick Chiluba issued a decree banning the print edition of the Feb. 5 issue of the independent daily *The Post* as a "prohibited publication" under Section 53 of the Penal Code, and warning that any citizen found in possession of the issue could be charged with committing a criminal offense. The issue contained articles revealing the Zambian government's plan to hold a referendum in March to promulgate a controversial draft constitution.

Editor in chief M'membe, managing editor Mwape, and special projects editor Phiri were arrested on Feb. 6 and charged with possession of a banned publication and possession of state secrets, a violation of Section 4 of the State Security Act.

The three journalists were released on US$350 bail on Feb. 7, the same day that Chiluba ordered, by decree, the removal of the Feb. 5 issue from *The Post's* World Wide Web site, marking the first act of censorship on the Internet in Africa.

On March 18, the High Court revoked the journalists' bail and *The Post's* lawyers immediately filed an appeal with the Supreme Court. At the time of the bail revocation, M'membe and Mwape were already in prison on other charges. In addition to writing a letter to President Chiluba urging him to reverse the ban and drop all charges against M'membe and his colleagues, CPJ launched a media campaign in March to bring world attention to the Zambian government's systematic harassment of the country's independent press.

On Aug. 14, M'membe, Mwape, and Phiri pleaded not guilty in the Lusaka High Court to the charges that they had received and published classified information. The trial, which began on Oct. 18, continues. The state dropped the charge of possession of a banned publication because it could not prove "beyond [a] rea-

sonable doubt that the three accused were found in possession of a state document containing information on the constitution."

February 21
Fred M'membe, *The Post,* IMPRISONED
Bright Mwape, *The Post,* IMPRISONED
Lucy Banda Sichone, *The Post,* THREATENED, LEGAL ACTION
Managing director and editor in chief M'membe, managing editor Mwape, and columnist Sichone (with her three-month old infant) went into hiding on Feb. 23 to avoid imprisonment on charges of contempt of Parliament. On Feb. 21, the Zambian National Assembly had found the three journalists guilty of violating the National Assembly Powers and Privileges Act, a colonial law prohibiting nonmembers of Parliament from criticizing proclamations made by members of Parliament. The National Assembly Standing Orders Committee sentenced the three journalists to detention until they publicly apologized for breach of Parliament.

In the Jan. 29 edition of *The Post,* M'membe, Mwape, and Sichone wrote articles commenting on the vice president's criticism, in Parliament, of a Supreme Court ruling that the clause of the Public Order Act requiring citizens to obtain police permits for demonstrations and other public gatherings is unconstitutional.

On March 4, M'membe and Mwape surrendered to parliamentary authorities, explaining that they would not apologize to the Parliament. M'membe pleaded with the speaker of the National Assembly to absolve Sichone, who remains in hiding, of blame. Attorneys for *The Post* petitioned the Supreme Court with a writ of habeas corpus challenging the National Assembly's use of the Powers and Privileges Act to arrest and detain their clients. M'membe and Mwape were held in separate maximum security prisons for 24 days. On March 27, Supreme Court Judge Kabazo Chanda ruled that it was unreasonable to imprison M'membe and Mwape indefinitely, and ordered that they be released on bail. But Judge Chanda also ruled that M'membe's and Sichone's articles were in contempt of Parliament. Mwape was absolved of any charges of contempt. Judge Chanda advised Sichone to appear before Parliament.

CPJ protested the charges and arrests in letters to President Chiluba and to Robinson Nabulyato, speaker of the National Assembly, and launched a letter-writing campaign to secure the journalists' release.

November 19
Zambia National Broadcasting Corp. (ZNBC),
HARASSED
Ten members of the opposition Zambia Democratic Congress (ZADECO) forced their way into the Kitwe television studios of state-owned ZNBC. They demanded to appear on live television to declare their objections to alleged manipulation of the Nov. 18 presidential and parliamentary elections. Police based at ZNBC persuaded the ZADECO protesters to leave the TV studios.

November 22
Monitor, HARASSED
Police searched the offices of the Monitor newspaper and seized 13 computer diskettes, letters to the editor, and various press releases from international organizations. Police searched the offices of the Committee for a Clean Campaign (CCC), which is the Monitor's publisher, the Inter-Africa Network for Human Rights and Development (AFRONET), and the Zambia Independent Monitoring Team (ZIMT) on the same day. They were looking for bank books, statements, certificates of registration, computer disks, pamphlets, and magazines. The authorities did not disclose why they were conducting the searches. Both the CCC and ZIMT reportedly had declared that the presidential and general elections of Nov. 18 were not free and fair.

November 25
Mundia Nalishebo, Zambia Information Service (ZIS), CENSORED

Abias Moyo, Zambia National Broadcasting Corp. (ZNBC), CENSORED
Gershom Musonda, ZNBC, CENSORED
Dominic Chimanyika, ZNBC-Kitwe, CENSORED
Chibamba Kanyama, ZNBC, CENSORED
Charles Banda, ZNBC Radio 2, CENSORED
ZIS deputy director Nalishebo; television station ZNBC's commercial manager Moyo; ZNBC subeditor Musonda; ZNBC-Kitwe news editor Chimanyika; ZNBC producer Kanyama; and ZNBC Radio 2 manager Banda were suspended indefinitely pending an investigation into allegations that they conspired with a local election monitoring group, the Zambia Independent Monitoring Team (ZIMT), to discredit the Nov. 18 presidential and general elections. ZIMT was among three independent monitors of the elections that declared that the victory of President Frederick Chiluba's Multiparty Movement for Democracy (MMD) was "not free and fair."

November 25
Emmanuel Chilekwa, Chronicle, HARASSED
Onassis Mandona, Chronicle, HARASSED
Chronicle managing editor Chilekwa and assistant editor Mandona were detained and interrogated at the Lusaka Central Police offices. They were questioned about a story printed in the Nov. 22-25 issue of the privately owned biweekly, which quoted opposition Zambia Democratic Congress (ZDC) leader Dean Mung'omba as calling for the "isolation" of President Frederick Chiluba. On Nov. 22 and 23, two Criminal Investigations Department (CID) police officers had visited the editorial offices of the newspaper seeking to interrogate Chilekwa and Mandona about their sources.

November 26
Kunda Mwila, The Post, THREATENED
Zambia's Electoral Commission chairman, Bobby Bwalya, threatened to order the arrest of Post reporter Mwila for asking why some polling stations had reported results for the Nov. 18 national election a week late. Two days

later, Bwalya threatened Mwila again, this time for inquiring about the national election results and for asking when local elections would be held.

November 26

Chibamba Kanyama, Zambian National Broadcasting Corp. (ZNBC), HARASSED
Kanyama was dismissed from ZNBC because he had been working at the same time for his own news agency, the Chibamba Kanyama Media Agency (CKMA), and because he had accepted 21 million kwacha (about US$16,000) from the Committee for a Clean Campaign. He allegedly used the money to produce a series of television-debate programs on the topic of the November presidential and general elections.

December 26

George Jambwa, *Chronicle*, IMPRISONED,
LEGAL ACTION
Army officers arrested Jambwa, a journalist for the privately owned newspaper *Chronicle*, for allegedly "trespassing into the army barracks." Jambwa had been attempting to verify reports that Zambia's army commander, Lt. Gen. Nobby Simbeye, was under house arrest. Rumors had linked Simbeye to an alleged coup attempt against the government of President Frederick Chiluba. Interrogators pressured Jambwa to reveal his sources.

Jambwa appeared before the Lusaka Magistrate Court on Dec. 30 to answer charges of "criminal trespass" under section 306 of the Penal Code. He pleaded not guilty and was released later that day on 50,000 kwacha (US$38) bail, plus two sureties of 50,000 kwacha each. The court scheduled a trial for Jan. 21, 1997.

Zimbabwe

Zimbabwe's April 8 general elections extended President Robert Mugabe and his ZANU-PF Party's 15-year rule for an additional six-year term. The government's strategy for suffocating political dissent during the election campaign hinged on a systematic assault on the press through the use of broad anti-defamation laws and the Parliamentary Privileges and Immunities Act. The state routinely invoked colonial-era laws such as the Official Secrets Act, which criminalizes receiving official information from unauthorized government officials, to prosecute journalists.

The Zimbabwean Union of Journalists (ZUJ), which has consistently criticized the system of secrecy institutionalized at the highest political levels, called for an overhaul of undemocratic laws that are used to harass members of both the state and the private media. In November, the ZUJ demanded that the government transfer control over national newspapers to an independent authority, reiterated its request for constitutional amendments to protect press freedom, and called for the repeal of a law that empowers the state to require journalists to disclose the identity of their sources. Justice Minister Emmerson Mnangagwa's response that "Unrestricted freedom would lead to disorder and anarchy and would harm social and national interests," indicates that the government has no plans to change Zimbabwe's media laws.

The state assumed direct control of the country's largest media group, the Zimbabwe Mass Media Trust (ZMMT), by invoking an April 29 amendment to the ZMMT deed which grants the government the authority to oversee ZMMT's operations. The state's monopoly over the broadcast media has restricted access to information for the majority of the population. In light of President Mugabe's strict control over all broadcast media, it is unlikely that liberalization of the airwaves will appear on the national agenda in the coming year.

March 27
Chris Chinaka, Reuters, THREATENED
While attending a government reception in
Harare, Reuters bureau chief Chinaka was told
by the secretary general of the Indigenous Business Development Center (IBDC), Enoch
Kamshinda, that he should have been killed for
writing stories critical of President Robert
Mugabe. Kamshinda advised Chinaka to stop
writing such articles in the future, adding that
the matter had been discussed by government
officials and that Chinaka and other reporters
were on a "hit list."

July 24
Gay and lesbian publications, HARASSED,
  CENSORED
The government banned Gays and Lesbians of
Zimbabwe (GALZ) from setting up an exhibit
at the Zimbabwe International Book Fair. On
July 31, the Zimbabwe High Court ruled the
prohibition invalid, and the organization was
allowed to participate in the book fair. At the
end of the exhibition, a mob of University of
Zimbabwe students ransacked the stand at
which GALZ was displaying its literature.

November 7
Elias Rusike, Modus Publications,
  LEGAL ACTION
Trevor Ncube, *Financial Gazette,*
  LEGAL ACTION
The Zimbabwe High Court upheld the convictions of Rusike, managing director of Modus
Publications and publisher of the independent
weekly *Financial Gazette,* and Ncube, the
Gazette's editor. In August 1995, the two had
been found guilty of criminal defamation and
ordered to pay high fines for a story claiming
that President Robert Mugabe had secretly
married his former secretary. The *Gazette* had
already published a retraction, in July 1995, saying that the paper had been misled by a state
intelligence agent.

November 13
Farayi Makotsi, *Financial Gazette,* HARASSED
Zimbabwe's minister of health, Timothy
Stamps, ripped the tape from an audio recorder
belonging to Makotsi, news editor of the privately owned *Financial Gazette.* The incident
occurred at a news conference in Harare where
the minister was discussing an ongoing strike by
doctors and nurses.

November 27
Horizon, LEGAL ACTION
The Zimbabwe High Court awarded Z$40,000
(US$4,000) in damages to former army com-
mander Gen. Solomon Mujuru in a defamation
suit he brought against independent monthly
magazine *Horizon.* Mujuru charged *Horizon*
with defamation after an article in the October
1991 issue implied that Mujuru had been "dis-
honest" in his business dealings. *Horizon* has
filed an appeal.

Clampdown in Addis: Ethiopia's Journalists at Risk

by Kakuna Kerina

Ethiopia's independent journalists and the government of Meles Zenawi, the country's first freely elected prime minister, eye each other with mutual suspicion and distrust. Journalists labor under a restrictive press law and penal code, and, as a result, more journalists have been jailed in Ethiopia in the past three years than in any other African country. Africa program coordinator Kakuna Kerina and CPJ board member Josh Friedman embarked on a fact-finding mission to Ethiopia in May 1996 to better understand how the press law and other legal measures are used against journalists.

Based on their discussions with more than 50 Ethiopian journalists, government officials, and other sources, Kerina wrote "Clampdown in Addis: Ethiopia's Journalists at Risk," a report that documents how the Meles government, which still maintains a monopoly on broadcast media, uses restrictive provisions of the 1992 Press Proclamation to quash opposing viewpoints and limit the news the independent press may report.

The following is an excerpt of that mission report, which CPJ released on Oct. 7—the day the Ethiopian Parliament reconvened in order to discuss, among other things, key media issues. That same week, U.S. Secretary of State Warren Christopher made his first official visit to Ethiopia. The secretary and his staff were sent advance copies of the report, and as a result of his review of CPJ's findings, Christopher declined the Ethiopian government's invitation to hold a joint press conference upon his arrival in Addis Ababa. Instead, the secretary elected to hold a press conference at his hotel, inviting both official and independent media as well as the traveling press. In a public statement, Christopher told reporters: "Ethiopia has made progress in human rights during the past five years, but the United States wants to see more. One of the areas of our concern is the freedom of the press and the treatment of journalists."

Despite the assurances in May of Prime Minister Meles and other senior Ethiopian government officials to CPJ delegates that key media issues were to be reviewed in the current parliamentary session, to date, no significant changes have been made in the restrictive Press Proclamation of 1992. The government monopoly on broadcast media remains intact, and a repressive climate still exists in which journalists are routinely harassed, censored, and jailed under the provisions of the press proclamation, bringing the number of imprisoned journalists—the majority detained without charge—to a high of 18 by year's end.

The government subsequently rescinded the privileges it accorded to the independent press at the time of Secretary Christopher's visit; independent journalists are still denied access to government officials and their agencies, as well as to official state press conferences. CPJ continues to closely monitor and protest abuses against journalists, and to encourage the government to take aggressive steps to ensure press freedom in Ethiopia.

AFTER CENTURIES OF FEUDAL RULE, 17 years of communist dictatorship, almost three decades of civil war, and no tradition of an independent press before 1992, Ethiopia is at a crossroads.

As one of the African continent's youngest exercises in democracy, Ethiopia can serve as an example of a true democracy—one that does not sacrifice freedom of expression and human rights as its leaders establish order. Or, it can join the ranks of neighbors whose leaders assumed office promising respect for press freedom and other civil rights, but who have since broken these and other pledges.

Following the fall of Col. Mengistu Haile Mariam's communist regime in 1991 and encouraged by assurances of press freedom by the newly installed Transitional Government of Ethiopia (TGE), a vociferous independent media exploded into existence, signaling what many hoped would be the end of tight government control over information.

One of the first acts of the TGE, led by then-President Meles, was passage of the Press Proclamation No. 34/1992 in October 1992. The law quickly put an end to the euphoria that fueled the country's new era of free speech as journalists realized how vulnerable they were under the proclamation, which is both restrictive and contradictory. The legislation prohibits, among other things, the dissemination of information the government deems dangerous, and requires the licensing of all journalists. Moreover, it classifies libel as both a criminal and civil offense, demanding penalties of payment in the amount of twice the value of a publisher's assets.

Criminal libel laws or indeed any statutes intended or used to insulate government officials from press criticism through the application of civil or criminal penalties have no place in democratic societies. The right to speak freely without fear of government reprisal is a core principle of democracy, and critical reporting must be tolerated and protected, not criminalized.

In late 1993, reeling from criticism from a growing number of newspapers and magazines about state policies and the political transition under way, the government cracked down on the press, starting with the detention of Tefera Asmare, editor of the independent newspaper *Etiopis*. In connection with an article titled "There's War in Gondar," Tefera was charged with "inciting people against the government" and "disseminating false rumors," under Article 10, Section 2 of the Press Proclamation. Tefera was later charged with 11 counts of libel under the press law; five counts were for the same story carried in different editions of *Etiopis*. In March 1994, he was convicted of all charges and sentenced to a two-year prison term. He was released on Sept. 27, 1995.

The irony of Tefera's arrest was that he was legally carrying out his responsibilities as a journalist according to the Press Proclamation's Art. 4, Sec. 2, which states that "the press gathers and disseminates news; expresses opinions on various issues; forwards criticisms on various issues; participates in forming public opinion by employing various other methods; [and] undertakes other activities necessary for the accomplishment of its purposes."

Tefera's case is emblematic of the double bind imposed on independent Ethiopian journalists—he is one of more than 50 who have been imprisoned for their work since 1993. By simultaneously using ambiguous articles of the Press Proclamation and provisions of the civil, penal, and criminal codes, many of which were created in the 1950s, the Meles government has put the media on notice that it will not hesitate to manipulate the laws to suit its own ends.

Ethiopia, which is a signatory to several regional and international charters guaranteeing press freedom, such as the African Charter on Human and People's Rights and the International Covenant on Civil and Political Rights (ICCPR), has rapidly become a country where reality belies the government's public proclamations about the need for a free press. Contradictory statements by government officials illuminate this gap between rhetoric and policy. "A free press is an essential ingredient of any democratic exercise [because it provides] information to the public so they can make informed decisions," Prime Minister Meles told CPJ's mission. During the same meeting, however, he also said that the government has to impose restrictions on the media to stave off ethnic strife and threats to national security.

The stance that Prime Minister Meles' administration chooses to adopt toward the independent press in the coming years will have significant repercussions. The existence of a free press in Ethiopia is dependent upon a clear commitment from the government to support the development of private media and to lift restrictions on reporting and private-sector competition. Ethiopia cannot claim to be a genuine democracy, nor should it be treated as one by Western donors such as the United States, unless the Meles government ceases its practice of subjecting independent journalists to repeated arrests, detention without trial, and excessive fines.

The Press Proclamation and the Prosecution of Journalists
Ethiopia's independent journalists currently work under threat of prosecution from three separate areas of government: a poorly trained police force that sometimes operates independently of the public prosecutor's office; an inexperienced, partisan judiciary operating in a severely backlogged court system; and overly sensitive government officials who are offended by public criticism of their actions. Journalists are granted certain rights by the Press Proclamation; yet at the same time the vagueness of these guarantees allows the government undue leverage to interpret editorial "intent" in published materials. This grants the government free rein to prosecute and punish journalists for perceived insults against the state and its officials. As a result, many independent publishers employ attorneys on retainer to conduct prepublication reviews of their newspapers and magazines to reduce their chances of becoming targets of government reprisals.

Journalists are often arrested in an arbitrary manner, either on the initiative of police, or when charges have been filed by the public prosecutor. In many cases, police officers decide independently that publications have acted illegally, and they arrest journalists before gathering evidence or filing charges in the courts.

The police often base their actions on the Press Proclamation's Art. 10, Sec. 10, which prohibits the media from "any defamation or false accusations against any individual, nation, nationality, people or organization," or "any criminal instigation of one nationality against another, or incitement of conflict between peoples and any agitation for war." Within 48 hours of an arrest, police can also request 14-day stays from the district courts, renewable for an additional 14 days, to remand journalists into custody while the police gather evidence.

In May 1996, when CPJ asked Justice Minister Mahteme Solomon about the government's expectations and plans regarding the establishment of a modern police force, he replied, "The police force is in its infancy. Many [police officers] were soldiers who protected the government, not the people." Modernization of the force would be "very expensive when compared to needs for food, medication, and education," he said. In early 1996, when the Ministry of the Interior was dismantled, the police force was placed under the jurisdiction of the Ministry of Justice. It remains to be seen, however, whether the police force will become fully accountable to the prosecutor and the courts.

The case of Lullit Gebre Michael, editor in chief of the independent daily *The Monitor*, exemplifies the danger of allowing police to subjectively interpret the Press Proclamation when they themselves have limited understanding of journalists' rights or the role of the media in a democracy.

In November 1995, Lullit and publisher Fitsum Zeab Asgedom were arrested at *The Monitor's* editorial offices and taken to the Criminal Investigation Department for questioning. The arrests were in connection with two wire stories *The Monitor* ran from the government-run news wire service, the Ethiopian News Agency (ENA). The stories, which ENA had received from the Panafrican News Agency and Agence France-Presse services, reported an assassination attempt on Col. Mengistu in Harare. Lullit tried to verify the information with the Ethiopian ambassador to Zimbabwe, and quoted him in a follow-up article. The ambassador said that he was unaware of the incident and asserted that the Ethiopian government was not involved.

In recounting her experience with the Ethiopian justice system, Lullit said that she realized the police had no knowledge of how the press operates. During questioning, she said, she had to explain to her interrogator that ENA was a government wire service and that *The Monitor*, like many other newspapers, paid a monthly fee for use of the wire's news reports. When Lullit went before the court the next day, the judge refused to hear her comments, said that he had not read the articles in question, and remanded her to custody. After nine days of detention, she was released without charge on a 10,000 birr bond (US$1,600). Five days later, Fitsum was released on the same conditions. The court ordered the newspaper to suspend publication for three weeks. In August 1996, the case was officially closed without explanation.

The state-run Ethiopian Television (ETV) also carried the ENA story on the Mengistu assassination attempt, but suffered no repercussions. *The Monitor's* case, however, was as much a turning point for state journalists as for the independent press because it marked the first time a government news story had been used as justification for prosecuting an independent journalist. As one state reporter told CPJ, "I was bitter when *The Monitor* editor was arrested for telling the truth. It was a deliberate misinterpretation of the news by the prosecutor."

Though legal harassment of government journalists is rare, the state press has not been immune to prosecution. In February 1993, editor Tesfaye Gebre Ab and columnists Tsegaye Hailu, Sileshi Tesserna, and Yeshtile Kokab of the government daily *Addis Zemen*, were detained and charged with "creating fear among the population." The arrests were in connection with an article discussing the positive and negative effects of democracy in Ethiopia. The journalists were eventually freed on a bond of 10,000 birr (US$1,600) each. In August 1993, after six months of litigation, the First Criminal Bench of the Central High Court acquitted them.

Protecting one's sources can also lead to prosecution and jail time in Ethiopia. Even though Art. 8, Sec. 4 of the Press Proclamation prohibits the state from forcing journalists to reveal their sources, the state may bring charges under the State Security Act against a journalist who refuses to do so. Conviction on such charges would result in a guaranteed prison sentence. As a result, many independent journalists use pseudonyms to avoid identification by police and the public prosecutor's office. One private publisher told CPJ that he insists on pseudonyms for reporters who cover controversial issues, like the economy and land lease programs, in the interest of the journalists' safety.

For attorneys representing the private press, the amorphous nature of the Press Proclamation prevents them from confidently advising journalists on how to protect themselves from future arrests and litigation. The Ethiopian court system is modeled on the Napoleonic Civil Law system, where each offense and penalty is decided on a case-by-case basis without regard to previous rulings in similar cases. Absent prior decisions to incorporate into their defense strategies, attorneys are at the mercy of individual judges' interpretation of the law.

In interviews with CPJ, a number of attorneys who represent journalists said that even if the court adhered strictly to existing laws and the constitution, the judiciary is not independent, and therefore could not be expected to reach objective decisions. These attorneys pointed out that the dismissal of the majority of Ethiopia's experienced judiciary in May 1996 landed the country squarely in a crisis. Today the court system is so severely backlogged that many defendants may spend more time in prison awaiting trial than they would if convicted of the charges against them. As one journalist told CPJ, "Christ, in his second coming, will see a judge sooner than the average Ethiopian citizen if the situation continues as it has until now."

The government's position that it was necessary to purge the judiciary of those loyal to Emperor Haile Selassie and Col. Mengistu is insufficient justification for citizens' prolonged imprisonment, in deplorable conditions, while awaiting trial. And the state's 30-year plan for the establishment of an independent judiciary is not a solution to the court crisis. The government should immediately appoint enough prosecutors, judges, and investigators to end the current state of indefinite pretrial detention.

Censorship and Libel
Although the government claims the Press Proclamation abolished censorship, it in fact bans dissemination of information that the government deems dangerous to the society. Hence, the law is often used as a government tool for post-publication censorship and punitive prosecution.

According to Art. 8 of the Proclamation, the news media may not publish:

• Information designated as secret by Parliament's Council of Representatives or the prime minister's cabinet, the Council of Ministers;

• Information that is held secret under the provisions of other laws;

• Information relating to any court case heard in camera, or information relating to a case pending before any court, unless the court decides otherwise; or

• Private information about a victim of a crime, unless the person consents.

The law leaves open for broad interpretation what information is designated as "secret" and does not offer specific guidelines on what constitutes a "criminal offense against the safety of the state, the administration, or national defense," the very charge leveled against journalists who are hauled into court for violating Art. 8. Without such specific guidelines, journalists are unable to protect or defend themselves.

In defense of the restrictive clauses of the Press Proclamation, Prime Minister Meles told CPJ, "What's considered free press may be inimical to democracy." The prime minister cited the role of "hate radio" in Rwanda's civil war as an instance where a government would be justified in restricting access to broadcast media. (Radio Mille Collines, the Rwandan radio station Prime Minister Meles was referring to, was a propaganda tool of the acting Rwandan government and was privately owned by members of that government. In CPJ's view, it is inaccurate to conclude that such a station is part of the independent news media.)

Ethiopian journalists run a high risk of punishment for reporting on national security issues and ethnic unrest. They are most frequently prosecuted under Art. 480 of the Penal Code, which prohibits "false rumors and incitements to the breach of the peace" and is punishable by fines of 1,500 birr (US$250) or up to six months' imprisonment. In court decisions where litigation against journalists was based on Art. 480, virtually all press reports and criticisms of conflict and ethnic violence have been characterized by the government as cases of spreading false rumors, supporting the state's historical denial of the existence of unrest in the country. Journalists are required to shoulder the burden of proof that their reports are true, whereas the public prosecutor need simply charge that their reports are false.

In cases of libel, the state targets both the editor in chief and the publisher of a publication when charging criminal liability. If the publisher is a corporate entity, all of the corporation's shareholders are considered liable. To enact stiffer penalties, the state usually charges journalists under the Penal Code, but fines them according to the Press Proclamation, which imposes substantially higher fines. In many cases, newspapers like *Etiopis*, *Muday*, and *Ruh* were forced into insolvency by such excessive fines, and eventually stopped publishing.

Post-publication punishment for violations of the penal and civil codes with respect to sedition, defamation, and copyright is commonplace; penalties range from fines of up to 50,000 birr (US$8,300), to a minimum of one year in prison, and/or injunctions against the publication.

Moreover, all publishers are required to submit two copies of each issue to the Ministry of Information within 24 hours of publication. The Ministry of Information then forwards one copy to the public prosecutor's office for review. Failure to comply with the requirement results in charges of publishing an illegal press product. Conviction on such a charge can result in a prison sentence of up to three years and/or a fine of up to 50,000 birr (US$8,300).

Freedom of Information
Art. 8, Sec. 1 of the Press Proclamation grants the press "the right to seek, obtain and report news and information from any government source of news and information," yet the private press continues to be denied access to government officials and their agencies. Moreover, independent journalists have been refused confirmation of information, or answers to questions posed to government representatives, in violation of Art. 19 of the Press Proclamation, which states that "government officials shall have the duty to cooperate with the press." As a result, many publishers use personal contacts and fellow journalists in both the state and independent media as sources for acquiring government information for their publications.

One independent journalist told CPJ, "They [government officials] know they have a duty to obey the law. Now when you ask for information they tell you, 'If I give you this information, all the other journalists will go against you because I didn't give it to them,' or, 'I've given [this information] already.' But they will never say 'no' outright."

The private press is also barred from attending government-sponsored press conferences, including those held by the diplomatic community in conjunction with the Ethiopian government. By complying with this restriction on the private press, the international community has sent mixed messages to the Ethiopian government, quite possibly undermining its own efforts on behalf of independent journalists. When CPJ asked Prime Minister Meles whether his administration has plans to grant the private press access to government information, he replied that an "official decision has not yet been made." Perhaps, he said, "we will have to relax, and every member of government will make his own individual decision about whom to speak with."

The question of access will be central in parliamentary discussions that begin in October 1996. Speaker of the Parliament Davit Yohannes told CPJ that decisions will be made regarding the appointment of a government spokesperson or the creation of a Department of Information, which would be responsible for informing the media about government policies and activities; and the establishment of a press council, accessible to all media, which would promote and offer support to the press.

CPJ strongly urges the Ethiopian government to appoint a government press secretary to disseminate information to all press. Such an appointment would leave independent journalists less vulnerable to charges of publishing false information.

Ushering Ethiopian Journalism into the 21st Century: Recommendations to the Ethiopian and U.S. Governments

Based on the comprehensive meetings held during the course of our mission, CPJ has identified several areas of continued concern. Improvements in these areas would contribute substantially to the creation of an environment within which members of Ethiopia's media can work freely and can develop into the skilled professionals that all of the journalists we met with aspire to become.

To bring about these improvements, CPJ calls on the Ethiopian government to:

- Immediately and unconditionally release all journalists who have been imprisoned for exercising their internationally recognized legal right to report the news.
- Eliminate all criminal libel statutes in the Press Proclamation, particularly those pertaining to seditious libel, which criminalizes critical commentary on public officials and government policies.
- Restore the right of detainees to apply for habeas corpus, as granted by Art. 19, Sec. 4 of the 1995 Constitution, to prevent indefinite pretrial detention.
- Abolish excessive bail, which primarily serves to render private publications financially insolvent.
- Train police officers, the judiciary, and government officials on the internationally recognized rights of journalists, the role of the press in a democratic society, and general human rights issues.
- Establish an equitable system that permits private ownership of broadcast media.
- Grant the private press equal and unrestricted access to government press conferences, including joint press conferences with foreign diplomatic representatives and international figures.
- Establish the already promised government press office so that the media can be informed about government policies and activities. It should also be this office's responsibility to respond to all inquiries from the press.
- Continue to provide the private press with equal and unrestricted access to government training programs and facilities.
- Accredit members of the press, both state and private, so that they may freely cover parliamentary activities.

The United States, which supports the Meles government and gives Ethiopia the second highest amount of U.S. aid allocated to sub-Saharan Africa, can greatly influence the development of a free press in this newly democratic society. CPJ calls on the U.S. government to:
- Give media training higher priority when allocating funds for democratization in Ethiopia
- Issue a public statement granting the private press in Ethiopia equal and unrestricted access to all press conferences involving U.S. officials and to all official U.S. embassy functions.
- Publicly encourage the Ethiopian government to give the private press access to government activities and officials.

• Fund training for the Ethiopian judiciary, police force, and regional government officials on the internationally recognized legal rights of journalists, the role of the media in a democratic society, and general human rights issues.

• Encourage and coordinate media funding by other foreign government representatives in Ethiopia.

• Expand the media analysis section on Ethiopia in the U.S. State Department's annual Country Reports on Human Rights Practices.

For information on obtaining a copy of the complete report, "Clampdown in Addis: Ethiopia's Journalists at Risk," see page 364.

The Americas

OVERVIEW
OF **The Americas**

by Suzanne Bilello

The Americas

BUOYED BY A TENACIOUS civil society anxious to realize the rewards of democratization, the press in Latin America continues to hold governments accountable and challenge corruption in the face of ongoing efforts by both public officials and criminal gangs to thwart these democratic impulses.

Despite the remarkable transition to democratic rule throughout Latin America, many of the region's fledgling democracies still lack vital governmental institutions to support these regimes. Legislatures and judiciaries are too often politically compromised, and many countries suffer from the absence of the rule of law. Moreover, there is a residual undercurrent of intolerance toward the news media on the part of governments throughout Latin America—a reminder of the not-so-distant past when journalists were frequent targets of assault, repression, censorship and the humiliating acquiescence of self-censorship under the region's numerous dictatorships.

But compared to the rest of the developing world, the press in Latin America today—with the exception of Cuba—has a remarkable breadth of freedom and, for the most part, a greatly diminished threat of imprisonment or physical attack.

At the time of the Committee to Protect Journalists' inception 15 years ago,

Suzanne Bilello *has been program coordinator for the Americas since February 1996. Prior to joining CPJ, Bilello was a staff reporter for* Newsday, *covering international business and immigration. She has written about Latin America for 15 years and was the Mexico City bureau chief for the* Dallas Morning News *from 1983 to 1987. She received several international awards for her coverage of the 1985 Mexico City earthquake. In 1988, she received an Alicia Patterson Fellowship to examine the roots of Mexico's political and economic crisis. She is fluent in Spanish and is a graduate of Barnard College and the Columbia Graduate School of Journalism.*

 Mira Gajevic, *a former research associate for the Americas, researched and wrote some of the 1996 cases for the region. She has a master's degree in political science from the University of Mainz in Germany and is fluent in German and Spanish. She is currently a reporter with Deutsche Presse Agentur in Germany.*

CPJ's work in the Americas in 1996 was funded in part by the Robert R. McCormick Foundation.

Latin America was the most dangerous place in the world to be a journalist. Government-sponsored death squads used violence and murder to control the press. In the 1980s, drug mafias waged brutal campaigns against journalists in Colombia, claiming scores of victims. And more recently, left-wing guerrillas and right-wing paramilitary groups in Peru and Colombia have stalked the press.

Today, the journalistic climate is arguably more benign, but the problems the press now confronts are far more complex. CPJ's work in Latin America now involves navigating in an environment of punitive civil and criminal libel suits, direct and indirect financial pressures against publications and broadcasters, and the ongoing threat of the criminal underworld and their protectors in corrupt criminal justice systems. Organized crime rings, paramilitary groups, and police continue to impede journalists' work and endanger their lives. In 1996, CPJ has confirmed the murder of a Colombian journalist. As this book goes to press, two murders in Guatemala are under investigation.

In Cuba, the only country in the hemisphere with no press freedom, the independent press movement has survived a crucial year. Despite threats, harassment and repeated detentions by the state security police, a small but growing group of Cuban journalists continues efforts to carve out a livelihood independent of the state-controlled media, yet at a comfortable distance from organized dissident factions at home and abroad.

Disturbingly, threats against the press in Latin America too often come from public officials in democratically elected regimes in the form of libel suits and restrictive press laws. In Peru, four journalists are currently in prison on trumped-up charges of collaborating with terrorists. In Brazil, the congress is considering dozens of bills that could restrict an otherwise free environment for the press. Many Brazilian journalists and media owners alike interpret the congress's efforts to pass restrictive press legislation as punitive, since the Brazilian press has aggressively reported on government corruption. In Argentina, President Carlos Menem, arguably the most litigious head of state in the hemisphere, has brought dozens of lawsuits against journalists. In a major victory for press freedom in Argentina at the end of the year, a judge ruled against Menem in a lawsuit he brought against columnist Horacio Verbitsky and the editors of the newspaper *Página 12*.

In delivering her December ruling before a courtroom filled with journalists and some of Argentina's intellectual luminaries, the judge upheld the right of the press to report, declaring that journalists have an obligation to inform society. A free press, she said, "is a necessity in a democracy." Although it's been 14 years since Argentina's military dictatorship collapsed and the nation ushered in democratic rule, the acquittal in Menem's suit against *Página 12* marked the first time an

The Americas

Argentine court so unequivocally acknowledged the centrality of a free press.

In 1996, Guatemala's 36-year civil war came to an end with the signing of a United Nations-brokered peace accord. Unfortunately, the accord's general amnesty is likely to leave the murders and disappearances of numerous journalists unresolved and unpunished and the culture of impunity that plagues many countries unchallenged. Similar accords in other countries, including Argentina, El Salvador and Chile, have resulted in a troubling irresolution and lack of accountability regarding journalists' fate.

Despite these vexing problems, the press in many Latin American countries enjoys unprecedented freedom and plays a vital role in setting the national agenda. Opinion polls in several countries reveal that the press is held in such high esteem by the public that it outranks all other national institutions, including the Catholic Church, in prestige and credibility.

In the absence of government safeguards, Latin American journalists are taking an increasingly active role in protecting themselves and press freedom in their respective countries. Independent associations now exist in Peru, Colombia, and Argentina to monitor press conditions and act on behalf of threatened or harassed journalists. These groups include the Peruvian Institute of Press and Society, which, since its inception in 1994, has helped fuel press freedom through its timely intervention in press attacks and the use of its moral weight to rally international support. In Argentina, the Association for the Defense of Independent Journalism, founded one year ago, succeeded in drawing national and international attention to President Menem's legal assaults on the press.

The robust growth of media companies throughout Latin America is another indicator of expanding press freedom in the region. New outlets, including radio programs and publications in indigenous languages, are emerging, increasing the diversity and accessibility of the news media.

In a recent discussion on the press in Haiti, a country that is slowly emerging from the trauma of decades of dictatorships, a foreign correspondent who has covered the country for years said that while overall conditions have vastly improved for the press, the shadow of the past is never far away. He emphasized the need to be vigilant of what gains had been achieved, and that his remarks could apply to the press throughout Latin America. "People are still very sensitive to any gathering of the clouds," said the reporter, who is based in Port-au-Prince. "We are not that far from hell, so we feel the heat."

Antigua and Barbuda

The Constitution of Antigua and Barbuda provides for freedom of the press and free speech, and the government of Prime Minister Lester B. Bird, whose Antigua Labor Party (ALP) has controlled the government since 1976, generally respects these provisions.

Nevertheless, the government wields enormous influence over news coverage through its active presence in the electronic media: It owns the country's only television station and one of its two radio stations. According to the U.S. State Department's human rights assessment of Antigua and Barbuda, government domination of the electronic media "effectively denies equal coverage to opposition parties."

The only daily newspaper, the *Daily Observer*, does provide critical coverage of the government, over which it has clashed with officials.

January 26
Samuel Derrick, *Daily Observer,* LEGAL ACTION
Winston Derrick, *Daily Observer,*
    LEGAL ACTION
Robert Potter, *Daily Observer,* LEGAL ACTION
Samuel Derrick, publisher of the *Daily Observer*, Winston Derrick, the newspaper's editor, and Potter, a salesman for the daily, were charged with "printing and distribution of a false statement concerning the Prime Minister of Antigua and Barbuda, which is likely to undermine public confidence in the conduct of public affairs." The criminal charges were brought by a government official and stemmed from an article published on Jan. 19 that dealt with the alleged detention of a person employed by Prime Minister Lester Bird. On Feb. 8, one day after CPJ and other press freedom organizations wrote to the Antiguan government protesting the

charges, the prosecution withdrew them, and the case was dismissed.

Argentina

Argentine journalists in recent years have played a more active role in safeguarding their own freedoms, and the press now plays a vital role in setting the national agenda. Many Argentines decry what they see as corruption and social inequities under the 14-year-old democratic government. They say they consider the judiciary and legislature to be unable to redress grievances and expect the press to fill the vacuum by in effect playing the role of investigator, prosecutor, and judge.

The public's expectations have created an enormous responsibility for the press. Journalists fear that the continued failure of society at large to resolve its political problems could backfire and lead to frustration and disenchantment with the press itself. "Argentine journalists are aware that the press can investigate problems, set ethical standards, and suggest alternatives, but we can neither solve the issues at stake nor punish those responsible," said Horacio Verbitsky, a columnist with the daily newspaper *Página 12*.

Along with its new higher profile, the press experienced a proportionate rise in hostility and threats. President Carlos Menem fired a legislative offensive against the press, bringing lawsuit after lawsuit, although so far the targets have successfully fended off his assaults. Menem and other government officials have also launched poisonous verbal attacks. In May, for example, the president labeled as "traitors" journalists who had filmed slum dwellers grilling cats for food.

In an important victory, on Dec. 17 Menem lost a libel suit he had brought

97

against *Página 12* in 1994. Menem had sued after *Página 12* published an article questioning the veracity of the president's claims that he had been tortured under Argentina's military dictatorship. In the suit, the president named Verbitsky, the columnist who wrote the article, and the newspaper's editors, Ernesto Tiffenberg and Fernando Sokolowicz. Journalists, writers, artists, rabbis, bishops, and union and political leaders were present in the courtroom during the hearing, a clear sign of the widespread support in Argentina for an independent press.

On Nov. 13, the Supreme Court, in a unanimous decision, acquitted the political columnist and commentator Joaquín Morales Solá in a libel case brought by a former government official. Dante Giadone, a special secretary to former President Raúl Alfonsín, had sued Morales Solá for defamation for Morales Solá's description of an alleged conversation between Giadone and Alfonsín. The passage had originally appeared in the newspaper *Clarín*, but Giadone sued after it was reprinted in a 1990 book.

The Association for the Defense of Independent Journalism, an independent press freedom group, vigorously monitored press conditions during the year and acted on behalf of threatened or harassed journalists. The association, spearheaded by Verbitsky, one of Argentina's most distinguished journalists, reflects a trend in Latin America of journalists coming together to use their collective moral weight to promote freedom of the press. Formed in December 1995 to defend journalists under attack and to alert Argentine authorities and the international community to any pressures on the press, the organization has been an effective advocate. It played a pivotal role in a libel and defamation case against Jacobo Timerman, a founding member of the group. After pressure from the association, Menem in April dropped the charges he had brought in 1988.

And in December, an appeals court overturned the slander conviction of Eduardo Kimel, who had accused a judge of deliberately failing to investigate five slayings during Argentina's military dictatorship. Kimel's book, *The St. Patrick's Massacre*, describes the July 4, 1976, murder of three priests and two seminary students.

February 6
Héctor Arroche, Free-lancer, ATTACKED, THREATENED
Unidentified men with machine guns fired several shots at the studio of free-lance photojournalist Arroche in the middle of the night. The studio was empty at the time, and no one was hurt. The attack came just hours after a judge assigned a police officer to guard Arroche in response to a complaint the journalist filed about receiving threatening phone calls. Prior to the attack, Arroche, who works for the daily *Crónica* and the official news agency Telam, had received several anonymous death threats after photographing a Jan. 22 police crackdown on a prison mutiny in Córdoba, which resulted in the death of three inmates. The callers warned Arroche to destroy all the negatives of the photos he took during the rebellion.

February 21
Hernán Ramos, Canal 13, ATTACKED
Julio Bazán, Canal 13, ATTACKED
Mariano Paccioco, *Telefé*, ATTACKED
Jorge Sagastume, Televisión Selectiva de La Plata, ATTACKED
Marcelo Clausel, Crónica TV, ATTACKED
Fernando Menéndez, *Telefé*, ATTACKED
Six journalists were beaten by policemen and plainclothes officers while covering a student demonstration that turned violent in La Plata, the capital of the Buenos Aires province. Ramos, a cameraman for the television station Canal 13, was shot by police in an effort to prevent him from filming the police beating demonstrators and journalists. He was hospitalized and had to have five rubber bullets surgi-

cally removed from his leg. Four police officers were placed under criminal investigation for the shooting of Ramos, and eleven were suspended for their brutality and misconduct during the demonstration.

March 22
Jacobo Timerman, LEGAL ACTION
Police tried to arrest Timerman, one of Argentina's most respected journalists and former director of the now-defunct daily *La Opinión*, on charges of libel. Two police officers went to the offices of the newspaper *El Buenos Aires Herald* with an arrest warrant for Timerman, who now lives in Uruguay. The newspaper is the provisional address of the journalists' organization Asociación para la Defensa del Periodismo Independiente, of which Timerman is a founding member. The warrant stemmed from charges of libel and defamation brought against him in 1988 by the then-presidential candidate Carlos Menem, charges of which Timerman was acquitted in two separate trials. However, about a year-and-a-half ago, the Supreme Court of Argentina, acting on President Menem's request, reopened the case. In a letter to President Menem, CPJ strongly protested the continued persecution of Timerman despite his acquittal in two trials and requested that the case be dropped. On April 10, a week after CPJ sent the letter, Menem announced that he would not pursue the charges against Timerman.

April 9
Cristian Dzwonick, *La Nación*, ATTACKED, THREATENED
Dzwonick, Argentina's leading newspaper cartoonist, who, under the name "Nik" drew biting political cartoons for the daily *La Nación*, was held at gunpoint for 30 minutes by two men who warned him to "quit all your rubbish." A week earlier, he had appeared on a television show about the 1976-83 rule of the military regime. The attack came during a wave of violence and threats against other journalists, schools and airlines coinciding with the 20th anniversary of the last military coup.

November 13
Joaquín Morales Solá, *La Nación* and *Telefé*, LEGAL ACTION
The Supreme Court of Argentina, in a unanimous decision, acquitted Morales Solá on appeal of defamation charges. A criminal tribunal on Feb. 22, 1995, had given Morales Solá a three-month suspended sentence and a fine of US$30,000 for his description of an alleged conversation between former Argentine President Raúl Alfonsín and Dante Giadone, a special secretary to Alfonsín. Giadone had sued when the description appeared in a 1990 book, even though the passage had already been published in the daily *Clarín*.

December 17
Página 12, LEGAL ACTION
Horacio Verbitsky, *Página 12*, LEGAL ACTION
Fernando Sokolowicz, *Página 12*, LEGAL ACTION
Ernesto Tiffenberg, *Página 12*, LEGAL ACTION
President Carlos Menem lost a libel suit he initiated in 1994 against *Página 12*, columnist Verbitsky, and top editors Sokolowicz and Tiffenberg. Menem was ordered by Judge María Laura Garrigós de Rébori to pay all the legal costs of the trial. In issuing her ruling, the judge said that in a democracy the press has an obligation to keep the public informed.

Menem had sued *Página 12* over an Oct. 30, 1994, article by Verbitsky that questioned the veracity of the president's claims that he had been tortured under Argentina's military dictatorship. Menem accused the daily and local human rights groups of plotting together to undermine his leadership.

Bolivia

Bolivian journalists began to take a more vig-

ilant role in promoting press freedom, along with journalists throughout Latin America, who are reacting more vigorously to threats against their colleagues and official efforts to intimidate the press. The Bolivian press has become more aggressive, reporting cases of government corruption. National opinion polls have revealed that the general public feels the press has more credibility than other national institution, including the Catholic Church.

But the press's more aggressive posture resulted in a death threat against one journalist and a libel suit against another. On March 15, Osvaldo Calle, a reporter with the La Paz daily *Ultima Hora*, received an anonymous death threat at the newspaper's office. The newspaper received several calls from a man inquiring about Calle's schedule. Calle, a reporter with the financial section, had reported on Bolivia's privatization of state enterprises.

On June 25, Ronald Méndez Alpire, a journalist and author, was sentenced to two years in prison for libel. In his book, *Financial Puzzle*, Méndez Alpire alleged that a former bank regulator was responsible for actions that led to two bank failures. The charges against the bank official were confirmed in a report by the controller general. News organizations and members of Congress protested Méndez's sentence. Méndez is free, pending an appeal.

March 19
Osvaldo Calle, *Ultima Hora de La Paz,*
THREATENED
Calle, a reporter with the daily *Ultima Hora de La Paz,* received an anonymous death threat sent to his newspaper's office. Also, since March 15, the receptionists at the daily received several anonymous phone calls from a man inquiring about the hours when Calle arrived and left the office. After the newspaper publicized the incident, the threats stopped. Calle, who works for the paper's financial section, had reported on

the involvement of politicians in two high-profile bank bankruptcy cases two years ago.

June 26
Ronald Méndez Alpire, LEGAL ACTION
Méndez Alpire, a journalist and author of three books on corruption in the Bank Supervisory Board, a federal regulatory agency, was sentenced to two years in prison for libel. The charges stemmed from Méndez Alpire's book *Financial Puzzle,* in which he alleged that a former bank regulator, Luis del Rio Chavez, was responsible for actions that led to two bank failures and cost the Bolivian treasury US$200 million. An official report by the controller general's office later accused del Rio of the same offenses, but a judge found Méndez Alpire guilty of libel anyway. Several news organizations and members of Congress called the sentence illegal and demanded an investigation. Méndez Alpire is currently free, pending his appeal.

Brazil

Brazil's feisty press faced off with a hostile Congress. The lawmakers considered scores of bills that threaten to restrict the current atmosphere of unfettered press freedom that Brazil has fostered since the country's 21 years of military rule ended in 1985.

Brazil's 1988 constitution abolished all forms of censorship and does contain a broad provision similar to the First Amendment, guaranteeing freedom of speech and a free press. The current legislative obsession with press laws is due in part to a broad congressional effort to update laws still on the books that date to the military dictatorship. The 53 bills aimed at the press, however, represent a possible encroachment on press freedom in Brazil—and, in fact, comprise the most formidable legislative assault against the press in Latin America.

Many Brazilian journalists and media owners alike interpret the legislators' efforts to pass draconian press legislation as punitive, punishment for a press that has cultivated a tradition of aggressive investigative reporting, often exposing scandal and official corruption.

Protests from media companies and journalists did manage to derail two of the more draconian measures under consideration. One of the withdrawn bills, under consideration by the Chamber of Deputies (the lower house of Congress) included provisions that would have allowed judges to order jail time for journalists convicted of libel and defamation of character and permit fines on media companies of up to 20 percent of their annual revenues. The two controversial measures were dropped after protests from the press, but scores of other provisions that would give judges significant leeway in ruling on press cases remain under consideration.

Arnaldo Jabor, a commentator for TV Globo, the country's largest network, raised the ire of legislators in May when he characterized the congress as a " supermarket," where "a guy can arrive with a suitcase full of money" and buy votes in exchange for political favors. A few days after he made his remarks, congress moved to expedite some of the new press legislation.

"We will not accept this kind of treatment from the Brazilian press," declared Luis Eduardo Magalhaes, the president of the Chamber of Deputies. "We need a legal instrument that can repel those who attack us without proof, those who seek to denigrate us."

Brazil's regional press, like that of other Latin American countries, was more vulnerable to threats and attacks from local power brokers and criminals because of its isolation in provincial areas.

Overall, however, the Brazilian press continues in its role as society's watchdog, resolving problems that the political system cannot, reporting on issues ranging from banking scandals to the murder of street children.

March 28
José Ronaldo, Rede Globo, ATTACKED
Nelson de Brito, Rede Globo, ATTACKED
Alexandre Wendel, Rede Globo, ATTACKED
Rioting prisoners in the state of Goias took about 40 people hostage, including members of a camera crew from Rede Globo television who were accompanying state officials and judges on their inspection of the prison. Ronaldo, a reporter with Rede Globo; de Brito, a cameraman; and Wendel, de Brito's assistant, were held hostage for eight hours. During that time, inmates assaulted the journalists, and forced Ronaldo to hand over his cellular phone, watch and wallet.

April 17
Marisa Romeo, TV Liberal, HARASSED
Jonias Cardoso, TV Liberal, HARASSED
Raimundo Marinho, TV Liberal, HARASSED
Romeo, a reporter with the television station TV Liberal; Cardoso, a cameraman with the station; and Marinho, Cardoso's assistant, had their video material confiscated by police and were forced to leave the area after they had filmed a confrontation between the police and landless peasants in the northern state of Para. Following widespread protests in the Brazilian press, the videotapes were returned and then broadcast on television.

May 30
Arnaldo Jabor, *O Globo,* TV Globo, *Folha de Sao Paulo,* THREATENED
Jabor, a filmmaker and political satirist, was threatened with a lawsuit by Bonifacio de Andrada, a member of the country's Chamber of Deputies who also serves as an attorney for the lower house of parliament. Jabor writes for several Brazilian newspapers, including *O Globo* and *Folha de Sao Paulo*, and airs weekly commentaries on TV Globo, Brazil's most popular

The Americas

101

television network.

De Andrada said that he would start legal proceedings for defamation and slander against Jabor for comments he made during a news show on TV Globo. Jabor had likened the Chamber of Deputies to a marketplace where votes were traded for favors. De Andrada also demanded that TV Globo broadcast a statement repudiating Jabor's comments. Several international organizations, including CPJ, sent letters of protest to Brazil's President Fernando Henrique Cardoso. At the end of June, no litigation against Jabor had begun.

December 20

Antonio Stelio de Castro, *Página 20*, ATTACKED, THREATENED

Altino Machado, *Jornal do Brasil,* THREATENED

Roberto Filho, a legislative representative for the state of Acre in northern Brazil, entered the office of the newspaper *Página 20* in Rio Blanco with a pistol and threatened to kill Stelio de Castro, the editor of the paper, and Machado, a correspondent for the Jornal do Brasil news agency, according to the Inter American Press Association (IAPA) in Miami. Filho also assaulted Stelio de Castro. Machado had written an article for *Página 20* about alleged fraud in entrance exams at the Federal University of Acre. The article incriminated Filho's wife, as well as other politicians and local authorities.

Chile

Government restrictions continue to threaten free speech in Chile, despite the return to democratic rule in 1990. A national security law enacted during Chile's military dictatorship, which imposes a maximum five-year prison sentence on anyone convicted of defaming an elected official, the military, the judiciary, or the police, remains in effect. Some people charged under this law, however, were able to muster enough public out-

rage to force officials to drop charges.

In October, a military court dropped sedition charges against the editor in chief of the weekly *Punto Final*. The charges stemmed from a 1991 front-page cartoon of army head Gen. Augusto Pinochet. Editor Manuel Cabieses told CPJ that he had received support from journalists and many other people who believed the charges were a threat to free speech. In recent years there has been "more concern and more public debate among Chileans about free speech and democracy," Cabieses said.

Journalists and news organizations in Chile continued to debate whether media companies should give preference in hiring to applicants with a degree in journalism from a Chilean University and who belong to the Colegio de Periodistas, a journalists union. The National Congress decided to remove such a requirement from the draft of a controversial press law the Congress has been considering for several years.

September 10

Manuel Cabieses, *Punto Final*, HARASSED, LEGAL ACTION

Punto Final, ATTACKED

Cabieses, editor in chief of the weekly *Punto Final*, was charged by a military court with "inciting sedition." Police, armed with a warrant for his arrest, raided his home and *Punto Final*'s offices. Cabieses went into hiding for 18 days while his attorney filed a writ of habeas corpus. The court on Oct. 10 dropped the charges on the grounds that the Santiago Appeals Court in 1995 had absolved Cabieses of the same charges and dismissed the case.

The case against Cabieses began in 1991, after he published a front-page cartoon in the Sept. 9 issue depicting then army leader Gen. Augusto Pinochet cleaning his bloody nose with the Chilean flag. The caption, "Cynicism and sadism," alluded to comments made by Pinochet about a secret grave site in which bodies had been buried two-by-two. Pinochet had said, "This represents a savings for the state."

Colombia

A Colombian journalist was assassinated, and others braved death threats, physical attack, bombings and kidnapping at the hands of a broad range of players—drug barons, the military, paramilitary groups and guerrilla terrorists—all intent on silencing them.

Moreover, in a continuing pattern of remarkable intolerance, Colombian government officials, including legislators, the judiciary and the president of the republic, maintained a hostile posture toward the press because of its hard-hitting reporting on official corruption and government links to drug trafficking.

The most controversial story of the year revolved around charges by a former cabinet minister that President Ernesto Samper knowingly accepted drug money to help financial his presidential campaign. In a bold gesture that illustrates the Colombian press's increasingly independent stance, several journalists called upon Samper to resign. It was the first time the Colombian press has openly challenged the legitimacy of a democratically elected head of state.

In a move that is widely interpreted as a punitive action against the press for its criticism of Samper and other reports of official corruption, the Congress in December passed a bill that would allow the government to revoke a television station's license if it finds that the programming does not conform to a standard of "objectivity, impartiality or balance."

Drug-mafia violence against the press has been steadily decreasing, reflecting a national decline in drug-related violence. But a series of death threats against several reporters early in the year by members of the notorious Cali drug Cartel sparked concern that the drop could be an aberration.

El Espectatador, the nation's oldest daily newspaper, continues to grapple with serious financial problems that date, in part, to the 1989 bombing of the newspaper by the Medellin cocaine cartel. The bombing, ordered by the late cartel leader Pablo Escobar, caused extensive damage and was intended to cripple the newspaper's main production facility. In 1986, Escobar was behind the assassination of Guillermo Cano Isaza, editor of *El Espectador*.

On the positive side of the ledger, the Colombian press has been taking significant steps toward monitoring press freedom and professionalizing journalists. With the support of CPJ, several prominent journalists in February formed the Foundation for the Freedom of the Press in Bogotá. The Foundation for New Journalism, an educational group headed by Nobel laureate Gabriel García Márquez, organized a series of journalism training workshops for young professionals.

The Americas

January 26
Jorge Ramos, Univisión, THREATENED
Patsy Lloyd, Univisión, THREATENED
Angel Matos, Univisión, THREATENED
Ramos, a newscast reporter and anchorman of the Miami-based television channel Univisión; Lloyd, a producer with Univisión; and cameraman Matos were threatened with death after Univisión aired Ramos's interview of former Minister Fernando Botero. In the interview, Botero confessed that he knew about President Ernesto Samper's alleged acceptance of drug money for his presidential election campaign. Ramos, who normally works out of the network's headquarters in Miami and had come to Colombia to report on the political crisis triggered by the allegations against the president, fled the country fearing for his life. Matos left Colombia with Ramos; both subsequently returned.

March 16
Raúl Benoit, Univisión, ATTACKED,
  THREATENED
Benoit, a Bogotá correspondent for the Miami-based television network Univisión, was shot at by two unidentified gunmen while driving with his wife and children in northwestern Bogotá. The assailants, on motorcycles, fired shots at Benoit's car but were greeted in return with a hail of gunfire from the journalist and his two bodyguards, whom he hired after an assassination attempt in 1990. No one in Benoit's car was injured. Prior to the attack, Benoit received death threats after filing a series of stories on the Cali drug cartel and the political crisis in Colombia. In a letter to Colombian President Ernesto Samper, CPJ urged him to issue a public statement condemning all attacks and threats against the press and to conduct an immediate investigation into the attempted assassination of Benoit.

May 10
Ana Lucia Betancur, Noticiero Nacional,
  IMPRISONED
Betancur, a prominent reporter for the television news program "Noticiero Nacional," was kidnapped by leftist rebels in the southwest city of Cali. She was released unharmed five days later with a message from her kidnappers to the government of President Ernesto Samper. In the fall of 1995, after unknown gunmen killed three-time presidential candidate Alvaro Gómez Hurtado, the government declared a state of emergency and enacted measures that prohibited the media from carrying any statements made by leftist guerrillas.

August 15
Hector Mujica, El Espectador, HARASSED
Mujica, a correspondent for the daily El Espectador in Puerto Asis, in the department of Putumayo, was ordered by an armed man to give a verbal explanation of articles he had written about an ambulance set on fire during protests by producers of coca. The coca producers were

demonstrating against a government campaign to prohibit cultivation of the crop.

August 20
Edison Parra, El Tiempo, THREATENED
Jaime Arias, El Tiempo, THREATENED
Reporter Parra and photographer Arias, both of whom are special correspondents for the Mocoa daily El Tiempo, in the Putumayo department, were threatened by a group of civilians, who forced them to attend a demonstration against a government campaign to prohibit coca cultivation by small-scale local producers.

August 22
Amparo Jimenez, QAP Noticias, THREAT-
  ENED, HARASSED
José Coronado, QAP Noticias, THREATENED,
  HARASSED
Jimenez, a reporter, and Coronado, a cameraman, both with television station QAP Noticias, were detained by police after covering the occupation of the Hacienda Bellacruz by farm workers. They were stopped by the police in the nearby city of Pelaya and ordered to turn over their footage of the occupation. They refused and were allowed to leave, but were stopped again by members of an armed paramilitary group, who stole some of their equipment. The paramilitary group later issued death threats against the journalists. CPJ wrote to President Ernesto Samper and urged him to publicly condemn the threats against Jimenez and Coronado.

August 23
Television news programs, CENSORED
The National Television Committee (CNT) ordered television news programs not to transmit unofficial information that "aggravates public order." The government decree was in response to television coverage of clashes between soldiers and coca farmers demonstrating against government prohibitions on cultivation of the crop in the towns of Caqueta and Putumayo.

Some members of the Colombian Congress, apparently angered by news reports, lobbied for an amendment to Television Law 182 in an effort to delay the extension of the current licenses of the news programs.

August 29
Luis Alberto Miño, *El Tiempo,* ATTACKED
Camilo Chaparro, Noticiero CM&, ATTACKED
Gloria Tisnés, Noticiero Nacional, ATTACKED
Jaime Orlando Gaitán, Caracól 7:30, ATTACKED
Maribel Orsorio, QAP Noticias, ATTACKED
Miño, a reporter for the Bogotá daily *El Tiempo,* and four reporters for Bogotá-based television stations—Chaparro of Noticiero CM&; Tisnés of Noticiero Nacional; Gaitán of Caracól 7:30; and Orsorio of QAP Noticias—were fired upon by soldiers in the village of Morelia in the Caquetá department of Colombia. The reporters were covering a demonstration by coca cultivators against government prohibitions of small-scale local producers. They were clearly identified as journalists by brightly colored flak jackets bearing the names of their respective news organizations. No one was injured. CPJ wrote a letter on Aug. 30 to President Ernesto Samper urging him to publicly condemn the attack and begin an investigation.

August 29
Luis Gonzalo Vélez ("Richard"), Cadena 1
ATTACKED
Vélez, a cameraman with "Colombia 12:30," a news program carried on television station Cadena 1, was beaten repeatedly by three soldiers with the butts of their G-3 rifles while he was covering a demonstration by coca cultivators in the village of Morelia in the Caquetá department.
The soldiers also tried to confiscate film from Vélez's camera. He had taken pictures of the soldiers firing upon farm workers. Vélez was taken to the hospital for treatment and later transported to Bogotá. CPJ wrote a letter to the Colombian government denouncing the beating.

August 29
Yesid Cristancho, Cadena A, HARASSED
Cristancho, a cameraman for the television program "CM" on the public channel Cadena A in Bogotá, was forced to jump into the Bodoquero River after finding himself surrounded by security forces and protesters during confrontations between soldiers and coca producers in the Caqueta department in southern Colombia. The coca producers were opposing government prohibitions on cultivation of the crop. Cristancho was not able to escape via a metal bridge nearby because it had been electrically charged by the soldiers to prevent anyone from fleeing the area.

October 18
Norvey Diaz, Radio Colina, KILLED
Diaz, director of the program "Rondando por los Barrios" on Radio Colina, was killed in Girardot, a resort town 135 kilometers from Bogotá. Diaz, who was last seen alive on a street in the company of a young woman, had left home to attend a meeting. His body was found with a bullet wound in the nape of his neck and a cigarette butt and necklace in his hand. Investigators believe that his murder was carefully planned by professionals.
Six years ago, Diaz had received frequent funeral wreaths ("coronas mortuarias") and letters warning him "to hold his tongue, otherwise something unfortunate would happen to him." In 1990, Diaz had reported on the alleged involvement of police officials in the murder of street people, as well as on the apparent investments made by drug traffickers in vacation resorts in the city. Colleagues stated that although Diaz had always reported on irregularities in society, he had, for the past few months, lessened the virulence of his reports. Shortly before his murder, Diaz had been named by Todelar, the company which owns Radio Colina, to a post which would have taken him away from his journalistic duties.

The Americas

105

December 16
Juan Gómez Martínez, *El Colombiano,* ATTACKED
A van packed with dynamite exploded in Medellín outside the home of Juan Gómez Martinez, an owner of the daily *El Colombiano.* Gómez is a former mayor of Medellín and a former state governor. A few days before the bombing, an anonymous telephone caller told the newspaper to "keep quiet" and that its journalists had "big mouths." Officials speculated that the bomb was planted by drug terrorists, but spokesmen for *El Colombiano* said in an interview that the perpetrators had not yet been identified.

December 16
Colombian press, LEGAL ACTION
As part of a broader constitutional reform, the Colombian Congress passed a bill that could permit the National Television Commission to revoke television licenses or place conditions on the issuance of TV channels. The bill empowers the Commission to evaluate the content of news programs every six months and to ensure that they conform to standards of "objectivity, impartiality, and balance." The measure was widely interpreted as a punitive action and raised concerns that it could force networks to exercise self-censorship or risk losing a license.

December 22
Voz, ATTACKED
A bomb loaded with 20 kilos of dynamite exploded in Bogotá outside the offices of the weekly *Voz,* the official publication of the Colombian Communist Party, causing extensive damage. Authorities do not know who planted the bomb.

The newspaper's director, Manuel Cepeda Vargas, was murdered in 1994. Police attributed his assassination to a paramilitary group calling itself Colombia Without Guerrillas.

December 28
EL Tiempo, ATTACKED
A bomb containing five kilos of dynamite exploded outside the offices in Medellín of the Bogotá-based daily newspaper *El Tiempo.* Police officials speculated that the bomb was planted by members of the guerrilla group Colombian Revolutionary Armed Forces, better-known by its initials, FARC. Police said they had found leaflets with FARC's name on them near the site of the attack. The leaflets derided the news media for its coverage of the conflicts in the banana-cultivating region of Urabá, where guerrillas and paramilitary groups operate. The guerrillas oppose the government and also plantation owners, some of which are foreign companies. The explosion injured a security guard and damaged the newspaper's offices and surrounding buildings.

Costa Rica

In an unprecedented ruling on June 7, the Constitutional Court of Costa Rica decided that a congressman who had sued the San José-based daily *La República* had the right to reply to a news article about him. The ruling raised serious concerns about editorial autonomy. The ruling stemmed from a lawsuit brought by Carlos Fernández, deputy chief of the Social Christian Unity Party, according to a report by the Inter American Press Association (IAPA). In its April 18 edition, *La República* published an article saying that Fernández, an attorney, had been suspended for a year from practicing as a notary public as a result of complaints from clients. Fernández had appealed the decision. After the article was published, the suspension was reduced to eight days. Fernández, who did not respond to reporters' telephone calls prior to the article's publication, demanded that *La República* print a correction written by him in the news section of the paper, where the original article had appeared. Instead, *La República* published Fernández's response on its opinion pages.

In the June 7 decision, the court ruled that the paper had to run the correction, along with a photograph of Fernández, on the same page as the original article. The newspaper complied on July 12.

In another development, Costa Rican President Jose Maria Figueres signed an executive decree, effective May 7, classifying as "state secrets" some documents related to police efforts to control drug trafficking and money laundering. According to the IAPA, the decree carries a penalty of up to six years in prison for anyone who makes these documents public.

The good news for journalists was that the Costa Rican Supreme Court upheld its May 1995 landmark decision declaring the licensing of journalists unconstitutional, despite appeals to overturn the decision.

Cuba

Cuba's fledgling independent press movement suffered an unrelenting wave of harassment by Cuban state security police but still managed to survive a crucial year, recruiting many new members and publishing articles regularly in the United States and Latin America.

Journalists within Cuba's official government news organizations also began to collaborate with the independent press, albeit anonymously, for fear of losing their jobs. By the end of 1996, there were eight groups of independent journalists, four operating in Havana and four others in provincial regions

The year began with the Cuban government's large-scale crackdown in January against "Concilio Cubano," an umbrella group of various pro-democracy organizations. Authorities detained dozens of human rights advocates and independent journalists, searched their homes, and confiscated typewriters, foreign publications, and correspondence.

Conditions for the independent press worsened in the wake of the Cuban air force's downing of two private aircraft flown by Cuban-Americans opposed to the Castro regime on Feb. 24, killing all four people aboard. In a speech the following month, Vice President Raúl Castro told the Communist Party Central Committee that the regime would not tolerate any democratic opening and absolutely no press freedom. "This so-called glasnost that undermined the Soviet Union and other socialist countries consisted of handing over the mass media, one by one, to the enemies of socialism," Castro said. "Cubans maintain and will maintain that a really free press is one serving the people, not the exploiters waiting to ambush from Miami."

Two independent journalists were forced into exile after state security police issued a verbal ultimatum that they either leave the country or face prison sentences for their activities. Rafael Solano, the director of Havana Press, was incarcerated for 42 days. He was released on April 8, following a campaign for his release by CPJ and other press freedom organizations. A month later, he left Cuba for exile in Spain. Roxana Valdivia, a founder of the agency Patria, in Ciego de Avila, left for exile in Miami on June 4, after she had been threatened with incarceration.

Cuba's state security apparatus attempted to marginalize independent journalists through a campaign of threats of reprisal that targeted family members as well as supportive neighbors and colleagues. The extraordinary pressure and harassment is intended to take a psychological toll on the journalists and to ruin them financially.

A debate has emerged among journalists over their role in Cuba's political future. Many reject the label "dissident" and strive to professionalize journalism with an eye toward the post-Castro era. This debate has spilled over into the journalists' often-con-

The Americas

107

tentious relationship with Radio Martí, the U.S. government's Office of Cuban Broadcasting which broadcasts to Cuba. Several unpaid stringers for the station have charged that Radio Martí has censored their reports, fueling the resentment of those journalists who feel the U.S. government is using them as political pawns.

One of the Cuban government's most common harassment techniques has been the suspension of telephone service, sometimes for weeks at a time, as an apparent reprisal for reporting activities. Independent journalists are also denied access to facsimile machines and computer modems.

In addition, state security police confiscated articles, manuscripts, foreign publications, typewriters, and writing materials, including pens, from several journalists. Harassment also took a new, troubling turn in July when police detained a member of the Cuba Press agency and stole $700 in cash he had received from the French press group, Reporters Without Borders.

Despite all these government hurdles, the four Havana-based news agencies—Independent Press Agency of Cuba (APIC), the Independent Press Bureau of Cuba (BPIC), Cuba Press, and Havana Press—continued to operate and disseminate news articles through representatives in Miami and Puerto Rico. In addition, four new independent press agencies were formed in 1996 in provincial areas: Agencia Centro Norte del Pais (CNP) in Villa Clara; Agencia de Prensa Libre Oriental (APLO) in Santiago de Cuba; Patria, in Camaguey and Ciego de Avila; and Pinar Press, in Pinar del Rio. And, in a real triumph over the Castro regime's repressive agenda, the news agencies' U.S. supporters succeeded in widely distributing their Cuban colleagues' articles through various World Wide Web sites. (See special report on Cuba, p. 133.)

January 10

Yndamiro Restano, Bureau of Independent Journalists of Cuba (BPIC), HARASSED
State security agents detained the parents of Restano, who is the director of BPIC, and questioned them for seven hours about letting their home be used as the BPIC office. Restano's parents, who are both in their 70s, are not involved in any journalistic or political activities. In a statement issued while traveling in Venezuela, Restano said he feared his parents' detention was a sign that he would not be allowed to return to work as a journalist in Cuba.

January 14

Raúl Rivero, Cuba Press, HARASSED
Juan Antonio Sánchez, Cuba Press, HARASSED
Rivero and Sánchez, both journalists with the independent news agency Cuba Press, were arrested by State Security agents in a spate of government actions against journalists and members of a newly formed coalition called the Concilio Cubano (Cuban Council). Cuba Press is a member of the Cuban Council, an umbrella organization for a broad range of dissident groups. Rivero and Sánchez were arrested in Rivero's home in Havana. They were taken to a police station and then transferred to Villa Marista, the headquarters of the Department of State Security. They were released the next day. No charges were filed.

January 19

Luis Solar Hernandez, Bureau of Independent Journalists of Cuba (BPIC), THREATENED, HARASSED
Roxana Valdivia, BPIC, THREATENED, HARASSED
Solar, who covers religion for BPIC, was detained in the town of Ciego de Avila by Cuban state security agents while waiting for a train to Havana. Solar was threatened, and his address book and other personal belongings were confiscated. He was released the next day. State security agents also threatened Valdivia, a BPIC colleague Solar was visiting in Ciego de

Avila, and summoned her to appear at the state security offices for violating orders not to receive dissidents in her house. In a press release, CPJ condemned the government's campaign of harassment against independent Cuban journalists.

January 20
Olance Nogueras, Bureau of Independent Journalists of Cuba (BPIC), HARASSED
Nogueras, a journalist with BPIC, was expelled from a press briefing held by the Ministry of Foreign Relations. He had tried to attend the weekly briefing, which was open to the foreign press corps, requesting that independent Cuban journalists be allowed to participate. Police accused him of participating in news conferences at government entities without having the proper government-issued journalism credentials. In a press release, CPJ condemned the government's treatment of Nogueras.

February 15
Bureau of Independent Press in Cuba (BPIC), HARASSED
State security agents surrounded the offices of BPIC in Havana and cut off all communications with and access to the offices, which also serve as the residence of the parents of its director, Yndamiro Restano. Restano's parents and family were prohibited from leaving the building and no one was allowed to enter. Police also intercepted Lorenzo Paez Nuñez, a BPIC reporter, as he was approaching the BPIC building, and confiscated material he was carrying. In the afternoon, security agents raided the offices of BPIC and confiscated 50 articles written by BPIC journalists. CPJ wrote to President Fidel Castro, requesting that BPIC be allowed to operate freely.

February 27
Rafael Solano, Havana Press, IMPRISONED, LEGAL ACTION

Solano, president of the independent news agency Havana Press, was arrested by state security on charges of alleged "association with persons with the intent to commit a crime." A request by his lawyer to free him on bail was denied by Cuban State Security even though, according to his lawyer, there were no legal grounds for his imprisonment. During Solano's detention, his health deteriorated seriously. He lost a considerable amount of weight and was running a high fever. On March 12, CPJ wrote to President Fidel Castro to express its concern about the continued incarceration of Solano and the pattern of harassment against Cuba's independent journalists. On April 8, a day after the *New York Times* ran an article on his case and the challenges facing the Cuban independent press, Solano was freed but the case against him was still pending. CPJ sent another letter to President Castro, welcoming the release but urging him to drop the charges against Solano and to close the case. Solano said that upon his release from jail he was given an ultimatum; emigrate or face a possible prison sentence. On May 8, he left Cuba for exile in Spain.

March
Roxana Valdivia, Bureau of Independent Press of Cuba (BPIC), THREATENED, HARASSED, EXPELLED
Valdivia, a BPIC reporter, was given a verbal ultimatum by Cuban authorities at the beginning of March warning that if she did not secure a visa to emigrate by the end of the month she would be incarcerated on charges of refusing to obey orders to stop her work as an independent journalist. On March 20, she was granted a visa by the U.S. government. During the three weeks Valdivia was seeking a visa, her phone lines were frequently cut, at one point for as long as a week. In October 1995, she was detained for one day by state security in Havana and then was forced to return to her home in

The Americas

Ciego de Avila. She remained under police surveillance and was not allowed to leave her province without securing official permission. In a March 12 letter to Cuban President Fidel Castro, CPJ condemned the harassment of Valdivia and urged Castro to allow independent journalists to operate freely without the threat of harassment and imprisonment.

On June 4, Valdivia arrived in Miami with her family after being forced to emigrate. CPJ sent a letter to Cuban President Fidel Castro, protesting what it considers to be the defacto expulsion of independent journalists from Cuba.

April 23
Olance Nogueras, Bureau of Independent Cuban Journalists (BPIC), IMPRISONED
Nogueras, a reporter with BPIC, was detained by agents of the political police in the city of Cienfuegos, where he planned to meet with Danielle Mitterrand, president of the French human rights organization France Liberté. In a letter to President Fidel Castro, CPJ requested that Nogueras be released immediately. He was released two days later, after Mitterrand had left the country.

April 26
Bureau of Independent Press of Cuba (BPIC)
ATTACKED, HARASSED
Police raided the BPIC headquarters in Havana, confiscating BPIC's files, correspondence, magazines, typewriters, a computer, and pens and pencils. The office was set up in the home of Julio Restano Suárez, BPIC director Yndamiro Restano's father. Yndamiro Restano lives in Miami. CPJ wrote a letter to the Cuban government denouncing the raid.

On May 2, State Security agents detained Julio Suárez for about 10 hours at Villa Marista, Cuban State Security's headquarters. Police ordered Julio Suárez to stop allowing his home to be used as BPIC's office, and told him that BPIC had to cease its work immediately. In response, BPIC closed down the office; BPIC

members now operate from their respective homes.

May 24
Lázaro Lazo, Bureau of Independent Press of Cuba (BPIC), IMPRISONED, THREATENED
BPIC reporter Lazo was arrested in Havana by two agents of Cuban state security. He was detained for four days in Villa Marista, the main prison of the state security agency, then released. Agents warned Lazo to stop working for BPIC and to leave Cuba.

May 31
Joaquín Torres, Havana Press, THREATENED, HARASSED
Torres, president of the independent news agency Havana Press, was threatened in his home by two members of the state security police, who told him that he would be incarcerated if he continued to write for the agency. Initially, the police informed him that he had received authorization to emigrate and should prepare to leave the country. Torres told authorities, however, that he never sought to emigrate and had no intention of leaving Cuba.

June 3
Cuban independent journalists, HARASSED
CPJ, in a June 3 letter to Javier Garza Calderon, chief executive of the Mexican corporation Grupo Domos, condemned what it views as Grupo Domos' complicity in the Cuban government's ongoing campaign of harassment and intimidation of independent Cuban journalists. In 1994, Grupo Domos entered into a joint venture with the Cuban government, buying 49 percent of the state telephone company, ETECSA, for US$750 million. The Cuban government has systematically interrupted or denied telephone service to independent journalists, often as a reprisal against reporting activities. CPJ urged Grupo Domos to work toward granting or restoring telephone service to all Cuban citizens, regardless of their occu-

pation or purported political beliefs.

Journalists are not permitted to own or operate facsimile machines or computer modems. But some journalists in Cuba, both foreign correspondents and local reporters, do use the machines, and the government has confiscated some of them. The restrictions are a direct violation of Article 19 of the Universal Declaration of Human Rights, which guarantees the freedom "to seek, receive, and impart information through any media regardless of frontiers."

June 9
José Rivero García, Cuba Press, THREATENED
Rivero, a reporter for the independent news agency Cuba Press, was threatened by State Security officials with imprisonment or exile because of his activities as an independent journalist. The security officials, who came to Rivero's home and confiscated a file of press clippings, reportedly were angry about some of his coverage for Cuba Press. They also threatened to cut off his telephone if he continued to file reports to Radio Martí, a U.S.-based radio station funded by the U.S. government.

June 12
Rodrigo Alonso, Telemundo, ATTACKED
Alonso, a reporter for the Miami-based Telemundo network, was abducted by four men outside his hotel in the Vedado section of Havana. While the men drove Alonso around Havana in their car for approximately four hours, his hotel room was burglarized.

The incident began when Alonso received a phone call in his room at the Cohiba Hotel and was told that he had a visitor. When he went outside to meet the supposed visitor, he was approached by two men who asked him if he was Rodrigo Alonso. When he said yes, they pushed him into the car, and two other men entered the vehicle, blocking his exit. During the four-hour drive, he was asked several times what he was doing in Cuba. One of the men hit Alonso on the back of his head and poked his right eye several times with a sharp object.

Alonso had traveled to Cuba on June 10 with two other representatives of Telemundo to research material and conduct interviews for a program about the life of the revolutionary leader Ernesto Ché Guevara. CPJ urged the Cuban government to investigate Alonso's abduction and the burglary.

June 19
Suzanne Bilello, Committee to Protect Journalists (CPJ), HARASSED, EXPELLED
Bilello, CPJ's program coordinator for the Americas, was arrested at 10:30 p.m. in her room at the Hotel Nacional in Havana by two plainclothes Interior Ministry officials and a uniformed immigration officer. She was brought to the Interior Ministry, where she was interrogated for three hours about her activities in Cuba and her contacts with independent journalists in Havana. She was also questioned about the modest gifts she brought the journalists she met with, including pens, notebooks and medicines—all of which had been approved by Cuban Customs officials—and small advance payments from private sources to help underwrite news-gathering costs for the coming months. Bilello's interrogators seized her notebooks, personal papers, and other private documents, along with rolls of exposed film and other possessions. At 2 a.m. on June 20 she was informed that she was being expelled for "fomenting rebellion." She was then placed aboard a 7 a.m. flight to Cancun, Mexico.

Bilello had traveled to Cuba from Mexico on June 16 on a tourist visa. During her four-day stay she met with reporters and editors of five newly established independent Cuban news agencies.

In a June 20 press release, CPJ strongly protested "the unjustified seizure of Ms. Bilello's personal papers and other belongings as an unconscionable invasion of privacy, and as a violation of press freedom."

June 24
Lázaro Lazo, Bureau of Independent Press of

Cuba (BPIC), HARASSED

Lazo, BPIC's interim director, was summoned
to the offices of the Department of State Security in Villa Marista, Havana. He was held for
nine hours and interrogated about his work
with BPIC and other independent news agencies. He was also questioned about the visit of
CPJ staff member Suzanne Bilello, who was
expelled from Cuba a week earlier after speaking with independent journalists there. In a letter to President Fidel Castro, CPJ expressed its
grave concern about the interrogation of Lazo
and the harassment of other independent journalists.

June 26
Norma Brito, Bureau of Independent Press of
Cuba (BPIC), HARASSED

Brito, a BPIC spokesperson, was summoned to
the offices of the Department of State Security
in Villa Marista, Havana, and interrogated
about her work with BPIC. She was also questioned about the visit of CPJ staff member
Suzanne Bilello, who was expelled from Cuba a
week earlier after speaking with independent
journalists there. Brito was released after several
hours. In a letter to the Cuban authorities, CPJ
protested the harassment.

July 12
Jacques Perrot, Reporters Sans Frontières
EXPELLED

Perrot, a journalist working in the Americas
department of the French press freedom group
Reporters Sans Frontieres (RSF), was denied
entry to Cuba. When he arrived at the José
Martí International Airport in Havana, a police
officer told him he would have to return to
France on the next available flight because his
passport was allegedly not in order. Perrot, who
had entered Cuba on a tourist visa issued in
France, was escorted by police to a plane headed for Paris.

According to a statement published by RSF,
an agent of the Cuban Interior Ministry
claimed that Perrot was an "undesirable"

because of a previous trip he had made to Cuba.
Perrot had visited Cuba with an RSF delegation
from May 16 to May 20. The delegation met
with independent journalists and provided them
with funds to finance news reporting.

Cuba's refusal to allow Perrot into the country came three weeks after CPJ staff expert
Suzanne Bilello was expelled from Cuba. In a
letter to President Fidel Castro, CPJ denounced
the Cuban government's treatment of Perrot.

July 12
Joaquín Torres, Havana Press, HARASSED

Torres, a reporter with the independent agency
Havana Press, was arrested in his home, taken
to a police station in the Havana neighborhood
of Caballo Blanco, and incarcerated there until
the morning of July 14. Torres was interrogated
briefly about his work by an official of the State
Security Agency, which maintains a bureau in
the Caballo Blanco police station. CPJ strongly
denounced the arrest in a letter to President
Fidel Castro.

July 13
Orlando Bordón Galvez, Cuba Press, HARASSED

Bordón, a reporter with the independent news
agency Cuba Press, was interrogated for four
hours at the police station in the Havana neighborhood of San José about his activities as an
independent journalist.

July 15
Nestor Baguer, Cuban Association of
Independent Journalists (APIC)
THREATENED, HARASSED

Baguer, head of the Cuban Association of Independent Journalists (APIC,) was summoned by
the state security police at Villa Marista, where
he was charged with distributing false information and enemy propaganda. Baguer was interrogated for several hours about his work with
APIC and about a recent visit to Cuba by CPJ
staff expert Suzanne Bilello.

On July 16, Baguer reported back to Villa
Marista as ordered. He was detained briefly. He

told CPJ that security police threatened to bring him before a criminal tribunal if he continued to write articles that they considered "enemy propaganda." CPJ protested his detention and the harassment of several other independent journalists in a letter to Cuba's president, Fidel Castro.

July 15
Mercedes Moreno, Bureau of Independent Press of Cuba (BPIC), THREATENED, HARASSED

Moreno, a BPIC reporter, was summoned to the state security agency at Villa Marista in Havana and charged with distributing false information and enemy propaganda. She was questioned about CPJ staff member Suzanne Bilello's visit to Cuba, though she never met with Bilello. Moreno was also threatened with criminal prosecution. In a letter to Cuban President Fidel Castro, CPJ expressed its deep concern about the charges against Moreno and the wave of harassment against independent journalists in Cuba.

July 30
Juan Antonio Sanchez, Cuba Press, THREATENED, HARASSED

Sanchez, a photojournalist with the independent news agency Cuba Press, was apprehended by Cuban Security Agents as he left a currency exchange booth at the Havana Libre Hotel, where he had changed US$700 from large denominations into smaller bills. The money had been sent to Cuba Press by the French press freedom advocacy group Reporters Sans Frontières, to support news-gathering efforts.

The officials drove Sanchez to the sixth police unit, in the Mariano section of Havana, where he was detained for six hours. They confiscated the money and told Sanchez he had to sign a written statement that he had "received money from the American government in order to finance domestic counterrevolutionary activities." Sanchez refused to sign the statement.

The officials threatened him, saying, "This is nothing compared to what could happen to you." He was then released.

August 1
Ramon Alberto Cruz Lima, Patria, THREATENED, HARASSED

Cruz, a reporter for the independent news agency Patria, was arrested in Ciego de Avila at the home of Hector Valdivia. Valdivia is the father of Roxana Valdivia, a Patria journalist who was forced into exile with her family in June. Hector Valdivia was also arrested but released soon after.

Cruz told CPJ that he was detained and interrogated at the headquarters of the State Security Department for four hours. During the interrogation, Cruz was questioned about CPJ staff member Suzanne Bilello's visit to Cuba in June. At the time of his arrest, police confiscated articles that Cruz had written and threatened to use them as evidence in a criminal prosecution, but Cruz was not formally charged with anything.

On Aug. 7, Cruz was summoned to the State Security headquarters and interrogated again, this time for six hours. The police threatened Cruz with charges of enemy propaganda, conspiracy, and practicing journalism illegally. In a letter to President Fidel Castro, CPJ urged the Cuban government to halt the harassment of Cruz and other independent journalists, which appeared to be part of an ongoing campaign against Patria.

August 12
Bernardo Fuentes Camblor, Patria, IMPRISONED
Magaly Pino García, Patria, IMPRISONED
Jorge Enrique Rives, Patria, IMPRISONED

Fuentes Camblor, Pino García, and Rives, reporters for the independent Cuban news agency Patria, were arrested in their homes in the city of Camaguey by members of the Cuban State Security police. The reporters were incarcerated in State Security's provincial headquar-

The Americas

ters in Camaguey, where they were interrogated about their activities as independent journalists and CPJ staff expert Suzanne Bilello's visit to Cuba in June.

In a letter to President Fidel Castro, CPJ urged Cuban authorities to release the journalists immediately. All three were released on Aug. 16.

August 14
Jorge Olivera Castillo, Havana Press, HARASSED
Olivera Castillo, a reporter for the independent news agency Havana Press, was interrogated by two State Security officials about the source of a news report he had filed for Radio Martí in early August. The officials came to his home at 10 a.m. and interrogated him for 30 minutes about the source for his report about the Instituto Cubano de Radio y Televisión, where tape-recording equipment had recently been damaged by an acid-like substance.

The two officials told Olivera Castillo that they would continue to visit him until he revealed his sources. Olivera Castillo himself had been an editor with the Institute for nine years before he was forced to resign in 1993.

Dominican Republic

The media met some resistance from political parties vying in the watershed May 16 presidential election and in a second round of voting in June, scheduled because none of the candidates received an outright majority in the first round. The campaign was widely considered the most reserved and civilized in the Dominican Republic's three decades of democracy. But supporters of the ruling Social Christian Reform Party (PRSC), one of the three principal political parties, assaulted a reporter for the Rahitel television sta-

tion and her cameraman at a press conference. Journalists for other media outlets reported some minor skirmishes with members of political parties after news organizations endorsed candidates.

The press suffered a significant setback when one of the Dominican Republic's most prestigious journalists was convicted of defaming the head of a telecommunications company. On June 19, a criminal court found Juan Bolívar Díaz guilty of libeling another journalist, Generoso Ledesma, in *Electoral Trauma*, a book about the Dominican Republic's 1994 general elections. Bolívar received a six-month prison sentence and a fine of approximately US$233,000. Bolívar has appealed the conviction and is awaiting a new trial.

In other developments, the police officer accused of shooting and killing *Ultima Hora* journalist Juan Carlos Vasquez in June 1995 went on trial for murder.

May 23
Victoria Espinosa, Rahitel, ATTACKED, HARASSED
Rentería Montero, Rahitel, ATTACKED, HARASSED
Espinosa, a reporter with the television station Rahitel, and Montero, her cameraman, were assaulted and their television equipment was destroyed by those attending a press conference called by the ruling Partido Reformista Social Cristiano (PRSC) on the eve of the presidential elections.

June 19
Juan Bolivar, Teleantillas, LEGAL ACTION
Bolivar, news director of the private television station Teleantillas and one of the most respected journalists in the Dominican Republic, was convicted of defaming Generoso Ledesma, the head of Comunicaciones Ltd., a telecommunications company. The charges stemmed from a paragraph in Bolivar's book *Electoral Trauma*, in which Bolivar claimed that Ledesma had divert-

ed funds from Comunicaciones Ltd. to the 1994 electoral campaign of President Joaquín Balaguer.

Bolivar was sentenced to six months in prison and fined US$233,000. The sentence specifically stated that he would have to go to prison even if he planned to file an appeal. But the Santo Domingo prosecutor general suspended the sentence, calling it "excessive and hasty." While most trials in the Dominican Republic run for several years, Bolivar's trial was completed in one day. Bolivar has appealed and is awaiting a new trial.

Ecuador

Since President Abdalá Bucaram Ortiz came to power on Aug. 10, Ecuadorian journalists have complained that there has been a deterioration in official tolerance of the media that has taken a toll on press freedom.

In a televised address to the nation on Dec. 1, Bucaram diverged from the substance of his speech on political and economic strategy to attack the daily newspaper, *Hoy*, which has been one of the regime's harshest critics. *Hoy* has reported extensively on political patronage in the current and previous presidential administrations.

Shortly after the president's vociferous attack on the newspaper, a series of television commercials that journalists and others believed were backed by the president urged a boycott of the newspaper.

Energy Minister Alfredo Adum has also targeted *Hoy* for attack, publicly stating that he was buying shares in the daily newspaper with the intention of taking it over. In a letter published in the newspaper, Adum attacked all journalists, saying a journalist's life "means sitting around drinking coffee, taking on the phone, being a pain to everyone else, winning themselves a bribe from time

to time and ultimately talking and writing stupidities."

Responding to the alarming press conditions in Ecuador, the International Federation of Journalists, a Caracas, Venezuela-based press group said in a statement: "The intolerance of the government and civil servants towards the media investigations, reports and criticism has systematically manifested itself in verbal public attacks, insults, smear campaigns and direct threats against journalists and media outlets."

El Salvador

Officials, police, and an underground political organization continue to target journalists in El Salvador with scattered threats and attacks as the country strives to nurture its democratic institutions.

In June and July, several national and foreign journalists and media outlets received a communiqué from a clandestine right-wing political group called FURODA, accusing them of trying to destabilize the government of President Armando Calderon Sol. FURODA, or Fuerza Nacionalista Mayor Roberto D'Aubuisson, is named for the late founder of the ruling National Republican Alliance (ARENA) political party. The ARENA Party issued a statement saying it had nothing to do with FURODA and that it regretted the threats.

On Sept. 4, Juan José Domenech, former head of ARENA, verbally and physically attacked Liliana Fuentes and Margarita Cerna, reporters for the daily *La Prensa Grafica* when they attempted to interview him in the city of San Miguel. Domenech and his bodyguards seized press credentials from the journalists, grabbed a camera, and tore out the film.

Community radio stations in El Salvador continued efforts to gain licensure from the

The Americas

National Telecommunications Administration (ANTEL). In January, the Supreme Court ruled that ANTEL's seizure a month earlier of equipment from 11 community radio stations was unconstitutional and ordered ANTEL to return the equipment. ANTEL complied, but in March the Supreme Court ruled that the stations themselves were illegal, because they had not been licensed. The World Association of Community Radio Broadcasters (AMARC) reported that ANTEL had harassed the station during the year. The radio stations at issue are located in villages that were controlled by insurgent guerrilla groups during El Salvador's civil war. Moves to legalize the stations began in 1992, when the armed conflict ended.

Early February
Segundo Montes, CENSORED
Izcanal, CENSORED
Ulua, CENSORED
Cooperativa, CENSORED
Victoria, CENSORED
Suchitlan, CENSORED
Excel, CENSORED
Teo-Radio, CENSORED
Nejapa, CENSORED
Radio Sumpul, CENSORED

The Supreme Court of El Salvador suspended a Dec. 4, 1995, order by the Salvadoran National Civil Police (PNC) that closed 10 community radio stations and confiscated their equipment. The closure was carried out at the request of the president of ANTEL, the state agency charged with regulating broadcasting and telecommunications. ANTEL interpreted the Supreme Court's decision to mean only that the equipment had to be returned, not that broadcasting should be allowed to resume, and the agency has refused to grant licenses to the radio stations.

June 26
Channel 12, THREATENED
CNN, THREATENED

Co-Latino, THREATENED
Diario Latino , THREATENED
Radio Mayavisión, THREATENED
Radio Sonora, THREATENED
Radio YSKL, THREATENED
Domestic and foreign press, THREATENED

Fuerza Nacionalista Mayor Roberto D'Aubuisson (FURODA), a right-wing underground political group, sent a communiqué to several media outlets issuing death threats against journalists, priests, and politicians. The communiqué accused them of being behind a "frantic opposition" campaign against the government of President Armando Calderon Sol. It also accused the foreign press of being "sinister and conveying a wrong image abroad of El Salvador and its government."

FURODA, named after the late founder of the ruling National Republican Alliance (ARENA) party, then sent a second communiqué in which it threatened to take action against journalists. The statement accused both the domestic and foreign press in El Salvador of negative coverage of the government and its privatization process.

July 12
Francisco Elias Valencia, *Co-Latino*
LEGAL ACTION

Valencia, editor in chief of the newspaper *Co-Latino*, was detained for six hours on defamation charges, then released on 10,000 colones (US$1,150) bail. He was ordered not to leave the country. A hearing on the charges has not yet been scheduled.

Valencia was charged with defaming Rafael Antonio Gonzales Garciaguirre, formerly the head of the criminal investigations division of the National Civil Police, in a Feb. 6 article about corruption in the division. Valencia refused to reveal his sources for the article or to provide the names of any witnesses who could corroborate his allegations against Garciaguirre. Garciaguirre was removed from his position, investigated, cleared of the charges of wrongdoing, and reassigned as the subcommissioner of the Department of Criminal Investigations in the Oriente province.

On July 26, Fuerza Nacionalista Mayor Roberto D'Aubuisson (FURODA), an underground right-wing political group, issued a threatening communiqué to the media, saying that the charges against Valencia were "only the beginning." FURODA claims that it can find ways to stop Valencia and others from continuing to be "the voice of the Communists."

Guatemala

Guatemala was once again one of the most perilous places for journalists in Latin America. The nation's judicial institutions remained ineffective in safeguarding the media and implementing a general rule of law, and the press, which has aggressively pursued stories on corruption, contraband, and kidnapping rings, was subjected to threats and violent assaults.

The murders of two journalists last year remain unsolved, a chilling reminder that despite a transition to democratic rule over the last decade, the culture of impunity that has long plagued Guatemala continues to be a serious concern. While the government's overt censorship and the press's self-censorship have diminished, there persists a troubling undercurrent of intolerance on the part of the government toward the news media. Journalists complain that the government continues to restrict the press's and public's access to official information.

In December, the government and former guerrilla insurgents signed a historic peace accord mediated by the United Nations, ending the longest civil war in Latin America. The 36-year conflict had ravaged much of the country, claimed more than 100,000 lives, most of them civilian, and resulted in the disappearance of thousands more. Under the terms of the accord, a general amnesty was approved that will most likely leave the murder or disappearance of numerous journalists unresolved and unpunished. CPJ denounced the amnesty in a letter to President Alvaro Arzú Irigoyen, saying that, "Contrary to contributing to national reconciliation, a general amnesty would further aggravate the reigning climate of impunity." The family of Jorge Carpio, the former publisher of the daily *El Gráfico* and leader of the National Centrist Party who was murdered in 1993 and whose death is still unsolved, also denounced the amnesty.

The Guatemalan media have matured and diversified. Radio programs and publications in Mayan languages and other new media outlets have emerged, broadening the range of the news media in Guatemala and providing information to sectors of the population that had been excluded because of language barriers. In addition, two new daily newspapers have begun publication, including *El Periódico*, started by José Ruben Zamora Marroquin, former editor of the newspaper *Siglo Veintiuno*. "The press became more professional in 1996, was more openly critical of the government, and wrote about massacres committed during the civil war, drug trafficking, and a series of topics that were once taboo," said Haroldo Shetemul, an editor with *Crónica*, the country's leading newsmagazine.

February 2
José Ruben Zamora Marroquín, *Siglo Veintiuno*
THREATENED
Zamora, editor in chief of the independent daily *Siglo Veintiuno*, received several anonymous death threats after his newspaper published the transcript of a videotaped interview with a former military officer. In the interview, the now-exiled officer accused a group of high-ranking military officers of participating in organized crime activities, including drug trafficking and car theft.

February 28
Vinicio Pacheco, Radio Sonora, ATTACKED, THREATENED

Pacheco, a reporter with the radio station Radio Sonora, was abducted in the center of Guatemala City by unidentified men who forced him into their vehicle. Pacheco, who covers the judicial system for his station, was freed only after being beaten and tortured for several hours. His captors blindfolded him and burnt him with cigarettes, and they played recordings of his reports on a wave of car thefts, kidnappings and drug trafficking. Before he was released several miles outside of Guatemala City, they slashed his feet. According to Radio Sonora's director, Eduardo Mendoza, the captors held a gun to Pacheco's head and told him, "The only reason we won't kill you is so that you will give this message to other journalists." In a letter to President Alvaro Árzu, CPJ called on the government of Guatemala to order an investigation into the incident and to bring those responsible to justice. Three weeks after his abduction, Pacheco left Guatemala for Costa Rica due to continuing threats directed at Radio Sonora.

March 8
Haroldo Shetemul, *Crónica Semanal,* THREATENED
Gustavo Berganza, *Crónica Semanal,* THREATENED
Estuardo Zepeta, *Crónica Semanal,* THREATENED
Mario Alberto Carrera, *Crónica Semanal* THREATENED
Marta Altolaguirre, *Siglo Veintiuno* THREATENED
Carlos Rafael Soto, *El Gráfico,* THREATENED

Berganza, director of the weekly magazine *Crónica Semanal;* Shetemul, its deputy director; its columnists Zapeta and Carrera; Altolaguirre, a columnist for the daily *Siglo Veintiuno;* and Soto, a columnist for the morning paper *El Gráfico,* were named in an anonymous death list distributed by an unidentified organization in Guatemala City. A notice with the list stated that the journalists named would be put to death for having "betrayed the fatherland." The group sent the list to each journalist listed and announced that it would reveal its name once it had carried out the first execution. CPJ urged the government to investigate the death threats.

April 11
Juan José Yantuche, TV Noticias, KILLED
Oscar Mazaya, TV Noticias, THREATENED

Yantuche, a reporter with the cable television news program "TV Noticias," died from injuries inflicted by gunshots. The gravely injured Yantuche was found in his car in the city of Mixco one week earlier. He was hospitalized and remained in a coma until he died. Yantuche's murder came a few weeks after an anonymously penned death list of journalists was circulated in Guatemala City. His name, however, was not on that list.

One week after Yantuche's assassination, Oscar Mazaya, the director of "TV Noticias," reported receiving anonymous death threats. In a letter to Guatemalan President Alvaro Arzú, CPJ protested the lack of thorough police investigations into Yantuche's murder and the death threats against Mazaya.

May 15
José Rubén Zamora Marroquín, ATTACKED

Zamora, former editor in chief of the independent daily *Siglo Veintiuno* and a recipient of CPJ's 1995 International Press Freedom Award, was dining at a Guatemala City restaurant when unidentified assailants in a moving vehicle threw two grenades at his car parked out front. One exploded, damaging the car. The assailants, two men and a woman, escaped. Two days prior to the attack, Zamora had resigned as editor in chief of *Siglo Veintiuno* over conflicts with the board of directors. Zamora told CPJ that he believes the attack was intended to deter him from launching another newspaper in Guatemala. He also believes that the attack was a warning to his yet-to-be-named successor at

Siglo Veintiuno. In a letter to Guatemala's President Alvaro Arzú, CPJ expressed its deep concern about the incident and urged Arzú to ensure that the police conduct a thorough investigation into the matter.

December 10
Israel Hernández Marroquín, *Infopress Cen-*
troamericano, KILLED
Hernández Marroquín, editor of the weekly newsletter *Infopress Centroamericano,* was found murdered on the outskirts of Guatemala City. According to police reports, Hernández Marroquín, who also taught economics at San Carlos University, had been shot once in the head. Police said he had been driving in his white Nissan automobile when the unknown assailants stopped him and then shot him. His car was found near the site of the murder.

Haiti

Physical attacks against the Haitian press diminished significantly as Haiti entered its second year of democratic rule, edging further away from the decades of political turmoil that had traumatized the country and stifled the press. Two of the main protagonists of violence against the press—the now-demobilized Haitian military and right-wing paramilitary groups that supported past dictatorial regimes—have largely receded from the political landscape.

The Haitian media focused on building professionalism in the industry by forging economically viable press institutions that can provide information in both French and Creole. In addition, some media institutions began to explore educational programs to train professional journalists.

Haiti re-established press freedom in Sept. 1994, when a U.S.-led multinational invasion ousted the 3-year-old military regime. But a general lack of openness in the government of President René Préval, limited access to information, and a reluctance on the part of the population to engage in criticism remain significant impediments to press freedom. Some troubling incidents during the year reminded journalists that they are not far removed from the period of repression and absence of press freedom. On several occasions, national police obstructed reporters' and photographers' access to news events. "People are still very sensitive to any gathering of the clouds," said one reporter based in Port-au-Prince. "We are not that far from hell, so we feel the heat."

Honduras

Honduran journalists have became more aggressive in pursuing investigative stories about official and private sector corruption. But the press's efforts to deepen its coverage also led to several attacks on journalists during the year.

The Committee for the Defense of Human Rights in Honduras (CODEH) reported that Sandra Maribel Sanchez Escoto, a reporter who covers the Congress for Radio América, a national radio station, received numerous telephone death threats as a result of her investigative reporting on corruption among officials and the military.

CODEH also reported that on Nov. 3, a reporter and photographer for the Tegucigalpa daily *La Tribuna* were assaulted by the spouse of a public official and political candidate. Jimmy Macoto, the husband of Gloria Oqueli de Macoto, executive director of the National Institute of Retirement Pensions for Public Employees, assaulted reporter Emma Calderón and photographer Julio Cesar Atunez after they covered a political rally outside the capital and took a picture of the couple's sportscar, an Alpha Romeo.

February 15
Guilmor García, *La Prensa,* THREATENED
García, a photographer with the daily newspaper *La Prensa*, was threatened by an agent of the Criminal Investigation Division (DIC) of the Public Ministry in San Pedro Sula. When García photographed the back of a DIC agent as he was inspecting a car recovered after a robbery, the agent warned García not to publish the picture. Then he asked for García's press card and took down his name. The DIC later issued an apology.

September 4
All journalists, LEGAL ACTION
The Honduran National Congress approved reforms to Article 295 of the penal code, increasing prison sentences and fines for anyone who "within the country or abroad publishes or in any manner discloses false, exaggerated, or tendentious news which places at risk the national economy or public credit." Individuals found guilty under this amendment now face a three- to six-year prison sentence, up from one to three years, and may be fined 20,000 to 50,000 lempiras (US$1,600 to $4,000), up from 500 to 2,000 lempiras.

Journalists and human rights advocates denounced the changes to the legislation. In response, the Congress on Sept. 11 made the law even broader, removing from the text any reference to publishing or disclosing news and making the law applicable to anyone who "places at risk the national economy or public credit." The Commission for the Defense of Human Rights (CODEH) issued a statement saying that the reforms to Article 295 violate Hondurans' constitutional right to free expression.

October 8
Jorge Luis Monroy, *La Voz de la Frontera*
    ATTACKED, THREATENED
Monroy, a news commentator for the radio station *La Voz de La Frontera* in Ocotepeque and a five-year veteran of the daily program "Las Ver-

dades del Aire," was attacked by two assailants while on the air. Monroy was transmitting his program from the broadcast booth when, during a discussion on local political issues and the recent results of an internal election within one of the two major Honduran parties, two men entered the station and forced their way into the broadcast booth.

During the live broadcast, one of the men punched Monroy in the face, breaking his nose, and the other pummeled him with more than 15 blows to the head and body. Monroy was told he would be killed if he did not stop spreading lies or if he reported who his attackers were. The two men have been identified by Monroy as businessman Luis Manuel López and orthodontist César Pinto Valle. A complaint was filed with local police and with the National Commission on Human Rights, but both men are still at large.

Jamaica

A damaging libel verdict by a Jamaican jury against the island's leading newspaper has jolted the press and dampened the general atmosphere of press freedom in Jamaica.

A jury in July ordered the Gleaner Company Ltd., owners of the island's oldest newspaper, the *Daily Gleaner*, to pay an unprecedented US$2.5 million in damages for libel to Eric Anthony Abrahams, a former minister of tourism.

The case stems from an article originally published in 1987 by the Associated Press news agency that was picked up by the *Daily Gleaner* and its afternoon tabloid, *The Star*. The report contained allegations that Abrahams had accepted bribes from a U.S. advertising firm in return for the island's advertising and public-relations contract.

Calling the award "manifestly excessive," the 162-year-old Gleaner Company is appealing the decision to the Jamaica Court

of Appeals, which could hear the case early in 1997. In the meantime, the award amount and attorneys fees remain in escrow.

The decision of the seven-member jury has had a chilling effect on the entire Jamaican media. Observers predict that the case will deter journalists from aggressive reporting for fear that a libel suit could result in ruinous damages. "This is a time of mourning for us in the media," Desmond Allen, editor of the *Jamaica Observer* told the Inter Press Service.

The verdict has sparked debate among journalists, media owners and policy-makers over the adjudication of libel cases and whether there should be a cap on the amount of monetary damage awards. There is discussion of placing libel cases under the jurisdiction of a judge instead of a jury.

July 17
Daily Gleaner, LEGAL ACTION
A Jamaican jury ordered the Gleaner Company Ltd., owner of the island's oldest newspaper, the *Daily Gleaner*, to pay an unprecedented US$2.5 million in damages for libel to Eric Anthony Abrahams, a former Minister of Tourism. The case stems from an article that was published by the Associated Press news agency in 1987 and picked up by the *Daily Gleaner* and its afternoon tabloid, the *Star*. The report contained allegations that Abrahams had accepted bribes from a U.S. advertising firm in return for the Jamaican government's advertising and public relations contract.

Mexico

The Mexican press has been moving away from collusion with public officials, a decades-old tradition among many Mexican journalists and news organizations that in the past has diminshed the intergrity and independence of the press.

Mexican journalists covering controversial stories in provincial areas generally are susceptible to attacks from political and criminal elements about whom they report. This is the case in the cities along the U.S. border, where narcotics traffickers proliferate, as well as in the politically volatile states of Tabasco, Oaxaca, and Chiapas.

Unlike their counterparts in some Latin American countries, the Mexican press has not moved toward the formation of professional associations aimed at protecting journalists and denouncing violations of press freedom. But the September kidnapping of a journalist who had written about a recently emerged guerrilla organization in the state of Oaxaca did prompt widespread concern among the press about both personal safety and the implications for press freedom in general.

While the trend among Mexican journalists is toward increased independence and professional integrity, the media remain vulnerable to government influence through official advertising and the control of broadcast licensure.

There were also some milestones for press freedom in 1996. The weekly news magazine *Proceso*, begun by a group of journalists who had been forced out of the daily newspaper *Excelsior* in 1976 by then-President Luis Echeverria Alvarez because he did not like their independent posture, celebrated its 20th anniversary. The independent editorial stance of *Proceso* and other notable publications—including the news weekly *Zeta* of Tijuana; the daily newspaper *El Norte* of Monterrey; and more recently *Reforma* of Mexico City—has inspired a new generation of well-trained, enterprising journalists that is providing Mexicans with more balanced coverage of the news.

In contrast to the officials of many other Latin American nations, the Mexican government has responded to all of CPJ's protests and inquiries about attacks against Mexican journalists. Yet it remains unable or unwilling to resolve the cases of 10 murdered journalists who CPJ has determined were killed because of their work as journalists. Among these cases, which occurred between 1984 and 1995, is the 1988 assasination of Héctor Félix "El Gato" Miranda, the columinst and co-publisher of *Zeta*.

In an Oct. 15 ruling, a panel of the Organization of American States condemned the Mexican government for jailing a general who publicly criticized the armed forces. The Inter-American Commission on Human Rights called for the release of Brig. Gen. José Francisco Gallardo Rodríguez, who has been in a military prison since November 1993. Gallardo has claimed that his imprisonment stems from an essay he wrote, in which he detailed several crimes committed by Mexican troops and urged the creation of a civilian-appointed military ombudsman. The panel concluded that the Mexican military had jailed Gallardo "with no reasonable, logical or justifiable purpose."

Despite this ruling, the Mexican government, which has accused Gallardo of stealing public monies, refused to reconsider Gallardo's case.

January 28
José Barrón Rosales, Radio Huayacocotla
ATTACKED
Barrón, a reporter for Radio Huayacocotla, a radio station that serves indigenous communities in Texcatepec, Veracruz, was attacked by his neighbor Aquilino Mendoza. Mendoza insulted and threatened Barrón, accusing him of spreading rumors and false information about land issues on the radio station's broadcasts. He then fired a shot at Barrón, but missed, injuring Barrón's dog instead. Mendoza's wife intervened and prevented him from firing again. Citizens of the indigenous communities in the region reported the incident to the Public Ministry, the president of the Texcatepec Municipality and the state governor of Veracruz but no

immediate action was taken. In a written response to CPJ's letter of protest to President Ernesto Zedillo regarding the lack of an investigation into the matter, the general prosecutor of Veracruz stated that Mendoza had been charged with attempted murder.

February 2
Ninfa Deandar Martinez, *El Mañana*,
THREATENED
Deandar, the publisher of the independent daily *El Mañana* of Nuevo Laredo, in Tamaulipas State, received anonymous threats by telephone at her home. The unidentified caller told Deandar that she would be killed and threatened to harm her four sons, three of whom work at the newspaper. In Nuevo Laredo's town hall on Feb. 20, unidentified people distributed a leaflet carrying a photo of Deandar, stating that she was a "mercenary, gangster, and prostitute of journalism."

February 13
Raymundo Ramos, *El Mañana*, HARASSED
Ramos, a reporter for the daily newspaper *El Mañana* of Nuevo Laredo, reported that he was harassed because of articles he wrote that were critical of the government of the state of Tamaulipas. Ramos said he received a call from an unidentified man who said he had a "warning" that he wanted to convey to Ramos in person, and told him to come outside. Ramos said he left the newspaper office and was met by two unidentified men, who told him to accompany them in their vehicle. Ramos went with them; for two hours, they drove around Nuevo Laredo. During this time Ramos said the men told him to stop writing articles criticizing the state government. CPJ wrote to Mexican President Ernesto Zedillo and the governor of the state of Tamaulipas, Manuel Cavazos Lerma, urging them to conduct an investigation into the incident.

March 26
Gina Batista, Channel 40, ATTACKED
Batista, a reporter and anchorwoman for Corporation de Noticias e Información, Channel 40, was attacked and shot at by unidentified men while she was driving her car in the Bosque de Chapultec section of Mexico City on her way to Channel 40. A vehicle she identified as a Ram Charger pulled alongside and attempted to cut her off. A shot fired by one of the men in the Charger penetrated the left passenger door of Batista's automobile. Batista heard one man shout that she should "stay out of matters that don't concern [her]." In a letter to President Ernesto Zedillo, CPJ expressed concern that Batista may have been targeted because of her journalistic work and asked for a thorough investigation of the incident.

May 7
XERA, ATTACKED
XEOCH, ATTACKED
Supporters of the Zapatista rebels in the southern state of Chiapas occupied two local radio stations, XERA, in San Cristobal de las Casas, and XEOCH, in nearby Ocosingo. After occupying the stations for 24 hours, they left peacefully but not before warning that they would carry out more takeovers unless the government released from prison two men recently jailed for allegedly belonging to the Zapatistas.

June 23
Oswald Alonso, Radio Rama, ATTACKED
Alonso, a reporter with Radio Rama in Cuernavaca, Morelos, was kidnapped from his home by three unidentified men. He was beaten and tortured for 24 hours, and then released in Teloloapan, Guerrero. Alonso, who covered the police beat and had publicized several incidents of police corruption, suffered a dislocated collarbone, a broken shoulder, and bruises. His colleagues believe that he was attacked for his work. Radio Rama is known for its independent political coverage.

June 26
XEVA, ATTACKED
Sergio Sibilla, XEVA, HARASSED
XEVA, a popular radio station in the state of Tabasco, was taken over for two hours in the early morning by dozens of supporters of the ruling Institutional Revolutionary Party (PRI). They accused the station and "Telereportaje," the news program they interrupted, of using their programming to destabilize the state and incite violence. The PRI supporters took the microphone away from "Telereportaje" host Sergio Sibilla, and read political statements on the air.

The takeover occurred a day after riots by PRI opponents disturbed a visit by Mexican President Ernesto Zedillo to Tabasco. The rioters were protesting Zedillo's support for Tabasco's governor, a PRI member. During the previous 18 months, PRI supporters had occupied XEVA four times, accusing it of being a mouthpiece for the opposition Democratic Revolutionary Party (PRD).

August 13
Alberto Flores Casanova, *El Mañana,* ATTACKED
Flores Casanova, a reporter for the daily *El Mañana* in the city of Nuevo Laredo, near the Texas border, was attacked while driving to the newspaper's offices just after midnight. Two unidentified men stopped Flores Casanova at an intersection about two blocks from the newspaper. One of the men pointed a handgun at Flores Casanova, who managed to push it away as it went off. A shot hit the vehicle's dashboard, and bullet fragments lodged in Flores Casanova's right leg. The motive for the attack is unknown. Flores Casanova has written critically about the government of the state of Tamaulipas. CPJ wrote a letter to Mexican authorities urging them to pursue an investigation.

September 12
Juan Francisco Ealy Ortiz, *El Universal*
HARASSED, LEGAL ACTION
The Mexican government sent an estimated 40

armed federal judicial policemen to the office of the Mexico City daily *El Universal* to arrest Ealy Ortiz, the newspaper's owner, for alleged tax evasion, but he was not there. Ealy Ortiz peacefully turned himself in to the attorney general's office the following morning. He posted bail and was freed pending a judicial proceeding. On Sept. 17, Ealy Ortiz was formally charged with tax evasion.

In a letter to President Ernesto Zedillo, CPJ stressed that it had no information about the veracity of the tax evasion charges against Ealy Ortiz but that it questioned the government's extreme show-of-force in its attempt to arrest him at his office, especially at a time when the Mexican press is becoming increasingly independent and is playing a crucial role in Mexico's economic and political evolution. CPJ also pointed out that it is widely known that *El Universal* hired some of Mexico's most prominent journalists, some of whom had been critical of the government.

September 17

Razhy González Rodríguez, *Contrapunto*

IMPRISONED, ATTACKED, THREATENED
González Rodríguez, director of the Oaxaca-based regional weekly magazine *Contrapunto*, was abducted in Oaxaca City at 11 p.m. González Rodríguez was walking along Bustamante Street in the center of Oaxaca with a friend, Pilar Monterubio, when two armed men, wearing black hoods and carrying handguns, forced González Rodríguez into the back of an automobile and waved a pistol at Monterubio, signaling her to leave. Two other men were in the front of the car, and after González Rodríguez was in the car, they sped off, driving against traffic on a one-way street. Their car was followed by a man on a motorcycle.

González Rodríguez was taken to an undisclosed location, gagged, blindfolded, and bound with handcuffs to a chair for 44 hours. He was mentally and physically tortured, his life and the lives of his family were threatened, and he was accused of being a collaborator with the

Ejercito Popular Revolucionario (EPR), a terrorist guerrilla army that has recently emerged in Southern Mexico. González Rodríguez, who was one of a group of journalists to interview EPR representatives in Oaxaca on Sept. 13, was interrogated about his reporting on the EPR's activities. He believes his interrogators were members of the federal police force because they released him only after he agreed to notify authorities if he received any more information from the EPR.

Nicaragua

The Nicaraguan National Assembly considered controversial press legislation that would require media organizations to hire journalists who belonged to a Colegio de Periodistas, a trade union. The move prompted a national discussion among journalists along political lines. The Nicaraguan Journalists Union, which is largely supportive of the Sandinistas, backs the legislation; the Nicaraguan Journalists Association, formed by anti-Sandinistas, opposes it.

February 29

Sabhja Hamad, Channel 12 Televisión, ATTACKED

Ernesto Rizo, Channel 6 Televisión, ATTACKED

Mario Sanchez, *Barricada*, ATTACKED

William Roiz, *Barricada*, ATTACKED

Carlos Durán, *Barricada*, ATTACKED

Manual Alvarez, *Barricada*, ATTACKED

Ernesto Pineiro, Channel 4 Televisión, ATTACKED

Oscar Roiz Martínez, Extravisión, ATTACKED

Benito Tellez, Channel 12 Televisión, ATTACKED

Nine journalists were injured while covering a confrontation between police and lottery ticket vendors. Hamad, a reporter with Channel 12 Televisión, had to be hospitalized after several rocks were thrown at her. Rizo, a cameraman for Channel 6 Televisión, also had to be hospitalized after a tear-gas bomb thrown by police exploded near him. Sanchez, Roiz, Durán and Alvarez, all reporters with the daily *Barricada*, and television reporters Pineiro, Roiz Martínez and Tellez were beaten by vendors and policemen.

June 6
Radio La Corporación, ATTACKED, THREATENED
Fabio Gadea Mantilla, Radio La Corporación, HARASSED

Former Nicaraguan contras, anti-Sandinista resistance fighters, took over Radio La Corporación, reportedly by order of ex-contra Leonardo Zeledon, a member of the Nicaraguan Resistance Party (PRN). The group occupied the station for 15 hours, demanding that Radio La Corporación owner Gadea Mantilla, who is also president of the PRN, register specific candidates in upcoming general elections. Gadea Mantilla refused. Police June 7 apprehended Zeledon and other PRN members on charges including "illegally occupying private property, [making] death threats, and terrorism." Zeledon, who is confined to a wheelchair, was placed under house arrest.

According to Gadea Mantilla, the same group on June 9 threatened to destroy the station. Gadea Mantilla said that when he received the threats by telephone he immediately notified police, asking for protection for the station's downtown Managua offices and for the station's transmitter in Tipitapa, 22 kilometers north of Managua.

Panama

In a move to replace restrictive press laws that date to Panama's military dictatorship, representatives of news organizations helped draft a new bill that went before the Legisla-tive Assembly, but the assembly took no action. Under current Panamanian law, the government can muzzle the press by exercising prior censorship. The Interior Ministry has the authority to impose sanctions on the media in the form of fines and closure of media outlets.

The bill under consideration includes provisions that guarantee freedom of the press and shield journalists from being forced to reveal their sources. Press organizations plan to lobby lawmakers to include the decriminalization of slander and libel as well. The Legislative Assembly is scheduled to review the bill again when it convenes in March 1997.

Aggressive press coverage, particularly by the daily *La Prensa*, of allegations that government officials had ties to drug traffickers raised the ire of President Ernesto Pérez Balladares, who unleashed verbal attacks on the national and foreign press. In June, Pérez Balladares accused journalists of waging "a campaign of disinformation."

Paraguay

The press continued to play an important role in Paraguay's fledgling democracy by reporting on government corruption, political turmoil, and the ongoing problem of drug trafficking.

In January, the head of Paraguay's army, Gen. Lino Oviedo, publicly attacked the press for reporting that he was involved in the activities of a political party, despite a constitutional ban against military participation in politics. Oviedo's political ambitions became apparent in April when it was revealed that he was behind a threatened military coup.

Journalists covering drug trafficking continue to suffer reprisals for their work. Reporters based in remote provincial areas were particularly vulnerable to such attacks. In January, a fugitive drug trafficker shot a correspondent for the national newspaper *ABC Color*, mistaking the correspondent, who is based in the city of Pedro Juan Caballero, on the border with Brazil, for another *ABC Color* reporter. *ABC Color* has aggressively covered the activities of Brazilian drug cartels.

In Asunción, another *ABC Color* reporter received death threats after the publication of articles about alleged corruption among members of the national police.

January 29

Cándido Figueredo, *ABC Color,* THREATENED, HARASSED

César Dauzacker, *ABC Color,* ATTACKED

Dauzacker, a correspondent in Pedro Juan Caballero for the Asunción-based daily *ABC Color*, was shot at by Dionicio Vázquez, a fugitive drug trafficker. The reporter was covering an attack against a police station by Vázquez. Figueredo, a correspondent for *ABC Color* who has been threatened frequently for his reports on local drug traffickers and has been under police protection since the summer of 1995, said Vázquez had mistaken Dauzacker for him. One day after the attack, Figueredo's brother was kidnapped and briefly detained by three captors. They released him with a warning that he and his family would be killed if Figueredo continued to report on drug trafficking. Although Vázquez was taken into custody on Jan. 30, he continued to threaten Figueredo from prison. CPJ wrote to President Juan Carlos Wasmosy urging him to issue a public statement condemning the threats and to take all necessary precautions to guarantee Figueredo's safety.

September 10

Vladimir Jara, *ABC Color,* THREATENED, HARASSED

Unidentified individuals entered *ABC Color* reporter Jara's apartment, ransacking his family's belongings and looking through their papers. The intruders left behind a picture of Jara with an "X" inscribed on it. There was no sign of forced entry, even though the door had been locked. Jara changed the locks, but another break-in occurred soon after the first, and for two weeks both Jara and his wife received telephone death threats and other harassing calls.

Jara covers the courts for *ABC Color*, a daily, where he has reported on police participation in the trafficking of stolen cars. He was also due to publish a book dealing with wide-ranging police corruption and with the assassination of Gen. Ramón Rodriguez, who had directed the police force's anti-drug investigations.

The calls included offers to Jara of 500 million guarani (US$250,000) to stop his investigations. A fellow reporter who happened to be shopping for an inexpensive used car also received a phone call, offering him a new Porsche if he would convince Jara to accept the money. When Jara and his wife moved to her parents' home to escape the harassment, they started receiving calls there, and what appeared to be bullet holes surfaced on the outside of the house. After Jara reported the harassment to the police, the telephone calls stopped, but he has continued to receive indirect death threats.

Peru

The Peruvian press enjoys considerable freedom, but remains vulnerable to the country's precarious form of democracy and faces intimidation and harassment by national and regional government officials, the military, and criminal gangs.

Four journalists unfairly convicted of subversion under Peru's draconian anti-terrorist laws are currently in prison, serving sentences of up to 20 years. President Alberto Fujimori granted special presidential pardons to four others in 1996. And while Fujimori acknowledged that the journalists—

as well as others who had been convicted of subversion—were unjustly imprisoned, their criminal record stands and they cannot claim damages for the state's error. One of the freed journalists, Jesús Alfonso Castiglione Mendoza, a respected radio journalist, had received his 20-year sentence after a ten-minute trial—the work of Peru's infamous "faceless court," a panel of judges hidden behind a one-way mirror.

The increasingly independent stance of the Peruvian press has made it a much more politically formidable institution. According to public opinion polls, only the Catholic Church has greater credibility. Moreover, in a significant shift in society's view of the media, Peruvians have turned to the press for support in their quest to make government institutions accountable. There is widespread distrust of elected officials and skepticism about the judiciary's and legislature's independence from the president. "The institutional crisis has obliged the press to take on the role of accountability," says Francisco Miró Quesada, executive editor of El Comercio, the country's oldest and most influential major newspaper.

At the same time, Peruvian journalists are becoming more self-critical, conscious that ethical lapses could taint the media's public image.

New tensions between the press and Fujimori have arisen in the wake of the dramatic takeover of the Japanese embassy by members of the armed Tupac Amaru Revolutionary Movement, a leftist guerrilla group, that began on Dec. 17. At the rebels' invitation, journalists slipped past police security on Dec. 31 and entered the besieged compound to conduct interviews with rebel leaders. Such actions have raised concerns that the hostage crisis could result in a setback to prospects for the elimination or reform of special tribunals and other anti-terrorist laws that the Fujimori government have used against the press.

In 1992, Fujimori showed just how fragile democracy is in Peru when he suspended the constitution, dismissed the Congress, and assumed near-dictatorial powers, including direct executive control of the judiciary. Fujimori won a second five-year term in the 1995 election, and his party secured control of the congress. The president had promised the October dismantlement of the faceless court system, which he had established during the "self-coup." But in a troubling setback on Oct. 11, the Congress approved a bill extending the system for another year.

In a positive development, the Congress, at Fujimori's request, granted amnesty in December to a retired general who had been detained in a military prison after a television interview in which he denounced human rights abuses by the military. In the interview, the retired general, Rodolfo Robles, alleged that a military death squad had blown up the transmission tower of Global Television , a local station in Puno that has been critical of the government. The military court—which claims jurisdiction over all active and retired military personnel—charged Robles with insubordination.

April 2
Carlos Maravi, *La República,* THREATENED
Maravi, editor-in-chief of the daily *La República*, received an anonymous threatening letter that was also sent to other media outlets. The letter accused the daily of defending the former president of Peru, Alan García, and stated that Maravi would be put in "his rightful place" along with others involved in an alleged meeting to draw plans to exculpate the former president of charges of embezzlement that were to be heard by the Supreme Court. In particular, the letter alleged that Mirko Lauer, a columnist at *La República*, had taken part in the meeting.

May 3
José Llaja, Canal 5, ATTACKED,
THREATENED

The Americas

Enrique Cuñeo, *El Comercio*, ATTACKED,
HARASSED

Javier Zapata, *Caretas*, ATTACKED, HARASSED

Llaja, a cameraman with Canal 5 television;
Cuñeo, a photographer with the daily *El Comercio*; and Zapata, a photographer with the weekly
magazine *Caretas*, were beaten by security
guards at Lima's City Hall. The journalists were
covering a labor dispute between municipal
employees and the mayor's office when security
personnel tried to prevent them from filming
the event by beating them and destroying the
cameras of Cuñeo and Zapata. The mayor later
issued a public apology to the journalists and
announced that there would be an investigation
into the matter. In a report issued at the end of
May, the commission that investigated the incident concluded that the head of the Lima
police, José La Madrid Ponce, was to blame for
the aggressive behavior of the officers at the
demonstration. The commission also said that
the police reacted inappropriately and used
excessive force. La Madrid's handling of the
affair will now be the subject of a judicial
inquiry.

June 6

Miguel Pérez Julca, Radio Oriental,
IMPRISONED, LEGAL ACTION

Pérez, a reporter with Radio Oriental, was
arrested after he refused to appear before a tribunal in Chiclayo, in northwestern Peru, on
charges of terrorism. He was released two days
later after protests by a Peruvian congresswoman, local press freedom organizations, and
colleagues.

Pérez had been arrested in 1991 on the same
charges and had spent two years in prison
awaiting trial. In 1993, he was acquitted, but
that decision was later annulled.

Under Peru's anti-terrorism law, a person
acquitted of terrorism can be summoned to
court on the same charges if the court annuls
the acquittal.

June 14

Teobaldo Meléndez Fachin, Radio Oriente,
Panamericana Televisión, ATTACKED,
HARASSED

Meléndez, a reporter for Radio Oriente and
Panamericana Televisión, was assaulted by soldiers from the Peruvian air force in the city of
Yurimaguas in Callao province. Meléndez was
covering the arrival of the bishop of Callao,
Miguel Irizar Campos, at the Yurimaguas airport. When Meléndez tried to get close to the
bishop to interview him, he was beaten by soldiers, who also confiscated his camera. They
threatened to detain Meléndez if he resisted.
The soldiers later returned the camera. The air
force issued a statement about the incident, saying that Meléndez had verbally abused one of
the soldiers. Meléndez denied that accusation.

June 20

Julio Alberto Quevedo Chavez, *El Tarapotino*,
LEGAL ACTION

Luis Humberto Hidalgo Sánchez, Radio Tarapoto,
LEGAL ACTION

César Herrera Luna, *El Achichito*,
LEGAL ACTION

Quevedo, director of the magazine *El
Tarapotino*; Hidalgo, director of Radio Tarapoto;
and Herrera, director of the magazine *El Achichito*, were charged with defaming the former
manager of the water treatment service in the
city of Tarapoto. The charges stemmed from
comments the three journalists had made about
a 50 percent increase in the cost of drinking
water in Tarapoto. The journalists also alluded
to the water treatment service manager's alleged
links to the guerrilla group Sendero Luminoso
(Shining Path). A judge imposed a 10 p.m. curfew on all three journalists and issued a "conditional freedom" order, which obligates them to
ask for permission to leave Tarapoto. Quevedo,
Hidalgo, and Herrera are currently awaiting
trial.

October 18
Global Television, ATTACKED
Radio Samoa, ATTACKED
The Institute for Press and Society (IPYS) reported that the branch office of Global Television in Puno, which also houses the local radio station Radio Samoa, was the target of a bomb attack that damaged sound and transmission equipment and broke the windows of 19 houses nearby. A police investigation found that three packages of explosives had been placed at the entrance of the three-story building, and that the bombs exploded at intervals of 10 and 15 seconds. The owner of the two stations, Mariano Portungal Catacora, said that the attack slightly injured three members of his family who live with him on the third floor of the building.

October 19
Gisu Guerra, Peruvian News Channel (CPN), HARASSED
Security police detained Guerra, a reporter for the radio station CPN, for several hours, according to the Institute for Press and Society (IPYS). She had gone to the Casimiro Ulloa Hospital in Lima to interview an alleged member of Peru's National Intelligence Service (SIN), who later died. The police held her at the hospital, although she identified herself as a journalist, and then took her to a local branch of the National Criminal Investigations Unit. She was asked to give police a statement and then released.

October 24
Nicolas Lucar, Channel Four, HARASSED
Alamo Perez Luna, Channel Four, HARASSED
Lucar and Perez Luna, director and reporter for the program "La Revista Dominical" on the Channel Four television network, reported that they have been harassed by unidentified men who staked out Channel Four's offices in vans with tinted windows. The journalists believe the harassment is related to news reports about a prominent airline executive's alleged ties to

drug traffickers. Lucar told the Institute for Press and Society (IPYS) that the same vehicles have parked outside of his home and that he has received anonymous calls on his unlisted cellular telephone from an unidentified caller who asks for Lucar by name. Perez Luna said that similar vehicles had followed him from the Orson Welles Journalism Institute, where he teaches.

Trinidad and Tobago

The press became ensnarled in Trinidad and Tobago's racially charged politics, with the daily *Trinidad Guardian* at the center of the controversy. On Feb. 2, Prime Minister Basdeo Panday barred *Guardian* reporters from access to government information in an effort to force the paper's owners to fire editor in chief Jones P. Madeira, whom the prime minister had called a racist. The ban lasted until Feb. 7. Panday has been very critical of the media since he took office in November 1995, and has clashed with Madeira over the *Guardian's* editorials. In April, several senior staff members, including Madeira and managing editor Alwin Chow, said that the paper's owners, the Trinidad Publishing Co., had forced them to resign. Chow told CPJ that Trinidad Publishing, either willingly or under government pressure, sought to appease officials by ousting the journalists. The chairman of the publishing company denied Chow's charges.

In May, Chow, Madeira and several former *Guardian* journalists started a new weekly newspaper, the *Independent*.

The specter of a 1990 failed coup attempt still haunts the country. In a conference on the media and democracy held in Port of Spain in August, former Prime Minister A.N.R. Robinson cautioned that "the whole society will be destroyed" if the government interferes with media coverage.

United States

On Oct. 30, a Brooklyn Federal Court judge sentenced two remaining defendants in the Manuel de Dios Unanue murder trial for their role in the 1992 assassination of the renowned Cuban-American journalist and former editor of New York City's *El Diario-La Prensa*.

De Dios, who built his reputation on muckraking exposés of drug traffickers in two upstart magazines he distributed in Queens, was shot to death in 1992 in a Queens restaurant at the direction of leaders of the Colombian Cali cocaine cartel.

The de Dios murder case prompted a CPJ investigation into attacks on immigrant journalists in the United States. The investigation culminated in a special report titled *Silenced: The Unsolved Murders of Immigrant Journalists in the United States*, published in December 1993.

The two defendants sentenced in October had pleaded guilty and turned against others involved in the murder, in exchange for leniency in sentencing. Juan Carlos Velasco received a 15-year sentence. He had faced a maximum sentence of life in prison for recruiting other conspirators involved in the murder and for killing two other men in a separate case. Elizabeth Castaño, Velasco's wife, received an 18-year sentence for helping to identify de Dios to the gunman.

In all, seven people were indicted for de Dios' murder. Five, including Velasco and Castaño, pleaded guilty. All except Velasco received 18-year sentences. A sixth person, Wilson Mejia Velez, the gunman, was convicted in 1994 and is serving life in prison. A seventh, Guillermo Leon Restrepo Gaviria,

who prosecutors said received $50,000 for his role in the assassination, remains a fugitive.

On March 6, José Santacruz Londoño, a top leader of the Cali cartel who was an unindicted co-conspirator in the case, died in a shoot-out with police in Colombia. De Dios had angered Santacruz Londoño with his exposés of the Cali cartel's operations in Queens.

Also in October, President Clinton signed the Intelligence Authorization Act for Fiscal Year 1997. The act contains the first congressional sanction of the use of journalists as CIA agents. CPJ's staff and board members were active in the debate over the passage of this amendment, which, although it limits the use of journalists as CIA agents, still allows the CIA director or the president to waive the prohibition to address the overriding national security interest of the United States. CPJ and others continue to make the case that such a waiver option jeopardizes the independence of the American press and leaves all reporters under suspicion (see "Subverting Journalism," p. 141).

In general, however, CPJ's work in the United States is limited. Since its founding in 1981, CPJ has, as a matter of strategy and policy, concentrated on press freedom violations and attacks on journalists outside U.S. borders. Indeed, we do not systematically monitor problems facing journalists in any of the developed industrial democracies. We devote most of our efforts to those countries where journalists are most in need of international support and protection.

While CPJ recognizes that press freedom requires constant vigilance and aggressive defense at home as well as abroad, we are able to rely within the United States on the thorough, professional efforts of organizations with a primarily domestic focus, such as the American Society of Newspaper Editors, the Society of Professional Journalists, the Reporters Committee for Freedom of the

Press, the Electronic Frontier Foundation, the American Civil Liberties Union, and the National Association of Broadcasters, among others. We recommend to journalists and other researchers the bulletins and annual reports of these and similar organizations, as well as the ongoing coverage of First Amendment issues provided by the *American Journalism Review*, the *Columbia Journalism Review*, *Editor & Publisher*, and other specialized publications.

On U.S. policy issues directly affecting the ability of American reporters to work safely and legally abroad, CPJ works with other American journalism organizations to effect constructive change. One such initiative—by CPJ and the American Society of Newspaper Editors, the Inter American Press Association, the National Newspaper Association, and the World Press Freedom Committee—led in 1995 to the easing of financial restrictions on U.S. journalists reporting from Cuba and the end of a 26-year ban on Cuban reporters in U.S. territory.

CPJ's overriding concern in the United States continues to be the cases of journalists who are murdered for reasons related directly to their profession. As a U.S. organization that forcefully urges governments around the world to investigate and prosecute the assassinations of local journalists, we believe that it is essential to hold our own government equally accountable when similar crimes are committed at home.

Since the widely publicized 1976 murder of *Arizona Republic* reporter Don Bolles, at least 11 other American journalists have been murdered because of their work, including de Dios in Queens. In all but one case, the victims were immigrant journalists working in languages other than English. Seven of those 10 homicides remain unsolved. Most received little or no national media attention. Limited local police investigations were carried out with only minimal federal law-enforcement assistance—despite strong indications in several cases of possible interstate and even international criminal conspiracies.

Uruguay

Various media and journalists' organizations called on government officials to reform a national press law that provides for a "right of reply." Under this law, which mirrors a troubling regional trend, a court can decide how editors must respond to complaints from people who feel they have been aggrieved by a news report, eroding the editorial independence of the news media to decide how to publicize a correction or response.

In May, the editor in chief, managing editor, and two reporters with the Montevideo daily *La República* were convicted of violating press laws and insulting a head of state, and received a two-year jail sentence. The editors were imprisoned immediately; the reporters were out of the country. In a significant act of solidarity, the Uruguayan press strongly condemned the convictions. *La República* editor in chief Federico Fasano Martens, in an article in the Uruguayan magazine *Noticias*, described how he continued to edit the newspaper from his jail cell. On June 7, authorities released the editors.

May 23
Federico Fasano, *La República.* IMPRISONED, LEGAL ACTION
Carlos Fasano, *La República,* IMPRISONED, LEGAL ACTION
Pedro Casademunt, *La República,* LEGAL ACTION
Ricardo Canese, *La República,* LEGAL-ACTION
Federico Fasano, editor in chief of the Montevideo-based daily *La República*; his brother Carlos, managing editor of the paper; and Canese and Casademunt, two *La República* correspondents in Paraguay, were convicted of violating

press laws and insulting the honor of a foreign head of state. All were sentenced to two years' imprisonment. Federico and Carlos Fasano were taken into custody immediately, and an arrest warrant was issued for Canese and Casademunt, who both live in Paraguay.

The charges against the four men were brought by Paraguay's President Juan Carlos Wasmosy in response to a Feb. 2 article in *La República* about Wasmosy's alleged involvement in mismanagement and corruption during the construction of the hydroelectric power plant at Itaipu, a dam on the border between Paraguay and Brazil. During the trial, the judge did not allow the journalists to present evidence supporting the accuracy of the article. In a letter to Uruguay's President Julio María Sanguinetti, CPJ expressed its concern about the sentencing and urged Sanguinetti to instruct the proper authorities to overturn the convictions and to order the journalists' immediate release from prison. Federico and Carlos Fasano were released on June 7.

Venezuela

The vociferous debate over Venezuela's controversial 1994 licensing law for working journalists continued, as several publishers tried unsuccessfully to challenge the rule. The law requires media companies to employ journalists with a degree from a Venezuelan university and membership in the Colegio Nacional de Periodistas, a national journalists' guild.

Publishers fear that the press law is hobbling publications that specialize in areas such as business, medicine, and international affairs. Media owners have tried unsuccessfully to challenge the constitutionality of the 1972 law that established the Colegio.

In one important case in Venezuela, a court on Nov. 26 sentenced William Ojeda, author of a book titled *How Much is a Judge Worth?*, to one year in prison for defamation. Two judges mentioned in the book initiated the lawsuit in 1995. The book examines the Venezuelan justice system in the wake of high-level corruption and government-initiated reforms. Ojeda does not have the right to appeal to the Supreme Court. His sentence was scheduled to begin on Jan. 23, 1997. CPJ sent an appeal to President Rafael Caldera urging him to grant Ojeda a presidential pardon.

Cuba's Independent Journalists Struggle to Establish a Free Press

by Suzanne Bilello

The following is an excerpt from the testimony of CPJ Americas program coordinator Suzanne Bilello before the U.N. Human Rights Commission on Aug. 27. She offered similar testimony at a joint hearing of the Congressional Subcommittee on International Operations and Human Rights and the Subcommittee on the Western Hemisphere on June 27.

AN INDEPENDENT PRESS IS STRUGGLING to establish itself in Cuba. Dozens of independent journalists who were fired from their official jobs because of irreverent thinking about the revolution and its future are behind Cuba's struggling free press movement.

In just over a year, five upstart news agencies have been formed in Cuba. These agencies market stories about Cuba to news outlets in the United States and Europe. Since their founding, many of the agencies' journalists have endured waves of harassment. Several have been detained on charges ranging from "dangerousness" and "disrespect" to spreading "enemy propaganda." These are journalists whose sole aim is to carve out a livelihood that is independent of state-controlled media yet a comfortable distance from organized factions at home and abroad.

The catalyst for Cuba's fledgling independent press movement was the release of Yndamiro Restano from prison in June of 1995. A decade earlier, in 1985, Restano had challenged the concept of state-controlled media and was banished from official journalism, forcing him to work in menial jobs. He went on to found Cuba's first non-official journalism organization in 1987. He later founded a human rights movement seeking peaceful political change and was sentenced to prison for distributing information about it. A campaign by the Committee to Protect Journalists and other press freedom organizations, and the direct intercession of Danielle Mitterrand, wife of France's former president, led to Restano's release. At the annual meeting of the Inter American Press Association (IAPA) on

Oct. 15, 1995, leading Latin American and U.S. publishers accepted the journalists' application for membership.

Those in Cuba who are trying to establish a free press face significant internal obstacles, including a lack of rudimentary supplies, such as pens and notebooks, inadequate financial resources and virtually no exposure to the workings of independent media. In addition, fax machines and modems are illegal unless authorized by the state. And most important, independent journalists face the absolute opposition of Fidel Castro.

Since the beginning of this year, the Castro government has intensified its campaign of harassment and intimidation of these independent journalists. We have repeatedly expressed our outrage at these incidents. Mr. Castro's stepped-up anti-press campaign coincided with a crackdown on the dissident group Concilio Cubano and the shooting down of two planes piloted by the Miami-based, anti-Castro organization Brothers to the Rescue. In a visit to Cuba in June, I was able to learn more about these problems first-hand in discussions with the independent journalists there, and in my own encounter with Cuban authorities.

I traveled to Cuba on June 16 to speak with representatives of all five news agencies. Four days after I arrived, however, I was arrested in my hotel room by Interior Ministry and immigration officials and taken in for interrogation. During the eight hours I was detained, I got a taste of the Kafkaesque ordeal that many independent Cuban journalists have experienced. It was chilling. One of my captors said, "We will never allow to happen here what happened in Eastern Europe when groups of a so-called civil society brought down those regimes."

◆ ◆ ◆

CPJ is also very troubled by what is emerging as a pattern of forcing independent journalists into exile. The Cuban government earlier this year issued verbal ultimatums to Rafael Solano of Havana Press and Roxana Valdivia of Patria, to leave Cuba or face jail sentences for their activities as independent journalists. This Solzhenitsyn-style solution for silencing independent journalists by effectively expelling them from the country resulted in Solano's exile to Spain and Valdivia's departure for the United States.

One of the most formidable barriers facing the Cuban journalists currently struggling to establish an independent press is that they have been labeled dissidents by political forces in both the United States and Cuba. And their effort has become a tool in the arsenal of both political sides. It is important to keep in mind that most of Cuba's independent journalists do not think of themselves as dissidents. The willingness of these men and women to sacrifice so much stems from their desire to establish a free, objective, independent, uncensored press in their island-nation.

Fidel Castro Presents Greatest Obstacle to Free Press in Cuba
Castro remains the chief obstacle to freedom in Cuba for local and foreign journalists alike. Today, Cuba stands alone in the hemisphere as the only country that tolerates no independent newspapers, magazines or news broadcasts. That brings frequent criticism in international human rights forums, and it has earned Castro a spot on the Committee to Protect Journalists' enemies list of world leaders who pose the gravest threat to press freedom.

Under increased international scrutiny and sorely in need of economic partners, Cuba is poised for historic change. Whether the transition is to democracy hinges largely on whether Cuba has a free press that gives it citizens the basis for informed decisions about how they want to be governed.

CPJ works to support the efforts of Cuba's independent journalists and news operations. In addition to our letters of protest regarding individual cases of censorship, harassment, imprisonment or expulsion, we continue to appeal to the Cuban government to reform its policies toward journalists. We have called on President Castro to allow:

• Independent journalists to receive funds from overseas news organizations;

• Independent journalists to own fax machines, computers and other tools of their trade;

• Independent journalists to operate freely without the threat of harassment or imprisonment;

• Cuba to open its doors to American news bureaus; and

• Foreign news organizations to employ and pay Cuban employees directly.

U.S. Policy Inadvertently Limits Growth of Free Press in Cuba
♦ ♦ ♦

Ironically, the United States has become an unlikely ally in Castro's efforts to justify keeping independent journalists isolated and vulnerable, subject to the whims of the state and cut off from potential foreign patrons. Essentially, independent journalism and its practitioners in Cuba are being held hostage to the political conflicts between the United States and Cuba. CPJ is concerned that America's policies are doing more harm than good in the fight to establish the most fundamental democratic institution of all—a free press.

In our efforts to promote the spirit of Article 19 we have been vigilant of all parties in the Cuba debate. In July CPJ reproached the U.S. State Department for its decision to deny travel visas to two members of the state-owned Cuban media who were invited to participate in a conference in Puerto Rico.

U.S. policy should support independent Cuban journalists in their struggle to be autonomous, unfettered by the political demands of any government. To this end, in an appeal to the U.S. Congress in June, CPJ urged policy-makers to ensure that U.S. policy:

• Makes it easier for Western journalists and news organizations to work in Havana and employ Cuban citizens;

• Recognizes that Cuba's independent journalists are not dissidents and should not be supported by U.S. aid.; and

• Ensures that Radio and TV Martí's editorial content not compromise Cuban journalists' credibility and independence.

Reexamine Section 114 of the Cuba Liberty and Democratic Solidarity Act of 1996 (Libertad Act)
In October of 1995, following a major campaign by CPJ and other news organizations and press freedom groups, the Clinton Administration rescinded the 26-year-old ban on Cuban news bureaus in the United States and lifted Treasury Department restrictions on expenditures in Cuba by U.S. news-gathering organizations. CPJ urged President Castro to follow suit and permit U.S. news organizations to reopen bureaus in Cuba.

We urged President Clinton to take this action because, in the words of CPJ Honorary Chairman Walter Cronkite, "It could lead to huge dividends in the most valuable of all commodities—information, in this case about a neighbor on the brink of fast and far-reaching changes."

Unfortunately, a little-noticed provision in The Cuban Liberty and Democratic Solidarity Act of 1996 overrides President Clinton's executive order.

Section 114 of the law authorizes the president to establish and implement an exchange of news bureaus between the U.S. and Cuba, if certain conditions are met:

• The exchange is fully reciprocal;

• The Cuban government agrees not to interfere with the establishment of news bureaus or with the movement in Cuba of journalists of any U.S.-based news organization, including Radio Martí or TV Martí;

• The U.S. Department of Treasury is able to ensure that only accredited journalists regularly employed by a news-gathering organization travel to Cuba; and

• The Cuban government agrees not to interfere with the transmission of telecommunications signals of news bureaus or with the distribution of publications of any U.S.-based news organization that has a news bureau in Cuba.

Under the rubric of "reciprocity," The Cuba Liberty and Democratic Solidarity Act of 1996 allows President Clinton to authorize a mutual reopening of news bureaus only if Cuba permits "distribution" on the island of all print or broadcast reports by news organizations stationed there. Since President Castro will not likely allow the distribution of all these materials as long as he is in power, the ultimate impact of this condition will be to prohibit the operation of U.S. news bureaus in Cuba.

As a further assurance that an exchange of reporters would be "fully reciprocal," the law sets as a precondition the opening of a Cuban office of the U.S. government's Radio and TV Martí. For Mr. Castro, this is unthinkable, given that he believes the ultimate goal of Radio and TV Martí is to destabilize his government. The law's supporters contend that Radio and TV Martí are the only functional equivalents of Prensa Latina, Cuba's official international news agency. But in the U.S. system, as a matter of principle as well as law, it is the private media, not state-run information services, on which we rely for news.

Another facet of Section 114 that hinders the advance of press freedom in Cuba is the requirement that U.S. Treasury officials determine which bona fide "accredited" journalists will be allowed to work in the island-nation. Only people "regularly employed with a news-gathering operation" need apply. This provision excludes free-lancers, including the distinguished writer Tad Szulc, Castro's biographer. This sets a dangerous international precedent. In Latin America and elsewhere, leftist media unions backed by Cuba have fought for years for similar state licensing procedures, failing only because of the effective resistance of private journalism organizations backed strongly by the U.S. government.

Whatever the broader merits or demerits of The Cuban Liberty and Democratic Solidarity Act of 1996, the inadvertent impact of Section 114 is to hinder the exposure of Cubans (journalists and non-journalists) to the peaceful workings of a free and independent media, and to limit the information about Cuba available to Americans.

Many of the Cuban journalists I spoke with in June agreed with CPJ's position that the establishment of U.S. news bureaus in Cuba would bring about a radical improvement for the island's independent journalists. The creation of job opportunities—for stringers, reporters, editors, cameramen, and other newsroom positions— would give Cuba's independent journalists much-needed training in how to operate as effective and objective professionals.

CPJ has urged the U.S. Congress to reevaluate Section 114 of The Cuban Liberty and Democratic Solidarity Act of 1996 in light of our analysis of its impact on the establishment of a free press in Cuba.

Ensure Editorial Independence of Radio and TV Martí
The Committee to Protect Journalists does not take a position on the political content of Radio and TV Martí. We recognize that Radio Martí fills a void in providing news and information to citizens of Cuba. Our fundamental concern is for the independent journalists in Cuba who work as stringers for Radio Martí.

In my meetings in Cuba, journalists raised several concerns about Radio Martí. It should be noted that the station does not pay any of these independent journalists for news reports. Several complained to me that Radio Martí is almost exclusively interested in news about detention of dissidents. In fact, they said they experienced outright censorship from the station's editors. Others remarked that they felt the tone of some of the broadcasters was patronizing, making fun of the daily plight of Cubans.

Anthony DePalma of *The New York Times* correctly character-ized the political dangers for Cuban stringers for Radio Martí in an article published on April 17, 1996. DePalma writes, "The Cuban Government considers Radio Martí an American attempt to over-throw Fidel Castro. Cuban officials said men like Mr. Solano (one of Cuba's leading journalists who formed Havana Press, an indepen-dent news agency, in May of 1995) are subversives, not journalists, and their association with Radio Martí constitutes a crime against the state."

The journalists I met with expressed fear that, in its pending move from Washington, D.C., to Miami, Radio and TV Martí could become more overtly political. If so, Cuba's independent jour-nalists who provide stories for the news organization can expect even greater vilification by Castro's government.

From CPJ's perspective and that of many of the independent journalists I met with in Cuba, Radio and TV Martí will be a more effective agent of democratization if its editorial content remains balanced. We urge Congress to closely examine the current editorial control policy of Radio and TV Martí to ensure that, following the move to Miami, the station continues to provide credible, profes-sional information to the citizens of Cuba. This is more important than ever since Radio Martí is virtually the only source of informa-tion for Cubans about events in Cuba as well as the world.

Forego U.S. Aid to Independent Journalists
Section 109 of The Cuban Liberty and Democratic Solidarity Act of 1996 authorizes the U.S. government to furnish assistance, financial and other support, for individuals and independent nongovernmen-tal organizations to support democracy-building efforts for Cuba. The intention of this provision is to support the dissemination of information in Cuba on democracy, human rights, and market economies, and to support the individual dissidents and their fami-lies, and dissident groups, which circulate this information.

CPJ is concerned that this provision will be broadly interpreted to include Cuba's independent journalists. It would be a serious mis-take—and one with significant consequences—to consider these men and women dissidents and therefore eligible for U.S. aid. CPJ urges the United States to refrain from offering this type of assistance to independent journalists.

As I learned firsthand on my recent visit, Cuba's independent journalists do not consider themselves dissidents. Their aim is to carve out a livelihood that is independent of state-controlled media yet a comfortable distance from organized factions at home and abroad.

Financial assistance from the United States government to Cuba's independent journalists will endanger their safety and discredit their effort to establish an independent press. Moreover, these payments would compromise the small press freedom gains already attained.

I personally learned how grave a matter this is. I carried with me a modest amount of cash, raised exclusively from private funds, as well as reporters' notebooks, pens and medicine, to distribute to the journalists I met with. After my arrest, however, my Cuban interrogators seized on the donations. Again and again, I was asked about their source and purpose. Despite what I told them, they were of the unshakable belief that these donations came from U.S. government funds, and that the recipients of those funds are clients of U.S. interests. Some critics of CPJ's position may argue that Cuba's independent journalists do not have to accept these private donations if offered. But given the state of Cuba's economy and the difficulty people face in trying to make a living as independent journalists, the offer of financial assistance is hard to turn down.

Subverting Journalism:
Reporters and the CIA

by Kate Houghton

AMERICAN JOURNALISTS have long been bitterly opposed to the recruitment of reporters by U.S. intelligence agencies, and the fraudulent use of journalism credentials by intelligence operatives. Since the mid-1970s, journalists and others—including some of the nation's top foreign policy-makers—believed that the CIA could no longer recruit reporters as spies. They shared a widespread but inaccurate assumption that the U.S. government had banned such objectionable practices as part of a package of reforms revamping codes of conduct for covert intelligence operations adopted in response to recommendations of the 1976 Church Committee report. In its investigation of U.S. foreign and military intelligence operations, the committee—the Senate Select Committee on Intelligence, chaired by Senator Frank Church (D-Idaho)—found that more than 50 American journalists had worked clandestinely as CIA agents during the Cold War era. The committee's final report strongly condemned this practice and unequivocally called on the intelligence community to "permit American journalists and news organizations to pursue their work without jeopardizing their credibility in the eyes of the world through covert use of them."

In fact, during the subsequent two decades, the CIA merely curtailed the practice.

The issue was spotlighted anew in the spring of 1996 by the release of a Council on Foreign Relations task force report on U.S. intelligence-gathering policies and practices—which in turn inadvertently prompted the passage of the first U.S. law explicitly permitting the practice. Ironically, many of the members of Congress who supported the new statute thought they were effectively prohibiting the covert use of journalists by the CIA.

Kate Houghton *has been board liaison and assistant to the executive director of CPJ since July 1996. She has a bachelor's degree in history from New York University.*

The episode could be written off as yet another example of the Law of Unintended Consequences—were the consequences not so potentially calamitous. The perception that American journalists are agents of the U.S. government compromises their professional integrity, impedes their ability to function in many parts of the world, and often puts their lives in jeopardy. Yet the CIA's endorsement of the new law, coupled with the agency's admission that it reserves the right to use this practice as an avenue for clandestine information-gathering, can only magnify these suspicions. Thus, CPJ and other leading journalism and press freedom organizations are pressing for an unambiguous statutory prohibition of all uses of journalists and journalism credentials by U.S. intelligence agencies. A CPJ task force co-chaired by Terry Anderson and Walter Cronkite is spearheading the fight.

IN FEBRUARY 1996, an independent task force of the Council on Foreign Relations led by Richard Haass, a former senior director for Near East and South Asian Affairs of the National Security Council in the Bush administration, proposed taking a "fresh look...at limits on the use of non-official 'covers' for hiding and protecting those involved in clandestine activities." Haass later publicly expanded on this point, challenging what he characterized as the prohibition on the use of journalists as undercover intelligence agents. The outcry among journalists—including many who are members of the Council of Foreign Relations—led council president Leslie Gelb to distance himself and the council from the task force and its recommendations.

The reaction to the controversy among U.S. intelligence professionals, however, was quite different—and far more disturbing to journalists. John Deutch, director of Central Intelligence, appeared before Congress and said there was no need to change U.S. policy as Haass had advocated, since the CIA already had the power to use U.S. reporters as spies. Under the terms of the guidelines adopted after the Church Commission report, the CIA director retained the right to approve such recruitment if he judged it necessary, Deutch explained. Deutch received public support for his interpretation of the CIA's prerogative from Stansfield Turner, the CIA chief in the Carter administration. Speaking to a gathering of the American Society of Newspaper Editors, Turner revealed that he had authorized the use of journalists in intelligence operations three times during his tenure as CIA director.

Journalists, shocked to hear that a practice most thought had been banned was in fact still permitted, were not mollified by Deutch's assurances that the CIA "will not use journalists...American journalists, except under, very, very rare circumstances." Louis Boccardi, president of the Associated Press, and Tom Johnson, president of CNN, met with Deutch and asked him to pledge publicly that he would never call on journalists to gather information clandestinely for U.S. intelligence services. Boccardi pointed to the case of Terry Anderson, who had been taken hostage by the Hezbollah in Lebanon while a foreign correspondent for Associated Press on the false accusation of information-gathering for the CIA and held for almost eight years. And Johnson noted that a CNN crew assistant in Baghdad had been tortured by Iraqi security forces seeking to extract a confession of his and CNN's purported collaboration with the CIA. "The CIA should say it's not going to use the cover of journalism for the work that is does," Boccardi declared before the meeting. "They have a function, we have a function, and I think mixing them exposes our people all over the world to a level of danger that's extremely worrisome."

In response, Deutch refused to reject the practice categorically. "As Director of Central Intelligence," he said he told Boccardi and Johnson, "I must be in a position to assure the president and the members of his National Security Council and this country that there will never come a time when the United States cannot ask a willing citizen to assist in combating an extreme threat to the nation."

Amidst this controversy, then-Congressman William B. Richardson of New Mexico proposed an amendment to the pending intelligence services appropriations bill that would ban the use of reporters for U.S. news organizations in covert intelligence operations unless the president gave written authorization to the House and Senate intelligence oversight committees certifying that a particular exception to the policy was justified by "overriding national security concerns."

Richardson said he hoped to "ensure that neither the independence guaranteed to the press by the Constitution nor the lives of journalists are endangered by blurring the distinction between reporters as commentators on government and reporters as instruments of government."

While Richardson's initial intent may have been to put an end to the CIA's covert use of journalists, in subsequent debate he agreed to add language to his amendment stating that the ban would not preclude "voluntary cooperation...with the United States Intelligence Community [sic]." Given that any such collaboration in a democracy would presumably never be compulsory, this caveat effectively rendered the other restrictions meaningless.

Passed overwhelmingly in a 417-to-6 House vote, the Richardson amendment to the Intelligence Authorization Act for Fiscal Year 1997 (H.R. 3259) stated:

(a) Policy—It is the policy of the United States that an element of the Intelligence community may not be used as an agent or asset for the purposes of collecting intelligence any individual who—1) is authorized by contract or by the issuance of press credentials to represent himself or herself, either in the United States, or abroad, as a correspondent of a United States news media organization; or (2) is officially recognized by a foreign government as a representative of a United States media organization.

(B) Waiver—The President may waive subsection (a) in the case of an individual if the President certifies in writing that the waiver is necessary to address the overriding national security interest of the United States. The certification shall be made to the Permanent Select Committee on Intelligence of the House of Representatives and the Select Committee on Intelligence of the Senate.

(C) Voluntary Cooperation—Subsection (a) shall not be construed to prohibit the voluntary cooperation of any person who is aware that the cooperation is being provided to an element of the United States Intelligence Community.

The Senate Select Committee on Intelligence convened a hearing on July 17 to discuss the use of journalists in CIA operations. Terry Anderson, a CPJ board member and former AP Bureau Chief in Lebanon; Ted Koppel, anchor of ABC's "Nightline"; and Mortimer B. Zuckerman, chairman and editor in chief of *U.S. News and World Report* and chairman and co-publisher of *The Daily News*, testified before the Intelligence Committee about the threats that this policy represented—to the physical safety and professional integrity of members of the press, and to the very principles of press freedom. All three stated their absolute opposition to the use of journalists in CIA operations and demanded on behalf of their colleagues around the world that an absolute and unalterable ban be set in place. In his testimony, Anderson told of the life-threatening dangers for a journalist in an atmosphere of suspicion and mistrust. "I have been accused of being a spy, not just on the occasion of my captivity, but on other occasions in various places. I was told by a number of people that I was on a list of CIA agents kept by the fundamentalist Shiites who captured me. That is a perception that is very difficult to disprove. It's hard to argue with them. They are very suspicious people."

"The damage has already been done," continued Anderson, "I believe, most prominently by Director Deutch's acknowledgment that there were exceptions to the general rule and that such things have happened in the past. So, the best thing we can do is try to repair the damage by a greater prohibition, without exceptions. We are talking about a real danger; this is not imaginary. A statement of formal exception—no matter how hedged or restricted—would simply be an acknowledgment to those who suspect us of being spies that 'Yes, on occasion, you're right.'"

Ted Koppel cautioned the Intelligence Committee of the implications and limitations of this new policy. "If the CIA must, on occasion, use the role of an American journalist to conceal one of its operatives and to protect the greater national interest, it will do so, regardless of what is decided by Congress. But let that continue to be in the knowledge that a free press is being endangered and that American law is being broken," he said. "How often the CIA would actually use such cover is beside the point," he stressed. "The relevant question is how often it would be assumed, both at home and abroad, that American reporters are working with a second, secret agenda."

LEGITIMATE REPORTERS RISK serious repercussions when they work under suspicion of being intelligence operatives. In a July letter of protest sent to all members of the U.S. Senate, CPJ Chair Kati Marton urged them to support a "complete and unalterable ban on the use of journalists as intelligence operatives, and on the fraudulent use of journalistic credentials and agency affiliation as cover for espionage activities." Marton included in the letter the story of her parents' 1955 arrest in Hungary on false charges of affiliation with the CIA. Her parents, Hungarian nationals and correspondents for the Associated Press and United Press International, were imprisoned for reporting the truth to the rest of the world about the Stalinization of their country. Sentenced to 25 years in prison on groundless charges, they were forced to leave their young daughter to the care of strangers until their case was brought to international attention almost two years later. "My parents' arrest has had an unlimited impact on my work," said Marton. "I'm drawn to debunking oppression. I started out in a part of the world where, if you strayed from imposed views you lost your job or your life or both. In my parents' case it was a loss of freedom." She concluded by underscoring that "Journalists like my parents and Terry Anderson know from their own personal experience that a policy which permits the use of journalists in intelligence operations jeopardizes the safety of all journalists working in dangerous and repressive countries."

Senator Robert Kerrey, Vice-Chairman of the Senate Select Committee on Intelligence, replied to Marton's letter on Aug. 21, stating that "there are imaginable scenarios where only a member of the press, clergy, or the Peace Corps would have the access necessary to prevent the loss of life," and that the CIA should have access to the intelligence gathering potential of all professions if and when it is deemed necessary for national security. "When lives are at risk or vital interests are at risk, I don't see why any American patriot should be forbidden to cooperate with an American intelligence agency," Kerrey continued. Another Democratic Senator, John Kerry of Massachusetts, also expressed opposition to the flat ban that Richardson had proposed, but was more concerned about the impact on journalists of continued public discussion of the issue. As he put it, "if they weren't tainted before, they sure as hell will be tainted afterwards."

Senate Bill 1718, the Senate's version of the intelligence authorization act, contained no language on the issue of the CIA's use of journalists as spies. The conference committee, however, rolled in the House amendment virtually verbatim, but with one critical change: Not just the president, but the CIA director as well, could waive the ban on the use of journalists in covert operations by writing to the House and Senate intelligence oversight committees. This is the version of the bill that became law on Oct. 11, 1996, with President Clinton's signing of the 1997 Intelligence Authorization Act.

IN HER LETTER TO THE SENATE, Kati Marton warned that "The disturbing acknowledgment that the CIA has waived restrictions on the use of journalistic credentials in intelligence-gathering operations in the past and wishes to retain the right to do so again, may have already led some foreign leaders to believe that the CIA and leading U.S. policy-makers are actively urging an end to official constraints on the use of journalists for espionage."

The repercussions of this recent change in U.S. policy have already begun to inform the intelligence practices of other nations. The Russian daily *Izvestiya* published an article on Dec. 7, 1996, reporting that Russia's Federal Security Service planned to create a new department of intelligence operations to manipulate the news coverage of security issues, resulting from its failure to control public opinion during the Chechen war. On Dec. 20, *The Moscow Times* ran an article illustrating the dangers for Russian journalists already engendered by this policy. An unnamed source was quoted saying that "the FSB (Federal Security Service) is putting correspondents in danger especially in Chechnya. [They] are already convinced that we are all spies, without the FSB advertising that they use journalists as sources for their operations."

"There is no essential difference between the work of a spy and a journalist; both collect information in the same way—just the end consumers are different," said Maj. Gen. Yury Kobaldze of Russia's SVR, the Foreign Intelligence Service. "Journalists make the best spies; they have more freedom of access than diplomats. The Americans' moral stand on not using journalists is artificial, and not a little duplicitous."

Looking beyond the immediate threats to the lives of journalists, the threat this law poses to the integrity of journalism is profound. In the United States, the First Amendment protects the rights of the press to practice its craft without fear or favor from the government. If American journalists become agents of government rather than its critics, as they already are in so many countries, the practice will have a corrosive effect on our democracy. "Whatever gains may be justified and whatever grounds may be used to justify intelligence work by the press, in whatever form it may take, it seems to me that these gains must still be assessed in the context of what they do to the press as an institution in a free society," Zuckerman testified before the Senate Intelligence Committee. "To be the instrument of government rather than a constitutional check on government would undermine the good that independent journalism does for an open society."

Asia

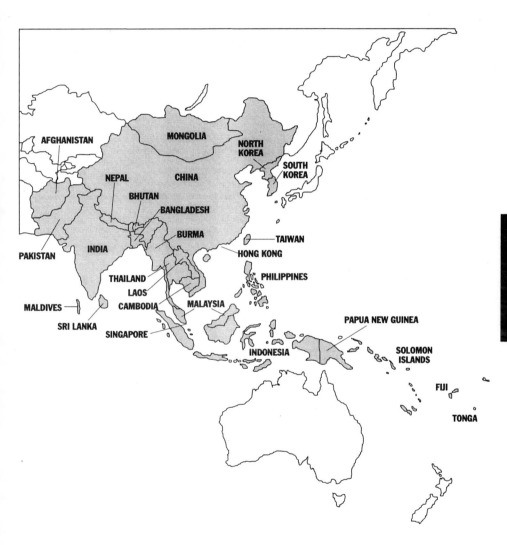

OVERVIEW
OF **Asia**

by Vikram Parekh

C IVIL STRIFE AND SEPARATIST WARS provided the backdrop to
most of the press freedom violations in South Asia, while the more autocratic regimes of East Asia impeded access to information through Internet censorship and the ongoing suppression of dissident journalism.

China blocked access to Internet sites run by Hong Kong- and U.S.-based
news organizations, including *The Washington Post*, *The New York Times*, and the
respected Chinese language daily *Ming Pao*. Singapore established a regulatory
body to police the Internet and required the city-state's three Internet providers
to install equipment capable of blocking access to banned sites. Vietnam—which
allows only limited access to the Internet, primarily to foreigners working in the
country—continued to vacillate on the question of legalizing broader Internet
use. As a preliminary step, the government drafted regulatory guidelines that
reportedly hold subscribers responsible for the content of both transmitted and
received communications, and permit the government to shut down service
providers if their subscribers transmit "offensive" or "subversive" material. These
and other press freedom issues formed the basis for ground-breaking discussions
betweenVietnamese officials and a CPJ delegation that visited Vietnam in September 1996. (See p. 183 for a special report on the CPJ delegation's findings.)

Crackdowns on dissident journalism proceeded apace in China and Indonesia.
A Beijing court sentenced a noted dissident, Wang Dan, to 11 years in prison for
conspiring to subvert the government, a charge based in part on articles that
Wang had written for the overseas press. And in a year marked by massive civil

Vikram Parekh *is the program coordinator for Asia. He holds a J.D. from Rutgers Law School and a B.A. in
politics from the University of California, Santa Cruz. Before joining CPJ, he was a Ford Foundation Fellow
at the International Center for Law in Development, and has worked both for the International Human
Rights Law Group in Washington, D.C., and the International Institute of New Jersey.*

James Bucknell, *the research associate for Asia, contributed extensively to this report.* **Paul Zielbauer,**
who was the research associate for Asia from January through May 1996, also contributed to the report.

unrest in Indonesia, President Suharto's regime stepped up its persecution of Indonesia's only independent journalists union, the Alliance of Independent Journalists (AJI). Authorities shifted two imprisoned AJI members, including CPJ's 1995 International Press Freedom awardee Ahmad Taufik, to a more remote facility after they smuggled out an interview with a fellow inmate, East Timorese leader José Alexandre ("Xanana") Gusmaõ. Indonesian police also raided a printing press used by the underground magazine *Suara Independen*, which was founded by AJI, and arrested two of its employees, charging them with the distribution of printed materials defaming Suharto.

With the handover of Hong Kong from Britain to China scheduled for July 1997, Hong Kong journalists looked warily across the border. What they saw was not encouraging. Senior Chinese leaders said publicly that Hong Kong journalists would not be allowed after the handover to advocate Hong Kong or Taiwanese independence, nor would they be able to publish what Chinese Foreign Minister Qian Qichen termed "personal attacks" on Chinese leaders.

Political turmoil in much of South Asia put journalists in danger of both physical and legal assault. In Bangladesh, many journalists were physically attacked early in the year after opposition parties boycotted elections called by the government. Police fatally shot a journalist for the weekly *Neel Sagar* as he attempted to cover an opposition protest, while the government charged the daily *Ajker Kagoj* with sedition and raided its offices. In Karachi, Pakistan's largest city, journalists for party organs and independent publications alike continued to be caught in the crossfire between a provincial government dominated by ethnic Sindhis and an opposition party of Urdu-speaking immigrants from India. One journalist who was put in prison in 1995 on charges of terrorism was still there at the end of 1996. Many of his colleagues believe he was framed. In India, inconclusive assembly elections in Uttar Pradesh, the country's most populous state, allowed a powerful political figure—whom all the major parties were courting in hopes of forming a coalition government—to lead a physical assault on a group of journalists without fear of prosecution.

India and Sri Lanka sought to contain separatist movements within their borders by imposing gags on the local press. In India's northern state of Jammu and Kashmir, the Indian government held elections for Kashmiri representatives to the national Parliament for the first time since 1989, when separatists in Kashmir began an armed uprising against Indian rule. During the elections, federally appointed state authorities in Kashmir issued a directive to the local press, warning journalists against publishing statements by separatist leaders, material deemed prejudicial to national unity, or articles that expressed a lack of faith in the elections. In Sri Lanka, the government for the second time in two years

Asia

introduced strict censorship of all reporting on the military in conjunction with an army offensive against the Liberation Tigers of Tamil Eelam (LTTE) on the country's northern Jaffna Peninsula.

Bangladesh

A political crisis in Bangladesh, emanating from long-standing tensions between the ruling Bangladesh National Party (BNP) and opposition parties led by the Awami League, led to severe and widespread attacks on the press. Journalists were variously assaulted, arrested, and in one case, murdered, because of their suspected ties to the opposition, their coverage of abuses by police and paramilitary Bangladesh Rifles (BDR) during the rioting, or simply because they were caught in the violence between the opposition and government forces or supporters.

Lawlessness and violence enveloped the Feb. 15 elections, boycotted by opposition parties. Yasin Kabir Joy, a photographer for the daily *Janakantha*, and Tapan Dey, a photographer for the daily *Khabar*, were beaten on Feb. 4 by pro-government students while covering a clash between rival student groups at Dhaka University. A week later, on Feb. 10, Joy and Shaiful Islam, a photographer for *Banglar Bani*, were severely beaten by BDR troops while covering a clash between the BDR and opposition supporters. BDR troops broke four of Joy's teeth and fractured his wrist and elbow. Law enforcement officials were also responsible for the death of Mohammad Quaruzzaman, a reporter for the weekly newspaper *Neel Sagar*, who was shot by police while he was covering their crackdown on a violent protest in the north of the country. The Dhaka-based daily *Ajker Kagoj*, a pro-Awami League paper, suffered sustained attacks. Masked intruders raided the offices of Ajker Kagoj on April 14, damaging property and threatening to kill the paper's editor, Kazi Shahid Ahmed. Ahmed, who had been charged with sedition on Feb. 29, was in hiding at the time.

The violence abated after a second round of elections on June 12 that brought the Awami League to power under Prime Minister Sheikh Hasina Wajed. In an address to the nation following her election, she promised to foster an atmosphere conducive to press freedom and to grant autonomy to state-owned media. Press freedom conditions have improved substantially since her government assumed office.

February 4
Yasin Kabir Joy, *Janakantha*, ATTACKED
Joy, a photographer for the daily *Janakantha*, Dhaka's largest newspaper, was assaulted while covering a clash at Dhaka University between student groups supporting rival political parties. According to a United Press International report, Joy and at least one other photojournalist were beaten as they tried to photograph pro-government students destroying microphones set up for an opposition group meeting. Joy's camera and eyeglasses were smashed during the attack.

February 19
Mohammad Quamruzzaman, *Neel Sagar*, KILLED
Police fatally shot Quamruzzaman, a reporter for the weekly newspaper *Neel Sagar*, while he was covering their crackdown on a violent protest against election results in the northern town of Nilphamari. According to several reports, police officers beat and kicked the journalist after having shot him. Although they initially refused to acknowledge his death, authorities later handed over Quamruzzaman's body to relatives. CPJ wrote a letter to Bangladesh authorities, urging them to launch an investigation and prosecute those responsible for the murder.

February 29
Syed Borhan Kabir, *Ajker Kagoj*, IMPRISONED, LEGAL ACTION
Kazi Shahid Ahmed, *Ajker Kagoj*, LEGAL ACTION
Kabir, a reporter for the daily *Ajker Kagoj*, was arrested at his office for publishing an article that Ministry of Home Affairs officials deemed

seditious and threatening to government security. He was denied bail and taken to the central jail in Dhaka. Police also attempted to arrest Kabir's editor, Kazi Shahid Ahmed, on charges of sedition, but he evaded arrest and went into hiding. In the offending article, published Jan. 29, Kabir had stated that the election commission's request to post army sentries at polling stations was unconstitutional. His report also said some members of the army had refused to comply with the request. Kabir was subsequently denied an appeal for a bail hearing.

June 19

S.M. Alauddin, *Ogrodoot,* KILLED

Masked gunmen shot Alauddin, editor of the weekly *Ogrodoot* and a former member of Parliament for the governing Awami League, in Satkhira, where *Ogrodoot* is published. The unidentified assailants entered the newspaper's office, just a few yards from the main police station in Satkhira, and shot Alauddin while he was watching the nightly news on television. Other journalists and political activists who were there at the time of the attack rushed him to a local hospital, but he died shortly afterward. Police told local journalists that the murder stemmed from a longstanding political feud, but they failed to provide further details.

Burma

Political arrests and repression have dramatically increased in Burma, as the State Law and Order Restoration Council (SLORC) maintains its tight rein on the flow of information, insuring that the Burmese media remain among the most repressed in Asia. The state, which controls virtually all Burmese media, added to its already comprehensive body of laws restricting the free flow of information. On June 7, SLORC introduced Law No. 5/96, making it an offense to instigate, protest, say, write or distribute anything that would

"disrupt and deteriorate the stability of the state, communal peace and tranquillity, and the prevalence of law and order." Persons convicted under the new law face prison terms of up to 20 years. The regime also made owning, using, importing or borrowing a modem or fax a crime punishable by up to 15 years in prison.

SLORC barred access to the residence of Daw Aung San Suu Kyi, leader of the opposition National League for Democracy (NLD) in late September and conducted mass arrests of NLD members and supporters. The blockade prohibited her weekly rallies, and also prevented foreign journalists from meeting with her. In addition, SLORC repeatedly cut off Suu Kyi's telephone lines to prevent interviews with the foreign media. Meanwhile, the government continued to jam Burmese language broadcasts by the BBC World Service and Voice of America, effectively denying its citizens any independent, reliable information on developments in their country. (The jamming of both radio services began in August 1995, after the BBC broadcast an interview with Suu Kyi.)

Student protests, which had been ongoing since October, peaked in early December, when police and military authorities beat and detained two journalists for a Japanese daily who were covering the story. After receiving a beating from police, *Yomiuri Shimbun* news assistant Myo Thant spent more than four hours in military detention on Dec 3. Upon his release, he spent five days in the hospital. On Dec. 6, police and soldiers beat Shigefumi Takasuka, a Bangkok-based reporter for the *Yomiuri Shimbun,* and detained him for questioning. Despite Takasuka's repeated identification of himself as a journalist, police and soldiers struck him repeatedly on the head and body, causing serious bruising.

December 3

Myo Thant, *Yomiuri Shimbun,* ATTACKED,

HARASSED

Police beat Thant, a news assistant for the Japanese daily *Yomiuri Shimbun*, while he was covering student demonstrations in Rangoon. Thant had passed through a blockade after receiving permission to do so, but police clubbed him repeatedly anyway, on the head and back. The beating continued after Thant identified himself as a journalist and showed his press card. Military authorities then took Thant to Yangon military district headquarters, where he was held for four hours. He had to be hospitalized for five days after his release.

December 7
Shigefumi Takasuka, *Yomiuri Shimbun,*
ATTACKED, HARASSED
Takasuka, a Bangkok-based reporter for the Japanese daily *Yomiuri Shimbun*, was beaten by police and soldiers and detained for questioning during student protests in Rangoon. Authorities arrested more than 250 people during the demonstrations. Despite Takasuka's repeated assertions that he was a journalist, police and soldiers wielding clubs struck him about 10 times on the head and body, causing serious bruising. Officers of the military intelligence department questioned Takasuka for two-and-a-half hours.

Cambodia

The fractiousness and volatility of Cambodia's political life was readily apparent throughout the year, as was the toll it has taken on the development of an independent press. During a mission to Cambodia and Vietnam in late September by Committee to Protect Journalists board member Peter Arnett and Asia program coordinator Vikram Parekh, the committee found a Cambodian press that for the most part was highly partisan, and vulnerable to violent reprisals for its commentaries on national politics. CPJ found

other disturbing conditions, including a judiciary and police forces that afford little security to the local press. (See also special report on Vietnam, p. 183.)

Newspapers supporting the Khmer Nation Party (KNP)—unrecognized by the government and led by Sam Rainsy, a civil liberties proponent who was expelled from the National Assembly in 1995—were conspicuous targets of legal and extralegal intimidation. Thun Bun Ly, the editor of *Odom K'tek Khmer* (Khmer Ideal), was shot and killed by unidentified gunmen in May, on the same day that the KNP was opening its first office outside Phnom Penh. Official investigations into Bun Ly's murder and those of three journalists killed in 1994 appear to have ground to a halt. In a meeting with Arnett and Parekh, however, First Prime Minister Prince Norodom Ranariddh did promise to address the murders. He described the lack of progress in the investigations as "unacceptable" and pledged to raise the issue with the country's Interior Ministry.

Like the editors of two other pro-KNP papers, Bun Ly had an appeal pending before the Supreme Court against a conviction for defamation and disinformation. While his murder effectively spelled an end to Bun Ly's case, the Supreme Court upheld the convictions of his colleagues, Chan Rotana of *Samleng Yuvachun Khmer* (Voice of Khmer Youth) and Hen Vipheak of *Serei Pheap Thmei* (New Liberty News). Both were sentenced to prison, but were released a week later, after international organizations condemned the convictions and King Norodom Sihanouk granted both journalists pardons. Cambodia in 1995 had adopted a press law that superseded the disinformation and defamation statutes used to prosecute the three journalists. The new press law dispensed with criminal libel, but the courts refused to apply the new law to Rotana's and Vipheak's appeals.

The 1995 press law included an article that barred the publication of reports threatening to the country's "national security" and "political stability." The provision's ambiguous wording has alarmed many Cambodian journalists, who fear it will be used to silence any critical commentary on the country's internal politics, relations with neighboring countries, and war of attrition with the remaining Khmer Rouge forces. Fueling their anxieties were remarks made in February by State Secretary for Information Khieu Kanharith, in which he warned local newspapers that they faced temporary closure if they published stories deemed demoralizing to the army. In response to CPJ's concern about the law, Information Minister Ieng Mouly told Arnett and Parekh that the government was drafting a subdecree aimed at clarifying the terms, and would present it to local and foreign journalists, as well as nongovernmental organizations, for comment.

Second Prime Minister Hun Sen continued to consolidate his position as Cambodia's most powerful official, and most of the country's nominally independent print and broadcast media now have a pronounced tilt in favor of his Cambodian People's Party. But while he is emerging as an influential figure in his own right, Hun Sen's sensitivity to the interests of the Vietnamese government, which has been his strong supporter, was startlingly evide·,t during the year. Between December 1995 and December 1996, the Cambodian government conducted a massive crackdown on anti-Communist ethnic Vietnamese residents of Cambodia, expelling several dozen across the border to Vietnam. Among them was Ly Chandara, the publisher of a Vietnamese-language newspaper in Phnom Penh, who was jailed for seven months in Vietnam before being allowed to return to Cambodia.

February 8
Ek Mongkol, FM Radio 90, ATTACKED
Mongkol, the host of two call-in music request programs and a biweekly political commentary

show on FM Radio 90, was shot shortly after leaving work. He was riding a motorcycle in downtown Phnom Penh when two men on another motorcyle approached from behind and opened fire, striking him twice in the chest and once in the neck. He was evacuated to a Bangkok hospital, where doctors expected him to make a full recovery. A member of the royalist FUNCINPEC party, which owns FM Radio 90, Mongkol had made statements prior to the shooting decrying what he termed Vietnamese aggression along Cambodia's eastern border. He also had been critical of official corruption in Cambodia. Some local journalists blamed the shooting on FUNCINPEC's pro-Vietnam coalition partner, the Cambodian People's Party (CPP). Others pointed out that Mongkol was widely known to have engaged female callers in flirtatious on-air banter, leading some to speculate that he may have been shot by a jealous husband or boyfriend.

March 9
Ly Chandara, *Tu Do*, EXPELLED
Chandara, the editor of *Tu Do* (Freedom), an anti-Communist Vietnamese-language newspaper published in Phnom Penh, was expelled by Cambodian authorities to Vietnam. He was among several dozen ethnic Vietnamese opponents of Hanoi—very loosely affiliated with one another, and collectively termed the "Tu Do Movement"—whom the Cambodian government expelled or threatened with expulsion between December 1995 and December 1996. Chandara was taken into custody at the Vietnamese border and incarcerated in Vietnam for seven months. He was released on Oct. 10 and immediately repatriated to Cambodia, after promising Vietnamese officials that he would not conspire against Vietnam or engage in any other political activity. However, Chandara said in late January 1997 that he was seeking permission from the Cambodian government to relaunch *Tu Do*. Human rights activists in Phnom Penh had questioned Cambodia's authority to expel Chandara, citing as evidence

of his Cambodian citizenship a voter registration card in his name for Cambodia's U.N.-supervised elections in 1993.

May 18
Thun Bun Ly, *Odom K'tek Khmer,*
KILLED
Thun Bun Ly, a contributor to and former editor of the opposition newspaper *Odom K'tek Khmer* (Khmer Ideal), was fatally shot by two unidentified gunmen while riding a motorcycle near a major commercial thoroughfare in central Phnom Penh. He was hit three times: once in the arm, and twice on his upper body. The assailants, who were also riding a motorcycle, fled immediately after the shooting. The attack came the same day that the Khmer Nation Party, of which Thun Bun Ly was a leading member, was to open its first branch office outside Phnom Penh.

Cambodian courts convicted Thun Bun Ly twice last year on charges of defamation and disinformation for printing articles, letters to the editor and political cartoons that criticized the government. As a result, *Odom K'tek Khmer* was ordered permanently closed, and Thun Bun Ly was fined a total of 15 million riels (US$6,174). If he did not pay the sum, he risked up to three years' imprisonment. Both the fine and the closure order were stayed pending appeals to the Supreme Court, and Thun Bun Ly's requests for amnesty from King Norodom Sihanouk, and Hun Sen.

In a letter to Cambodia's co-prime ministers, Prince Norodom Ranriddh and Hun Sen, CPJ expressed its alarm over the killing of Thun Bun Ly and called for a prompt and thorough investigation.

June 28
Chan Rotana, *Samleng Yuvachun Khmer,*
IMPRISONED, LEGAL ACTION
The Supreme Court upheld the disinformation conviction of Rotana, editor of *Samleng Yuvachun Khmer* (Voice of Khmer Youth), as well as his one-year prison sentence and fine of

5 million riels (US$2,000). Rotana was immediately arrested and imprisoned, but was released on July 5 under a pardon from King Norodom Sihanouk that was agreed to by co-prime ministers Prince Norodom Ranariddh and Hun Sen. Rotana had been convicted on Feb. 27, 1995, of violating Article 62 of the Criminal Code, which bars the publication in bad faith and with malicious intent of false news that "has disturbed or is likely to disturb the public peace." The charges related to an article in the paper's Jan. 12-13, 1995, edition, titled "Ranariddh is More Stupid than Hun Sen Three Times a Day," which accused Prince Ranariddh of naively following Hun Sen's dictates.

August 23
Hen Vipheak, *Serei Pheap Thmei,* IMPRISONED, LEGAL ACTION
The Supreme Court found Vipheak, editor of *Serei Pheap Thmei* (New Liberty News), guilty of disinformation and upheld his one-year prison sentence and fine of 5 million riels (US$2000). The court struck down a lower court's order for *Serei Pheap Thmei* to be closed. King Norodom Sihanouk on Aug. 30 granted Vipheak a pardon, consented to by co-Prime Ministers Prince Norodom Ranariddh and Hun Sen, and Vipheak was released the same day.

Vipheak had been convicted on May 20, 1995, under Article 62 of the Criminal Code, which outlaws the publication of false information in bad faith and with malicious intent that "has disturbed or is likely to disturb the public peace." The charges stemmed from a Feb. 6, 1995, article in *Serei Pheap Thmei* titled "Country of Thieves." It was a satirical commentary on corruption in the various branches of government. Vipheak was also charged for a cartoon that depicted Hun Sen holding a gun to Ranariddh's head.

An appeals court on Dec. 22, 1995, upheld his sentence, but Vipheak remained free pending his Supreme Court hearing. The Supreme Court refused to retry Vipheak under Cambodia's new press law, which supersedes Article 62

Asia

and does not include libel as a criminal offense.

China

While China's commitment to market reforms remains firmly in place, the Communist Party has signaled a desire to retreat to the rhetoric of Maoist ideology on social and political issues. At its sixth annual plenum, the party endorsed a resolution to tighten its grip on ideology and social control as part of a broad-ranging crusade to revive traditional socialist values. It ordered government agencies, social institutions, and state-run enterprises to subscribe to party publications. At the same time, Xu Guanchuan, the deputy head of the Propaganda Department, called for a crackdown on unauthorized publications and the closure of any publications defying the party line. Xu's directive was a clear signal of official intolerance toward an independent press, and a reminder that the media's only role is to be the party's mouthpiece.

Feverish activity at China's nascent Shangai and Shenzhen stock markets, coupled with the dearth of economic information in the state-owned press, has fueled the growth of several independent stock market newsletters. The official daily *Renmin Ribao* carried a strident denunciation of the newsletters, blaming the wildly overheated market on their sanguine predictions.

As part of its bid to further control the distribution of information, China blocked access to a large number of Internet sites run by Chinese and English-language media outlets. The government warned the domestic media not to cover sensitive issues, such as corruption scandals involving party officials and the arrest of dissidents such as Wang Dan, who received an 11-year prison sentence for plotting to overthrow the government. They could carry only reports issued by the official Xinhua News Agency.

These developments caused consternation among the Hong Kong media, who remain fearful for the prospects for press freedom after China assumes sovereignty from Britain in July 1997. Anxiety about the future of press freedom has given rise to self-censorship among members of the Hong Kong press seeking to avoid angering the Beijing government and incurring possible repercussions after sovereignty passes to China.

March 4
Jin Zhong, *Open Magazine*, EXPELLED
Jin, the editor of the Hong Kong-based *Open Magazine*, said in a newspaper interview in Hong Kong that Chinese immigration officials had revoked his permit to enter Shenzhen, a city in mainland China near Hong Kong. Jin said he was detained by immigration police on his way to visit relatives in Shenzhen. After keeping him in a room for 90 minutes, the immigration police told him he was not welcome to return to Shenzhen. *Open Magazine*, published since 1987, is known for its critical coverage of China's policies.

March 10
Shui An-teh, Taiwan Television Enterprise (TTV), HARASSED, EXPELLED
Chuang Chi-wei, TTV, HARASSED, EXPELLED
Chinese authorities deported the TTV reporters Shui and Chuang after detaining them for two days for allegedly videotaping Chinese troops conducting military exercises in southeastern Fujian Province. According to China's official Xinhua News Agency, the two journalists signed written confessions of their wrongdoing, a usual condition of release for foreign journalists detained in China. Upon arriving in Hong Kong, however, both reporters said they were unaware that they had been taping in a restricted area and maintained that they were engaged in ordinary reporting activities. In a press release, CPJ said Shui and Chuang's detention fit a pattern of continued harassment

by China of Taiwanese journalists.

June 4
Chito Romana, ABC News, HARASSED, CENSORED
Richard Tullis, ABC News, HARASSED, CENSORED
Beijing Security Police detained ABC News producer Romana and cameraman Tullis as they drove around Beijing University, filming the campus. Romana and Tullis, who were held for two hours, were forced to erase the footage they had shot. The detention of the television journalists came on the seventh anniversary of the military assault on pro-democracy demonstrators in Tiananmen Square. The demonstrations began in the Beijing University area.

July 1
Louis Wong, *South China Morning Post,* HARASSED
Journalist, *Oriental Daily News,* HARASSED, EXPELLED
Journalist, *Hong Kong Standard,* HARASSED
Journalist, *Apple Daily,* HARASSED
Journalist, Asia Television, HARASSED
Journalist, *Hong Kong Daily News,* HARASSED
19 other journalists, HARASSED
Chinese police detained 25 journalists at Beijing's international airport, where the journalists were attempting to cover the arrival in Beijing of eight Hong Kong legislators. The legislators had planned to deliver a petition to the Chinese government protesting China's plans to scrap the elected Hong Kong Legislative Council after the July 1997 handover of Hong Kong from Britain to China.

Beijing police boarded a Dragonair flight from Hong Kong that was carrying the legislators and 12 of the 25 journalists. The police expelled all the legislators and one journalist, who works for the *Oriental Daily News* in Hong Kong.

The other journalists who were aboard the plane were allowed to disembark. But they and a number of journalists who were already in the airport to cover the legislators' trip were detained on the tarmac, at the immigration counter, or inside the airport terminal. Immigration officials forced several of the journalists to sign statements of "repentance" after the officials found that they were carrying press releases and other documents issued by the Hong Kong legislators' coalition.

July 8
Voice of Tibet (VOT), CENSORED
Chinese authorities began jamming VOT, an exiled Tibetan radio station produced in Oslo and broadcast from the Seychelles since May 14. China Radio International began occupying VOT's bandwidth with Easy FM, an English-language music service. China Radio International until July 8 had been a domestic service and had never broadcast on a short-wave frequency. To avoid the jamming, VOT July 22 started transmitting on a different short-wave frequency, and since then authorities have not attempted to disrupt the service again. Easy FM continues to be broadcast on the old VOT frequency.

Late August
CNN, CENSORED
The Washington Post, CENSORED
The New York Times, CENSORED
Wall Street Journal, CENSORED
Los Angeles Times, CENSORED
Voice of America, CENSORED
Time, CENSORED
Ming Pao, CENSORED
China Digest News, CENSORED
Chinese authorities blocked access to a number of Internet sites run by Chinese- and English-language media organizations. Among those affected were Internet sites operated by CNN, *The Washington Post, The New York Times, The Wall Street Journal, The Los Angeles Times,* Voice of America, and *Time* magazine. Several Chinese-language news sites run from outside China, including *China Digest News* and the Hong Kong-based daily newspaper *Ming Pao,*

Asia

have also been screened out. These moves followed a government announcement in February that laws against pornography, social disturbances, and state security breaches applied to the Internet, and that all Internet servers must operate through the Ministry of Posts and Telecommunications, which controls China's two gateways to the Internet.

October 30
Wang Dan, IMPRISONED, LEGAL ACTION
Wang, a former student leader, pro-democracy activist, and frequent contributor to overseas publications was sentenced to 11 years in prison for conspiring to subvert the government. He had already been in detention at an undisclosed location since May 1995. Wang's offenses consisted of publishing articles in the overseas press that were deemed objectionable by Beijing and receiving donations from overseas human rights groups. Foreign reporters were barred from the courtroom during his trial, and the domestic press was prohibited from reporting on the trial. On Nov. 10, the Beijing Higher People's Court took 10 minutes to reject his appeal. He was immediately sent to a prison in remote Jinzhou, in Liaoning province, 500 kilometers northeast of Beijing. Wang had previously been jailed for three-and-a-half years after he led pro-democracy protests in Tiananmen Square in 1989.

Fiji

When Fijian officials detained Mike Field, a New Zealand-based correspondent for Agence France-Presse (AFP), for five hours at Fiji's international airport, they told him that it was because he was on a blacklist of journalists. The revelation that the government maintains such a list was a shock, coming four years after Fiji's return from a military dictatorship to an elected government. While the government apologized to Field and admitted that it had mistakenly detained him, Minister for Home Affairs Col. Paul Manueli affirmed the existence of what he termed a "watch list" of journalists.

Fiji's government, which remains racially biased, reserving parliamentary seats for indigenous Fijians and restricting the number of seats available for ethnic Indians in Fiji, retains broad discretionary powers to impose restrictions on press freedom. While it did not invoke any of these powers to curb the press during 1996, its harassment of the *Fiji Times*—one of Fiji's two daily newspapers—and *Times* columnist Ron Gatty showed that it was willing to push members of the press into censoring themselves. In July, the government announced plans to review mass media laws, and commissioned an independent British team to present a report before Parliament. Local journalists said they were confident the report would be fair.

March 22
Fiji Times, THREATENED
The Fijian government threatened to take legal action against the *Fiji Times* to compel it to disclose sources and other information the newspaper relied on for an article about a Fijian village whose economy was based on marijuana cultivation. The government demanded that the paper reveal both the location of the village and the identities of its sources. The *Fiji Times* refused to comply. Despite its threats, the government had taken no legal action by year's end.

May 20
Ron Gatty, *Fiji Times*, HARASSED, CENSORED
The immigration department ordered Gatty, an expatriate Australian, to cease writing a weekly column for the *Fiji Times* on the grounds that his work as a journalist breached the terms of his work permit, which allows him only to manage a spice farm. Home Affairs Minister Col. Paul Manueli later reversed the decision, after Gatty supplied a declaration stating that he received no financial remuneration as a journal-

ist, and so was not violating his work permit. Colleagues in the region viewed the actions as an attempt to intimidate Gatty, whose column is often critical of the government.

May 25
Mike Field, Agence France-Presse (AFP),
HARASSED
Immigration officials detained Field, a New Zealand-based correspondent for AFP, at Fiji's Nadi international airport. The officials said Field's name was on a blacklist of journalists who had abused immigration procedures in 1990 by working without a permit. Officials released Field after five hours and allowed him to enter Fiji and remain in the country for two days. Jone Tevita, Fiji's immigration director, said on May 29 that Field had been placed on the blacklist of journalists by mistake, and a letter of apology was sent to him by the Fiji government. Field has since visited Fiji on two occasions without incident.

Hong Kong

Concerns about China's assumption of sovereignty over the colony, which will be transferred from Britain in July 1997, dominated Hong Kong's press freedom debates. As the year progressed, serious doubts arose over China's commitment to the Basic Law of Hong Kong, a set of rules negotiated with Britain for the governing of Hong Kong after the handover. The Basic Law contains a guarantee of press freedom. Lu Ping, director of the Hong Kong and Macau Affairs Office of China's State Council, announced in an interview with CNN in June that press freedom would be limited under Chinese rule. In particular, Lu said that the press would not be allowed to advocate two Chinas.

China's treatment of journalists from Hong Kong and the domestic Chinese press compounded the anxieties of the Hong Kong

media. The Chinese Public Security Bureau detained 25 journalists, many of them from Hong Kong, at the Beijing airport. The journalists were attempting to cover the arrival in Beijing of Hong Kong legislators. China's Communist Party also cracked down on dissidents and began to exert more control over mainland publications in the name of a revival of Maoist ideology, sending an ominous warning to Hong Kong's media about their prospects for press freedom in 1997.

The Hong Kong media also faced serious domestic problems. Assailants severed the left forearm of Leung Tin-wai, a veteran Hong Kong journalist, in an attack at his office two days before the scheduled debut of his new tabloid newspaper, *Surprise Weekly*. Local journalists speculated that the attack may have been organized by competitors or distributors. Organized crime groups are heavily involved in newspaper distribution.

May 15
Leung Tin-wai, *Surprise Weekly,* ATTACKED
Assailants severed the left forearm of Leung, a veteran Hong Kong journalist, in an attack at his office two days before the scheduled debut of his new tabloid newspaper, *Surprise Weekly*. Two unidentified men entered Leung's office and asked to see him. Leung led them into a conference room and shut the door behind him. Shortly afterwards, staff members heard Leung cry for help. Upon opening the conference room door, a journalist with the paper was knifed as the two assailants ran out and exited the building. Leung was immediately taken to a local hospital where doctors reattached his arm. Two 18-inch knives, apparently used in the attack, were later found on the building's first floor.

Leung had recently assumed publishing duties at *Surprise Weekly*, which faces fierce competition for readership. Local journalists told CPJ that the attack may have been organized by competitors or distributors since newspaper distribution in Hong Kong is closely

Asia

connected with organized crime groups. In a letter to Hong Kong's Gov. Christopher Patten, CPJ urged the colony's authorities to conduct a thorough investigation into the attack.

May 31
All media, THREATENED

Lu Ping, director of the Hong Kong and Macau Affairs Office of China's State Council, in an interview with CNN said that when China assumes sovereignty over Hong Kong from Great Britain in July 1997, Hong Kong's media will not be allowed to advocate independence for Hong Kong or for Taiwan. In a speech at Japan's National Press Club on June 5, he said that press freedom would be guaranteed after the transfer of sovereignty, but he drew a distinction between reporting news and advocating action. "Advocating itself is not press freedom and is different from objective reporting," Lu said.

China's information minister, Zheng Jianhui, echoed Lu's position in a July 11 interview with the *Far Eastern Economic Review*, and suggested that Hong Kong journalists follow the example of their mainland Chinese counterparts: "If [Taiwanese President] Lee Teng-hui stands up and says something, you can report it just like we do. As long as someone else says it, that's okay."

October 16
All media, THREATENED

Chinese vice premier and foreign minister Qian Qichen, in an interview with the *Asian Wall Street Journal*, said that Hong Kong's media will not be allowed to print "rumors and lies" or personal attacks on Chinese leaders after China assumes sovereignty over Hong Kong in July 1997. Qian's remarks were echoed by a local Hong Kong Xinhua news agency official, Wen Xinqiao, who said on Oct. 21 that the Hong Kong media would not be allowed to publish reports on dissidents if the reports advocated opposition to the Chinese central government or the principle of "one country, two systems,"

or made personal attacks on Chinese leaders.

India

Assaults and restrictions on journalists in regions torn by separatist wars continued to tarnish India's vaunted tradition of press freedom. And the lack of a strong central government following parliamentary elections in May allowed powerful political leaders to attack the press with virtual impunity.

Two journalists were murdered during the year in Assam and Kashmir—states that have been marked by internecine warfare between Indian troops, separatist militias, and Indian-backed counter-insurgency forces. Parag Kumar Das—editor of *Asomiya Pratidin*, the leading daily in Assam, as well as a human rights activist and outspoken proponent of self-rule for the state—was shot dead by suspected counter-insurgents in Guwahati, the state capital. In Kashmir, Ghulam Rasool Sheikh became the sixth local journalist to lose his life since the beginning of an armed uprising against Indian rule in late 1989. The editor of two minor Kashmiri newspapers, Sheikh was abducted and slain by men whom his family describe as members of an Indian-backed militia.

Parliamentary polling in Kashmir, conducted for the first time since the insurgency began, was marred by a press gag imposed by the federally appointed state government and threats from pro-Pakistan separatists. In a directive sent to local newspapers, state authorities warned of criminal prosecution of editors who published material that was "prejudicial" to the state's unity or integrity, or indicated a lack of faith in the state or federal constitutions. Following a counter-threat by the Hizb-ul-Mujahideen—the most powerful separatist group in Kashmir—to take severe measures against editors who published government statements or adver-

tisements, the local press suspended publication for two months.

The parliamentary elections themselves marked a watershed in Indian politics: the routing of the long-ruling Congress Party, after several years of steadily waning support. But the result was a precarious alliance of regional and leftist parties rent by pronounced policy disputes. A coalition government was also mandated for Uttar Pradesh, India's most populous state, after elections there produced a hung state assembly. Frenetic negotiations between parties, aimed at forming a government in Uttar Pradesh, gave politicians with important vote banks unprecedented authority. This was borne out by the federal government's inaction when Kanshi Ram, head of the Bahujan Samaj Party and a leader of India's dalits (untouchables), and several supporters assaulted a group of journalists who had gathered outside his New Delhi home, hoping to obtain an interview. Authorities refused to press criminal charges against the assailants, while police harshly suppressed subsequent protest marches by local journalists.

Regional parties also behaved with unchecked hostility toward the press. In Mumbai (formerly Bombay), more than 500 activists from the ruling Hindu nationalist Shiv Sena party attacked the offices of the Marathi-language daily *Mahanagar*, one of the few vernacular publications in the city that openly criticizes the Shiv Sena and a repeated target of organized assaults by Shiv Sena party members. Police arrested six Shiv Sena members in connection with the attack, and then released them on bail.

March 4
Aftab, ATTACKED
Al-Safa, ATTACKED
Uqab, ATTACKED
Armed men claiming to be members of the Hizb-ul-Mujahideen militant group entered a

printing plant owned by the Srinagar daily newspaper *Aftab* and ordered its operators to immediately cease printing *Aftab* and its fellow Urdu dailies *Al-Safa* and *Uqab*. Srinagar's press community responded with a solidarity strike that was lifted two days later, after Hizb-ul-Mujahideen leaders denied responsibility for the closure order. CPJ condemned the raid in a press release and called on the Indian government and separatist leaders to cooperate in identifying the assailants.

March 6
Ghulam Nabi Khayal, Pakistan Television (PTV), ATTACKED
Khayal, a correspondent for PTV, survived a grenade attack on his house in the Rawalpora area of Srinagar, Kashmir. Three unidentified armed men stormed Khayal's residential compound and ordered him to leave with them. He refused and went into the house, closing the door behind him. The assailants opened fire on the house and threw two grenades at the building before leaving the compound. One of the grenades exploded, damaging the house but causing no injuries. The following morning, police recovered and defused the second, undetonated grenade. Though police officials claimed unspecified Kashmiri separatists were responsible for the grenade attack, Khayal told colleagues that Rawalpora is heavily patrolled by Indian troops and would have been difficult for armed separatists to enter. CPJ condemned the attack in a press release and called on Indian authorities and separatist leaders to cooperate in identifying the responsible parties.

April 10
Ghulam Rasool Sheikh, *Rehnuma-e-Kashmir* and *Saffron Times,* KILLED
The body of Sheikh, an editor of the Urdu-language daily *Rehnuma-e-Kashmir* and the English-language weekly *Saffron Times*, was found floating in Kashmir's Jhelum River. Sheikh had been missing since late March, when family members say he was kidnapped by an Indian-

Asia

backed militia. Local police, however, claim that he was abducted and slain by separatist guerrillas. Prior to his death, Sheikh had spoken out against an increase in killings and arson incidents in the vicinity of his hometown, Pampur. He was also the head of an Islamic trust that is responsible for the management of shrines and mosques in the area. Sheikh's colleagues in the Kashmiri press called for a judicial inquiry into his murder. In a press release, CPJ condemned the slaying and endorsed calls by Kashmiri journalists for an official investigation into Sheikh's killing.

April 17
Kashmiri newspaper editors, CENSORED
Kashmir's federally appointed state government sent a directive to local newspaper editors, warning them that they faced criminal charges if they published statements by separatist leaders, material deemed "prejudicial to the unity and integrity of the state and the country," or articles that "directly or indirectly express lack of faith" in the state and federal constitutions. The directive, issued a month before federal elections were to be held in Kashmir, also barred "inflammatory matter likely to foment regional tension" and, in a vaguely worded provision, appeared to ban reports that would deter government employees from participating in the election process. In a press release, CPJ charged that the directive potentially encompassed any criticism of the electoral process, silenced debate over the issue of sovereignty, and undermined India's commitment to free and fair elections in Kashmir.

On April 18, the pro-Pakistan Hizb-ul-Mujahideen, Kashmir's most powerful separatist group, warned Kashmiri editors that they would be "dealt with severely" if they published government statements or advertisements in their newspapers. Responding to the threat and to the restrictions on the press introduced the previous day by the state government, newspaper editors in Srinagar, Kashmir's summer capital, shut down their publications indefinitely. On

June 18, publication resumed after editors and publishers reached an agreement with the state government and separatist groups.

May 17
Parag Kumar Das, *Asomiya Pratidin,* KILLED
Das, editor in chief of *Asomiya Pratidin,* the largest circulation daily in the northeast state of Assam, was fatally shot by unidentified gunmen in Guwahati, the state capital. Das was picking his son up from school when three men drove up in a car and opened fire on them. Das was hit at least eight times, and his 7-year-old son, Rohan, was shot in the right hand and injured. The gunmen fled the scene immediately after the shooting.

A proponent of self-rule for Assam, Das had recently published an interview with the leader of the separatist group United Liberation Front of Assam (ULFA). Das' colleagues suspect that his assassination was carried out by a splinter group of ULFA that had alleged ties to the previous administration in the state. Das was also general secretary of the Assamese human rights organization Manab Adhikar Sangram Samiti (MASS) and publisher of its monthly newsletter, *Voice of MASS.*

State police had arrested Das twice, in March 1992 and February 1993, under the National Security Law and the Terrorist and Disruptive Activities (Prevention) Act. The arrests were in connection with his human rights reporting and articles about ULFA. In December 1993, police also raided Das' office and home, seizing copies of a book he had written about Assam and manuscripts of articles he had published in *Boodhbar,* the newspaper he was then editing.

In a letter to Indian authorities, CPJ urged them to conduct a thorough and impartial investigation into Das' murder.

May 23
Tauseef Mustapha, Agence France-Presse (AFP),
ATTACKED, HARASSED
Qaisar Mirza, Associated Press (AP), ATTACKED
Troops of the Border Security Force (BSF), a

paramilitary group of the Indian army, beat AFP photographer Mustapha and AP correspondent Mirza while they were covering demonstrations against local elections in Baramulla, north of Srinagar, in the state of Kashmir. The troops smashed two of Mustapha's cameras and confiscated his film. Protestors called the elections an attempt by India to legitimize its claim to Kashmir.

May 30

Santosh Gupta, *Hindustan Times,* ATTACKED
Ravi Batra, *Indian Express,* ATTACKED
Ali Mohammad Sofi, Press Trust of India (PTI), ATTACKED
Shankar Chakraborti, *Hindu,* ATTACKED
Meraj-ud-din, Associated Press Television (APTV), ATTACKED
Prabhat Banber, Press Trust of India (PTI), ATTACKED

Six journalists: Gupta, a reporter for the *Hindustan Times*; Batra, a reporter for the *Indian Express*; Chakraborti, a reporter for the *Hindu*; Meraj-ud-din, a camera operator for APTV; and Banber and Sofi, both photographers for PTI were beaten by troops of the Border Security Force (BSF), a paramilitary group of the Indian army. The journalists were in Srinagar, Kashmir, covering demonstrations against local elections in Baramulla, a Kashmiri town north of Srinagar. Protesters called the elections an attempt by India to legitimize its claim to Kashmir.

Sofi required two stitches in the head after being struck with a rifle butt. The journalists attempted to lodge a complaint with the election commissioner, but he refused to meet with them. In response, members of the media boycotted a press conference that evening by the State Chief Secretary of Kashmir.

July 8

Fayaz Ahmed, New Delhi Television, HARASSED
Gulzar Ahmed, *Uqab,* THREATENED
Masood Ahmed, *Wadi-ki-Awaz,* THREATENED

Shujaat Bukhari, *Kashmir Times,* THREATENED
Bilal Butt, Asian News International (ANI), HARASSED
Javed Farooq, *The Pioneer, Greater Kashmir,* HARASSED
Arshad Hussein, ZeeTelevision, HARASSED
George Joseph, Business India Television (BITV), HARASSED
Fayaz Kabli, Reuters, HARASSED
Meraj-ud-din, Associated Press Television (APTV), HARASSED
Sheikh Mushtaq, Reuters, HARASSED
Tauseef Mustafa, Agence France-Presse (AFP), HARASSED
Surinder Singh Oberoi, Agence France-Presse (AFP), HARASSED
Abdul Qayoom, *Uqab,* THREATENED
Maqbool Sahil, *Chattan,* THREATENED
Afzal Shah, *Kashmir Times,* HARASSED
Zahoor Shair, *Al-Safa,* THREATENED
Amin War, *Daily Excelsior,* HARASSED
Unidentified, *Chattan,* HARASSED

Gunmen for the Indian-backed militia Jammu and Kashmir Ikhwan abducted 19 journalists who were traveling together to a press conference in the Kashmir Valley. The gunmen intercepted the journalists at Anantnag, 50 kilometers (35 miles) south of Srinagar, and took them to the Ikhwan's nearby headquarters. There, Ikhwan commander Hilal Haider threatened to kill six of the journalists who worked for Kashmiri newspapers—reporters Gulzar Ahmed and Qayoom of *Uqab*, Masood Ahmed of *Wadi-ki-Awaz*, Bukhari of the *Kashmir Times*, Shair of *Al-Safa*, and photographer Sahil of *Chattan*—unless the editors of Srinagar's eight major dailies appeared before him by noon the following day. The editors had disregarded a "ban" that Haider had ordered on their newspapers the previous week for having given the Ikhwan inadequate coverage. The editors, who were informed of the threat to kill the journalists by phone, said they would not heed the summons. Seven-and-a-half hours after the abduction, the elite Indian commando unit Rashtriya Rifles intervened and secured the

Asia

release of all 19 journalists. CPJ in a July 9 statement condemned the abduction and called for the disarming of the government-backed militias.

August 1
Ashraf Shaban, *Al-Safa*, ATTACKED, THREATENED

Shaban, editor in chief of *Al-Safa*, an Urdu-language daily published in Kashmir, was abducted by three unidentified men—one armed with a pistol—from *Al-Safa's* Srinagar offices and forced into an auto-rickshaw taxi. Shaban was taken to a private residence in the town of Chadoora, about 12 kilometers (eight miles) north of Srinagar. For nearly 24 hours, Shaban's captors repeatedly beat him and threatened him with death. They released him at the insistence of a woman whom he suspected was the landlord of the house. He then made his way back to his office in Srinagar, where he fainted and was immediately taken to a local hospital. Doctors released him later that afternoon. Local journalists speculated that an Indian-backed militia may have been involved in the kidnapping, since the place where Shaban was detained is near the base camp of one such militia.

October 25
Isar Ahmed, BiTV, ATTACKED
Maya Mirchandani, New Delhi Television, ATTACKED
Renuki Puri, *Indian Express*, ATTACKED
Anil Sharma, *Pioneer*, ATTACKED
Ashutosh Gupta, Aaj Tak Television, ATTACKED
Other journalists, ATTACKED, HARASSED

Followers of Bahujan Samaj Party (BSP) leader Kanshi Ram assaulted at least five journalists in front of Ram's home. The five were among a group of reporters who wanted to question Ram about what his party planned to do after elections for the assembly in the northern state of Uttar Pradesh proved inconclusive. An enraged Ram slapped Gupta, a correspondent for Aaj Tak Television, and called on his followers to

beat and shoot the journalists. Ram's staff and security detail—which included plainclothes members of the Delhi police—immediately attacked the reporters. Two of them were severely beaten, including Gupta and BiTV correspondent Ahmed, who was hospitalized for chest injuries. Delhi Television correspondent Mirchandani, *Indian Express* photographer Puri, and *Pioneer* photographer Sharma were also assaulted. Police made no arrests, and the Home Ministry referred the matter to the Press Council of India, which has the authority to make only nonbinding recommendations.

On Oct. 26, local journalists organized a march to the Home Ministry to protest the government's failure to take action in response to the assaults. Delhi police violently suppressed the procession. When the protesters overran barricades the officers had set up, police fired tear gas shells and used a water cannon to disperse them. Two days later, police arrested and briefly detained 300 journalists who were attempting to hold a related protest march from the Indian Newspapers Society building to Parliament House.

December 14
Mahanagar, ATTACKED
Nikhil Wagle, *Mahanagar*, HARASSED, LEGAL ACTION
Nishikant Bahaleroh, *Mahanagar*, IMPRISONED, HARASSED, LEGAL ACTION

Some 500 activists from the Hindu nationalist Shiv Sena Party, which governs Maharashtra state, stormed the offices of the Marathi-language daily *Mahanagar* in Mumbai (formerly Bombay) after the paper published critical remarks by G. R. Khairnar, a former municipal commissioner, about Shiv Sena leader Bal Thackeray. While their fellow party members demonstrated outside, a number of activists entered the editorial office of *Mahanagar* through a rear window and disconnected phone lines, damaged office equipment, and attempted to set a fire. Six of the activists who broke into *Mahanagar's* office were arrested for causing a civil disturbance. All were released on bail. The police also registered charges against two editors of *Mahanagar*. On Dec. 18, the police charged Wagle, the paper's editor in chief, with defaming political leaders and causing civil unrest. Bahaleroh, an editor at *Mahanagar*, was charged on Dec. 20 with inciting civil unrest; he was held in jail for two days. Wagle said he viewed the charges merely as a form of harassment, and did not believe that either he or Bahaleroh would face trial.

Indonesia

Mounting opposition to the ruling Golkar Party erupted in the largest wave of demonstrations and rioting in Indonesia since President Suharto's cataclysmic assumption of power three decades earlier. Indonesian journalists—already battered by the banning of three leading weeklies and the jailing and blacklisting of activists from the country's only independent journalists union—were caught in the military crackdown that followed.

A government-engineered congress in June of the Indonesian Democratic Party (PDI), one of three officially recognized political parties in Indonesia, saw the ouster of its increasingly outspoken leader, Megawati Sukarnoputri, the daughter of Indonesia's first president, Sukarno. Her supporters within the party refused to vacate the PDI headquarters in Jakarta, precipitating a month-long standoff with the authorities that culminated in the July 27 army seizure of PDI's offices. Soldiers severely beat four local journalists who were covering the seizure and subsequent protest demonstrations, while two foreign broadcast news organizations had their footage confiscated. In the weeks prior to and following the seizure, senior army officers bluntly warned Indonesian editors against criticizing

Megawati's removal or the crackdown on her supporters.

Indonesia's only independent journalists union, known as the Alliance of Independent Journalists (AJI), was a conspicuous target of government repression, as it has been since its founding in August 1994. Two AJI members—Eko Maryadi and Ahmad Taufik, who is the union's president and a CPJ 1995 International Press Freedom Award recipient—had their three-year prison terms upheld by the Supreme Court in March, despite appeals for their release that were signed by more than three hundred American journalists and media executives and presented to Indonesian officials by CPJ. Taufik, Maryadi, and a third imprisoned journalist, Tri Agus Susanto Siswowihardjo, continued to write from prison, smuggling out articles—including an interview with a fellow inmate, East Timorese leader José Alexandre (Xanana) Gusmaõ—to underground magazines. Their persistence earned them an abrupt transfer to a more isolated prison facility.

In an unusual development for Indonesia, a journalist lost his life, for reasons that his colleagues say may have been related to his reports on land disputes and government corruption in Yogyakarta. A correspondent for the Yogyakarta daily *Bernas*, Fuad Mohammad Syafruddin, died on Aug. 16 of injuries sustained in a beating by unidentified assailants three days earlier.

March 19
***Reader's Digest*,** CENSORED
The Indonesian government banned all newsstand sales of the March issue of *Reader's Digest* magazine. The ban effectively removed 10,000 copies of the monthly from newsstands; the 2,300 subscriber copies delivered via post were not affected. *Reader's Digest* editors, who learned of the ban from a Reuter wire story, received no formal notice of the censorship action from the government. A spokesman for the magazine

said he presumed the ban was a reaction to a profile in the March issue of the Roman Catholic bishop and East Timorese human-rights advocate Carlos Belo.

March 27
Ahmad Taufik, Alliance of Independent Journalists (AJI), LEGAL ACTION
Eko Maryadi, AJI, LEGAL ACTION
The Indonesian Supreme Court upheld the prison sentences of AJI president Taufik and AJI member Maryadi. The two journalists were arrested on March 16, 1995, and convicted on Sept. 1, 1995, of violating Article 19 of the Press Law, which prohibits the publication of an unlicensed newspaper or magazine, and Article 154 of the Criminal Code, which bars the expression of "feelings of hostility, hatred, or contempt toward the government." They were sentenced to 32 months in prison each—terms that were later extended to three years. The Supreme Court also upheld the 20-month sentence of Danang Kukuh Wardoyo, an AJI office assistant who was convicted on the same charges as the two journalists. CPJ expressed its dismay regarding the Supreme Court's verdict in a letter to President Suharto, and reiterated its demand for the AJI members' immediate release. Taufik is one of CPJ's 1995 International Press Freedom awardees.

June 13
Tempo, LEGAL ACTION, CENSORED
The Supreme Court upheld a June 1994 ban on the weekly magazine *Tempo,* reversing two lower court decisions that ruled in favor of *Tempo* publisher Goenawan Mohamad. Mohamad had filed suit on Oct. 7, 1994, against Information Minister Harmoko alleging that Harmoko had wrongfully revoked *Tempo*'s publishing license, forcing it to close. In banning the weekly, the Information Ministry had declared its articles about political corruption to be incompatible with a "healthy" and "responsible press." The Ministry also accused *Tempo* of failing to adhere to national press guidelines

and disregarding prior government warnings. The banning of *Tempo,* which was Indonesia's largest circulation newsmagazine at the time of its closure, prompted widespread protest demonstrations throughout the country and sparked international condemnation.

July 27
Cecek Sutriatna Sukmadipraja, *Ummat,* ATTACKED
Kemal Jufri, *Asiaweek,* ATTACKED
Associated Press Television, CENSORED
Australian Broadcasting Corp., CENSORED
Soldiers attacked two photojournalists who were covering the army's seizure of the Indonesian Democratic Party (PDI) headquarters in Jakarta. When Sukmadipraja, a photographer for the local Muslim magazine *Ummat,* refused to turn over his film, the soldiers kicked him in the groin and beat him with rattan, wood, and metal objects until he collapsed. A colleague took him to the intensive care unit of a local hospital, where he was given a blood transfusion and stitches for neck and back wounds. Another soldier hit Jufri, a free-lance photographer who strings for Hong Kong-based *Asiaweek,* on the head as Jufri tried to photograph a civilian being beaten. Jufri's attackers smashed his camera and threw it into a sewage canal. Soldiers also seized video footage belonging to Associated Press Television and the Australian Broadcasting Corp.

July 28
Subechi, *Surabaya Post,* HARASSED
Adi Sutrawijono, *Surya,* HARASSED
Subechi, a reporter for the daily *Surabaya Post,* and Sutrawijono, a photographer for the daily *Surya,* were detained at the army district command while attempting to cover a protest by Indonesian Democratic Party (PDI) supporters in Surabaya, Indonesia's second-largest city. Although Subechi and Sutrawijono identified themselves as journalists, soldiers repeatedly beat and kicked them over a three-hour period, along with 10 protesters who had been taken

into custody. They were released when two officers determined that they were journalists, giving them 50,000 rupiah (about US$20) as "uang
damai," an Indonesian gesture of resolution.

July 28
All media, THREATENED
Kompas, THREATENED
Merdeka, THREATENED
Lt. Gen. Syarwan Hamid, the head of the
sociopolitical section of the military general
staff, summoned Jakarta-based editors and
bureau chiefs to a meeting where he advised
them to support the army crackdown on supporters of ousted Indonesian Democratic Party
(PDI) leader Megawati Sukarnoputri and other
opponents of the Suharto regime. Indonesian
authorities also issued warnings to two leading
dailies—*Kompas* and *Merdeka*—for their critical
coverage of the crackdown. Since June, senior
Indonesian army officers had repeatedly delivered explicit warnings to the local press about
reporting on the conflict with Megawati loyalists.

August 16
Fuad Muhammad Syafruddin, *Bernas,* KILLED
Syafruddin, a correspondent for the Yogyakarta
daily *Bernas,* died from injuries sustained during
a beating by unidentified assailants. Two visitors
to Syafruddin's house beat him with a metal
stick on Aug. 13, inflicting serious injuries to his
head and stomach. The assailants fled on a
motorcycle immediately after the attack.
Syafruddin was transferred to the intensive care
unit of a Catholic hospital in Yogyakarta, but
never regained consciousness. He died in the
hospital three days later. Local sources speculated that Syafruddin's death may have been related to his articles on land disputes and
government corruption in Bantul, the
Yogyakarta suburb that he covered for *Bernas.*
    Indonesia's National Committee on Human
Rights in October began an investigation into
Syafruddin's death. Earlier in the month, police
in Jogyakarta arrested a suspect. However,

Syafruddin's wife reportedly claimed that the
suspect is not one of the men she saw kill her
husband, and that the suspect is a foil to deflect
blame from the guilty parties.
    CPJ wrote to President Suharto to express
alarm over the murder. The Committee called
on the Indonesian leader to order a complete
investigation into Syafruddin's death as well as
public disclosure of the investigation's findings.

August 16
Ahmad Taufik, Alliance of Independent
    Journalists (AJI), HARASSED
Eko Maryadi, AJI, HARASSED
Tri Agus Susanto Siswowihardjo, *Kabar Dari Pijar,*
    HARASSED
Authorities transferred AJI president Taufik, AJI
member Maryadi, and Tri Agus Susanto Siswowihardjo, editor of the underground newsletter *Kabar Dari Pijar,* from Jakarta's Cipinang
prison to a less accessible facility in Cirebon,
200 kilometers east of the capital. The three
journalists were awakened during the early
morning and ordered at gunpoint to pack their
belongings and vacate their jail cell. Their family members were not informed in advance of
the move, and learned of the transfer only when
they attempted to visit the journalists on Aug.
17 in Cipinang. The transfer was reportedly in
retaliation for letters and articles that the journalists had written in prison and smuggled out
to various underground publications. Among
them was an interview with a fellow prisoner at
Cipinang, East Timorese leader José Alexandre
("Xanana") Gusmaõ, which appeared in the
underground magazine *Suara Independen.* CPJ
denounced the relocation in a letter to President Suharto, and reiterated its calls for the
release of the three journalists.

October 28
Suara Independen, CENSORED
Indonesian police raided the printing house
where the monthly newsmagazine *Suara Independen* is printed. During the raid, police confiscated 5,000 copies of *Suara Independen,* and

Asia

arrested Andi Syahputra, the printing house manager, and Nasrul, a press operator. After the two were taken into custody, security forces searched Syahputra's home in central Jakarta. Syahputra and Nasrul were later charged under Articles 134 and 137 of the Indonesian Criminal Code with the distribution of printed materials defaming President Suharto. If convicted, they face up to six years in prison each.

Suara Independen, published by the Melbourne-based Society of Indonesian Alternative Media (MIPPA), is the best-known of several underground magazines that have attempted to circumvent the government licensing regime. Its predecessor, *Independen*, was published by the Alliance of Independent Journalists (AJI), which is not officially recognized. Two AJI members—Eko Maryadi and Ahmad Taufik, a winner of CPJ's 1995 International Press Freedom Award—are currently serving prison terms for their involvement with the magazine. In a letter to Suharto, CPJ demanded the release of Syahputra and Nasrul and the withdrawal of all charges against them. CPJ also reiterated its calls for the release of Taufik and Maryadi.

Malaysia

Repressive laws continued to threaten opposition journalists in Malaysia, while regional political considerations prompted the government to suppress coverage of a conference on East Timor of non-governmental organizations (NGOs).

Two laws that have encouraged self-censorship by Malaysian journalists are the Printing Presses and Publications Act (PPA) and the Internal Security Act (ISA). Under the PPA, all domestic and foreign newspapers must obtain an annually renewable publication license, which may be withdrawn without notice or legal recourse for their reinstatement. The ISA permits the government to detain suspects for up to 60 days, for renewable periods of two years, without judicial review or filing of formal charges. Nasiruddin Ali, a director of the publishing firm Karya One, which published four magazines linked to the banned Islamic movement al-Arqam—*Tatih, O.K!, Ayu,* and *Dunia Baru*—was detained in May under Section 8 of the ISA with no indication of when he may be released, and no charges made public. Following Ali's arrest, Tamrin Ghafar, the publisher of *Tatih, O.K.!, Ayu,* and *Dunia Baru* indefinitely suspended publication of the four magazines in June.

Prime Minister Mahathir Mohamad's belief that economic development must take precedence over personal freedoms was made dramatically evident in early November. To avert souring relations with its trading partner Indonesia—which invaded East Timor in 1975—the government closed the Asia Pacific Conference on East Timor II (APCET II) in Kuala Lumpur by variously arresting or deporting more than 100 participants. Ten journalists were among those local participants detained and charged with illegal assembly and refusing to disperse, after 200 members of the youth wing of the ruling United Malays National Organisation (UMNO) stormed the conference room.

Ownership of all the major newspapers and radio and television stations is in the hands either of the government, or of leading political figures. The result is that there is little independent press and little critical coverage of government officials and government policies—although, in a dramatic departure with tradition, several mainstream publications criticized the government's handling of the APCET II conference.

Deputy Prime Minister Anwar Ibrahim, a likely candidate to succeed Mahathir, sounded an optimistic note for press freedom in September at the opening of a Chinese-language Malaysian newspaper, *Nanyang Siang Pau*. Anwar advocated a loosening of restrictions on the media and told journalists present, "We should have more confidence in our society's maturity in making objective assessments."

January 2
Patrick Teoh, Radio 4, CENSORED
Radio 4, CENSORED
The Radio 4 talk show program "Rhythm of the Nation" was taken off the air after Teoh, its host, discussed a case of alleged police bribery with a caller. After hearing Teoh's on-air comments, the head of the federal traffic-police agency lodged a complaint against him in Kuala Lumpur on Jan. 6, alleging defamation. Teoh's radio program remained off the air while police investigated the complaint.

May 6
Nasiruddin Ali, Karya One, IMPRISONED
Nasiruddin, a director of the publishing firm Karya One, which published four magazines linked to the banned Islamic movement al-Arqam—*Tatih, O.K!, Ayu,* and *Dunia Baru*—was arrested and imprisoned, at the Kemunting Detention Center in Perak. The magazines were suspended on June 4.

Authorities detained Ali for the 60-day period allowed under section 73(1) of the Internal Security Act (ISA), then on July 7 invoked section 8 of the ISA, which allows up to two years' imprisonment without trial. The charges against Nasiruddin have not been made public. However, the pro-government daily *New Straits Times* reported in May that Nasiruddin had been arrested along with three other Al-Arqam members for attempting to revive the activities of the sect, which the government banned in 1994 for allegedly deviating from true Islamic teachings.

June 4
Tatih, CENSORED
O.K!, CENSORED
Ayu, CENSORED
Dunia Baru, CENSORED
Tamrin Ghafar, the publisher of *Tatih, O.K!,*

Ayu, and *Dunia Baru,* all of which are magazines linked to the banned al-Arqam Islamic movement, suspended publication of the four magazines for an indefinite period. Tamrin acted after the government renewed its crackdown on the al-Arqam movement. Fourteen former members of Al-Arqam have been arrested under Section 8 of the Internal Security Act, which allows up to two years' imprisonment without trial.

November 9
Sonny Inbaraj, *The Nation,* IMPRISONED, LEGAL ACTION
Roger Mitton, *Asiaweek,* IMPRISONED, LEGAL ACTION
Catherine McGrath, Australian Broadcasting Corp., IMPRISONED, LEGAL ACTION
Mohamed Raslan, *Night and Day,* IMPRISONED, LEGAL ACTION
Jaqueline Ann Surin, *The Star,* IMPRISONED, LEGAL ACTION
Steve Gan, *The Sun,* IMPRISONED, LEGAL ACTION
Premesh Chandran, *The Sun,* IMPRISONED, LEGAL ACTION
Sheryll Stothard, *The Sun,* IMPRISONED, LEGAL ACTION
Sharaad Khuttan, Free-lancer, IMPRISONED, LEGAL ACTION
Debbie Stothard, Free-lancer, IMPRISONED, LEGAL ACTION
Ten journalists—Inbaraj, a reporter for *The Nation* of Bangkok; Mitton, a Malaysia-based correspondent for *Asiaweek*; McGrath, a Singapore-based correspondent for the Australian Broadcasting Corp.; Raslan, a correspondent for *Night and Day* of Kuala Lumpur; Surin, a correspondent for *The Star* of Kuala Lumpur; Gan, Chandran, and Sheryll Stothard of Kuala Lumpur's *The Sun*; and free-lancers Khuttan and Debbie Stothard—were arrested and detained in Kuala Lumpur 27 hours or longer. They were charged under Section 27A(1c) of the Malaysian Police Act with illegal assembly and refusing to disperse.

Asia

171

If convicted, they face a fine of 2,000-10,000 ringgits (US$800-US$4,000) and/or a one-year prison term. Police also arrested 48 local participants in the Second Asia Pacific Conference on East Timor (APCET II), held in Kuala Lumpur. The arrests occurred after 200 members of the youth wing of the ruling United Malays National Organization (UMNO) stormed the conference room, destroying property and threatening conference participants.

Before the conference Deputy Home Affairs Minister Datuk Megat Junid Megat Ayob summoned senior local media officials to a closed-door meeting Nov. 6 and attempted to discourage them from covering APCET II. CPJ condemned the arrests and called on the government to drop all charges against the journalists.

North Korea

While North Korea remained resolutely closed to the outside world, the state-run Korean Central News Agency (KCNA) took the unprecedented step of opening an Internet site that offered foreign audiences Pyongyang's unique perspective on world affairs. Using a fast Internet gateway in Japan, the KCNA site appeared aimed at countering international media focus on near-famine conditions in North Korea. The site also depicted labor unrest in Seoul, South Korea, as evidence of solidarity among workers in the two Koreas.

Pakistan

The dramatic deterioration in press freedom conditions that began in 1995 when ethnic and sectarian violence in urban centers worsened and then-Prime Minister Benazir Bhutto's Pakistan People's Party started to impose bans on media outlets, continued throughout 1996. President Farooq Ahmad Khan Leghari on Nov. 5, 1996, abruptly dismissed the Bhutto administration from office because of accusations against the administration of rampant corruption and economic mismanagement. Leghari formalized the army's role in government by creating a 10-member Council for Defense and National Security on Jan. 6, 1997, causing concern among many local human rights groups that Pakistan could revert to authoritarian rule.

Many of the press freedom abuses were centered in the city of Karachi, where the Sindh provincial government vies for control with the Mohajir Qaumi Movement (MQM), an armed group that draws support from the descendants of Urdu-speaking Indian immigrants. Clouding the picture is a breakaway faction of the MQM, as well as sectarian groups that have pitted the city's Sunni and Shi'a Muslim communities against each other. Pakistani intelligence agency personnel seized Sheikh Aziz, an editor at the English-language daily *Dawn*, outside his residence in Karachi and detained him for more than 20 hours. In a separate incident, four armed men in a vehicle bearing Sindh government license plates beat and attempted to abduct Aftab Syed, an editor of the English-language daily *The News*, from his Karachi home.

Press conditions were even worse in the rural areas of Pakistan, where journalists encountered unchecked abuses of power by local governments and feudal lords who act with virtual impunity. The federal government effectively sanctioned and facilitated local authorities' intimidation of journalists by introducing an ordinance that allowed provincial governments to use army and paramilitary rangers for law and order purposes, including arrest and interrogation.

In a case typical of dangers journalists face in rural areas, police and others severely beat Monis Bokhari, a reporter for the daily *Sindh* in Dokri, after he reported that a member of the Sindh provincial government had illegally purchased land belonging to the Sindh Forest Department. Elsewhere in Sindh Province, men employed by a local landlord kidnapped and sexually assaulted Mumtaz Sher, a correspondent for the daily *Bakhtar*, after his newspaper published an article about alleged misconduct by a school administrator who is also the landlord's wife.

July 23
Zahid Ali Qaimkhani, Pakistan Press
    International (PPI), *Sindh Sujhag, Barsat,*
    IMPRISONED
Qaimkhani, a correspondent for the private news agency PPI as well as the Sindhi-language dailies *Sindh Sujhag* and *Barsat*, was sentenced to five years in prison after being convicted of an arson attack on the telephone exchange in Kandiaro, in Sindh province. He was jailed immediately. In reaching the verdict, the court disregarded a note written by the magistrate of the Naushehro Feroze district to the public prosecutor saying that he had found no evidence linking Qaimkhani to the arson attack. Qaimkhani had been arrested for the attack on Jan. 22, after the official in charge of the Kandiaro telephone exchange filed a complaint against him. At that time, he was held for five days and then released on bail. Before his arrest, Qaimkhani had written articles alleging that certain local officials were corrupt. Qaimkhani was released from Sukkur jail on Jan. 21, 1997, after the Sindh High Court overturned the judgment of the lower court on appeal.

Papua New Guinea

Press freedom conditions in Papua New Guinea stood at a crossroad at year's end.

The country's small but largely independent media face serious threats from two proposed media bills, introduced in parliament in December, which the government hopes to swiftly pass.

The Media Commission Bill requires all journalists and media organizations to register annually. Unregistered journalists face fines of K1,000 (US$760) for a first offense and K2,000 (US$1,520) for subsequent offenses; unregistered media organizations face fines of up to K10,000 (US$7,600) while their directors face fines of up to K5,000 (US$3,800) and four years' imprisonment. A nine-member media commission, to be appointed by the head of state, has the power to refuse or renew an application for registration. A second draft law, the National Information and Communication Authority Bill, contains libel provisions that would force journalists to reveal their sources or face punishment, with no possibility of appeal.

According to the government of Prime Minister Sir Julius Chan, these measures are meant to "make the media more accountable to the government." But local journalists suspect that the new measures are intended to muzzle the media before national elections in 1997. Tellingly, the bills' framers looked to their neighbors in East Asia for models of repressive legislation. Ben Micah, the chair of the Constitutional Review Committee (CRC), which drew up the draft media laws, preceded the bills' introduction with a study tour of China, Malaysia, Singapore, and Indonesia—countries which possess particularly restrictive press laws.

Both the continued armed secessionist struggle on the island of Bougainville and serious crime problems on the mainland curtailed press freedom. Journalists were denied access to Bougainville, where a mid-year military operation by the Papua New Guinea Defense Forces failed to bring an end to the seven-year conflict on the island. And law-

and-order issues so dominated the government's agenda that officials imposed a curfew in Papua New Guinea's three main cities—Port Moresby, Lae, and Mount Hagen.

June 28
Benny Malaisa, EMTV, ATTACKED
Eiwana Kila, EMTV, ATTACKED
Police attacked Malaisa and Kila, camera operators for the Port Moresby station EMTV, while they were covering a student protest at the Waigani campus of the University of Papua New Guinea (UPNG). Six policemen kicked and punched Malaisa as he filmed police beating and arresting students. Malaisa sustained bruising, and his video camera was knocked to the ground and damaged. A police officer slapped Kila, who was acting as Malaisa's driver, in the face when he attempted to assist Malaisa. Deputy Commissioner of Police Luwick Kembu announced that an investigation would be conducted into the police actions at UPNG, in which police reportedly fired tear gas and live ammunition. No action had been taken by year's end.

Philippines

The level of press freedom in the Philippines, like the character of the press itself, varied widely by locale. Manila, the capital, has a flourishing press with approximately 25 daily newspapers, and reporters there operate in an environment largely free from government interference. In rural areas outside Manila, however, where radio is the dominant medium because of an undeveloped infrastructure and high illiteracy rate, the military, powerful local families who maintain feudal-like control of the areas, large corporations, and the government subjected reporters to serious abuses. Working conditions for journalists were particularly grim in the southern island

of Mindanao, where the Muslim separatist Moro National Liberation Front (MNLF) has been waging a violent struggle for autonomy.

The MNLF signed a peace agreement with the government in September, but the accord has yet to be implemented and fighting continues. Reporters are often caught between the interests of Muslim separatists, Christian groups opposed to an independent Muslim state, and government forces. Ferdinand Reyes, who frequently wrote about official corruption and human rights abuses in the Philippines, was shot and killed at his office in Dipolog, Mindanao. Two local reporters, Ali Macabalang and Nash Maulana, were shot in Cotabato, Mindanao, while traveling in a jeep near Macabalang's home.

February 13
Ferdinand Reyes, *Press Freedom,* KILLED
Reyes, editor in chief of the weekly newspaper *Press Freedom,* was shot in the head by an unidentified gunman as he sat at his office desk in Dipolog, about 425 miles south of Manila. The gunman then fled with an accomplice on a motorcycle. An attorney as well as a journalist, Reyes frequently wrote columns about official corruption and human rights abuses in the Philippines. He had also organized demonstrations against government policies that he considered unfair, such as the expansion of the value-added tax. Reyes had reportedly received death threats in the past, in response to his articles and activities. In a letter sent to the Philippine government the day after Reyes' assassination, CPJ called for a prompt and thorough investigation.

March 20
Ali Macabalang, Reuters, ATTACKED
Nash Maulana, *Philippine Daily Inquirer,*
ATTACKED
A gunman shot Macabalang, a stringer for Reuters, and Maulana, a correspondent for the *Philippine Daily Inquirer,* the country's largest

daily newspaper, as they sat in Macabalang's car in the southern city of Cotabato. Macabalang sustained a neck wound, while Maulana was shot twice in the leg. Macabalang, who also heads the media affairs division of the government of the Autonomous Region of Muslim Mindanao, appears to have been the intended victim in the attack, which occurred less than 200 yards from his home. He escaped more serious injury by accelerating the car as the gunman approached. Following the attack, the assailant fled on foot. Both men were taken to a nearby clinic for treatment. Cotabato lies in a region of Mindanao where Islamic rebel groups have been waging a violent campaign for self-rule.

December 15
Roberto Berbon, DZMM, KILLED
Berbon, a senior editor for the radio station DZMM, which is owned by the largest television and radio network in the Philippines, ABS-CBN, was shot and killed. At least two unidentified gunmen, armed with an automatic rifle and a pistol, fired several shots at Berbon in front of his house in Imus, 16 kilometers south of Manila. A stray bullet also wounded Berbon's wife, Sabrina, in her right thigh. The assailants fled immediately after the shooting, driving off in a waiting car. No motive has been established for the murder, but local media speculate that it may be linked to Berbon's leadership of an anticrime organization. CPJ, which is continuing to look into the case, called on the Filipino government to vigorously investigate Berbon's slaying and to publicly disclose its findings.

South Korea

The South Korean government appeared content to allow the continued growth of a free press that began after South Korea's return to elected civilian rule in 1993, after three decades of successive military-backed governments, and made few overt attempts to stem critical reporting. One notable exception was the Justice Ministry's refusal in February to renew the visa of *Australian Financial Review* correspondent Bruce Cheesman, who had written an unflattering biography of President Kim Young Sam, as well as several articles that were critical of Kim. In an effort to control coverage of North Korea, Kim's government announced in September that it would begin strictly enforcing the National Security Law (NSL), which provides for prison terms of up to seven years for those who "praise" or "benefit" North Korea, or engage in other ill-defined "antistate" activities. The announcement followed a massive police crackdown on left-leaning students at Seoul's Yonsei University.

February 14
Bruce Cheesman, *Australian Financial Review,* EXPELLED
The South Korean Justice Ministry refused to renew the visa of *Australian Financial Review* correspondent Cheesman, ending his nine years as a reporter in South Korea. Although the official reason for the denial was that Cheesman had breached the conditions of earlier visas, an Information Ministry official said in an interview with the British magazine *The Economist* that Cheesman's writing "sometimes went beyond the boundary of sound journalistic reporting." South Korean government officials privately told the foreign press that Cheesman had angered high-ranking officials by writing critical articles about President Kim Young Sam, as well as an unflattering biography of the president. For the past 14 months, South Korean authorities had issued Cheesman three-month visas, requiring him to leave the country every three months to apply for a new one.

Sri Lanka

Elected in 1994 on a platform that expressly included support for press freedom, the People's Alliance (PA) government continues to use the country's protracted ethnic civil war as a pretext to curb the media through emergency regulations and extra-legal devices. President Chandrika Kumaratunga has threatened the press in public speeches, while defamation suits against newspapers that have criticized Kumaratunga drag on in the courts.

Despite the miltary's success at the end of 1995 in retaking the northern city of Jaffna, a stronghold of the separatist Liberation Tigers of Tamil Eelam (LTTE), the ethnic civil war continues. The government used the continuing conflict as an excuse to reimpose censorship of coverage of all military and police affairs as part of a new round of emergency regulations which it issued on April 4. Whited-out words and paragraphs replaced with "censored" punctuated stories in Sri Lankan newspapers. Although the government lifted the censorship regime on Oct. 8, it retained tight control over press access to war zones in the north and east.

Appealing to the emergency regulations, authorities detained and questioned four Danish journalists for four days before expelling them on November 13. The four had traveled to Sri Lanka to report on the treatment of Chitra Rajendran, a Tamil woman who was refused asylum in Denmark and deported. The government claimed Rajendran had links to the LTTE.

In early April, President Kumaratunga issued a pointed threat to the media at a public rally in Nittambuwa. She warned that "newspapers which persist in publishing irresponsible and false material detrimental to the war effort and to the Security Forces will have to be closed down." She went on to declare, in unusually florid language, that "what these newspapers enjoy is not press freedom but freedom of the wild ass." She singled out two articles—published more than a year prior to her speech, in the English language daily *The Island* and the Singhalese-language *Divaina*—that reported soldiers in northern army camps lacked food and speculated over the main purpose of a state visit to India by President Kumaratunga. Defamation cases that the government's criminal investigation department brought against the *Sunday Leader* and the *Sunday Times* for reporting on the president's late-night appearance at a legislator's birthday party moved at a glacial pace, with no resolution in sight at year's end.

April 11
Maharaja Broadcasting Corporation (MBC), CENSORED
Sugi Senadheera, MBC, LEGAL ACTION
Ranjan Amerasinghe, MBC, LEGAL ACTION
The Media Ministry ordered Colombo-based MBC to suspend news broadcasts on its Singhalese- and English-language stations. The ban came as a result of an erroneous news bulletin on Singhalese-language Sirasa FM, one of MBC's radio stations, announcing that the government had just declared a national curfew. The government had in fact broadened its state of emergency regulations to cover the entire nation but had not declared a curfew.

Sirasa FM reportedly issued a correction seven minutes after the erroneous broadcast. In retaliation for the mistake, the government shut down not only Sirasa FM but also MBC's English-language radio station, Yes-FM. The ban on Yes-FM was lifted a few days later, and the ban on Sirasa FM was lifted on May 11. Two MBC journalists, Senadheera and Amerasinghe, were charged after the incident with slandering the government and broadcasting false news. At a hearing on June 6 both were ordered to surrender their passports and report monthly to the Criminal Investigation Department.

April 19
All media, CENSORED

The government imposed Emergency Regulation No. 1, which applied to coverage of military and police affairs, as part of a nationwide state of emergency announced on April 4. The regulation banned the printing, publication, distribution, and transmission of all military and police information by both local and foreign media. In practice, however, the ban has been enforced only on local media. The ban coincided with the launch of the government's military offensive, Riviresa II, against the Liberation Tigers of Tamil Eelam (LTTE) on the Jaffna peninsula in the north. Deputy Defense Minister Gen. Anuruddha Ratwatte on Oct. 8 announced that the ban was lifted.

August 4
All media, THREATENED

President Chandrika Kumaratunga, in a public speech in Nittambuwa, threatened to close down newspapers that she said hindered the war effort by misreporting the conflict between government forces and the rebel Liberation Tigers of Tamil Eelam (LTTE). Kumaratunga warned that "newspapers which persist in publishing irresponsible and false material detrimental to the war effort and to the security forces will have to be closed down." Kumaratunga singled out two articles published over a year ago in the English-language *The Island* and the Singhalese-language *Divaina*, both of which belong to the Upali press group, as examples of misreporting. She commented that "what these newspapers enjoy is not press freedom but freedom of the wild ass."

November 13
Jens Moellor, TV 2, IMPRISONED, EXPELLED
Ole Hoff-Lund, *Berlingske Tidende*, IMPRISONED, EXPELLED
Morten Jastrup, *Information*, IMPRISONED, EXPELLED
Nis Olsen, *Politiken*, IMPRISONED, EXPELLED
Four Danish journalists—Moellor, of the Danish national television station TV 2; and Hoff-Lund, Jastrup, and Olsen, all reporters with Copenhagen-based dailies—were expelled from Sri Lanka after being detained and questioned for four days by the Sri Lankan police. Moeller, Hoff-Lund, Jastrup, and Olsen had traveled to Sri Lanka to report on the treatment of a Tamil woman, Chitra Rajendran, who had been deported to Sri Lanka after Denmark refused to grant her asylum.

Sri Lankan police took the four journalists into custody on Nov. 9 under the prevailing Emergency Regulations, and detained them at the Beachway Hotel in the Mount Lavinia area of Colombo until their expulsion. While they were at the Beachway, the police searched their rooms at other hotels where they had been staying. The Sri Lankan Foreign Ministry said it expelled Moeller, Hoff-Lund, Jastrup, and Olsen because they failed to obtain press accreditation from the Department of Information.

Asia

Taiwan

Despite dramatic improvements in press freedom conditions in recent years, Taiwan's ruling Kuomintang (KMT) continues to limit critical coverage of the party, relying on lawsuits and a license regime to achieve that objective. Although the government granted a license to Taiwan's first private television network in 1995, the station's owners have yet to meet a requirement to raise a prohibitively high amount of capital. The requirement ensured that broadcast coverage of Taiwan's presidential election campaign in early 1996 was weighted in favor of the incumbent president, the KMT's Lee Teng-hui.

Taiwan's pirate radio stations, which are overwhelmingly critical of the KMT, no longer face massive police raids as they did through early 1995, but the most popular of those

stations—Voice of Taiwan—remains mired in legal battles. The High Court in late 1996 overturned an eight-month prison sentence imposed on Hsu Rong-chi, the station's owner and operator, for breaching the Parade and Assembly Law, but placed him on a five-year probation. Hsu's alleged offense was inciting taxi drivers to protest an increase in car insurance fees by massing in front of the Ministry of Finance. Hsu also faces a separate charge of breaching the Parade and Assembly Law for inciting a demonstration against electricity shortages in front of President Lee's house.

In a move supported by senior members of the KMT, Lui Tai-ying, director of the KMT's Business Management Committee, filed a libel suit in November against Ying Chan and Hsieh Chung-liang over an article in *Yazhou Zhoukan* (Asia Weekly), a Hong Kong-based Chinese-language newsweekly. The suit elicited objections from CPJ, other press freedom groups, and prominent U.S. journalists and news organizations, but it remained on the docket at year's end.

November 7
Ying Chan, Free-lancer, LEGAL ACTION
Hsieh Chung-liang, *Yazhou Zhoukan,*
    LEGAL ACTION
Lui Tai-ying, director of the Business Management Committee of Taiwan's ruling Kuomintang, filed a criminal libel suit against Chan, an American journalist who writes for the *Daily News* of New York, and Hsieh, senior editor of the Hong Kong-based *Yazhou Zhoukan* (Asia Weekly). The suit stemmed from an article in the Oct. 25 edition of *Yazhou Zhoukan* that alleged that during an August 1995 meeting with former White House staffer Mark Middleton, Lui had offered to donate US$15 million to the Democratic National Committee for U.S. President Clinton's re-election campaign.

If convicted, Chan and Hsieh face up to two years in jail. Lui's decision to sue the reporters has been defended by senior members of the Kuomintang. CPJ sent a letter to President Lee Teng-hui condemning the use of seditious libel suits and calling on his government to openly dissociate itself from Lui's suit. CPJ also urged Lee to ensure that no government or Kuomintang resources are used in the suit.

Thailand

Press freedom conditions in Thailand deteriorated dramatically, albeit temporarily, along with the plummeting fortunes of former Prime Minister Banharn Silpa-Archa and his Chart Thai Party mid-year. Banharn frequently accused the media of biased coverage and blamed them for his government's troubles, including allegations of corruption and incompetence. He also attempted to stifle reports critical of his performance. Parliament in September dismissed Banharn, who had held office only since July 1995, after the second of two no-confidence votes. Voters elected Chavalit Yongchaiyudh as the new prime minister.

When the press reported that the government had adjourned the first no-confidence vote before Parliament could reach a decision, authorities sent warning letters to six newspapers, claiming they had made inappropriate statements in their coverage. Officials also banned some radio and television programs, and applied pressure to have journalists dismissed. Boonradom Jitdon of the military-run Channel 5 lost his post as news chief after producing a segment that reportedly displeased Banharn. And the government-run Channel 11 dropped Chirmsak Pinthong's weekly political program, "Moon Tang Moon," after Chirmsak questioned Banharn about his controversial cabinet appointments.

Working conditions for the press improved markedly after Banharn's ouster, but journalists still face substantial obstacles in Thailand. Despite the country's return to democratic rule in 1992 from military dictatorship, the military continues to wield substantial influence over Thai politics—exerted in part through its control of much of the broadcast media. Radio and television stations in Thailand are government-licensed, and operated primarily by the government and the military. In one case, military officials pressured three television stations to dismiss reporters for questioning the legality and ethics of the military's purchase of armored cars from a French company.

Tonga

Tonga has a fledgling media system, with a small number of weekly or monthly newspapers and newsletters, and one government-owned radio station. The Tongan government—a constitutional monarchy in which the king, the nobility, and a few prominent commoners dominate political life—has repeatedly shown its intolerance of any criticism of authority or suggestions of democratic reform by the media.

Filokalafi 'Akua'ola, the deputy editor of *Taimi 'o Tonga*, received an 18-month suspended prison sentence for publishing letters critical of Minister for Police Clive Edwards. And 'Akua'ola and *Taimi 'o Tonga* editor Kalafi Moala, along with 'Akilisi Pohiva, a member of Parliament and pro-democracy leader, were each sentenced to 30 days in prison for contempt of Parliament. Pohiva's publication of the bimonthly newsletter *Kele'a* has garnered a string of libel cases.

February 23
Filokalafi 'Akau'ola, *Taimi 'o Tonga,* IMPRIS-
ONED, LEGAL ACTION
'Akau'ola, deputy editor of the weekly *Taimi 'o Tonga,* which is published in Auckland, New

Zealand, and distributed in Tonga, was arrested after the newspaper published letters to the editor on Feb. 21 that were deemed insulting to Tongan Minister of Police Clive Edwards. 'Akau'ola was charged with inciting violence against an officer of the government under Section 57 of the Tongan Criminal Code. 'Akau'ola was released on bail after two days in custody. On April 17, he was convicted and given an 18-month suspended prison sentence.

July 16
Mike Field, Agence France Presse (AFP),
CENSORED
Police Minister Clive Edwards, who is in charge of immigration matters, denied Field's written request to enter Tonga, claiming that Field, a New Zealand-based correspondent for AFP, had referred to the king of Tonga as a baboon. Edwards failed to substantiate his claim but warned Field that if he entered Tonga he would be charged with defamation, a criminal offense.

Field had applied for permission to attend the Pacific Islands News Association (PINA) convention from Aug. 6-9. Tonga normally permits journalists to enter freely without obtaining visas in advance. But after Field did a series of reports in 1993 on Tonga's pro-democracy movement and the sale of Tongan passports in Asia, then-police minister Noble 'Akau 'Ola informed him that he would have to apply in advance whenever he wished to visit Tonga.

September 20
Kalafi Moala, *Taimi 'o Tonga,* IMPRISONED
Filokalafi 'Akau'ola, *Taimi 'o Tonga,*
IMPRISONED
Moala, editor, and 'Akau'ola, deputy editor of the weekly *Taimi 'o Tonga* (Times of Tonga), published in Auckland, New Zealand, and distributed in Tonga, were sentenced to 30 days in prison for contempt of Parliament. The two were convicted of libeling the legislative assembly under Article 70 of the Tongan constitution. The charge stemmed from their Sept. 4 publication of the text of an impeachment motion

against Justice Minister Tevita Tupor before it was tabled in Parliament. 'Akilisi Pohiva, the member of Parliament who had drafted the motion and provided a copy of it to *Taimi 'o Tonga*, was also found guilty of contempt of Parliament and sentenced to 30 days in prison.

Moala, 'Akau'ola, and Pohiva were released from prison Oct. 14 after serving 24 days of their prison term. Nigel Hampton, chief justice of the Tongan Supreme Court, ruled that the legislative assembly had breached several constitutional provisions in convicting the three men of contempt of Parliament, and ordered their immediate release.

Vietnam

A CPJ delegation—consisting of board members Peter Arnett and Rick MacArthur, as well as Vikram Parekh, CPJ's program coordinator for Asia—visited Vietnam and Cambodia in September 1996 for a series of breakthrough discussions with senior government officials and local journalists about press freedom conditions. The delegation's findings in Vietnam are covered extensively in a special report on p. 183. (See also Cambodia, p. 155.)

Vietnam's Communist Party Congress in June left the country in a holding pattern. The Congress reinstated Vietnam's ruling triumvirate—General Secretary Do Muoi, President Le Doc Auh, and Prime Minister Vo Van Kiet—for another five-year term, ending months of political tension leading up to the Congress that reflected a major struggle between hard-liners and reformists. The government in 1995 jailed dissidents for their writings and launched an official campaign against "social evils," a euphemism for Western cultural influences. In the end, neither conservatives nor reformists had enough political strength to gain a decisive advantage over their rivals, and Vietnam was left with the status quo, a careful balancing act of regional, institutional, and ideological interests. The regime is sticking with its formula of limited economic liberalization coupled with stringent controls on civil liberties.

For local and foreign journalists in Vietnam, this means the continued risk of breaching the ill-defined boundaries of acceptable reporting. Three state-owned newspapers were investigated for allegedly disclosing state secrets in their coverage of business deals between Vietnam and foreign corporations. Officials ordered correspondent Adam Schwarz of the *Far Eastern Economic Review* to leave Vietnam in November. And Ly Chandara, an ethnic Vietnamese journalist who edited and published an anti-Hanoi newspaper in Phnom Penh, Cambodia, was expelled from Cambodia to Vietnam, then imprisoned there for seven months. Chandara returned to Cambodia after being released.

The three dissident writers who were jailed in 1995—Do Trung Hieu, Hoang Minh Chinh, and Nguyen Xuan Tu—were all released in mid- and late 1996 after serving their terms.

March 9
Ly Chandara, *Tu Do,* IMPRISONED
Chandara, the editor of *Tu Do* (Freedom), an anti-Communist Vietnamese-language newspaper published in Phnom Penh, was expelled by Cambodian authorities to Vietnam. He was among several dozen ethnic Vietnamese opponents of Hanoi—very loosely affiliated with one another, and collectively termed the "Tu Do Movement"—whom the Cambodian government expelled or threatened with expulsion between December 1995 and December 1996. Chandara was taken into custody at the Vietnamese border and incarcerated in Vietnam for seven months. He was released on Oct. 10 and immediately repatriated to Cambodia, after promising Vietnamese officials that he would not conspire against Vietnam or engage in any

other political activity. However, Chandara said in late January 1997 that he was seeking permission from the Cambodian government to relaunch *Tu Do*. Human rights activists in Phnom Penh had questioned Cambodia's authority to expel Chandara, citing as evidence of his Cambodian citizenship a voter registration card in his name for Cambodia's U.N.-supervised elections in 1993.

July
Hanoi Moi, HARASSED
Tien Phong, HARASSED
Kinh Doanh Van Phap Luat, HARASSED
The Interior Ministry began investigations of three newspapers, the daily *Hanoi Moi* (New Hanoi) and weeklies *Tien Phong* (Pioneer) and *Kinh Doanh Van Phap Luat* (Business and Law), for allegedly disclosing state secrets. All three newspapers are published by Communist Party or state organizations. In March, *Hanoi Moi*'s Sunday edition reported that Vietnam Airlines lost US$7.2 million when the Dutch aircraft manufacturer Fokker went bankrupt because under the airline's contract with Fokker, cash payments to the manufacturer were nonrefundable. *Tien Phong* and *Kinh Doanh Van Phap Luat* published articles in May and June suggesting that the state-owned Vietnam Oil and Gas Corp. was making excessive concessions to Broken Hill Proprietary Co., an Australian mining company that was attempting to renegotiate a production-sharing contract for an offshore oil field. Vietnam's criminal code prescribes prison terms of up to 15 years for intentionally disclosing state secrets, but does not define what constitutes a secret.

August 22
Nguyen Xuan Tu (Ha Si Phu), Free-lancer,
    IMPRISONED, LEGAL ACTION
A Hanoi court imposed a one-year prison sentence on Tu, a biologist and dissident writer whose pen name is Ha Si Phu, for violating Article 92 of the Criminal Code, a national security provision that outlaws possessing or divulging "state secrets." Tu received credit for time already served, and was released in December 1996.

Police had arrested Tu at his home in Dalat on Dec. 5, 1995. Two days later, they searched his house and confiscated thousands of pages of documents and manuscripts, including two issues of *Thien Chi*, a monthly Vietnamese-language journal published in Germany that had reprinted some of Tu's essays. Earlier in 1995, he had written an essay in which he called Marxism-Leninism an outdated relic that was harmful to the country's economic reforms. In a Dec. 4, 1995, radio interview on a California station, he called on Vietnamese-Americans to lobby the United States to withhold most-favored-nation trading status for Vietnam until that country's democracy was "well developed."

September 9
Dylan Martinez, Reuters, ATTACKED
Police severely beat Reuters photographer Martinez as he attempted to photograph a demonstration by market women in Hanoi. The demonstration, held outside the Hanoi city government offices, involved about 70 vendors who were protesting conditions imposed by the managers of a newly reopened market. A busload of police arrived while Martinez was photographing the demonstrators. As he walked away, a dozen policemen surrounded him, threw him to the ground, and repeatedly kicked and punched him. He was then thrown into a van, where police again kicked him, and taken to the local police station. Before being released, Martinez was forced to destroy seven rolls of unexposed film and sign a statement acknowledging that the incident was his fault.

October 31
Adam Schwarz, *Far Eastern Economic Review*,
    EXPELLED
Schwarz, the Hanoi-based Vietnam correspondent for the *Far Eastern Economic Review*, was expelled from Vietnam after the government refused to renew his visa. Schwarz's expulsion

followed heavy censorship of the magazine in
the last year, in which government authorities
blacked out articles, glued pages together, and
cut out articles from copies circulated in Vietnam. The censored material included an obituary of the late foreign minister, Le Mai, and a
special section on trade and investment in Vietnam. Despite Schwarz's expulsion, the magazine's Hanoi office remained open, and *Far
Eastern Economic Review* editors said they
planned to assign another correspondent to the
post. Schwarz had been in Hanoi for nearly two
years.

Controlling Interest: Vietnam's Press Faces the Limits of Reform

by Vikram Parekh

Introduction

Ten years ago, an isolated and impoverished Vietnam embraced a policy of economic reforms that the country's leaders termed *doi moi*, or renewal. Since then, the country's transition to a market economy has captured the attention of many observers and investors in Asia and the United States. Yet the corollaries to market reform—political liberalization, and with it, press freedom—have remained conspicuously absent from the government's agenda. Five dissidents, including CPJ's 1993 International Press Freedom Award winner Doan Viet Hoat, are presently in jail for publishing pro-democracy essays, while official media have periodically faced investigations, and even closure, for stretching the boundaries of acceptable reporting. Vietnam's reluctance to authorize visits by human rights groups has long been an obstacle to inquiry in these areas. In a pronounced and important departure from established policy, however, Hanoi accorded the Committee to Protect Journalists the rare opportunity last September to send a fact-finding mission to the country.

With the full cooperation of the government's Foreign Press Center, CPJ's mission team—board members Peter Arnett of CNN and *Harper's* magazine publisher John R. MacArthur, as well as Vikram Parekh, CPJ's program coordinator for Asia—enjoyed unprecedented access to a broad array of editors and government officials. Their relative openness allowed for a much-needed dialogue, especially after months of heightened political tension during the run-up to Vietnam's Eighth Communist Party Congress, held every five years to confirm appointments to the Politburo and signal major policy changes.

The Vietnamese authorities' willingness to receive CPJ's delegation was due in part to their familiarity with CPJ and its board. Arnett, a veteran correspondent in Vietnam, is highly regarded by many local officials and journalists for his impartial coverage of the Vietnam War, while CPJ board member Terry Anderson has undertaken reconciliation projects with other former United States Marines who served in Vietnam. And Vietnamese authorities had read with great interest a 1993 CPJ report on the unsolved murders of five Vietnamese-American journalists in the United States, citing the cases in discussions with U.S. diplomats on human-rights issues. At least three of the murdered journalists are believed to have been targeted by extremist factions in the Vietnamese-American community led by former Army of the Republic of Vietnam (ARVN) officers violently opposed to U.S. rapprochement with Hanoi.

In a series of meetings in Hanoi and Ho Chi Minh City, CPJ's mission team found an official press that prides itself on the independence that it has carved out, but which continues to face substantial impediments to investigative reporting. CPJ also found senior officials who were willing to speak frankly about the extent of press freedom in Vietnam, including specific cases of journalists such as Doan Viet Hoat, whom the government has jailed or placed under investigation. Their comments, however, were not always encouraging. Senior officials, including Deputy Foreign Minister Vu Khoan, maintained that state secrecy laws had to be enforced against journalists in order to protect Vietnam's trade and political interests, and that political stability necessitated the continued imprisonment of Hoat and his colleagues.

The government's simultaneous openness to CPJ and its reluctance to lift curbs on press freedom reflect Vietnam's conflicting impulses—to join the international community while seeking to control news coverage of Vietnam both within and without its borders. Such a policy can only result in stasis for the country.

Based on its findings, CPJ urges the Vietnamese government to take the following steps toward insuring a climate of media freedom:

• *Release Doan Viet Hoat and others jailed for their writings.* Doing so would send an important signal to journalists around the world that Vietnam recognizes their concerns about individuals whom they regard as colleagues. It would also serve as an encouraging sign that Vietnam has again embraced *doi moi* with the spirit in which it was originally promulgated.

• *Refrain from invoking state secrecy and subversion laws against journalists.* These laws, which have been used to interrogate the staff of licensed newspapers and jail underground press journalists, are by definition vague, and ripe for abusive interpretation. Moreover, the investigation or prosecution of journalists on charges of leaking state secrets or engaging in subversive activities has a chilling effect on all journalists and media organizations in the country.

• *Allow foreign correspondents to report freely on political and economic developments in Vietnam.* Foreign reporters based in Vietnam have said they face routine surveillance, wiretapping, and questioning about their sources, as well as prohibitions against residence in Ho Chi Minh City. One internationally respected correspondent—Adam Schwarz of the *Far Eastern Economic Review*—was expelled from the country when his visa expired in November 1996. CPJ urges the Vietnamese government to recognize the importance of objective international coverage of developments in Vietnam and cease practices that would deter such reporting. At a minimum, this would include ending the surveillance and wiretapping of foreign correspondents, respecting their right to protect their sources, and ceasing the practice of threatened or actual expulsion of foreign correspondents for reports seen as unfavorable to the government. The government should also lift its residency ban on foreign journalists in Ho Chi Minh City.

• *Do not hold Internet users liable for the content of received Internet communications.* Any attempt to police the content of information circulated on the Internet, through legal or technological means, would only serve to undermine the Internet's use as a communication and information tool. But to hold users liable for received material, as the government office supervising the Internet is reportedly planning, would pose an unjustified threat to the many prospective Internet users in Vietnam.

The Emergence of Reform Journalism
Inside the small, but bright Hanoi offices of *Vietnam Courier*—an English-language weekly aimed at foreign investors—are a dozen or so computers running Microsoft Windows, a young, energetic, predominantly female staff, and a relaxed, yet confident deputy editor in chief who speaks with enthusiasm about his fax news service and plans for an Internet edition. The deputy editor, Do Le Chau, occupies an unusual position among Vietnamese journalists; a former fellow at the East-West Center in Honolulu, he has had far greater exposure to the international press than most of his peers—a fact reflected in his embrace of electronic media.

Vietnam Courier is emblematic of the increasing diversity of the country's press, which has grown rapidly in recent years to number roughly 350 magazines and newspapers. The vast majority of these publications are wholly owned by various arms of the government, the few exceptions being collaborations with foreign publishers. Nevertheless, the coverage and tone of the news periodicals vary considerably. At one extreme are *Nhan Dan* (The People) and *Quan Doi Nhan Dan* (The People's Army), didactic party and army dailies that remain vigilant against foreign cultural and political encroachment. The other end of the spectrum includes the dailies *Lao Dong* (Labor) of Hanoi and *Tuoi Tre* (Youth) of Ho Chi Minh City, trade union and youth league publications that have won a large readership through their aggressive coverage of corruption and labor abuses, and—in the case of *Lao Dong*—by incorporating a brighter layout modeled on *USA Today*.

Without exception, the Vietnamese editors whom CPJ interviewed stressed the gains they had made over the past ten years. They have won responsibility for determining the content of their publications, the freedom to expose corruption in public offices, and discretion over which government actions to cover.

Several news organizations have transformed themselves into profit-making enterprises, independent of government subsidies; they include Hanoi's leading daily, *Hanoi Moi* (New Hanoi), as well as *Lao Dong*, *Tuoi Tre*, and *Saigon Giai Phong* (Liberated Saigon). And it is among these papers that the most far-reaching transformation of the Vietnamese press has taken place.

"Our paper was the first in the country to give up subsidies from the government," declared *Tuoi Tre*'s deputy editor in chief, Huynh Son Phuoc, with evident pride, during a meeting with CPJ in his paper's Ho Chi Minh City offices. "We work as professional businessmen—this is one of the main points in the history of our newspaper." But financial independence has also made his paper more accountable to its readers. "We have to answer readers' questions better, more fairly, and protect their interests," he said. For Phuoc, that not only meant exposing corruption, but printing critical commentary on the budget and "ensuring equality between foreign and domestic investors."

While government officials portrayed the press's increased independence as an outgrowth of *doi moi*, several of the editors whom

CPJ interviewed took pains to point out that the loosening of media controls was something journalists themselves had initiated and fought for.

"The change started in '84 to '85, even before renewal was officially declared," said *Vietnam Courier*'s Chau. "In 1985, *Tuan Tin Tic* (Weekly News) launched an exposé of a corruption case involving a provincial governor. At the time, we [reporters] thought the editor in chief was going to hell. Instead, the governor was stripped of his party membership, and Vietnamese journalists realized we had new power."

Much of the initial impetus for investigative reporting came from Ho Chi Minh City, where the media have tended to be more independent than their northern counterparts. In part, according to some editors, this was a result of continuity from pre-unification Southern reporting traditions. But it also reflected the subject matter available to the Ho Chi Minh City press, which in the early 1980s began covering experiments with market reforms—most of which were undertaken in the South.

Although they share an enthusiasm for reform journalism, the Southern journalists who spearheaded this movement come from diverse backgrounds. Phuoc told CPJ that he had been part of the pro-Hanoi resistance in Ho Chi Minh City, while *Tuoi Tre*'s editor in chief spent the war years in prison. By contrast, Ly Quy Chung, the former editor of *Lao Dong*, had been a member of the South Vietnamese parliament, and for a few feverish hours before unification, a cabinet member in the last government of South Vietnam.

Frustrated by the ideological orthodoxy of state journalism schools, many editors have taken on the task of training brasher, more probing reporters themselves. "All papers in Vietnam have opened their own departments to train journalists," one editor commented. "Journalism schools now are useless." But against this initiative, the frustrations that they experience are palpable. "We have to stay within the boundaries of the environment and the law," another editor ruefully noted.

Limits to Reporting by the Official Press
Housed in one of the French colonial buildings that give Hanoi much of its aesthetic appeal, the city's leading daily, *Hanoi Moi*, symbolizes the accomplishments and dilemmas of the Vietnamese press.

Its editors pride themselves on their independence and professionalism, the paper is financially self-sustaining, and several of its staff members have received journalism training in France.

But neither *Hanoi Moi*'s prominence nor its profitability have been enough to guarantee its survival.

In mid-1996, the paper ran a series of articles about a flawed contract for the purchase of two jet aircraft between Vietnam Airlines and the Dutch aircraft manufacturer Fokker, which had recently declared bankruptcy. Having obtained a copy of the contract, the paper's staff found a fatal defect: In the event of a bankruptcy, payments toward purchase of the aircraft would not be refunded. Consequently, when Fokker was forced to close its doors, Vietnam Airlines faced a loss of US$7.2 million—a sizable sum for the state-owned carrier to bear, especially when faced with the costly task of replacing its aging Russian-made fleet. Shortly after the stories ran, the Ministry of the Interior placed *Hanoi Moi* under investigation for leaking state secrets, questioning editors and reporters involved in the story's publication.

The matter remained in the hands of the Interior Ministry at the time of CPJ's visit, although no criminal charges had yet been filed. In addition, two other newspapers were under investigation for revealing state secrets in articles about Vietnam's oil industry; the weeklies *Tien Phong* (Vanguard) and *Kinh Doanh Van Phap Luat* (Business and Law) had covered attempts by the Australian firm Broken Hill Petroleum (BHP) to renegotiate its contract for an oil field whose output had proved disappointing.

All three cases would have to proceed through the state's administrative and legal machinery, senior officials told CPJ, although they challenged neither the substance of the articles nor the journalists' motivation. Instead, suggested Deputy Foreign Minister Vu Khoan, Vietnam's trade interests underlay the government's actions. "We want to solve every conflict with other countries by negotiation and dialogue," he said, adding, "BHP is a very important company—a joint venture in a prospecting area, and the incidents happened in a period when the government in Australia was changing."

A more sanguine interpretation came from Huu Tho, chairman of the Ideology Commission of the Communist Party's Central Committee and former editor of *Nhan Dan*. Tho told CPJ that in his personal opinion, while the journalists working for the three newspapers had made mistakes, their offenses weren't very serious. "If anything, they should be reprimanded or disciplined," he said. Tho also noted that in recent years, there had been only one instance in which a licensed journalist had received a prison sentence for his reporting—a case four years ago involving an article about a land dispute that appeared in *Tien Phong*. "At court, his sentence was reduced to sanctions, and he is still working as a journalist." Regardless of the outcome of these three investigations, the vagueness of the term "state secrets" will continue to pose a hazard to the local media, serving as a catch-all with which officials can snare and silence enterprising journalists. The press law sheds little light on the limits of secrecy; it simply enumerates sweeping areas— "...either military, security, economic, foreign relations or other secrets as set out by law"—in which journalists are prohibited from disclosing state secrets. During CPJ's visit, Vietnamese journalists cited this legal ambiguity as a chronic problem in defining the scope of their work. "Every newspaper has a staff lawyer," an editor noted.

The Vietnamese government, journalists suggested, could clarify the press law by effecting a variety of procedural changes, including formalizing and publicizing the process by which they register state documents as "secret," specifying the level and duration of secrecy, and exercising due precautions to prevent the disclosure of a registered secret. Unless the government institutes such measures, the ambiguity surrounding state secrecy is likely to continue to inhibit the media, and to cast doubt on the express intent of Vietnamese officials to expose corruption and mismanagement.

Several Vietnamese newspapers have in the past been closed for transgressing official directives. In early January 1995, the Information Ministry suspended the publication of *Nguoi Hanoi* (The Hanoian), after the paper ran an article about the social and economic implications of a recent government ban on firecrackers. The ministry also ordered local authorities to discipline the publication's editor in chief, as well as the other journalists involved in the article's publication; they were eventually forced to pen "self-criticisms."

Behind the investigation and closure of state-owned media lies a gulf between the authorities' view of the press as serving the interests of the party and state, as spelled out in the press law, and the media's growing recognition of their role as serving the public interest.

"Journalists used to mistake the role of reporter for that of educator," one editor said of his colleagues' past approach to their work. On the other hand, senior officials—while speaking approvingly of efforts by the press to impose accountability on government—appeared to perceive the media primarily as a means of communicating official policy. "Through information, we have to guide the public," said Phan Quang, president of the Vietnam Journalists Association and director general of Voice of Vietnam radio. "This doesn't mean forcing the public into views, but to educate and guide." Quang pointed out that the media also had an important role as a public forum. But later, during a candid exchange in French with CPJ board member John R. MacArthur, he asserted, "The interest of the state is supreme, and public opinion serves it."

Paradoxically, the state's continued efforts to control the domestic media limit its ability to reach a wider audience through those news organizations. Some editors, for instance, are prepared to launch Internet editions of their publications, but cannot move forward without government authorization of Internet access. *Courier*'s Chau is one of those who have already seen the potential of electronic information services; an internationally faxed bulletin that his staff produces is already the newspaper's main source of revenue. "The Internet would create more customers," says Chau, whose office is fully computerized.

Government authorities have been frank about their discomfort with the Internet; Luu Van Han, a Ministry of Culture and Information spokesman, said in late 1996, "The state must control the Internet so as to use its positive aspects and eliminate its negative influence." ("Vietnam's booming computer market still lacks Internet access," Deutsche Presse-Agentur, Hanoi, Nov. 10, 1996) The latter is seen by many observers of Vietnam as a reference to websites maintained by overseas anti-communist Vietnamese groups, which regularly post articles by dissidents, Ho Chi Minh City samizdats, and leaked party documents.

But with Vietnam now the only member of the Association of Southeast Asian Nations (ASEAN) lacking Internet access, and with the government officially committed to industrializing the country by the year 2020, the advent of electronic information seems inevitable. Officials privately concede that Internet authorization awaits finalized regulations from the Directorate General of Posts and Telecommunications and the installation of policing technology. Draft regulations reportedly hold subscribers responsible for both transmitted and received content, and allow the revocation of service providers' licenses—and the confiscation of their equipment—if their subscribers are found to have transmitted material deemed offensive or subversive. ("Vietnam Struggles with the Information Age," Reuters European Business Report, Ho Chi Minh City, Nov. 25, 1996)

Dissident writers
Somewhere in Ho Chi Minh City, an anonymous Vietnamese man intermittently issues photocopied tracts in which he sardonically comments on political developments in the country and predicts—with impressive accuracy—the rise and fall of party officials. "The Saigonese," as he refers to himself, has drawn a wide audience among the city's intellectuals and among overseas Vietnamese, who carefully transcribe and post his writings on the Internet ("Underground in Vietnam," *The Economist*, June 22, 1996, p. 39).

He carries out his work in clear violation of Vietnam's press law, which explicitly bars the circulation of unauthorized printed matter. The press law, promulgated in 1989, sets out the parameters of a strict licensing regime. Journalists, it states, must be accredited by the Ministry of Culture and Information, and must work for one of the media organizations licensed by the same ministry. The licenses themselves are narrowly defined, spelling out the organization's charter, objectives, audience, scope of distribution, and duration of publication; any attempt to redefine one of those terms requires an application for a new license (Press Law of Vietnam (1989), Chapter V, Article 20).

The tracts circulated by the Saigonese and others constitute something of a parallel, underground press. These *samizdats*—based primarily in Ho Chi Minh City—represent the only outlets for information and commentary in Vietnam that are completely unfettered by state controls. While these organizations exist outside of the Vietnamese government's narrow definition of "journalism," they fall squarely into the definition of journalism shared by CPJ and much of the international media.

For samizdat journalists, forsaking anonymity carries a heavy price. The noted Southern dissident Doan Viet Hoat is currently serving a 15-year prison term for publishing an unlicensed pro-democracy journal. Six years after Hoat's arrest—and despite repeated appeals by CPJ, human rights groups, and foreign governments for his release—Vietnamese authorities still appear unwilling to reconsider the case. "One of the experiences of East Asia is that political stability is one of the most important factors for economic development," said Deputy Foreign Minister Khoan. "These persons [Hoat and his associates] have been punished for violating Vietnamese laws, not for writing articles."

Hoat's periodical, *Dien Dan Tu Do* (Freedom Forum), was a mimeographed collection of essays advocating the democratization of Vietnamese political life that appeared in at least four installments between 1988 and 1990, circulating privately among a loose network of dissidents in Ho Chi Minh City.

On November 17, 1990, police seized Hoat at his home in Ho Chi Minh City and held him incommunicado for six months before his family was allowed to visit him. Authorities also detained seven other contributors to the journal without charge. On May 6, 1992, before any charges had been filed, the Ho Chi Minh City newspaper *Saigon Giai Phong* announced that a "reactionary group" led by Hoat had employed *Dien Dan Tu Do* "as a most important means of rallying forces to oppose and sabotage our country." The paper's invective was a significant portent of things to come, for political trials in Vietnam are often presaged by media condemnation of defendants.

The eight detained writers were finally tried on March 29 and 30, 1993 and found guilty of subversion. Hoat had been forced to represent himself, since Hanoi denied visas to the California-based attorneys whom his wife had approached to take up his case. The sentences were unusually severe, with Hoat receiving a 20-year term, and his colleagues anywhere from eight months—reportedly in the case of a defendant who "confessed"—to 16 years. At a June 3 appeal hearing, Hoat's sentence was reduced by five years, while the other *Dien Dan Tu Do* defendants also received slight reductions in their prison terms. The Vietnam News Agency attributed these reductions to the fact "that their plot had been nipped in the bud before causing any serious damage."

Hoat continued to write in the prison and labor camps at which he was interred over the next six months. Through contacts in the camps, he managed to smuggle out a few essays in which he discussed, among other topics, the relevance of international human rights to Vietnamese society. As a result, authorities have relocated him to progressively more remote facilities, where, family members fear, he is unable to receive necessary medical care. He is currently serving out his sentence in Thanh Cam prison, located in northern Vietnam, near the Laotian border, and normally reserved for serious criminal offenders.

Prior to last June's party congress, the government conducted a sporadically enforced, but nevertheless pointed campaign against what the regime terms "cultural evils." While the Western press focused primarily on the whitewashing of Eastman Kodak billboards and other advertisements for American corporations, the repressive measures had far more insidious consequences for Hanoi-based dissidents, such as the arrests of several prominent dissidents in connection with their writings, most of which had been circulated as privately printed essays, and in some cases, reprinted in overseas Vietnamese journals.

Among them were Do Trung Hieu and Hoang Minh Chinh, who were arrested in June 1995 and tried and convicted in November for violating the interests of the state by writing and distributing documents criticizing the government. Hieu was sentenced to 15 months in prison, while Chinh was sentenced to 12 months. In his pamphlets, Hieu had written about the government's attempts to disband the Unified Buddhist Church of Vietnam and had called for greater openness in the Communist Party. Chinh had written essays criticizing the party's monopoly on power and had demanded the rehabilitation of party members purged in the 1960s.

Both dissidents had experienced prior arrests for their writings. Hieu, the former party official in charge of religious affairs in Ho Chi Minh City, was arrested in 1990 and expelled from the party in 1992. The former director of the Institute of Marxist-Leninist philosophy, Chinh was jailed from 1967 to 1973, and from 1981 to 1987, for alleged revisionism.

In December 1995, police in Dalat arrested Nguyen Xuan Tu, a biologist and dissident writer whose pen name is Ha Si Phu. Two days later, authorities searched Tu's house and confiscated thousands of pages of documents and manuscripts, including two issues of *Thien Chi*, a monthly Vietnamese-language journal published in Germany that had reprinted some of his essays. Tu was charged with violating Article 92 of the criminal code, a national security provision that outlaws possessing or divulging "state secrets," and sentenced to one year in prison on August 22, 1996. In early 1995, he had written an essay in which he called Marxism-Leninism a relic that was harmful to the country's economic reforms.

Despite the radical stance that they adopted in their writings, all three received sentences that were far more lenient than those imposed on Hoat and most of the other *Dien Dan Tu Do* writers. Foreign correspondents in Vietnamese attributed the discrepancy to the northern provenance of the dissidents arrested in 1995 and their past association with the party. All three were released at various points in mid- and late 1996, after the completion of their sentences.

A more elusive case involves Ly Chandara (also known as Ly Ngoc), the editor of *Tu Do* (Freedom), an anti-communist Vietnamese-language newspaper published in Phnom Penh. Cambodia handed Chandara over to Vietnamese border authorities on March 9, 1996, despite evidence suggesting that he was a Cambodian citizen. He was among several dozen ethnic Vietnamese opponents of Hanoi—very loosely affiliated with one another, and collectively termed the "Tu Do Movement"—who were variously expelled, or threatened with expulsion, by the Cambodian government between December 1995 and December 1996.

According to Chandara, who resurfaced in Phnom Penh in late January 1997, he had been released by the Vietnamese in October after eight months in jail in exchange for a promise not to plot against the regime or involve himself in politics. He is seeking permission from Cambodian authorities to relaunch his paper.

Restrictions on the Foreign Press
Last November, Adam Schwarz, the Hanoi correspondent for the *Far Eastern Economic Review*, a Dow Jones publication, was expelled from Vietnam after the government refused to renew his visa. Recognized internationally as an authority on Vietnamese politics, Schwarz's detailed accounts of political and economic developments in Vietnam had evidently violated the government's own conception of the foreign media's role in the country. Throughout 1996, authorities had inked out articles, glued pages together, and cut out articles from copies of the *Review* meant for circulation in Vietnam. The censored articles included an obituary of the late foreign minis-

ter Le Mai and a special section on trade and investment in Vietnam. And, as Schwarz noted earlier in the year during a conference held in Hong Kong by the Arlington, Virginia-based Freedom Forum, he had regularly been admonished by officials and questioned about his contacts in response to reports that he had filed. At year's end, the *Review*'s Hanoi bureau remained open, although no correspondent had been assigned to the post.

Although the exhaustiveness of Schwarz's reports provoked particularly harsh retribution, all foreign journalists based in Vietnam work under similarly restrictive conditions. Some of the strictures are overt: They may maintain bureaus and residences only in Hanoi (although they are free to travel elsewhere in the country), and they are required to hire all support staff through the government's Foreign Press Center. In practice, these assistants act as informants for the government. They are required to attend weekly group meetings, where authorities remind them of their "obligations" to Vietnam, question them about their employers' meetings and correspondence, and encourage them to denounce each other for complicity in unapproved activities of the foreign press corps. Other obstacles to reporting by the foreign press are more subtle, including surveillance and wiretapping.

In a disturbing example of the government's intolerance toward enterprising foreign journalists, Hanoi police severely beat Reuters photographer Dylan Martinez as he attempted to photograph a demonstration by market women on September 9, 1996. The demonstration, held outside the Hanoi city government offices, involved about 70 vendors who were protesting conditions imposed by the managers of a newly reopened market. A busload of police arrived while Martinez was photographing the demonstrators. As he walked away, a dozen policemen surrounded him, threw him to the ground, and repeatedly kicked and punched him. He was then thrown into a van, where police again kicked him, and taken to the local police station. Before being released, Martinez was forced to destroy seven rolls of unexposed film and sign a statement acknowledging that the incident was his fault.

When CPJ raised the case during its meeting with Deputy Foreign Minister Khoan, the delegation was told that Martinez's case was an anomaly and "did not reflect our policy."

Khoan's statements, however, revealed a narrow view of the foreign press's role in Vietnam—one that cast it as an accessory to the state information apparatus. "We think foreign journalists can play a very important role for us because our media is very limited," he said. "They could help us provide information about Vietnam for the foreign press community."

While enjoying considerably more leeway in reporting than entirely state-owned media, two Hanoi-based publications linked to foreign publishers already serve this mandate: the weekly *Vietnam Investment Review*, produced in association with Australian publisher Kerry Packer, and the monthly *Vietnam Economic Times*, a collaborative venture with the Swiss firm Ringier AG. Both these publications fall substantially short of a true joint venture, reflecting the government's desire to maintain a broad measure of control over the portrayal abroad of Vietnam's economy. They function under an agreement known in Vietnam as a "business cooperation contract": Rather than forming an economic entity, each partner assumes separate responsibilities, with the Vietnamese editorial board in both cases maintaining final authority over content.

In a decree that took effect in January 1997, the government also moved to restrict private access to satellite dishes. Under the regulations, ownership of satellite dishes is restricted to select government offices, people's committees, hotels of three stars and above, and radio and television stations. Although prompted by the proliferation of satellite dishes in Vietnam—many cheaper dishes are illegally imported from China and sold for as little as US$1,000—some observers questioned the extent of the decree's impact on access to foreign broadcast news. According to one foreign correspondent in Hanoi, the English-speaking audience remains limited in Vietnam, and much of that audience will continue to have access through the existing exemptions and because of the difficulty in enforcing the decree.

Conclusion

Vietnam's press law, adopted in 1989 at the height of the *doi moi* reforms, consolidated important gains by local journalists, such as the right to disseminate information obtained through their own sources and limited protections of the confidentiality of sources. In so doing, the press law effectively recognized the right of journalists to engage in investigative reporting. But at the same time, the document explicitly stated that the role of the press was to serve as the voice of the party and state.

The tension between these two conceptions of the media's role was manifest during CPJ's mission to Vietnam. While recognizing that they work for state-owned media, Vietnamese journalists have received conflicting signals about the acceptable boundaries of reporting. Since the advent of reforms ten years ago, the government has officially encouraged the local press to expose corruption and mismanagement, and many publications have responded to those directives with enthusiasm and dedication. The investigations of Vietnamese newspapers for leaking state secrets or questioning official policies, however, have increased the level of confusion and insecurity for local journalists.

Thus, criminal prosecution in such cases would, from CPJ's standpoint, be unjust, because it would penalize journalists for fulfilling their professional obligations as spelled out and reiterated by authorities since the advent of *doi moi*.

With Vietnam's integration into the international economy, its interests have diversified. Countervailing state secrecy, for example, is the need to insure the flow of information—an essential component of the relationship between foreign investors and their Vietnamese partners. But the government's inclination to investigate local papers when they critically examine contracts between state agencies and foreign firms impedes this information flow. So does the monitoring—and, in the case of Adam Schwarz, expulsion—of foreign journalists who have attempted to present an independent assessment of the climate for business in Vietnam.

The reception accorded CPJ's delegation, and the accessibility and candor of the officials with whom CPJ met are difficult to imagine in neighboring countries such as China or Burma. They clearly reflect Vietnam's appreciation of the role of the international media in fostering relations between the United States and Vietnam, as well as the growing interaction of the Vietnamese press with the regional and international media.

Yet the continued imprisonment of Doan Viet Hoat and his colleagues paints a picture of Vietnam that is at odds with the one that the government has taken pains to present—both to CPJ and to numerous diplomatic missions. Although it was evident from CPJ's discussions with Deputy Foreign Minister Vu Khoan that Vietnamese officials do not see Hoat as a journalist, the international press community views him and the other samizdat publishers as colleagues. Hoat's release would send an important signal to journalists around the world that their concerns are taken seriously by the Vietnamese government.

While foreign journalists who periodically visit Vietnam have reported few difficulties in their work, those who are accredited as foreign correspondents in Vietnam have a strikingly different tale to tell. The depth of their coverage is in many ways restricted by surveillance that limits their interaction with Vietnamese citizens, questioning about reports that they have written in accordance with international reporting standards, and wiretapping that diminishes the confidence with which they can communicate with the agencies for whom they work. These conditions—coupled with the continuing prohibition against journalists' residence in Ho Chi Minh City despite the city's burgeoning foreign business community—stand in stark contrast to the desire, stated by Foreign Ministry officials in their conversations with CPJ, to have good relations with the foreign press. Foreign news agencies need to be allowed to establish permanent offices in Ho Chi Minh City.

Perhaps the most important channel for communication between Vietnamese media and their international counterparts will be the Internet. As a number of Vietnamese journalists recognize, it will enable the local media to reach vast new markets and gain access to information published by the international press for a modest financial outlay. With the eventual legalization of the Internet in Vietnam a foregone conclusion, it is important to insure that Vietnamese journalists themselves bear no criminal liability for received material over which they have little or no control. Such punitive provisions, currently being contemplated by the government as it prepares to initiate use of the Internet in Vietnam, would drastically curtail the Internet's use by local journalists and would forestall Vietnam's integration into an age marked by the preeminence of electronic information.

Several of the officials and editors with whom CPJ spoke cited the growing interaction between Vietnamese journalists and their counterparts elsewhere in the region since the country's admission as a full member of the Association of Southeast Asian Nations (ASEAN) in 1995. But by strictly controlling access to and dissemination of information, Vietnam is forestalling full integration into the regional community. Although there are widely varying approaches to media freedom in the ASEAN member countries—with Singapore and Malaysia as obvious examples of private ownership masking statist policies—none is so resolute as Vietnam in using subversion laws to regulate content, in restricting access to electronic media, and in limiting the freedom of foreign correspondents.

In contrast, some ASEAN countries, such as Thailand and the Philippines, offer models of a thriving, independent press. The relative influences that these countries bring to bear on Vietnam may play a significant role in determining whether a new generation of talented Vietnamese reporters, with a clear conception of their professional role, can further Vietnam's integration into the international community.

Central Europe and the Republics of the Former Soviet Union

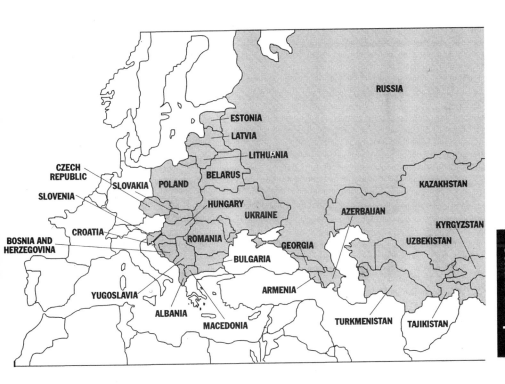

OVERVIEW
OF
Central Europe and the Republics of the Former Soviet Union

by Catherine A. Fitzpatrick

S ix years after the failed coup in the former Soviet Union, and eight years after the fall of the Berlin Wall and the Velvet Revolution, these historic events no longer serve as benchmarks by which to measure press freedom in the region that encompasses the republics of the former Soviet Union, the Baltic states, the Balkans, and Central and Eastern Europe. Significant privatization of the media throughout the region and the appearance of an independent and increasingly professional press even in the harshest climates mean that comparisons with the communist past are misleading.

While many of the region's societies have become freer, and some have even shrugged off repressive communist rulers they returned to power in post-revolutionary democratic elections, the problems of the defense of journalists and the protection and expansion of the media's freedoms remain paramount. Because the press has become so much stronger, it has attracted more enemies, and violence has become a method of persuasion.

While virtually every post-communist country heavily regulates the media

Catherine A. Fitzpatrick, *the program coordinator for Central and Eastern Europe and the former Soviet Union, has worked as a consultant to non-governmental organizations and foundations on civil society programs and for nine years directed research in the former Soviet Union department of Helsinki Watch. She is fluent in Russian and has published a dozen translations of the works of prominent Russian political figures and journalists as well as articles on politics, human rights, and the media in the region.*

Amanda Onion, *former CPJ research associate for Central and Eastern Europe, provided extensive assistance for this section and prepared many of the country summaries for Eastern Europe. Fluent in Russian, she has worked as a free-lance journalist in Moscow and New York.*

CPJ's work in Central Europe and the republics of the former Soviet Union in 1996 was funded in part by a grant from the John D. and Catherine T. MacArthur Foundation.

Central Europe

with press laws, a growing number have foregone exclusive state ownership of electronic media, and the use of prior censorship or anti-state laws to punish dissident writings. Brutal and long-term shut-downs of independent news outlets to maintain authoritarian control are still common in the Russian Federation, the Caucasus, and Central Asia, but less so in Central and Eastern Europe.

Government officials in the region and media scholars abroad generally feel that conditions are freer than they have ever been, with some important exceptions, such as Belarus, or Turkmenistan. But the effects of this growing press freedom on working journalists' safety are often paradoxical. Yes, conditions are far freer. The rule of law is better rooted than in the Soviet era; privatization of the media has meant less dependence on government; and many more emboldened and better-trained journalists in their twenties, who were teenagers during the revolutions, have appeared. Yet, a journalist's work has become more dangerous than it has been in decades. The threat of physical harm is considered part of the job description in many areas. The region's treacherous conflict zones, the explosion of mafia-style organizations, the unraveling of the old security and intelligence apparatuses, and the disintegration and corruption of the military-industrial complexes have all contributed to making journalism a most hazardous profession (see "Russia's Harsh Press Climate," p. 271).

The stakes are higher when the monolithic communist bureaucracies are no longer the known enemy and threats come from their rogue remnants as well as many other quarters. Killings, beatings, anonymous threats, and bankrupting libel lawsuits are unanticipated consequences of more freedom. The greater the free flow of information, the harder it is to stop it, and those who would try to suppress the news must either resort to brute violence or to increasingly devious and subtle methods (arcane tax inspections, well-timed electricity outages, induced paper shortages, sudden broadcast frequency auctions). These gambits require more painstaking monitoring and intervention from the international community; the press freedom battle has moved to a higher, more sophisticated plane.

Of the 10 killings of journalists in the region last year, nine are unsolved assassinations (in Russia, Ukraine, and Tajikistan), by and large following the pattern of the previous two years (11 in 1995 and 14 in 1994) in which organized crime or paramilitary figures are suspected in the deaths but only one case has come to trial. (The Moscow-based Glasnost Defense Foundation, the region's most reputable press freedom organization, reports 74 journalists killed in the former Soviet Union since 1993. CPJ's total is 56 because it does not include military journalists, nonjournalist media workers, and victims of crimes apparently unrelated to journalism, although some of the unsolved murders occur along the shifting borders between commerce and journalism in the newly privatized media.)

Central Europe

In past years, as the Balkan and Chechen wars and other conflicts raged, the number of reporters killed in crossfire was far greater. Last year brought a still fragile cease-fire to Chechnya, and an uneasy peace reigned in Bosnia and Herzegovina, but restriction of movement and hazardous working conditions persist in these heavily guarded zones. Four journalists were declared missing in Chechnya in 1996, bringing to 10 the total of those who have disappeared in the secessionist republic from December 1994 through January 1997.

Many reporters suffered serious injuries this year in police assaults, particularly in Albania, Belarus, Bosnia, Bulgaria, Russia, and the republic of Serbia in Yugoslavia—the result of covering mass public rallies where demonstrators were attacked by baton-wielding riot squads. Not all of these beatings resulted from indiscriminately violent crowd control: Security forces often deliberately targeted journalists, sometimes after a rally, or far from the action, with accompanying confiscation of film or destruction of equipment.

Currently, not a single journalist in the former Soviet Union and Central and Eastern Europe is in prison for his or her work. Reporters were held for only short periods, or, as in Russia and Kazakhstan, served some months in pretrial detention but were released after international campaigns in which CPJ played a prominent part. If there are a few journalists left imprisoned in the region, it is due to political activism or local statutes criminalizing "incitement to ethnic hatred," especially anti-Semitic or virulent nationalist expression. Such laws make CPJ uneasy, because they are all too readily used against journalists to punish the legitimate practice of their profession—such is the case of radical magazine commentator Valeriya Novodvorskaya of Moscow, still caught up in a judicial prosecution for calling Russians "lazy" on Estonian television. In the Gorbachev era, prosecutors failed to pin charges on her of insulting the president.

Even when democratically elected, presidents—who in some ways wield more power than the previous era's communist general secretaries—are among the greatest threats to press freedom in the region. The rulers of Russia and the regions Bashkortistan and Tatarstan in Russia, as well as the leaders of Belarus Croatia, Georgia, Kazakhstan, and Serbia, all became personally involved in either verbal or legal threats to noncompliant media, situations in which CPJ intervened. The presidents shamelessly hogged the airwaves, particularly at election time, firing controversial editors in electronic broadcasting and closing critical independent stations and other news outlets through a variety of means. Many presidents enjoy their "own" television stations, with those of Alyaksandr Lukashenka in Belarus or Slobodan Milosevic in Serbia or Saparmurad Niyazov in Turkmenistan at the extreme end of the spectrum of obsessive coverage of the Great Leader's every move and utterance, blackouts on the opposition's activities, and enormous pressure exerted on alternative broadcasters.

While the independent broadcasters faced formidable obstacles, some relatives of people in high places got their own television or radio stations, including the Kazakhstani president's daughter, Daraga Nazarbayeva, and the accused Serbian war criminal Radovan Karadzic's daughter, who runs an international press center and a Serbian Orthodox radio station in Pale. Other family members, cronies from various ministries, and communications officials have managed to parlay their proximity to power into actual possession of the means of communication. "We have a private radio station," a journalist from a former Soviet republic told CPJ. "It belongs to [a certain minister] who made his own personal investment in the station." A network of such television and radio stations controlled personally by presidents, ministers, and governors could stretch from the Adriatic Sea to the Bering Sea with few interruptions.

"Insult" laws (seditious or anti-government libel), usually deployed when presidents take umbrage, caused some of the region's worst legal threats to journalists, as when Croatia's President Franjo Tudjman threatened an editor and correspondent from *Feral Tribune* with prison for satirizing him; when two reporters from Romania's *Zuia* received prison sentences for making scandalous claims about then-President Ion Iliescu; or when the entire Slovak Cabinet of Ministers slapped the independent daily *Sme* with a comical but crippling lawsuit demanding a graduated table of fines, depending on the cabinet members' rank, for their "pain and suffering" caused by a reporter's critical comment.

Despite such obstacles by censorious rulers, 1996 was the year the Internet began to revolutionize the flow of information in Eastern Europe. A journalist in New York could talk to colleagues through Sarajevo On Line, run by the radio station Studio 99 and the news agency Oslobodjenje, or through other sites; monitor the Balkans; and swiftly discover what aired on the ruling parties' television stations in the ethnic enclaves of Bosnia. A reporter researching a story could tap into a search engine the names involved in Russia's "Kremlingate" scandals, and a dozen well-written articles by investigative journalists would spring up—in English or Russian—from many Web sites established by publishers of newspapers or news agencies in Russia. CPJ's and other supporters' Web pages helped defendants such as the Russian scientist Alexei Nikitin or the journalists from Croatia's *Feral Tribune* involved in precedent-setting cases of free speech and freedom of information obtain their release.

When Yugoslavia was swept up in mass rallies protesting annulment of democratic elections, Belgrade's brave Radio B92 provided a vital news link defying government blackouts. Although President Milosevic shut down the independent station for a few days, B92 stayed on the air in RealAudio, a sound program on

Central Europe

the Internet, publishing daily press releases on its Web site. B92's icon, an umbrella under the falling snow, was linked to other Internet sites around the world. It reminded viewers of a B92 reporter covering the demonstrations with wet shoes, a crumpled notebook, and an umbrella raised against the freezing elements, who became the symbol of the hardiness of Eastern European journalism.

Despite President Lukashenka's gagging of the media on the eve of a controversial referendum, journalists in Belarus kept a steady flow of pictures of beaten demonstrators and alternative information on several Web sites, but fared less well than B92 when unidentified hackers destroyed one site. Still, Webmeisters can circumvent the governments' nefarious use of the new technologies with mirrored pages on other servers abroad, re-posting of information to Internet discussion groups, and regular e-mail. In some cases this year, CPJ received its first tips about troublesome situations via e-mail, and responded with e-mail protest letters to governments or official news agencies.

Internet traffic mainly flows between these countries and the outside world. Within nations undergoing painful economic transformation, most people are increasingly unable to afford newspapers, let alone Internet access, and rely on state-dominated television to get their news. Foreign broadcasting, sponsored by the U. S. and Western European governments, continues to provide a valuable supplement for news-starved populations. The American-funded Radio Free Europe and Radio Liberty (RFE/RL) and Russian public and private television are still vital to the free media mix in the former Soviet Union and Eastern and Central Europe, although RFE/RL correspondents continue to suffer attacks, and Russian television has been reduced or discontinued in some states. The battle for possession of broadcasting frequencies is likely to pose the greatest risk to media freedom in the coming years.

Journalists' self-defense societies or associations of correspondents are beginning to emerge, but are still weak, and the structures based on the communist-era journalists' unions are often dormant, corrupt, or actively hostile to press freedom in some areas. Nevertheless, very encouraging signs of an increasing willingness and ability to advocate press freedom issues from an independent perspective can be seen in the work of the Glasnost Defense Foundation, Globus Press Syndicate, and the St. Petersburg League of Journalists in Russia; the Association of Independent Journalists in Croatia; the Free Press Association in Georgia; the Young Generation journalists' group in Azerbaijan; the Association of Professional Journalists of Albania; many other local committees with which CPJ cooperates; and the Western organizations Internews and Open Media Research Institute. We are grateful to all of them for information used in this report.

Albania

While Albania's entrance to the Council of Europe in June 1995 promised improved press freedom in the country, last May's parliamentary elections sparked a renewed crackdown on the opposition press, as the ruling party tried to limit critical coverage of the government. During the months leading to the elections, officials in President Sali Berisha's ruling Democratic Party impounded delivery trucks servicing *Koha Jone*, a leading opposition newspaper, and made sweeping arrests of *Koha Jone*'s staff for tenuous connections with a bombing in Tirana. After the bombing, authorities arrested and detained another journalist, who had written for the daily *Populli Po*, on the suspicion that an article she had written in November 1995 was related to the incident.

Radio and television news remains entirely state controlled, providing only one-sided, pro-government coverage. On election day, May 26, the Albanian government cut regular programming by a German news agency and continued to bar the broadcast for one week. Following the elections, which opposition parties and Western observers said had been manipulated, authorities again targeted print journalists, this time harassing and attacking them while they covered opposition rallies protesting the elections. Meanwhile, the Albanian government continued heavy monitoring of all radio and television broadcasts, often censoring programs from Western news agencies.

Most nongovernmental newspapers were directly affiliated with opposition parties. Several editors and writers from opposition newspapers ran for office in the May elections and in the Oct. 20 runoffs, in which the ruling Democratic Party claimed a landslide victory.

January 26

Koha Jone, HARASSED
Police impounded six delivery vans of the independent newspaper *Koha Jone*, claiming that they were defective or lacked proper registration documents. On March 3, the newspaper's publisher and editor announced that *Koha Jone* would have to permanently discontinue two of its smaller publications, *AKS* and *Sport Ekspres*, due to financial constraints caused by the impoundment of three additional delivery vans.

January 31

Altin Hazizaj, *Koha Jone,* IMPRISONED
Hazizaj, a reporter with Albania's largest independent daily, *Koha Jone*, was arrested for allegedly assaulting two police officers while trying to enter a building. Hazizaj was covering a police attempt to evict former political prisoners who were living as squatters in an unfinished building in Tirana. At the scene of the eviction, police also confiscated the film and camera of a *Koha Jone* photographer, Genc Shkullaku. On Feb. 2, after CPJ and other international organizations protested his detention, Hazizaj was released by court order. As the investigation against him continues, Hazizaj is required to report to authorities twice a week.

February 26

Koha Jone's staff, HARASSED
Shortly after an explosion that killed four and wounded 27 in the center of the Albanian capital, Tirana, police raided the offices of the independent daily *Koha Jone* and arrested all 33 staffers present. No arrest warrants were shown. The newspaper's staff, including publisher Nikoll Lesi, were taken to Tirana Police Station No. 2 and questioned individually about the bombing. Police also raided Lesi's apartment and confiscated a hunting rifle and a safe box containing tapes from a 1994 trial in which two journalists from *Koha Jone* were convicted of slander and revealing state secrets. Lesi was then charged with illegal arms possession. CPJ

sent a letter to President Sali Berisha expressing grave concern about the continued harassment of Albania's independent press and urged him to ensure that members of the independent media are not unfairly targeted during times of crisis.

February 26
Ylli Polovina, Free-lancer, IMPRISONED, LEGAL ACTION

Polovina, a well-known free-lance journalist, was detained by Albanian authorities shortly after an explosion that killed four and injured 27 in the center of Tirana, the Albanian capital. The arrest occurred after a news broadcast on Albanian State Television suggested a link between the day's bombing and a Nov. 29 article in *Populli Po* by Polovina titled "The Car Bomb in Skopje Could be 'Repeated' in Tirana." The article discussed a car bombing in Skopje, Macedonia, and suggested that a figurative "explosion" of corruption may occur in Tirana. On March 5, CPJ sent a letter to President Sali Berisha urging him to clarify the charges against Polovina, who remained in detention, and ensure that he be provided a speedy and fair trial with proper legal representation. On March 12, an Albanian court convicted him of inciting terrorism. Polovina was sentenced to pay a fine of 30,000 lek (US$300) and was then released.

March 14
Aleksander Frangaj, *Koha Jone*, LEGAL ACTION

Frangaj, editor in chief of the independent daily *Koha Jone*, was convicted on charges of publishing false information and fined US$1,000. The charges were brought by a former police chief from Gjirokastra who claimed that an article in *Koha Jone* contained false allegations about him, specifically that he was involved in corruption and was wanted by the authorities. Frangaj was convicted under Albania's widely criticized 1993 Press Law. A few days later, President Sali Berisha annulled the fine. The president offered no explanation for his move, but press reports speculated that it was a gesture by Berisha to ease tensions between the government and *Koha Jone*, which had been harassed frequently by authorities.

May 26
Deutsche Welle, CENSORED

The daily, 30-minute, Albanian-language broadcast by the German news agency Deutsche Welle was cut from Radio Tirana's programming on the evening of general elections in Albania and remained off the air for a week. Radio Tirana, a state-run station that broadcasts throughout Albania, offered no explanation for cutting the program and played music in its place. The station put the program back on the air only after reporters from Deutsche Welle lodged protests with the Radio Tirana director. But sources at the German news agency report that nearly all of the stories filed by their Tirana correspondents are censored, as well as those stories filed from Germany that are critical of the Albanian government.

May 28
Bardhok Lala, Dita Information Service, ATTACKED

Lala, a reporter for the independent Dita Information Service, was beaten by police during a rally in Tirana's Skanderberg Square, where opposition supporters were protesting alleged ballot manipulation in the May 26 parliamentary elections. President Sali Berisha's Democratic Party won an overwhelming majority of votes in the elections.

Lala said he was watching the rally when he was picked up by police and taken to a restaurant, where he was beaten and kicked. He was moved to a police station, dumped into a car with no license plates, beaten again, and threatened with a gun to his face. The police took Lala to a lake south of Tirana, stripped him, and beat him with batons and a revolver. They demanded to know the names of secret police officials who leaked information to newspapers, and fired a gun several times near his head. Lala, whose attackers eventually left him by the lake, injured, sought help in a nearby village.

International organizations reported that other journalists, foreign and Albanian, and protesters were also beaten at the rally. CPJ urged Albanian authorities to investigate the attack on Lala and hold the police officers involved accountable.

May 28
Gianfranco Stara, Associated Press Television (APTV), ATTACKED
Spiro Ilo, APTV, ATTACKED, HARASSED
Eduardo del Campo, *El Mundo*, ATTACKED
Stara and Ilo, both journalists with APTV, and del Campo, a reporter for Spain's *El Mundo*, were beaten by police while observing a political rally in Skanderberg Square in the center of the capital, Tirana. Police also smashed Ilo's video camera and destroyed his film. CPJ condemned the attack and urged the authorities to order an investigation into the police beatings.

Armenia

Press freedom eroded along with democracy in Armenia, as President Levon Ter-Petrossian reasserted autocratic rule and heavy media control despite a highly contested Sept. 22 national election that the Organization for Security and Cooperation in Europe and other international monitors declared fraudulent.

During violent protests over election results, the president's office and other government agencies censored and threatened foreign and local journalists, and riot police destroyed the cameras of several news organizations. Authorities shut down two independent radio stations and a television channel for several days, forcing editors from their offices. But in the case of HAI-FM, the

director herself sought police protection, fearing opposition reprisal for the station's favorable coverage of the president. Armenian media and administration officials censored Russian and Armenian television election footage. Police detained, interrogated, and beat Gagik Mrktchyan, political commentator for the Russian-language newspaper *Golos Armenii*, charging him with organizing mass unrest. Mrktchyan, who said he was punished for his journalistic rather than political activity, was released on his own recognizance after 10 days and his case was dropped.

Since the president's banning of the Armenian Revolutionary Federation (ARF), known as the Dashnak Party, in 1994, authorities have closed a dozen newspapers associated with ARF, including *Yerkir*, formerly the largest circulation daily. Other opposition and independent publications exist alongside the official press, but have little impact. The combined circulation of Armenia's seven daily newspapers totals 25,000-30,000 in a country of about 3.5 million people. In a climate plagued with libel lawsuits and official intimidation, "there are very few Don Quixotes; somebody must be behind every newspaper," as an editor of a newspaper with Western investors explained to Russia's *Nezavisimaya Gazeta*.

Prior to the election, state security agents warned leading newspapers not to criticize the president. Ter-Petrossian monopolized the airways, and opposition candidates received tendentious coverage from predominantly state-run electronic broadcasting or suffered last-minute refusals of paid television access. On Sept. 2, government radio executives fired the director of the State Radio Co. after an aggrieved state bread plant manager filed a libel lawsuit against him. Mass resignations at the station to protest the firing followed. Ter-Petrossian faulted the two sides in the dispute and urged the court to punish both.

Ter-Petrossian refuses to meet with local reporters and has not given an interview to a Western journalist in at least two years. In October, when an independent Armenian news agency reprinted an interview with the president from a Czech newspaper, Ter-Petrossian's office ordered the agency to distribute a longer version of the interview that had appeared in the Armenian government newspaper.

On a more encouraging note, Armen V. Sarkisyan, the new prime minister, told *The New York Times,* "Somebody has to say that the press is truly free and then stand by to guarantee it." Although Sarkisyan met with leading journalists on Nov. 7 to hear their views on relations between the government and the "fourth estate," he has been unable to change the president's harsh attitude toward a critical media.

April 22
Azg, CENSORED
The Ministry of Justice ordered a pro-government splinter group of the opposition party Ramgavar to take over the executive board of the opposition daily *Azg.* When the staff and board of *Azg* resisted the takeover, the ministry ordered their printing house to cease publication of the newspaper. On May 21, a court ruled that the ministry's attempt to change ownership was unlawful, and the paper resumed publication.

September 26
Vladimir Nazaryan, Russian Public Television (ORT), ATTACKED, HARASSED
A1+, THREATENED
Defense Ministry soldiers seized a Betacamcorder from Nazaryan, the Yerevan correspondent for ORT, four days after turbulent presidential elections in Armenia, an independent observer said. Nazaryan had filed a story to his Moscow bureau on election violence. The story, aired on ORT's prime-time evening news program "Vremya," described how the Armen-

ian opposition stormed the parliament building on Sept. 25 to protest ballot-box tampering.

When Interior Ministry police returned the camera to Nazaryan 10 hours after it was confiscated, Defense Ministry soldiers on the scene immediately grabbed him, beat him, and then returned him to his office, warning him not to file such reports. A Defense Ministry major told Nazaryan that his footage should not have shown tanks on the streets. The major warned another television company, A1+, which shared studios in Yerevan with ORT, that it could suffer reprisals as well if it did not "keep in line."

Azerbaijan

Despite the authoritarian government's willingness to use military force to quell unrest, it has permitted independent and opposition papers to exist in Azerbaijan. Nevertheless, reporters must labor under both government and military censorship. The Soviet-era censor, an administrative body known as Glavlit, still operates in the government, in tandem with a special unit in President Heidar Aliyev's office, vetting articles before they appear and providing strong guidance and criticism to editors. In November, the National Assembly (the legislature) adopted the Law on State Secrets, which was condemned as overly broad by lawyers and journalists, since it deems certain information on subjects in the public interest—industry, transport, communication, and infrastructure—to be classified. A draft law on the media before the legislature in December contained a proposal to re-register all news outlets with "appropriate executive bodies."

Dozens of critical papers have thrived, some with support from neighboring Turkey, but many have small circulations of 10,000-20,000. Several with larger runs are dependent on government printing presses. In at least one case, an opposition group was banned and some members arrested in a coup attempt, although the newspaper associated with it was tolerated, albeit with threats of removal of its printing license for satirical commentary.

At least one opposition newspaper, *Avrazia*, a weekly that converted to a daily in early 1996, was shut down for a prolonged period, then resumed publication under new management. Others, like *Azadlig*, a respected independent paper that converted to a daily in September, as well as *7 Days* and *Mukhalifat*, are repeatedly censored, seized, or threatened. The publications are forced to run cartoons in their issues, since the censors forbid publishers to run blank space to show where an article was removed.

Topics that have fallen under the censors' scissors are government corruption, the human rights situation, relations with Russia, the treatment of Azeri citizens in Russia, the Russian military presence, the conflict with Armenia over Nagorno-Karabakh, Azerbaijan's relations with Iran, the assassination attempt against President Aliyev, and disparaging commentary about the president or other high officials. On Dec. 3, the new speaker of Parliament stripped an *Azadlig* reporter of his accreditation for an article critical of the Parliament. It was the reporter's second such removal from parliamentary coverage. Reporters have also occasionally been detained for several hours and questioned when covering demonstrations.

Prominent political figures, including government officials in office, frequently use the courts to file libel suits against critical journalists. Some newspapers have been compelled to pay heavy fines, crippling their work, but in a few instances, newspapers have been acquitted. A local cultural official filed suit against the newspaper *Sugovushan*, after that publication characterized him as indifferent toward refugees. The official initially obtained a judgment in his favor with substantial financial compensation for "offense to honor and dignity," but the Supreme Court overruled the verdict.

Azeri journalists have been particularly active in their self-defense. The Yeni Nesil (New Generation) group within the Union of Journalists has organized protest on behalf of colleagues and sought remedy in the courts to reopen newspapers or fight libel suits. The group has also raised Azerbaijan's censorship issues in an English-language bulletin and has covered the press situation in neighboring states.

The government monopolizes television broadcasting, and the Ministry of Communications has generally refused to grant licenses to independent stations. Applicants are told of the need for approval from the presidential administration, which the president's office denies, thus leaving independents without any recourse, because there is no broadcasting law to use to mount a challenge through the courts. Local executive authorities have closed down independent television stations indefinitely until the passage of media legislation. Some stations continue to broadcast illegally, showing great ingenuity with homemade equipment, and resourcefulness in covering local news. One station uses women reporters in the theory that government troops will be less likely to attack them.

March 16

Azer Husseinbala, *Azadlig,* CENSORED
Taptig Farhadoglu, Turan News Agency, CENSORED
Gunduz Tairli, *Azadlig,* HARASSED
Kenaan Aliyev, *Azadlig,* HARASSED
Husseinbala, a parliamentary correspondent for the opposition newspaper *Azadlig,* and Farthadoglu, a reporter for the independent news agency Turan, were stripped of their parliamentary press accreditation after President Heidar Aliyev's brother Djalal Aliyev, a member of Par-

liament, publicly criticized the independent media in Azerbaijan. Husseinbala had recently written an article critical of the Parliament. Turan news agency's monthly parliamentary bulletin had come under fire from Djalal Aliyev shortly before Farthadoglu lost his credentials. Djalal Aliyev has called for the closure of all opposition newspapers.

This is the second time this year that journalists from *Azadlig* have been disciplined by the government. On Feb. 7, Gunduz Tairli and Kenan Aliyev, two other *Azadlig* journalists, were summoned to the prosecutor's office and were urged to publish a retraction of an article on government corruption they had written for the paper. When the journalists refused, they were warned that the next time they published such material they would be brought to trial.

July 26
Metin Yasar Oglu, *Mukhalifat,* HARASSED
Yasar Oglu was detained by police while attempting to cover a demonstration in front of the Russian Embassy in Baku, the Azeri capital. The demonstrators were protesting the reported mistreatment of Azeris in Moscow and other Russian cities. Police dispersed the rally. Yasar Oglu was held for four hours. His camera and other equipment were damaged.

November 25
Elchin Saljug, *Azadlig,* CENSORED
Azadlig,CENSORED
The chairman of the Main Department for the Protection of State Secrets in the Press ordered the newspaper *Azadlig* to remove reporter Saljug's articles concerning the dismissal of the prime minister and speaker of Parliament. On Nov. 26, the newspaper printed a cartoon instead of Saljug's articles, in compliance with the government's prohibition on leaving blank spaces where editorial material has been censored. CPJ appealed to President Haidar Aliyev to reinstate Saljug's accreditation and to ensure that any further censorship of the media be stopped.

December 3
Azer Husseinbala, *Azadlig,* LEGAL ACTION
Husseinbala, a correspondent for the newspaper *Azadlig* (Liberty), was stripped of his accreditation by order of the new speaker of the Parliament, Murtuz Aleskerov. The action was in violation of Article 37 of the Law of the Azerbaijan Republic on the Mass Media, whereby a journalist cannot be stripped of his or her accreditation without a court order. Aleskerov tried to justify the move by saying that Husseinbala had "negatively assessed the processes taking place in the republic" in several satirical articles. Aleskerov threatened to take the same action against other reporters who criticized the Parliament or its members. When a group of 23 Azeri journalists appealed to Aleskerov to reverse his decision, he told them their appeal was "false."

Belarus

Belarus slides further into dictatorship, as reforms lag under President Alyaksandr Lukashenka, a former communist bureaucrat. The president tightened the gag on the media when he insisted on holding a public referendum Nov. 24 on conflicting new drafts of the constitution, despite resistance from the legislative and judicial branches. In the run-up to the referendum, state-owned broadcasters carried reports largely flattering to Lukashenka, barred the parliamentary opposition from getting any air time, and remained silent about large protest rallies and police violence. Local independent news organizations and the foreign media, which did cover the opposition, were repeatedly accused by the president and other top officials of "nonobjectivity."

The Lukashenka government employed a variety of repressive methods from the Soviet past to control the media, such as banning or blocking broadcasts, denouncing

out-of-favor journalists on national television, forcibly appointing government loyalists to state-owned media, and threatening to expel noncompliant foreign reporters. Just as in the Soviet era, the Belarusian public often relied on foreign broadcasters to learn about events in its own country. Some journalists, such as Svetlana Alexeyich, a frequent contributor to Russia's *Izvestiya* and a frequent target of officially supported libel suits in Belarus, were compelled to publish abroad.

Throughout the year, spurious tax inspections and nuisance lawsuits under vaguely worded press laws that punish libel, "insult of the head of state," "incitement of social intolerance," and "undermining of national security" plagued a dozen opposition newspapers. They were fined thousands of dollars for alleged violations of tax regulations, and were prevented from mailing copies to subscribers, or sometimes from publishing at all in Belarus. Resourceful editors found printers in the neighboring Baltic countries and quietly brought their press runs back to Belarus, but risked detention and confiscations at the border.

In August, the government shut down the only independent radio station. Speaking in Parliament, on television, and elsewhere, the president lambasted the Russian television stations ORT, NTV, and RTR for covering public controversies. On Nov. 19, Lukashenka issued a decree cutting off ORT and NTV's communication lines to Belarus, but revoked the decision after the Russian government objected. During the week of the referendum, electronic mail to and from Belarus was blocked, and the independent Web site www.belarus.net, which carries the on-line version of the daily *Vecherniy Minsk* and other information, reported that an unidentified hacker had damaged its server on Nov. 22. In December, the Belarusian Foreign Ministry again threatened that foreign journalists who "distort reality" would lose accreditation, and the Belarusian Security Council accused the Russian media of "inciting political tension in society."

March 19
Nikolai Galko, *Narodnaya Gazeta,* HARASSED
Galko, editor of the parliamentary daily *Narodnaya Gazeta,* was fired by order of President Alyaksandr Lukashenka. The president cited Galko's "failure to carry out his duties" as the reason for his dismissal. One year earlier, on March 17, 1995, Galko's predecessor, Iosif Seredich, was dismissed by the president for "inciting violence and political unrest." *Narodnaya Gazeta* is known for its criticism of the president's policies and its liberal slant.

April 26
Eduard Terlitsky, Radio Liberty, ATTACKED
Elena Lukashevich, *Imya,* ATTACKED
Leonid Sveridov, Russian State Television (RTR), ATTACKED
Oleg Trizno, Free-lancer, IMPRISONED
Vladzimir Dzyuba, Belarus Radio, IMPRISONED
Oleg Bebenin, *Imya,* ATTACKED
Oles Mikolaichenko, *Nasha Slova,* ATTACKED
Tsesary Golinsky, *Gazeta Wyborcha,* ATTACKED
Police who were dispersing participants in an unauthorized protest march marking the 10th anniversary of the accident at the Chernobyl nuclear plant beat and detained several journalists. Terlitsky, a reporter for Radio Liberty in Minsk, was clubbed by a policeman and received head injuries that required several stitches. Lukashevich and Bebenin, reporters for the Belarusian independent newspaper *Imya*; Sveridov, a reporter for Russian state television (RTR); Mikolaichenko, a reporter for the Belarussian independent newspaper *Nasha Slova*; and Golinsky, a reporter for the Polish daily *Gazeta Wyborcha*, were all also beaten by police. The free-lance journalist Trizno, who contributes to several banned Belarusian opposition papers, was arrested and sentenced to five days in jail on charges of "insulting a policeman." He was released on May 2. His wife was also required to pay 75,000 rubles (US$6) to

Central Europe

cover the cost of his stay in jail. Belarus Radio correspondent Dzyuba was arrested and sentenced to 10 days in jail on administrative charges of "disturbing the peace." According to his colleagues, Dzyuba is conducting a hunger strike to protest his detention. In a letter to President Alyaksandr Lukashenka, CPJ protested the policemen's treatment of journalists and urged Lukashenka to order the immediate release of Trizno and Dzyuba.

May 3
Alexander Kushner, Free-lance photographer, HARASSED
Alexander Stupnikov and crew, NTV, ATTACKED, CENSORED
Leonid Sveridov, Russian State Television (RTR), HARASSED

Government security agents harassed and attacked several journalists who were covering May Day rallies in Minsk attended by opposition leaders and Communist and trade union activists. Members of President Alyaksandr Lukashenka's security detail stopped Kushner, a free-lance photographer, as he was attempting to photograph them and exposed his film. Stupnikov, a correspondent for the independent news television station NTV, was stopped by plainclothes agents who refused to present identification. The men attacked Stupnikov's crew, beating one cameraman until a crowd began to gather. As a result, NTV was unable to file a story about the rally. As he was driving home from the event, Sveridov, an RTR correspondent, was followed by several men driving in a car with tinted windows. The driver of the car cut him off and forced him to stop. The men got out and showed Sveridov their identification so quickly that he was unable to read it. They threatened to smash his windows unless he got out of his car. He refused to cooperate, and eventually they drove away. Shortly thereafter, Sveridov interviewed the deputy head of President Lukashenka's administration, Uladimir Zamyatalin, who told him that Russian television companies were filing "inflamma-

tory reports" and that "the most serious measures would be taken."

June 22
Yury Drakokhrust, Radio Free Europe/Radio Liberty (RFE/RL), THREATENED

Galina Drakokhrust, the wife of RFE/RL correspondent Yury Drakokhrust, was attacked in Minsk by unidentified assailants, who issued a threat against Yury during the assault. Three men forced their way into the Drakokhrusts' locked apartment at 2 a.m. and attacked Galina, beating her and warning her to "tell your husband about this." The RFE/RL correspondent was in Poland on a business trip when the break-in occurred. His wife was knocked unconscious by her assailants, and awoke in a bathtub full of hot water. Nothing had been stolen from the apartment. Galina called the police, who took fingerprints, although she had noticed that at least one assailant was wearing gloves.

Yury Drakokhrust, who is known by the pseudonym Marat Dymov, regularly reports on Belarusian news and politics for RFE/RL, an international radio station funded by the U.S. Congress. He said he believes the Belarus government sanctioned the attack on his wife in retaliation for his coverage of a recent government crackdown on opposition political parties and media. Specifically, he had reported incidents in which police assaulted journalists attempting to cover demonstrations against the government of President Alyaksandr Lukashenka or to publish independent newspapers, which are either suspended or banned altogether in Belarus.

August 19
Belaruskaya Delovaya Gazeta, HARASSED, LEGAL ACTION
Belaruskaya Gazeta, HARASSED, LEGAL ACTION
Belaruski Rynok, HARASSED, LEGAL ACTION
Imya, HARASSED, LEGAL ACTION
Nasha Niva, HARASSED

Narodnaya Volya, HARASSED
Semida, HARASSED
Svaboda, HARASSED, LEGAL ACTION
Svabodnie Novosti Plus, HARASSED
BelaPAN, HARASSED
Minsk Economic News, HARASSED

Tax authorities began imposing penalties, including stiff fines, on Belarus' leading independent or opposition weekly newspapers for alleged tax infractions. As of November, at least nine newspapers had been affected: *Belaruskaya Delovaya Gazeta* (BDG), *Belaruskaya Gazeta, Belaruski Rynok, Imya, Nasha Niva, Narodnaya Volya, Semida, Svaboda,* and *Svabodnie Novosti Plus.* BelaPAN, the country's only independent news agency, was subjected to a tax inspection, and another weekly, *Minsk Economic News,* the only English-language newspaper in Belarus, was warned that it, too, would be penalized by the tax inspectorate.

BDG, Belaruskaya Gazeta, Belaruski Rynok, Imya, and *Svaboda* were handed fines ranging from 600 million to 2 billion Belarusian rubles (approximately US$42,000 to $118,000), and their bank accounts were temporarily frozen. Officials charged *BDG* and other newspapers with writing off unsold copies as a loss, instead of reporting them as a "hidden source of profit." *Imya* was penalized for taking cash directly from subscribers, rather than following the usual procedure of having the post office accept the subscription payments, but authorities had already prohibited the post office from assuming that function. *BDG* and others managed to get their accounts released on Sept. 10, but they still must pay the fines. Some of the papers have appealed to the Supreme Economic Court to overturn the fines.

Most of the newspapers continued to publish in spite of the penalties, but those with frozen bank accounts had no funds to buy newsprint and faced the depletion of their stocks within a few issues. Although Belarusian law prohibits employers from withholding payrolls even when the government has suspended the employers' accounts, at least one paper was unable to pay its workers. All opposition papers in Belarus continued to have difficulties distributing their publications through state-run kiosks and were forced to use unauthorized vendors. CPJ on Sept. 11 wrote to President Alyaksandr Lukashenka to express concern about the government crackdown.

August 31
Radio 101.2 FM, CENSORED
The Ministry of Communications disconnected the state-owned transmitter rented by the popular independent station Radio 101.2 FM in Minsk. On Aug. 30, the ministry had faxed to the station a copy of an internal memo claiming that "in order to eliminate interference in the reception" of Radio Altai, a government station, Radio 101.2 FM could no longer operate the transmitter. The independent station has appealed the suspension, but the government has refused to allocate another frequency.

Officials suggested that Radio 101.2 FM temporarily broadcast with a weaker signal or move its antenna to a suburban site. Both actions would reduce the station's audience of more than a million listeners, and moving the antenna would be costly and time-consuming. Editors at the station said that in more than a year of operation, they had received no complaints from the ministry concerning interference. Radio 101.2, the only nongovernmental station broadcasting in the Belarusian language, went on the air July 21, 1995, offering mainly musical programming, news, and retransmissions of BBC, Deutsche Welle, and other foreign programs.

September 14
Pavel Sheremet, *Belaruskaya Delovaya Gazeta,*
THREATENED
ORT, THREATENED
Sheremet, then editor in chief of the biweekly *Belaruskaya Delovaya Gazeta* and a free-lancer for ORT, Russia's public television channel, was warned by Uladzimir Zamyatalin, President Alyaksandr Lukashenka's deputy chief, that

ORT's Minsk bureau would be closed if Sheremet's material were broadcast. The material was aired anyway. CPJ on Sept. 11 wrote to Lukashenka to express concern about the ongoing government crackdown on the media.

September 19

Svaboda, THREATENED, LEGAL ACTION
The State Committee for the Press, the body which grants Belarusian newspapers their licenses, informed the opposition newspaper *Svaboda* that it was in violation of the press law and began proceedings against the paper in a Minsk commercial court. The action stemmed from an article that ran under the headline "The Devil's Bible" on Sept. 17. The article, written by Alexander Starikevich, a correspondent for the Russian daily *Izvestiya*, allegedly libeled the Belarusian head of state and other officials.

On Oct. 24, Ihar Hermenchuk, editor of *Svaboda*, was warned by the deputy public prosecutor that his newspaper might be suspended because of the article. The prosecutor threatened to take action if *Svaboda* committed similar violations within a year. CPJ appealed to President Alyaksandr Lukashenka on Nov. 18 to cease any further harassment of the press.

October 30

Brest Kuryer, THREATENED
The prosecutor of the Brest region issued an official warning to the newspaper *Brest Kuryer* on allegations of unspecified "incitement of social intolerance," a violation of Article 5 of the press law. The alleged violation was in connection with articles that were critical of Belarus' president. The warning noted that if the newspaper continued such violations, authorities would launch proceedings to close it. CPJ appealed to President Alyaksandr Lukashenka on Nov. 18 to cease any further harassment of the press.

November 13
Pavel Sheremet, ORT, THREATENED

Alexei Stupnikov, NTV, THREATENED
In a speech to the Belarusian Parliament, and again in television appearances Nov. 14 and Nov. 17, President Alyaksandr Lukashenka called for the expulsion of Sheremet, the Minsk correspondent for ORT, Russia's public television channel, and Stupnikov, correspondent for NTV, Russia's independent television station. Lukashenka also threatened to ban Russian broadcasting in Belarusian territory. He claimed that the journalists were not accredited and denounced them as "enemies." Sheremet, who is also deputy editor of a leading independent newspaper, *Belaruskaya Delovaya Gazeta*, is a native of Belarus. Stupnikov has permanent resident status in Belarus. Both have publicly displayed their accreditation from the Belarusian Interior Ministry. ORT and NTV ran shots of their press cards on Nov. 14.

CPJ appealed to President Lukashenka on Nov. 18 to cease any further harassment of the press.

November 19
NTV, CENSORED
ORT, HARASSED, CENSORED
President Alyaksandr Lukashenka issued a decree cutting off the transmission lines connecting the Russian public television channel ORT and the Russian independent channel NTV with Belarus. Lukashenka justified the move by saying that the Russian channels were not objective in their news coverage. The restrictions were removed later the same day.

ORT earlier had been ordered by the Belarusian Television and Radio Co. to vacate the Minsk studio it rents from the company by Nov. 10. Local ORT correspondent Pavel Sheremet and his staff refused to leave the premises because ORT's contract was valid until Dec. 31. CPJ appealed to Lukashenka on Nov. 18 to cease any further harassment of the press.

Bosnia and Herzegovina

After the signing of the December 1995 Dayton Peace Accords, local media geared up to cover the campaigns for the fall 1996 elections. As illustrated in CPJ's *Briefing on Press Freedom in Bosnia and Herzegovina Before the September 14 Elections* (see excerpt), the state and ruling parties largely controlled coverage inside Bosnia during the campaigns, and censorship plagued the minimal independent coverage. Authorities placed severe restrictions on freedom of movement for both foreign and local reporters among the three entities of Bosnia: the Republic of Bosnia and Herzegovina (the Sarajevo-based government); the Federation of Bosnia and Herzegovina (the Muslim-Croat Federation, including the Croat-controlled "mini-state" of Herzeg-Bosna, which was officially dismantled in December); and the Republika Srpska (Serb Republic).

After the elections, conditions remained tense among the ethnic groups, and journalists were often victims of the unrest. In October, Serb police attacked Mike Kirsch, an American free-lance journalist, while he was filming a destroyed Muslim village in Republika Srpska, confiscating his film and camera. The Peace Implementation Force (IFOR) later retrieved and returned Kirsch's camera.

Legal maneuvers also silenced journalists. When Bosnian Serb President Biljana Plavsic sacked the Bosnian Serb military leader Ratko Mladic in November, authorities also shut down an independent radio station with close ties to Mladic, and confiscated its equipment. The station had a reputation for critical reporting on the Bosnian Serb ruling party. Also in Republika Srpska, officials of the ruling party brought a libel suit against two reporters from *Alternativa*, a weekly independent newspaper, for an article that described corruption among officials of the governing Serbian Democratic Party.

A new television network, sponsored by the European Union, the United States, Japan, and the Open Society Institute in an effort to overcome heavily biased state-sponsored reporting, seemed to gain momentum by the end of the year. Planners originally intended to provide a single Bosnia-wide source of campaign coverage during the fall, but the Open Broadcasting Network (OBN) took longer than expected to overcome the Sarajevo-based Bosnian government's bureaucratic obstacles and difficulties with personnel in order to link four smaller stations in Sarajevo, Mostar, Tuzla, and Zenica. The network officially went on the air with only a week to spare before the elections, and outside the Federation of Bosnia and Herzegovina, its broadcasts reached only the large cities in Republika Srpska, and Herzeg-Bosna. By year's end, the project was close to linking an additional bureau in Republika Srpska.

February 8
Srdjan Ilic, Associated Press (AP), HARASSED
Hidajet Delic, Bosnian Government News
Agency, IMPRISONED
Ilic, an AP photographer based in Belgrade, and Delic, a photographer with the Bosnian Government News Agency who also works for AP, were arrested near a bridge connecting Serb- and Bosnian government-held parts of Sarajevo. Both journalists were taken first to Grbavica, a Bosnian Serb-controlled suburb of Sarajevo, and then to Serb police headquarters in Pale. Ilic was released the next day, but Delic, who was carrying negatives of photographs taken in Bosnian President Alija Izetbegovic's office, was kept in detention.

Bosnian Serb authorities accused Delic of having served in the Bosnian government's army in 1992 and of having ordered the murder of a Serb that summer. Delic's colleagues at AP's

Central Europe

217

Belgrade office informed CPJ that the accusations were false since he was excused from military service due to his work at AP.

CPJ wrote a letter of protest to Bosnian Serb leader Radovan Karadzic, urging him to release Delic immediately and to respect the status of journalists as civilian noncombatants. CPJ Chair Kati Marton then wrote to Serbian President Slobodan Milosevic, calling on him to make every effort to ensure Delic's immediate release.

On March 25, Delic was set free in Pale, less than 24 hours after a Serb reporter, Ninko Djuric, was released by the Bosnian government. Djuric, who works for the Pale-based Bosnian Serb weekly *Javnost*, was arrested on Sept. 10, 1995, on the battlefield in Vozuca in central Bosnia. No reasons were given for his arrest.

March 29
Srecko Latal, Associated Press (AP), ATTACKED, HARASSED

Latal, a Bosnian reporter for AP, was attacked by a crowd of Serbs when he went to investigate clashes between Serbs and Bosnian Federation police near Sarajevo. The crowd then forced Latal into a Serb police car. At this point, Italian soldiers with the Peace Implementation Force (IFOR) reportedly intervened and took Latal out of the Serb police car. The soldiers searched him, took him inside an armored personnel carrier, handcuffed him, and returned him to the Serb police, despite the fact that an Agence France-Presse reporter at the scene shouted that Latal was a member of the press. Latal was released three hours later in Serb-held Lukavica. In a letter to IFOR, CPJ protested the Italian soldiers' treatment of Latal.

June
Foreign correspondents, HARASSED

Officials at the press center in Republika Srpska, the Bosnian Serb enclave, were pressuring foreign journalists to accept the translation and escort services of a "bodyguard," who func-

tioned as the government's informer, for a fee of DM100 (US$67). The press center was also charging DM20 (US$13) for a seven-day press pass, according to Frank Havlicek, vice president of industrial relations for the *Washington Post*, who was in Bosnia and Herzegovina to teach a course. Havlicek said that the purpose of the bodyguard was ostensibly to look out for the numerous land mines remaining in the region, but journalists who refused the service were pursued and harassed by a press center employee sent to enforce the rules.

June 4
Studio 99, CENSORED

The telephone wires of "Hyde Park," a popular call-in talk show broadcast twice a week by Sarajevo's independent radio station Studio 99, went dead just as listeners attempted to discuss the controversial issue of the existence of two armies in the Muslim-Croat Federation. On June 6, the lines went dead again just before a scheduled debate on plans to send an official Bosnian delegation to Belgrade, Yugoslavia, for negotiations on establishing relations with Serbia.

June 30
Miguel Gil Moreno, Associated Press Television (APTV), ATTACKED

Gil Moreno, a cameraman for APTV, was knocked unconscious after being hit in the head and stomach by unidentified assailants while he was filming the arrival in Mostar of Serbs who had been displaced from their homes there. The Serbs were coming to Mostar to vote on whether the city, now divided between Muslims and Croats, should be unified or kept divided. His colleagues said that police who witnessed the beating did nothing to stop it. The colleagues also said they could not identify Gil Moreno's attackers. Gil Moreno, who suffered a minor concussion from the attack, was back at work by July 2.

August

Radio Zid, HARASSED

Radio Zid editors discovered that a new officially sponsored station, Orthodox Radio St. John,
broadcasting from Republika Srpska (Serb
Republic), was using its frequency, 89.9 FM. As
a result, Radio Zid listeners could not tune in to
the station. Initially, Radio Zid increased its
kilowatts, but it received a letter from the commander of IFOR, the peace implementation
force, saying that Radio Zid was interfering
with military communications. The radio station then appealed to the Organization for
Security and Cooperation in Europe (OSCE),
but was told that the OSCE could not stop the
Serb station from broadcasting. The radio executives then appealed to the Bosnian Ministry of
Culture to give them a new, unused frequency,
89.7, but they received no answer.

August 6

Zivko Savkovic, *Alternativa,* LEGAL ACTION

Pavle Stanisic, *Alternativa,* LEGAL ACTION

Editor in chief Stanisic and managing editor
Savkovic, of the weekly independent newspaper
Alternativa in Doboj, in Republika Srpska, were
charged in connection with a July 17 article that
claimed officials of the ruling Serbian Democratic Party (SDS) of Republika Srpska had
blocked several opposition election meetings in
Grbavica. A Doboj court convicted Savkovic on
Nov. 7 under Article 80, Paragraphs 1 and 2 of
the Criminal Code of Republika Srpska, for
transmitting false material injurious to the
"honor and reputation" of another. Savkovic
was handed a one-month suspended sentence.
Stanisic was found not guilty.

August 12

Free Election Radio Network (FERN), CENSORED

The Bosnian Serb Ministry of Transport and
Communications banned the Free Election
Radio Network (FERN), sponsored by the
Organization for Security and Cooperation in
Europe (OSCE), from broadcasting its election
radio program via the Lisina transmitter, which

reaches Banja Luka and surrounding Serb-controlled areas. The ministry said that an "inspection revealed the transmitter was being used
without the permission of the respective
Republika Srpska ministry."

FERN employees told CPJ that they continue to broadcast and that the transmitter in
question is protected by IFOR, the peace
implementation force, so that media groups
may use it. FERN also said that the Bosnian
Serb ministry has not proceeded with any further action since FERN ignored the ban.

August 15

Azenina Mulahuseinovic, *Oslobodjenje,* HARASSED

Nedzad Mulahuseinovic, the husband of Azenina Mulahuseinovic, a correspondent in the
Muslim-controlled town of Tesanj for the Sarajevo daily *Oslobodjenje,* was severely beaten by
unidentified assailants in Tesanj. Azenina had
reported several stories about the harassment of
local opposition political parties. Her editors
believe that her husband was targeted because
of her coverage of violence leading up to Sept.
14 national and regional elections.

August 28

IN-TV, HARASSED

Police in Sarajevo surrounded and blocked
entry to the main studios of IN-TV, a new for-
eign-sponsored Bosnian station that links five
existing stations together in one network.
When IN-TV moved its operations to another
building, Bosnian officials warned the new landlord not to cooperate with the station.

IN-TV, known as "Carl Bildt TV," after High
Representative Carl Bildt, had been plagued
with other difficulties as well before finally
going on the air Sept. 7, one week before general elections in Bosnia and Herzegovina. The
chief obstacle to the project was the Bosnian
government's temporary refusal to suspend a
regulation that prevented IN-TV from linking
the frequencies of the five smaller private stations. The regulation also prohibited IN-TV
from using several transmission points to pro-

Central Europe

vide wider reception.

October 11
Mike Kirsch, Free-lancer, ATTACKED,
 HARASSED
Kirsch, an American free-lance journalist and
cameraman working for Insight News Television Ltd. (INTV) of Great Britain, was attacked
by 10 Serb police officers with AK-47 assault
rifles. Kirsch was videotaping a destroyed house
in Jusici, a Muslim village now under the control of the Bosnian Serb Republic, when Serb
security police rushed toward him from around
the house, ordered him to stop filming, and
threatened to shoot him. They then shoved and
kicked him while they tried to take his camera.
Kirsch said police knocked him to the ground,
spit on him, and pointed their guns at him. He
said he tossed his camera to a Danish International Police Task Force (IPTF) officer, but a
Serb policeman pointed his gun at the Danish
officer and ordered him to give up the camera.

A U.S. Army cameraman, operating under
the command of the Peace Implementation
Force (IFOR), filmed the entire scene. IFOR
also retrieved Kirsch's camera the next day and
returned it to him, but the videocassette he had
been using to film the house was missing.

Kirsch and INTV requested copies of IFOR's
videotape of the incident, but their requests
were denied. CPJ appealed to top officials at the
Organization for Security and Cooperation in
Europe (OSCE), IFOR, the Pentagon, the U.S.
Army, and the U.S. Secretary of State to ensure
that the IFOR video of the attack be released.
CPJ also wrote to Serb Republic President
Momcilo Krajisnik, condemning the attack,
demanding that Kirsch's video be returned, and
calling for an end to any further attacks on
members of the press.

On Oct. 23, IFOR officials informed CPJ
that they released copies of the IFOR video to
Kirsch and INTV and that disciplinary action
would be taken against the local police commander responsible for the officers who
attacked Kirsch.

November 13
Radio Krajina, CENSORED
Bosnian Serb police shut down Radio Krajina,
an independent station with close ties to the
recently sacked military leader Ratko Mladic,
and confiscated the station's transmitter. Radio
Krajina was run by Lt. Col. Milovan Miluti-
novic, formerly Mladic's spokesman. Mladic and
other Bosnian Serb army officers were dismissed on Nov. 9 by Republika Srpska President Biljana Plavsic. The radio station began
broadcasting in the summer of 1995 and was
critical of the Bosnian Serb ruling party and
authorities.

Bulgaria

**Voters elected anti-Communist opposition
candidate Peter Stoyanov, a pro-market liberal, to the presidency on Nov. 3, after Stoyanov defeated Zhelyu Zhelev, Bulgaria's first
non-Communist head of state, in a primary in
June. The Socialist-dominated Parliament did
not face elections in 1996, and it was the
Parliament that showed its willingness to
keep the press in check when its members
in September attempted to introduce a new
electronic media law. The Parliament overrode Zhelev's veto to pass the law, but the
Constitutional Court of Bulgaria ultimately
rejected it.**

**The Constitutional Court invalidated the
main provisions of the law on Nov. 14. The
law would have severely restricted both
state-run and private radio and television stations. The draft called for a National Radio
and Television Council to oversee programming, staffing, and licensing of state-run stations, and would have monitored general
programming of the private radio and television stations.**

**Widespread complaints of censorship,
specifically by journalists at Bulgarian
National Radio (BNR), prompted several BNR**

staffers in December 1995 to found Bulgaria's first press freedom association, called Svobodna Slovo (Free Word). More than 100 journalists, translators, and sociologists officially established the organization on Jan. 8, defining it as politically independent and committed to the defense of free speech.

While Bulgaria has a number of nationwide independent newspapers and journals, including a newsmagazine that started publishing in January, the country's poor economy limited the spending power of most Bulgarians to buy print media. A poll in the local newspaper *Standart* found that the vast majority of Bulgarians get their domestic news via state television or radio. The poll also found that the majority of respondents felt that the state media's news coverage and commentary were politically biased.

February 20
Valentin Hadzhiev, *24 Chasa,* HARASSED,
 LEGAL ACTION
Mitko Shtirkov, *Trud,* HARASSED,
 LEGAL ACTION
Hadzhiev and Shtirkov, reporters for the independent dailies *24 Chasa* and *Trud,* respectively, were detained in the city of Smolyan on charges of slander. The two journalists were released the next day, but the charges against them still stand. On Feb. 19, Hadzhiev and Shtirkov had published articles stating that a newly appointed prosecutor in the city of Devin had been dismissed from the Devin police force in 1992 for bribery. A district prosecutor in Smolyan accused the journalists of reporting false facts and charged them with slander under Articles 146 and 148 of the Bulgarian Criminal Code. CPJ wrote to President Zhelyu Zhelev and Prime Minister Jan Videnov, urging them to drop the charges against the journalists.

September 5
All radio and television, LEGAL ACTION
The Bulgarian Parliament passed a bill outlining the formation of a new National Radio and Television Council, which was to be responsible for monitoring broadcasts and appointing directors to state-run radio and television. The Parliament overrode President Zhelyu Zhelev's veto against the bill. Zhelev submitted the law to the Constitutional Court of Bulgaria for further examination.

On Nov.14, the Constitutional Court invalidated 15 provisions of the electronic media law. The judges declared unconstitutional the formation of an 11-seat National Radio and TV Council based on political criteria and on parliamentary representation. The provisions that such a council, which would have been a state organ, approve program schemes and program content and have the right to cancel programs, were also declared unconstitutional. The court also invalidated articles that would have deprived the judiciary of free airtime and banned journalists from giving "subjective" commentaries.

Croatia

This was an unstable year for press freedom in Croatia. The passage of two amendments to the Croatian Criminal Code unleashed a string of libel cases against independent journalists. The amendments greatly facilitated the process by which journalists could be charged with libel against five top government officials.

In June, in the first trial under this law, two journalists from the satirical weekly *Feral Tribune* were charged with libeling President Franjo Tudjman. CPJ selected the case as emblematic of the use of seditious libel, or anti-government "insult" charges, against journalists in Croatia as well as throughout the former Yugoslavia and Eastern Europe, and prepared a legal brief condemning the statute and the indictment CPJ board member James C. Goodale presented the brief to the court trying the case.

Goodale noted that the use of such seditious libel laws was "fundamentally antithetical to the values of a democratic society." The September acquittal of the two journalists, an editor and a reporter, was hailed as a victory for domestic journalists' groups as well as for CPJ and other international press freedom advocates. By year's end, the state had appealed the acquittal, and at least two other cases under the new amendments were pending. (See special report, p. 263)

CPJ Chair Kati Marton met with several independent journalists and with President Tudjman during a six-day fact-finding mission to the Balkans in April. During Marton's meeting with Tudjman, he insisted that no government leader would tolerate the satirical criticism he faces from the Croatian press, but Marton told him that democratic leaders would permit it. Tudjman, a former Communist general who himself was once imprisoned for his writings, repeated his comments in public and followed them up with a rash of incidents of harassment of print and broadcast media.

Tudjman's ruling Croatian Democratic Party refused to renew the license of Radio 101, an independent radio station that once aired Tudjman's dissident views about Communist authorities. When the government gave the popular Radio 101's frequency to another station, at least 6,000 people gathered in Zagreb's center to show their contempt for the decision. Taxi drivers circled the station's offices, honking their horns in support of Radio 101. Authorities softened their stance, and by year's end they were re-evaluating the status of Radio 101 and its frequency.

Although Tudjman actively sought Croatia's entry into the Council of Europe, the council delayed admitting the country, largely because of the government crackdown on the media, begun in March. But the Council reconsidered Croatia's status after the Croatian parliament passed a more liberal media

law on Oct. 2, and Croatia was admitted to the Council on Nov. 6.

While the new media law sets more lenient guidelines for journalists, its wording is ambiguous. For example, the law absolves publishers of liability for information causing "offense," but only if the material is considered to be reported in good faith and in the public interest. Furthermore, the new law authorizes the government to force newspapers to run corrections and clarifications.

Throughout the year, Croatia's ruling party continued to use arcane and often spurious legal maneuvers, such as tax inspection and restriction of broadcast licenses, to silence critical, independent voices in the media. The main national newspapers and Croatian radio and television remained under the control of the ruling party.

March 26
All media, LEGAL ACTION
The Croatian Parliament passed two amendments to the Penal Code, reinstating laws previously abolished in 1991. The laws restrict press freedom and strengthen the position of the ruling Croatian Democratic Union (HDZ) by making publication of criticism of top officials and state secrets criminal offenses. Under these provisions, journalists convicted of criticizing the president of Croatia, the prime minister, the president of Parliament, the president of the Constitutional Council, or the president of the Supreme Court or of divulging ill-defined classified information could face six months to three years in prison.

While Justice Minister Miroslav Separovic claimed the laws met European standards, independent commentators called them a means to suppress media freedom and said they were designed to keep the press from airing internal party struggles and criticism of President Tudjman.

These amendments had to be promulgated by President Tudjman in order to be incorporated in the Penal Code. Despite intense protest, he

declared the amendments law. The public prosecutor was thus empowered to launch investigations of any journalist alleged to have offended
or slandered the highest officials. CPJ urged
President Tudjman to repeal the amendments.

March 28
Novi List, LEGAL ACTION
Novi List, an independent newspaper, was fined
US$2.5 million for using printing equipment
from Italy that the Croatian government
claimed was reserved for Italian-language
minority newspapers in Croatia. According to
Novi List reporters, agreements signed by members of the Croatian and Italian governments in
1992 contained no such restrictions. Not only
has *Novi List* used the equipment freely in the
past, it has also provided and paid for space to
house the machinery. In addition to the US$2.5
million fine for past usage, the Croatian government ordered *Novi List* to pay a monthly fee
for the equipment. These financial penalties
have forced the paper to raise its price from 3.5
kuna to 4 kuna and to reduce staff salaries by 25
percent. CPJ urged the Croatian government to
drop the fine against *Novi List.*

On May 10, the Croatian minister of finance
decided to suspend the fine even though, by
law, *Novi List* must pay the penalty first and
then appeal the decision. On June 6, the Croatian Parliament began drafting a law to regulate
the use of printing houses in the country. *Novi
List*'s editor in chief told CPJ he was optimistic
that the fine against the newspaper would be
suspended indefinitely.

April 25
Panorama, CENSORED
The Croatian government closed down the
offices of the independent newspaper *Panorama*
for allegedly violating property and environ-
mental laws. The newspaper's deputy editor,
Andrej Rora, stated that the government's move
was in response to *Panorama*'s critical coverage
of President Franjo Tudjman. CPJ wrote to
President Tudjman and urged him to reopen

the offices of *Panorama* and ensure that it be
permitted to resume publishing. On May 10,
authorities permitted *Panorama* to reopen.

May 3
Viktor Ivancic, *Feral Tribune,* LEGAL ACTION
Marinko Culic, *Feral Tribune,* LEGAL ACTION
Ivancic, editor in chief of the independent
weekly newspaper *Feral Tribune,* was taken to a
police station in Split and informed that a criminal case had been opened against him and
Culic, a *Feral Tribune* reporter. They were
charged with slandering President Franjo Tudjman in the April 29 issue of the paper. The
charges were in connection with an article titled
"Bones in the Mixer," and a photomontage,
labeled "Jasenovac: The Biggest Croatian
Underground City." The article criticized the
president's proposal to rebury the remains of
World War II Fascists alongside their victims.
This case was the first to be brought under legislation passed on March 29 that effectively
criminalizes any critical reporting or satirical
commentary on five top officials. The legislation allows for punishment of up to three years
in prison for those convicted. In a letter to
President Tudjman, CPJ urged that the charges
against Ivancic and Culic be dismissed.

On June 14, the criminal trial of the *Feral
Tribune* journalists was unexpectedly adjourned
on its opening day—apparently in response to
the international outcry over President Tudjman's efforts to muzzle Croatia's independent
media.

The judge scheduled the trial to resume on
Sept. 25, in order, he said, to call new witnesses.

CPJ board member James C. Goodale, who
traveled to Zagreb to show support for the journalists, presented the judge with a legal brief
prepared at the request of defense counsel. The
CPJ brief condemned the prosecution as an
example of seditious libel, a legal concept that
runs counter to the standards for press freedom
in democratic societies. The judge explained
that he could not enter the brief into the record
because the Croatian legal system had no pro-

Central Europe

cedures for filing such documents. But he did agree to meet with Goodale at a future date to hear CPJ's concerns. After the hearing, Goodale and other representatives from press freedom groups and local NGOs held a public meeting and press conference where they denounced the statutes used to prosecute the journalists, citing international practice regarding criminal libel.

On Sept. 25, the criminal trial resumed for the *Feral Tribune* journalists. On Sept. 26, the judge acquitted both Ivancic and Culic of all charges. In a press release following the verdict, CPJ hailed the decision as a victory for press freedom in Croatia, but called again for the elimination of the legislation that was used against Ivancic and Culic and is now being used against other journalists.

May 23
Feral Tribune, LEGAL ACTION
Nevenka Kosutic, the daughter of Croatia's President Franjo Tudjman, filed a civil libel suit against *Feral Tribune*, demanding 3.5 million kuna (US$635,000) in damages. Kosutic claims that *Feral Tribune*, a satirical and investigative weekly, slandered her by publishing allegations that she set up a prosperous business using her government connections. According to the state news agency HINA, Kosutic's lawyer, Zeljko Olujic, has asked the court to order the provisional withdrawal of the money from *Feral Tribune*'s bank account pending a verdict. CPJ, which had sent a May 7 letter to Tudjman concerning a criminal libel suit brought against two *Feral Tribune* journalists, sent another letter to the president, urging him to repeal revisions to the Penal Code on criminal slander and to cease all legal harassment of the *Tribune* and other independent media.

May 30
Globus, THREATENED
In an ongoing government campaign of harassment and intimidation against the independent press, the ruling Democratic Party of Croatia (HDZ) announced its intention to sue the

weekly independent newspaper *Globus*. The HDZ leaders cited a May 21 article, written by the paper's editor in chief, Davor Butkovic, which contends that the ruling party has drafted a list of opposition politicians whom they plan to publicize as public enemies. The HDZ leaders denounced the article, saying it contained "speculation and lies." CPJ urged President Franjo Tudjman to ensure that the HDZ does not file charges against *Globus*.

On June 3, the Council of Europe announced five conditions that Croatia had to meet for admission to the council, one of which was that the Croatian government drop all its pending cases against the independent news media.

July 2
"Slikom na Sliku," CENSORED
The editor of the television news program "Slikom na Sliku" (Frame by Frame) told CPJ that he had been informed by officials at the government television channel HTV, Croatia's only nationwide channel, that HTV would no longer air the popular program. No explanation was given for the program's cancellation. CPJ wrote to Croatian President Franjo Tudjman, urging him to allow "Slikom na Sliku" to continue broadcasting.

The show, which began running in January 1992 and aired five times a week, was a 45-minute program containing interviews with prominent newsmakers and broadcasts from abroad. It was the only television news program in Croatia to cover the June trial of *Feral Tribune* journalists Viktor Ivancic and Marinko Culic, who were charged with slandering President Franjo Tudjman. In April, CPJ's chair, Kati Marton, appeared on the program to discuss press freedom issues in Croatia.

July 15
Radio 101, LEGAL ACTION
The Croatian Telecommunications Council for the second time denied Radio 101, a local station in the Zagreb area, a permanent license to use the FM frequency it has been broadcasting

on since 1983. Radio 101's first application, submitted in January, had been rejected by the Council because of missing documentation. Although the station was able to provide the missing information in the second application, the Council refused to grant the license anyway. Meanwhile, the popular, award-winning Radio 101 has paid fees amounting to more than DM50,000 (US$32,000) for three temporary licenses, the last of which expired on Nov. 15. Editors there believe the Council's reluctance was politically motivated because Radio 101's news is often critical of the government and most of the nine members on the Council are also members of the ruling Croatian Democratic Party (HDZ).

On Nov. 20, the Council voted to give the frequency, 94.3 FM, to Radio Globus, a station that had been vying for the frequency but until that time had existed only on paper. Zagreb's citizens responded with mass demonstrations, and Radio Globus declined the frequency in support of Radio 101. CPJ and other international groups, the U.S. State Department, and even members of the HDZ also denounced the Council's move, and on Nov. 21 the Council revoked its judgment and decided to conduct another round of bidding for the frequency. Radio 101 was able to continue broadcasting.

On Jan. 24, 1997, the Croatian Telecommunications Council voted 6-2 in favor of granting Radio 101 its permanent license to broadcast on its current frequency, 94.3 FM. The Council stipulated, however, that the station would have to submit additional paperwork by Oct. 31; then the station would be able to sign a formal contract with the telecommunications ministry.

September 3
Veljko Vicevic, *Novi List*, LEGAL ACTION
Tihana Tomicic, *Novi List*, LEGAL ACTION
The Croatian Democratic Union (HDZ), the ruling party of Croatia, brought libel charges against Vicevic, editor in chief of the independent daily *Novi List*, and Tomicic, a columnist for the newspaper. The charges stemmed from

a recent column by Tomicic in which she compared the political climate in Croatia before its first regional elections, held in 1990, to the situation in Germany just before Adolf Hitler became chancellor. The charges were filed under Article 71 of the Croatian Criminal Code, which forbids the publication or broadcasting of information deemed to be false and considered injurious to the "honor and reputation" of public officials. The law mandates up to three years in prison for offenders. CPJ wrote to President Franjo Tudjman on Sept. 4 to express concern over the charges against the *Novi List* journalists and others accused of similar offenses.

September 3
Ivo Pukanic, *Nacional*, LEGAL ACTION
Srecko Jurdana, *Nacional*, LEGAL ACTION
The Croatian Democratic Union (HDZ), the ruling party of Croatia, brought libel charges against Pukanic, editor in chief of the weekly independent newspaper *Nacional*, and Jurdana, a columnist for the paper. The charges were filed under Article 71 of the Croatian Criminal Code, which forbids the publication or broadcasting of information deemed to be false and considered injurious to the "honor and reputation" of public officials. The law mandates up to three years in prison for offenders. In filing the charges, the HDZ did not cite any specific articles published by *Nacional*, but it did single out Jurdana, who is known for frequently writing columns critical of HDZ leaders. CPJ wrote a letter to President Franjo Tudjman on Sept. 10 to express concern about the charges.

November 18
Nacional, CENSORED
When the leading independent weekly *Nacional* attempted to issue an early edition with coverage of President Franjo Tudjman's visit to the United States for medical treatment, editor in chief Ivo Pukanic was told the newspaper's printer, which is state-run, had run out of paper and could not complete the job. Pukanic

learned, however, that there was an ample paper supply at the printing house. A senior official in the Croatian government called Pukanic and told him that *Nacional* had to wait one day before publishing the edition, saying that the paper should not publish news about the president's health just as he was returning to Croatia from a Washington, D.C., hospital. *Nacional* published the edition the following day.

November 29
Vesna Jankovic, *Arkzin*, HARASSED
Croatian police questioned Jankovic, the editor of the independent biweekly *Arkzin*, about a Sept. 13 article about the assets of President Franjo Tudjman's family. Jankovic was pressured into signing a statement saying that she was responsible for the article, but no formal charges have been filed against *Arkzin*.

The public prosecutor launched the investigation under Articles 71 and 72 of the Croatian Penal Code, the same legislation that was used against *Feral Tribune* journalists Marinko Culic and Viktor Ivancic.

Georgia

Georgia's community of independent newspaper editors, reporters, and broadcasters continue to expand their horizons, despite frequent government interference from President Eduard Shevardnadze and his political associates.

Georgian lawmakers debated changes to a controversial draft media law that would adversely affect journalists if enacted and also considered amendments to the criminal code that journalists feared would curtail their freedom. Journalists' groups lobbied vigorously against restrictive features of the proposed media law. The Free Press Association, a group made up of several of the major newspapers (*Alia, Resonance, Droni,* and others), issued a statement on June 20 noting that at a government meeting that day, Shevardnadze had accused the media of bias and libel and called on law-enforcement agencies to protect the government from the press. The association urged that the judicial system handle such cases under the rule of law and vowed to appeal official "insult" suits to the courts.

Journalists were also concerned about a clause in the proposed media law that would create a "National Press Council" to regulate advertising and impose journalistic ethics. At year's end, the journalists had managed to defeat a draft of the law in the national legislature that would have enabled the council's members to be selected largely by the government and the ruling party in Parliament.

In another victory for press freedom, some journalists successfully lobbied to eliminate some of the subjects that another piece of pending legislation would classify as "secret," because publication would "damage national security."

The government's arbitrary broadcast licensing procedures prevented Rustavi-2, an independent television station, from securing a permanent license, effectively forcing the station off the air. The government's stance on Rustavi-2 may stem from the independent electronic media's increasing competitive edge in a field formerly dominated by state-run channels.

The press felt the effects of the ongoing civil war in Abkhazia, a region of Georgia seeking autonomy. During an election campaign carried out amid violence in the region, the Glasnost Defense Foundation in Moscow received reports of a number of attacks on news organizations. On June 5, for example, equipment was stolen from the news agency Abkhazpress, and on Nov. 2 an explosion damaged the printing house in Gal District that typesets Abkhazia's main newspaper.

July 17

Rustavi-2, CENSORED

Rustavi-2, the leading nongovernment TV station in Tbilisi, with an audience of more than one million viewers, was forced off the air by the Georgian Ministry of Communications. The ministry revoked Rustavi-2's license, claiming that its parent company, Gamma Plus Agency, Ltd., is not authorized to broadcast on a television frequency.

Independent observers expressed concern that the sudden withdrawal of the license was designed to pressure independent broadcasters, and that Rustavi-2's coverage of controversial stories on politics, ethnic relations, and organized crime may have been a factor in the decision. CPJ wrote a letter on July 24 to President Shevardnadze, urging him to investigate the case and to allow Rustavi-2 to continue its daily broadcasts until the matter is examined through due process of law.

On Nov. 4, the Supreme Court of Georgia ruled that Rustavi-2 had been unlawfully denied a broadcasting license. But the Ministry of Communications has delayed the return of the license. The station remains off the air and its status is still unclear.

Kazakstan

President Nursultan Nazarbayev moved to increase his control over the media, most likely in anticipation of the presidential elections scheduled for the year 2000. In January, Nazarbayev decreed a reorganization of the National Agency for Press and Mass Media, according to which only he can appoint or dismiss the agency's chairman. Journalists viewed the move as consolidating presidential leverage over state-subsidized media.

Journalists continued to suffer detention, harassment, and even imprisonment for their work, while lawsuits and bureaucratic obstacles pressured independent newspapers and broadcasters. Some attacks on the press reflected the Kazak government's increasing concern with the presence of a large and vocal Russian population. Several Russian correspondents based in Almaty, such as *Izvestiya*'s Vladimir Ardayev, were threatened with the loss of accreditation when their coverage appeared to challenge the Nazarbayev government.

In some cases, reporters fought back and upheld their freedoms. *Komsomolskaya Pravda* was threatened with criminal prosecution and closure for carrying a controversial piece by Alexander Solzhenitsyn. But after campaigns by domestic and international press freedom advocates, including CPJ, authorities opted for a lighter penalty, requiring the newspaper to print an expression of regret. In another case, Batyrkhan Darinbet of Radio Liberty's Kazakstani Service, detained by police July 5 while attempting to cover an unauthorized anti-nuclear demonstration, sued the government for wrongful arrest and was awarded damages, although the government was not required to pay the damages.

Five independent radio and television stations—all of whom rent transmitters from the government—were informed Nov. 9 in writing that they were "interfering with air traffic communications" and that they would need special clearance to enter their studios. All the stations were intermittently shut down. In December, the Association of Independent Electronic Mass Media of Central Asia reported that law-enforcement officials in several provincial cities had conducted hostile inspections of television and radio companies, all of which are members of the association.

Meanwhile, the president's daughter, Dariga Nazarbayeva, received her own semi-privatized television station, Khabar, whose programming does not present a challenge to the government. Nazarbayeva was also instrumental in registering another "independent" channel, NTK, whose founders include high government officials. In December, the government announced a public tender of broadcast frequencies (including those already leased) at prices far out of the range of any truly independent company's ability to pay. The alternative media feared that only groups close to the government would gain control of the frequencies, since only such companies would have access to the necessary funds for licenses, at least US$30,000 for an investment in an FM radio frequency and US$64,000 for a VHF television frequency, plus annual fees of at least US$12,000.

January 23

Sergei Vasilyev, IMPRISONED, LEGAL
ACTION

Vasilyev, formerly a reporter for the Kazakstani edition of the Russian newspaper *Argumenty i Fakty,* was arrested and placed in detention. On July 10, he was found guilty of libeling a public official by the Medeus District Court in Almaty, the Kazak capital. He was sentenced to five months in prison, a term less than the time he had already spent in pretrial detention, and released.

On Aug. 10, 1994, Vasilyev had published a brief item alleging that the ex-governor of the East Kazakstan region had been detained by Moscow customs authorities for attempting to smuggle gold across the border. The item was based on an account from a source in the KNB (Kazakstan National Security), but the information turned out to be false, reportedly planted by other officials in an attempt to discredit the governor.

After Vasilyev was notified that he was under investigation for criminal libel, he returned to Russia in 1995, even though he had signed a statement promising not to leave Kazakstan. On Jan. 23, 1996, when Vasilyev returned to Kazakstan at the request of his editors, he was promptly arrested in his apartment in the city of Ust-Kamenogorsk. He spent about two months

in a local prison without charge and was then transferred to Almaty, where he spent more than three months in an isolation cell until his trial. *Argumenty i Fakty* did not rehire Vasilyev, and he has been unable to find work in journalism since his release from prison.

March 10

Erik Nurshin, formerly of *Dozhivyom do Ponedelnika,* LEGAL ACTION

A criminal libel case was opened against Nurshin, a prominent Russian journalist who lives in the capital of Almaty and had edited the now-defunct newspaper *Dozhivyom do Ponedelnika* (Let's Survive Until Monday). The investigation was in connection with the newspaper's criticism of the chairman of Kazakstan's Supreme Court and of law-enforcement officials, and its reporting of rape accusations against the governor of the Dzambul region. Article 191-1 of the Kazakstani Penal Code essentially prevents reporters from investigating allegations of official corruption or criminal acts until after a court renders a decision on the allegations. In July, authorities closed the case "due to lack of evidence."

Dozhivyom do Ponedelnika stopped publishing in December 1995 after authorities, unhappy with an article blaming high officials for Kazakstan's agricultural failures, ordered the founder of the paper to shut it down, and the founder fled the country. Eventually editor Nurshin and his staff from *Dozhivyom do Ponedelnika* started up a weekly television program called "Versiya" on TV M, a commercial channel. Although the criminal case against Nurshin was dropped, he and his television show continued to come under pressure from officials and the government press. By year's end the station was facing closure.

May 29

Komsomolskaya Pravda, THREATENED

Editors at the Almaty office of the Russian daily *Komsomolskaya Pravda* and a local district court judge were summoned to the office of the prosecutor general of Kazakstan and told that the prosecutor general was calling for a ban on the newspaper. The prosecutor general charged that *Komsomolskaya Pravda* had violated Kazakstan's constitution, which forbids incitement of ethnic hatred and violation of territorial integrity. The charges cited an April 23 article by Alexander Solzhenitsyn calling for the reunification of the northern districts of Kazakstan with Russia. *Komsomolskaya Pravda* later published letters opposing Solzhenitsyn's view.

The allegations were first made by the Union of Writers of Kazakhstan, which brought the case to the district court. When the district court judge dismissed the charges, the union then brought the allegations to the prosecutor general, who ordered another hearing. CPJ wrote a letter to the president and prosecutor general of Kazakstan urging that the case be dropped, noting that the charges were in serious violation of free press standards.

Meanwhile, Altynbek Sarsenbaev, chairman of the government's National Agency for Press and Mass Media of Kazakstan, petitioned the prosecutor general to close the newspaper for six months because of the alleged constitutional violations.

On July 17, the district court ordered the newspaper to print an apology about the incident within a week. *Komsomolskaya Pravda* printed a statement of regret the next day, and the case was dropped on July 24.

November
Radio/TV M, HARASSED
Radio NS, HARASSED
Radio Totem, HARASSED
Radio RIK, HARASSED
KTK TV, HARASSED
Several independent television and radio stations were harassed by Kazakstani officials during the first two weeks of November, apparently in anticipation of a mass opposition rally scheduled for Nov. 17 but eventually banned by the government before it could take place. Radio M, Radio NS, Radio Totem, and Radio RIK

were shut down for periods ranging from several hours to several days, and on Nov. 4, transmission of TV M and KTK TV reportedly was stopped. On Nov. 8, most of the radio stations received letters from the newly formed State Frequency Commission alleging that their broadcasts were interfering with air traffic communications at the airport. Air traffic control officials denied that the broadcasts were causing any difficulties.

Also in November, independent broadcasters were notified by the State Property Committee and the Ministry of Transport and Communications that the elevated area where both the government-owned transmitter and the studios of nongovernment stations are located had been declared a "controlled facility," requiring a special entry pass.

November 25
Radio/TV M, THREATENED, HARASSED
Electric and telephone wires to the studio for independent radio and television station M were cut, making work there virtually impossible. The station managed to continue broadcasting six hours a day to special three-channel receivers in customers' homes. On Dec. 5, an official from President Nursultan Nazarbayev's administration called M's directors and said, "For two years you have been the mouthpiece of the opposition, and therefore we are closing you down." Members of the administration later denied that anyone had made that statement, even though the phone conversation had been taped and broadcast. The officials claimed that the station had been closed "due to technical reasons." The station's license expired on Jan. 1, 1997, and unable to compete in a high-priced government auction of frequencies, M was forced to close.

Kyrgyzstan

Although many observers consider Kyrgyzs-

Central Europe

229

tan's president Askar Akayev to be the most democratic leader of the newly independent Central Asian states, he compromised his reputation for liberalism in 1996 when his government replaced the heads of major news organizations by decree, continued to harass the only remaining independent newspaper, Res Publika, and sentenced one of its journalists to jail for "defamation" of the president. Rysbek Omurzakov of *Res Publika* had been charged with insulting the president and with "defamation in printed form combined with commission of a crime against the state" for his political leaflets, which he had distributed at a protest rally. The same charges have been used in the past to harass other reporters and political activists.

In October, Uchkun, the state publishing house, refused to print an edition of Res Publika, ostensibly because of an outstanding debt. Yet Kyrgyzstan's leading government newspaper had a far greater debt and continued to print. The stalwart *Res Publika* was already operating under duress, managing to put out issues throughout 1996, even though its top editors in 1995 had lost a libel suit brought by President Akayev, resulting in their suspension from practicing journalism for 18 months.

Akayev in March appointed a former Communist Party ideological secretary to head Kyrgyz State Radio and Television. Given the small circulation of even state-owned newspapers, most people rely on government-sponsored television for their news.

The editors at the government's main newspaper, *Slovo Kyrgyzstana*, including editor in chief Alexander Malevanny, lost their jobs after they attempted to establish an independent newspaper, which the government refused to register.

Poland

The November 1995 transfer of power from 15-year incumbent President Lech Walesa to ex-Communist Aleksandr Kwasniewski affected the local media mainly in the sphere of public broadcasting.

Poland's public television station underwent many changes after the former director, identified with the station's independent-minded programming, resigned and Ryszard Miazek, a member of the ruling Polish Peasant Party, took charge. During his first month on the job, Miazek was quoted in a local newspaper as saying, "Society is the state and its democratic structures, and television should offer its services to them. It should not aspire to expressing independent opinions because such opinions are formulated by parliament and other representatives of the state." Miazek eliminated independent political programs from public programming and appointed new program directors closer to the views of the ruling party. Viewer ratings plummeted.

Meanwhile, private newspapers, journals, and television and radio stations remained largely independent, strengthened by Poland's growing market economy. But the independent media were subject to harassment by libel laws. Local and international media strongly criticized the guilty verdict in the only documented Polish government-sponsored civil suit against a journalist, which the court eventually annulled.

February 6
Jerzy Urban, *NIE*, LEGAL ACTION
Urban, editor in chief of the satirical weekly *NIE*, was convicted of publishing secret documents and given a one-year suspended prison sentence, fined US$4,000, and banned from managing a publication and acting as a journalist for one year. Urban's conviction stems from

a 1992 article in *NIE* that included secret documents of the Communist political police. CPJ protested the conviction and sentencing of Urban in a letter to President Aleksander Kwasniewski.

On Sept. 26, the Appeals Court in Warsaw annulled the February verdict of the Warsaw District Court. The presiding judge for the appeal said that the District Court "had no grounds" for handing down its sentence, as "the prosecution's case had not been proven." The Appeals Court returned the case to the office of the Warsaw district prosecutor, who now has the option of either preparing new legal proceedings or discontinuing the case.

Romania

The November election of opposition candidate Emil Constantinescu to the presidency had a nearly immediate effect on some Romanian media. About a week after Constantinescu's election, for example, police dropped an ongoing investigation into vague charges against Costel Bobic, a reporter with the independent daily *Ziua*, who had written about government corruption.

The presidential campaign revealed a thriving media, which provided insightful reporting and analysis about all of the candidates. While the majority of Romanians watch the widely accessible Romanian state television, and half rely on the state station for radio news, private broadcasters' audiences burgeoned during the campaign, especially in the larger cities, thanks to their comprehensive coverage of the candidates' speeches and debates.

In May, threatening to suppress some of these independent news outlets, Adrian Nastase, the president of the Romanian Chamber of Deputies, announced that the BBC coverage was unfairly favoring the opposition. Nastase proposed that the National Audiovisual Council "reconsider" the frequency allocations of those FM stations that broadcast the BBC. The threat generated much criticism from the international community, including CPJ, which appealed to Romanian authorities to allow stations to broadcast the BBC, and in the end, none of the stations lost its frequency.

Prior to the election, members of the ruling party had brought libel charges against independent newspapers voicing support for Constantinescu and the opposition party. At the close of the year, libel sentences against four such journalists remained unsettled. Two journalists in the city of Constanta lost their second appeal of libel convictions stemming from suits by former members of the city council. Their seven-month prison sentences and fines remained indefinitely suspended, however. Two other journalists, with *Ziua*, faced 12- and 14-month prison sentences for libel against former President Ion Iliescu. They are appealing their convictions, but a hearing date has not been set.

In October, after much debate and protest from opposition media, the Romanian Senate and Chamber of Deputies passed four amendments to sections of the Romanian penal code that affect freedom of the press. Articles 205, 206, 238, and 239 of the draft penal code allow for fines and imprisonment for those convicted for libel. After pressure from opposition media and protests from international organizations, including CPJ, the lawmakers dropped early versions of the amendments, which mandated heavy fines for journalists convicted under the legislation. The Constitutional Court of Romania was reviewing the legislation's final draft at press time.

April 12
***Bursa*, THREATENED**
Bursa, an independent financial weekly known for its groundbreaking coverage of the black

Central Europe

market and the emerging Romanian securities market, was threatened with legal action by the National Securities Council (CNVM). The CNVM issued a statement declaring that the "trading [of] shares listed or unlisted on the Bucharest Stock Exchange by unauthorized persons through ads published in the newspaper *Bursa* could be defined as a violation of Law No. 52/1994, Art. 114." This law forbids offering securities without authorization and is punishable by a fine or a prison term of three months to two years. In November 1995, *Bursa* published an article critical of the CNVM, leading some observers to conclude that the threat of legal action against the paper was motivated by a desire to suppress such reporting.

CPJ wrote a letter to President Ion Iliescu urging him to ensure that the CNVM and other state authorities refrain from attempting to censor or curtail legitimate publishing activity. CPJ pointed out that threats against news outlets covering free markets, whether in news stories or in advertising, signal a clear intention to suppress the independent media.

After receiving the letter, a presidential aide visited *Bursa* and—improbably—asked the editors to help draft Iliescu's reply to CPJ. A second presidential counselor then visited, and legislation was drafted to remove the vagueness in the law that led to the original charges, which have since been suspended.

May 4
Independent radio stations, HARASSED
BBC Romanian service, HARASSED
Adrian Nastase, president of the Chamber of Deputies, announced that the BBC Romanian service was violating Romania's electoral law by "obviously favoring the opposition in its campaign coverage." Nastase called for the National Audiovisual Council to "reconsider" immediately the frequency allocation of those Romanian FM stations that broadcast the BBC program. He added that "the BBC, being a British organization, should broadcast news about England and cover what happens in Lon-

don, not in Romania." While no radio stations canceled the BBC program, experts feared this would happen. Radio broadcast news is an important source of information in Romania since the vast majority of the country's television news programs are state-run. In a letter to Nastase and Romania's President Ion Iliescu, CPJ urged the government to ensure that Romanian radio stations are able to continue broadcasting independent news.

July 11
Radu Mazare, *Telegraf,* LEGAL ACTION
Constantin Cumpana, *Telegraf,* LEGAL ACTION
Mazare, editor of the Constanta-based daily *Telegraf,* and Cumpana, a reporter with the paper, were each sentenced to seven months in prison and a 25 million lei (US$82,000) fine for libel. The journalists were sentenced after the Romanian Supreme Court rejected their second appeal of the libel conviction. The first appeal had been rejected by a district court.

The charges stemmed from a 1992 article in *Telegraf* about corruption in the Constanta city council. The former deputy mayor of the council, Dan Miron, was forced to step down two months after the article appeared. Revi Moga, another figure named in the article and a former attorney for the city council, filed libel charges against Mazare and Cumpana in April 1994. (Moga is now a judge in a local Constanta court.)

On July 15, Romania's chief prosecutor suspended the jail sentences until Aug. 30 pending a re-examination of the case. The suspension followed protests by CPJ and other international and Romanian human rights organizations. At year-end the sentences remained suspended.

September 30
Mihai Antoci, *Ziua,* HARASSED
Razvan Savaliuc, *Ziua,* HARASSED
Marius Ghilezan, *Romania Libera,* HARASSED
Dan Preisz, *Romania Libera,* HARASSED
Flroin Esanu, *Romania Libera,* HARASSED
Oana Bratu, Radio Contact, HARASSED

Ovidiu Patrascanu, *Evenimentul Zilei,* HARASSED
Andreea Munteanu , *Azi,* HARASSED
Marius Huc, ABC, HARASSED
Mircea Marian, *Medifax,* HARASSED

Ten reporters from various news outlets were ordered by a member of the local branch of the Party of Social Democracy (PDSR), Romania's ruling party, to give up notes, videotapes, and any other material related to their reporting about an allegedly fraudulent polling station.

Earlier that day, the 10 journalists had entered the offices of the polling station, where PDSR members reportedly were using slanted questions to conduct voter polls in an effort to influence the voters in favor of President Ion Iliescu, who was running for re-election Nov. 3. On Oct. 3-4, after the story became public, several of the journalists were summoned by police for questioning, often late at night. CPJ appealed to Iliescu to put a stop to any further harassment of the journalists.

October 25
Sorin Rosca-Stanescu, *Ziua,* LEGAL ACTION
Tana Ardeleanu, *Ziua,* LEGAL ACTION

Ziua managing director Rosca-Stanescu and investigative reporter Ardeleanu were found guilty of "offense against authorities," a charge that was brought on Aug. 18, 1995, under Article 238 of the Romanian Penal Code. A Bucharest Court judge sentenced Rosca-Stanescu to one year in prison and Ardeleanu to one year and two months. The judge also stripped Rosca-Stanescu and Ardeleanu of their rights to practice journalism. The charges stemmed from a series of articles *Ziua* had published that claimed President Ion Iliescu had been recruited by the KGB when he was a student in Moscow.

Russia

The continuing pattern of anonymous threats, beatings, and murders of Russian journalists—particularly because they are rarely prosecuted or solved—serves as a stark reminder of the vulnerability of the press's newly won freedom (see special report, p. 271). Nevertheless, many reporters, particularly those who work in the provinces, face more mundane forms of pressure.

While many news outlets in the larger cities have carved out a "fourth estate" free of direct government interference, they are still heavily dependent on the state for tax breaks, newsprint, access to printing presses, satellite time, and distribution and sales channels. President Boris Yeltsin decreed in December that media outlets and publishers were exempt from import tariffs on foreign paper and equipment and excused from customs duty on the import and export of their publications. City governments in Moscow, St. Petersburg, and other towns bailed out the print media again this year by subsidizing their spiraling production costs and compensating for their plummeting circulation. Ties between editors and journalists schooled in the Soviet media and officials in the Russian government are still so strong as to make the line between the second and fourth "powers" (as they are known in Russia) very fluid. *Vertushki,* Soviet-era direct phone lines to government offices, are said to remain in the offices of many major print and broadcast editors.

Major media such as the national dailies and the independent television stations have achieved some financial independence through an infusion of investment capital from Russia's top banks and corporations—mainly the "Big Seven" businesses (Most-Bank, Menatep, LogoVAZ, Stolichny Bank, and others) that are close to the Yeltsin government. Although some of the Big Seven initially called on Yeltsin to postpone the July presidential elections, these corporate investors eventually used their media outlets to ensure Yeltsin's victory. Ironically, their partisan use of the media sparked criticisms of bias and unprofessionalism against the very editors and reporters who had sought private investment as a hedge against government pressure.

New, smaller-circulation newspapers without access to such powerful financial backers, attempting to reach communities of reform-minded entrepreneurs, farmers, and young people, face a variety of obstacles, especially in towns where Communist officials retain power.

In Chuvash Republic, financial ministers urged the removal of a noncompliant editor of *Biznes-Sreda*. Officials in the Republic of Kalmykia manipulated reregistration of *Sovetskaya Kalmykia* to place government loyalists in control of the paper. And in Bashkortistan, printing houses refused to produce *Vecherniy Neftekamsk* after the prosecutor accused the paper's editor of insulting the president of that republic.

During the elections, paper-starved provincial newspaper editors were startled when copies of a government-supported anti-Communist paper, *Ne Dai Bog!* (God Forbid!) flooded mailboxes. Some editors in provincial areas achieve a curious independence by attempting to serve two masters, a local Communist-leaning mayor and a Yeltsin-appointed governor.

Prepublication censorship of the print media has generally become a rarity. The more critical, muckraking newspapers, such as *Moskovsky Komsomolets* or *Obshchaya Gazeta* in Moscow, or *Nevskoye Vremya* or *Chas Pik* in St. Petersburg, have such relatively small circulations that authorities may not perceive them as a threat. Controversial television programs are the more common targets of the authorities' wrath, visited in the form of cancellation, dismissal of critical executives or editors in state-run television, and the closure of some independent provincial broadcasting stations. In November, the head of the private national channel TV6 canceled two episodes of "The Scandal of the Week," the first concerning ex-presidential bodyguard Alexander Korzhakov, who had been making public charges of campaign funding violations against Yeltsin supporters, and the second about *Izvestiya's* claim of the alleged dual nationality of Boris Berezovsky, the new deputy of the security council. The show was suspended temporarily in December.

As in many countries making the transition to greater press freedom, Russia's courts are clogged with libel suits that bedevil editors and journalists determined to serve the public's right to know. According to Professor Andrei Richter, the editor of *Zakonodatelstvo i Praktika v Smi* (Media Law and Practice), there were 2,827 media-related defamation lawsuits in 1995, three times as many as in 1990, most of them from irate government officials or public figures seeking substantial financial retribution for insults to their "honor and dignity" under the Russian civil or penal codes and the press law. According to *Obshchaya Gazeta*, the media lost such libel suits in more than 60 percent of the cases.

The Judicial Chamber on Information Disputes (a controversial body within the executive branch of government initiated by Yeltsin and unrelated to the court system whose decisions are not legally binding) continues to examine complaints filed by citizens, public figures, organizations, and media outlets disputing the content of news and commentary or seeking enforcement of regulations under media law. The Chamber dispensed dozens of decisions on libel, hate speech, and ownership, and recommended prosecution in many instances. Some journalists see the chamber as an effective bolster for the sluggish, overwhelmed court system. According to this view, the chamber works to control the noxious expression of dozens of fascistic groups, which have gained access to state printing presses and national air time through the largesse of sympathetic officials and talk show hosts. Moreover, they view the chamber as a potential ally for the liberal newspapers that frequently receive threats from such violence-prone groups. Other commentators regard the chamber's pronouncements as unacceptable intrusions on editorial independence and journalistic freedom, but cooperate when it summons them for testimony to avoid eventually dealing with the courts. The bolder publications, such as *Moskovsky Komsomolets*, simply ignore the summonses and do not appear to suffer consequences. Most journalists agree that as a creature of the executive branch, the Chamber has no credibility as a neutral arbitrator within their profession or the broader public.

Russian journalists comment that while they may have freedom of the press, they do not have freedom of information, particularly on military, security, and economic matters, both because many topics are classified as state secrets and because government officials are reluctant to go on the record, regardless of the secrecy status of an issue. The Parliament passed the first reading of a draft law on freedom of information that it was still debating at year's end. Reporters are skeptical of such a law's efficacy, because so far its draft has failed to grapple with ministers' discretion to classify many types of information. Some journalists have noted that Russia does not have a tradition of investigative journalism as it is known in the West; rather, reporters are recipients of targeted leaks that serve the purposes of various government agencies. In some instances, such as the Yerofeyev case (see case summary below), they serve as pawns in skirmishes between warring agencies,

often ending up as the scapegoats of vindictive officials.

(For a lengthier report on press freedom in Russia, see *Briefing Paper on Press Freedom in Russia Before the July Elections*, available from CPJ.)

January 25
Oleg Slabynko, Russian Television Channel 2, KILLED
Slabynko, a producer of the news programs "Moment of Truth" and "Forgotten Names" on Russian Television Channel 2 and a general manager of the advertising agency Time Moves Forward, was shot to death by two men in the doorway of his Moscow apartment late at night. Before showing up at his home, the assassins had called Slabynko to make sure he was there. The next day, CPJ urged Russian authorities to conduct a thorough investigation into the murder and bring to justice those responsible. A month later, the office of Russia's general prosecutor responded in a letter stating that a police task force was assigned to the case and that investigations were also under way in the murders of journalists Vladislav Listyev, Dmitry Kholodov and Vadim Alferyev. At year's end the case was still not solved and CPJ was unable to confirm that Slabynko's murder was related to his journalism.

February 12
NTV, HARASSED, CENSORED
Executives of NTV, Russia's only independent television news network, received a call from the presidential press service saying that NTV correspondents henceforth would not be allowed to cover events at the Kremlin. The call came after NTV's Feb. 11 broadcast of the second of two interviews with President Boris Yeltsin's former press secretary Vyacheslav Kostikov, in which Kostikov spoke very critically of Yeltsin. CPJ urged President Yeltsin to lift the ban immediately. After much publicity, Yeltsin's press secretary Sergei Medvedov denied banning the station from covering

Central Europe

events and allowed NTV correspondents access to Kremlin events the following day.

February 20
Aleksandre Minkin, *Moskovsky Komsomolets,* ATTACKED

Minkin, a political columnist for the Russian daily *Moskovsky Komsomolets,* and his wife were awakened early in the morning by the sound of glass breaking on the balcony of their second-story apartment. As two masked intruders stumbled over wiring from the Minkins' television, Minkin rushed out and called to neighbors to contact the police. By the time police arrived at the scene, the intruders had fled. This is the second time Minkin has been physically attacked: last September, Minkin was assaulted and suffered a broken nose. CPJ urged Russian authorities to investigate the attack on Minkin.

February 23
Aleksandre Krutov, *Moskovskiye Novosti,* ATTACKED

Krutov, a correspondent in the Volga region city of Saratov for the Russian weekly *Moskovskiye Novosti,* was beaten by two men. Krutov's Moscow-based editor, Mikhail Shevelov, confirmed reports that the men approached Krutov in Saratov's central district in the evening and struck him more than 10 times on the head with metal pipes. Shevelov reported that Krutov has recovered and is back at work, but he had no information about possible motives for the attack. However, a Feb. 23 NTV news broadcast suggested that the attack may have been linked to an article Krutov wrote in *Moskovskiye Novosti*'s Feb. 4-11 issue. The article, titled "The Chechen Syndrome in the Volga Region," exposed the ways in which local Saratov government leaders have exploited ethnic issues to advance their political and business aims.

February 26
Felix Solovyov, Free-lancer, KILLED

Solovyov, a free-lance photojournalist who con-tributed to the German newspaper *Bild am Son-ntag,* was shot and killed by unidentified gunmen in central Moscow. The Russian news agency Itar-Tass reported that police found two pistols with silencers and eight cartridges at the scene of the murder. In 1994, Solovyov's picture portfolio on mafia groups in Moscow was published in *Bild am Sonntag* and two other newspapers in Germany. A *Bild am Sonntag* journalist said that Solovyov was an occasional contributor and that it did not believe his murder was related to the 1994 publication of the portfolio but could be related to other subjects he had photographed. *Bild am Sonntag* also said that Solovyov had discussed story ideas with the newspaper in a trip to Germany two weeks before his death. CPJ urged Russian authorities to open an immediate investigation into Solovyov's death and bring to justice those responsible.

March 8
Journalists in Chechnya, CENSORED

During a raid by Chechen rebels in the center of Grozny, Russian officials prevented journalists from entering the city. Television crews already inside Grozny were forbidden to film or move around the city. A well-marked van of a television crew from Russia's Independent Television Network (NTV) was fired upon and damaged by snipers. No passengers were killed. The raid began on March 6 and ended in a cease-fire on the afternoon of March 9. Once the cease-fire was declared, journalists were allowed access to the site where the fighting had taken place.

March 11
Viktor Pimenov, Vaynakh, KILLED

Pimenov, a cameraman for Vaynakh, the Chechen television station controlled by pro-Moscow forces, was killed in Grozny, Chechnya's capital. The Russian state news service Itar-Tass reported that Pimenov was shot in the back by a sniper hiding on the roof of a 16-floor building on Lenin Street. Pimenov was filming the aftermath of the Chechen insurgents' raid on Grozny, which lasted from March 6 to March 9. During the raid Russian military officials had prevented all journalists from entering Grozny.

March 30
Nadezhda Chaikova, *Obshchaya Gazeta,* KILLED
Chaikova, a correspondent with the daily *Obshchaya Gazeta,* was shot and killed by unidentified gunmen. Residents of the Chechen village of Gekhi discovered her body on March 30 near a sewage pipe on the outskirts of town. According to a report from the Chechen prosecutor, the villagers then buried Chaikova in a corner of their local cemetery. On April 11, Chaikova's body was exhumed and identified by *Obshchaya Gazeta* colleagues. Photos taken before her burial and a forensic examination of her body after exhumation suggest that she was battered, blindfolded, forced into a kneeling position and shot in the back of the head. Chaikova had been on assignment in Chechnya since March 6 and was last seen by colleagues in Sernovodsk on or about March 20. She was reported to have left Samashki with refugees on March 21. Chaikova, who had frequently travelled to Chechnya and the surrounding regions, was known for her hard-hitting coverage of the war and issues such as the use of special "filtration" prison camps by Russian authorities to control the population. CPJ urged the Yeltsin government to launch a federal investigation into the matter, but to date no investigation has been opened.

In a follow-up conversation on June 11, Chaikova's colleagues at *Obshchaya Gazeta* reiterated to CPJ that the federal Russian prosecutor's office still has not opened an investigation into her death and that the local Chechen village prosecutor who originally took up the case could not go far because of limited resources. The editors of *Obshchaya Gazeta* have mounted their own investigation and discovered that Chaikova was known to have videotaped the destroyed village of Samashki. They learned that she was attempting to transmit the film out

of Chechnya and was also reported to have been seen with a television cameraman in a Chechen village on March 24.

April 10
Ali Tekin, *Selam,* IMPRISONED,
   LEGAL ACTION
Talip Ozdemir, *Selam,*
   IMPRISONED, LEGAL ACTION
Tekin, managing editor of the Turkish Islamic weekly *Selam,* and Ozdemir, an Ankara representative for the weekly, were given the maximum possible sentence of three years in prison for attempting to enter Chechnya illegally from Azerbaijan via Dagestan, in violation of Article 83 of the Russian Penal Code. They had been detained since Nov. 2, 1995, when Russian border guards arrested them at the Chechen border with Dagestan and accused them of not holding the proper visas. After appeals from their lawyer and CPJ, an appeals court on July 5, 1996, overturned the sentence, acquitted the journalists of charges of "border and custom violation" because they were considered to be "journalists on duty," and released them.

May 9
Nina Yefimova, *Vozrozhdeniye,* KILLED
Yefimova, a reporter for the local Russian-language newspaper *Vozrozhdeniye* (Revival) in the Chechen capital of Grozny, was found dead from a pistol shot to the back of her head. According to the state news agency ITAR-TASS, Yefimova and her mother were abducted from their apartment on the outskirts of Grozny on the night of May 8. Yefimova's body was discovered the morning of May 9 in Grozny's Leninsky District, and her mother was found that night in a deserted canned food factory in the city. A local law enforcement official, who declined to give reporters his name, claimed that Yefimova's murder was committed "for private reasons." But journalists in Grozny and Moscow believe that her murder was related to stories she had published about crime in Chechnya. CPJ urged President Boris Yeltsin to

Central Europe

launch an immediate investigation into the case and prosecute those responsible for the murders.

May 12
Viktor Mikhailov, *Zabaikalsky Rabochy*, KILLED
Mikhailov, a crime reporter for the daily newspaper *Zabaikalsky Rabochy* in southeastern Siberia, was killed by unknown assailants in broad daylight in the city center of Chita. His mutilated body was identified the following day. Reports say Mikhailov had been covering crime and the work of law enforcement agencies at the time of his death. CPJ has urged Russian authorities to conduct a thorough investigation of the murder.

June 23
Valery Yerofeyev, *Vremya-Iks*, HARASSED, LEGAL ACTION
Yerofeyev, a former editor in chief of the Samara city newspaper *Vremya-Iks*, went on trial in Samara. He was charged with "pandering," or procuring the services of prostitutes, and with "producing pornography" under Article 226 of the Russian Penal Code.

Yerofeyev had been in prison since Sept. 25, 1995, when he was arrested on vacation in the Ukrainian city of Simferopol. On July 29, 1996, a Samara judge released Yerofeyev after sentencing him to 10 months in prison, the same amount of time he had already served in pretrial detention.

The case began in the spring of 1995, when Yerofeyev published a series called "People on Sidewalks" in *Vremya-Iks*. The series claimed that high-ranking police officers were accepting bribes from owners of so-called massage parlors, allegedly fronts for brothels.

Yerofeyev was first arrested on June 7, 1995, and detained for three days on suspicion of "procuring a prostitute." He was beaten while in police custody and warned by police officers to discontinue the series of articles. He proceeded with the series, however, and in September 1995, a special Samara police squad was

sent to Simferopol to extradite him. His attorney and the Samara chapter of the Journalists' Union filed petitions with the prosecutor's office to have Yerofeyev released on bail, but those petitions were denied.

In June 1996, and again in July, CPJ wrote to local and federal officials in Russia, including President Boris Yeltsin, urging them to release Yerofeyev and calling for an investigation of his prosecution and the conduct of police officers involved in the case. The Interior Ministry told CPJ it was looking into the matter.

June 24
All media in Tatarstan, CENSORED
The president of the republic of Tatarstan, Shaimiev Mentimer, issued a decree forbidding anyone from making slanderous remarks about the Tatarstani president or publicly insulting him. The decree imposes a fine of four million rubles (US$800)—equal to 20 times the minimum monthly wage—on those convicted of insulting or slandering the president. The decree states that any news organization that reports an insult against the Tatarstani president will be fined 30 million rubles (US$6,000) and that all copies of the offending issue or broadcast will be confiscated. Repeat offenders or those whose insults are printed or broadcast in the news media would face a fine of seven million rubles (US$1,400).

On June 27, CPJ sent a letter to President Mentimer condemning the decree as a form of seditious libel and urging him to repeal the decree immediately.

July 9
Yulia Kalinina, *Moskovsky Komsomolets*, THREATENED, HARASSED, LEGAL ACTION
Kalinina, a reporter for the daily *Moskovsky Komsomolets*, received a summons to the Judicial Chamber for Information Disputes regarding allegations that she had libeled officials in the Ministry of Construction. The charges stem from a free-lance article Kalinina had written

for the Russian weekly *Itogi*, alleging that state construction officials had accepted bribes to rebuild homes in Chechnya. The Judicial Chamber found her allegations to be unsupported and sent her case to the prosecutor's office, recommending that she be investigated. Kalinina has stood by her story and refused to reveal her sources.

Kalinina has received anonymous, threatening letters and phone calls since she began covering the war in Chechnya and corruption in the Russian military. In the letters and phone calls Kalinina has been accused of supporting the Chechen rebels, and has been threatened with rape and other violent assaults. After Kalinina published a free-lance story on military corruption in the Russian weekly *Obshchaya Gazeta*, on May 13, the calls and letters became more frequent. Kalinina's apartment was broken into and searched on May 24. She went into hiding for two weeks after the break-in.

July 16
Natalya Alyakina, RUFA and *Focus*,
KILLER SENTENCED

A military judge in the southern Russian city of Lermontov gave Sergei Fedotov, the Russian soldier accused of killing Alyakina June 17, 1995, a suspended sentence of two years for "involuntary manslaughter through negligent use of firearms." Alyakina was a journalist with dual Russian-German citizenship who was working for the German weekly magazine *Focus* and the radio news service RUFA at the time of her death. She had been given permission by Russian soldiers to cross a Russian army checkpoint leading into the southern city of Budyonnovsk, where she was going to report on a mass hostage-taking by Chechen rebels, but she was shot shortly after passing through the roadblock. Gisbert Mrozek, Alyakina's husband and an eyewitness to her death, lodged an appeal for Fedotov to be retried. Mrozek, himself a RUFA correspondent, repeatedly protested to Russian officials about the inept handling of evidence

and the refusal to call witnesses whose accounts differed from the official version of events. The soldier claimed in court that he had accidentally triggered a heavy machine gun with his foot as he entered an armored personnel carrier (APC), firing the two shots that killed Alyakina. The prosecutor demanded an acquittal, saying that Fedotov could not have known the safety catch was off and blaming the accident on a design fault in the APC.

August 1
Eduard Khusnutdinov, *Vecherny Neftekamsk,*
LEGAL ACTION

Khusnutdinov, editor in chief of *Vecherny Neftekamsk*, an independent newspaper formerly distributed in the Russian republic of Bashkortostan but now out of print, was notified by a Neftekamsk prosecutor that he is under criminal investigation for libel of Bashkortostan President Murtaza Rakhimov, and could face up to five years in prison. *Vecherny Neftekamsk* was one of the few private newspapers in Bashkortostan, an autonomous region in the Urals where the media have been heavily controlled by local leaders. Khusnutdinov is currently in Moscow.

The accusation reportedly stems from an article titled "No Smoke Without Fire," which alleged corruption in Rakhimov's administration. In the front-page key to the newspaper's stories, a summary of Khusnutdinov's story contained the phrase "bribe-taking in the staff of our hapless president." The article itself, however, dropped the words "in the staff." Khusnutdinov claims the mistake was a typographical error. Khusnutdinov's article was distributed just before the July 3 presidential run-off between Yeltsin and Gennady Zyuganov. Rakhimov supported Yeltsin in his bid for re-election.

August 6
Abrek Baikov, Russian State Television (RTR),
HARASSED
Yaroslav Malishev, RTR, HARASSED
Vladimir Seltsov, RTR, HARASSED

Central Europe

Andrei Klimov, ITAR-TASS, HARASSED
Andrei Khemelyanin, ITAR-TASS, HARASSED
Sergei Trofimov, ITAR-TASS, HARASSED
Mikhail Sotnikov, Russian Public Television
(ORT), HARASSED
Konstantin Tochilin, ORT, HARASSED
Oleg Nikifirov, ORT, HARASSED
Vladimir Trushkovsky, Radio Rossiya, HARASSED
Anatoly Shushevich, Radio Rossiya, HARASSED
Vasily Dyachkov, RIA-Novosti, HARASSED
Correspondent Baikov, cameraman Malishev,
and sound engineer Seltsov of RTR; Klimov,
Khemelyanin, and Trofimov, correspondents
for the Russian government news agency ITAR-
TASS; correspondents Sotnikov, Tochilin, and
Nikifirov of ORT; correspondent Trushkovsky
and sound engineer Shushevich of Radio
Rossiya; and Dyachkov of RIA-Novosti were
trapped in a hostel inside a government com-
pound in the center of Grozny. The journalists,
along with civilians, had taken refuge in the
hostel when the compound, which includes the
Chechen Interior Ministry, was surrounded by
Chechen rebels fighting Russian federal troops.
They were trapped for six days.

ITAR-TASS on Aug. 9 quoted a Russian official as saying that the journalists had been freed,
and Interfax later reported the same news. But
the journalists themselves, sending messages by
satellite telephone, contradicted those reports.

On Aug. 10, CPJ sent an alert urging both
Russian and Chechen forces to ensure the journalists' safe release. The group was freed by
Russian forces the night of Aug. 11 and was
taken to the airport at Khankala, in Chechnya,
then flown to Moscow. CPJ confirmed with
Radio Rossiya on Aug. 13 that the reporters
were unharmed.

August 8
Steve Harrigan, CNN, ATTACKED
Sergei Volkov, CNN, ATTACKED
Vladimir Ribalchenko, CNN, ATTACKED
Abdul Gudantov, CNN, ATTACKED
CNN producer/correspondent Harrigan; cam-
eraman Volkov; sound technician Ribalchenko;

and driver Gudantov were shot at by a Russian
military helicopter on the outskirts of Grozny,
the Chechen capital. They had been driving in
an armored Land Rover vehicle that was clearly
marked with the letters "T.V." on the roof and
sides. When they got out of the vehicle at a
Russian military checkpoint a Russian helicopter gunship flying overhead began firing at
the journalists. The crew scrambled back inside
their vehicle and drove away. No one was hurt
in the incident.

August 8
Andrei Babitskiy, Radio Liberty, ATTACKED
Vladimir Dolin, Spanish State News Agency
(EFE), ATTACKED
Erad Faist, Worldwide Television News
(WTN), ATTACKED
Sebastian Smith, Agence France-Presse (AFP),
ATTACKED
Babitskiy, a reporter for Radio Liberty; Dolin, a
correspondent for EFE; Faist, a WTN producer; and Smith, a correspondent for AFP, were
traveling in Chechnya in a Land Rover vehicle
owned by London-based WTN, when Russian
soldiers began firing at the vehicle from a nearby field. WTN told CPJ that the Land Rover
was clearly marked as a press vehicle. On their
way to Grozny, the journalists were stopped at a
checkpoint on the outskirts of the city. A Russian soldier told them to turn back and threatened to destroy their equipment if they did not.
When the journalists complied, they were fired
at again. A rocket-propelled grenade was then
shot at the van, but narrowly missed it.

Two hours later, as the crew tried entering
Grozny from another side, their vehicle came
under fire from Russian helicopter gunships and
automatic weapons on the ground. The journalists fled the vehicle to seek shelter in nearby
brush. Faist kept his video camera going
throughout the attack. The footage, which
showed the journalists seeking cover in the
woods, where they hid for about 20 minutes
while the helicopters continued firing at them
from both sides, was broadcast on international

television. No one was hurt in the attack, but the car was hit in three places.

August 11
Ramzan Khadzhiev, Russian Public Television (ORT), KILLED
Khadzhiev, chief of the Northern Caucasus bureau of Russian Public Television (ORT), was shot dead while attempting to leave Grozny, capital of the secessionist republic of Chechnya, with his wife and young son. Khadzhiev was shot in the head twice after being waved through a Russian military checkpoint.

NTV, Russia's only independent television station, and the state-owned television station RTR both broadcast an account by an unidentified man who said he was a passenger in Khadzhiev's car. The man said that Khadzhiev presented his ORT press credentials to Russian soldiers at the checkpoint and was waved through, but then Russian armored vehicles opened fire on the journalist's car, an unmarked Volga. ORT reported a different account, saying that Khadzhiev, an ethnic Chechen, may have been targeted by Chechen rebels because of his support for the current Moscow-installed government in Chechnya.

CPJ issued a press release about the murder, saying the Russian government's lack of reaction to the murder of journalists in Chechnya effectively condones further violence against journalists in the future. Khadzhiev was the 10th journalist to be killed in Chechnya since December 1994.

August 11
Vitaly Shevchenko, Lita-M. MISSING
Andrei Bazvluk, Lita-M. MISSING
Yelena Petrova, Lita-M. MISSING
Shevchenko and Bazvluk, journalists from Lita-M, a small television company in Kharkhov, Ukraine, were reported missing by their colleagues in early September. Fellow correspondents last saw the pair Aug. 11 in Grozny, during heavy fighting between Russian federal troops and Chechen fighters who had seized

control of Grozny on Aug. 6. Shevchenko and Bazvluk had traveled from their native Ukraine to Chechnya before warfare resumed in the capital.

A third journalist, Yelena Petrova, a senior executive of Lita-M, was also believed to be missing. She did not contact her studio after mid-August, according to a colleague. An anonymous informant called the Kharkhov station on Sept. 13 and claimed that Petrova was being held by agents of the DGB, the former security forces of the separatist Dudayev government, in a bank building in the Achkhoi-Martan district outside of Grozny. CPJ urged Russian authorities to undertake a search for the three journalists. At year's end colleagues had found no trace of them.

September 26
Valeriya Novodvorskaya, *Novoye Vremya* and *Stolitsa*, LEGAL ACTION
Trial proceedings against Novodvorskaya, a staff writer for *Novoye Vremya* and *Stolitsa* as well as a political activist, began in a Moscow municipal court. She was charged under Article 74 of the Russian Criminal Code for allegedly "inciting interethnic discord" and "disparaging the dignity of the Russian nation."

The charges against Novodvorskaya stem from an interview she gave to the Estonian television program "Pikanyaevaryukhm" and from two articles she wrote for the Russian newspaper *Novy Vzglyad* in 1994. The prosecution asked for 18 months' imprisonment, during which time she would also be banned from journalistic activity. A verdict had been expected on Oct. 22, but the judge delayed, requesting that the prosecution investigate further. CPJ on Oct. 11 wrote to President Boris Yeltsin to express concern about the prosecution of Novodvorskaya.

On Dec. 23, after lobbying by Parliament members, the Supreme Court lifted the restraining order on Novodvorskaya and she was permitted to travel outside Moscow. The investigation continued at press time.

Central Europe

241

September 27

Natalya Vasenina, *Respublika*, MISSING
Vasenina, editor in chief of *Respublika*, a local
Grozny newspaper, was abducted from her
home in central Grozny at 2:30 p.m. by two
unidentified masked people, who threatened
her with firearms and forced her into a car,
according to reports by the Russian wire services RIA/Novosti and ITAR/TASS. The
account of the abduction reportedly came from
a well-informed source close to the Moscow-
backed Chechen government of Doku Zavgayev. *Respublika*, one of the most popular
Russian-language youth periodicals in Chechnya, is described as "centrist" in opinion, which
means that it was not critical of the Zavgayev
government.

Slovakia

CPJ repeatedly engaged the Slovak government with concerns about deteriorating
press freedom conditions in Slovakia, particularly involving a draft "anti-subversion"
amendment to the penal code and a draft
press law containing serious restrictions on
journalistic freedoms. When CPJ included
Prime Minister Vladimir Meciar on its "enemies of the press" list for his promotion of
the ominous new laws, the Slovak government reacted with outrage. In a meeting
with Ambassador to the United States Bro-
nislav Lichardus in May 1996 in Washington,
D.C., he assured CPJ that parliamentary
debate on the controversial law had been
suspended indefinitely, and that the government's Legislative Council was floating a
more liberal draft of the press law. In follow-
up letters to the government, CPJ voiced
continued alarm about the proposed legislation as well as harassment of individual journalists and excessive government
interference in state-owned television and
radio.

Contrary to these high-level assurances
of improvement in law and practice, the
speaker of the Slovak parliament in October
again introduced the controversial legislation
for debate. He indicated that he intended to
push the amendment through to protect Slovakia's "national interests" by imposing stiff
penalties for the "spreading of false information abroad." The effort seemed motivated
largely by fear of demands for autonomy by
Slovakia's ethnic Hungarian population.

Government intrusion into the state-
owned daily *Slovenska Republika* prompted
12 journalists to quit their positions in October. They resigned in protest over the recent
appointments to top editorial posts at the
newspaper of figures directly linked to the
ruling party. Tatiana Repkova, editor in chief
of the privately-owned *Narodna Obroda,* was
fired by directors and shareholders close to
the Prime Minister after erroneous statements about Meciar's health were printed.
Repkova had refused to run an apology.

Despite restrictive libel laws, Slovakia's
beleaguered but hardy press corps demonstrated its great capacity for hard-hitting
investigative journalism in stories exposing
official malfeasance, a scandal involving the
abduction of the president's son, and the
unsolved murder of a police investigator.
Nevertheless, some independent reporters,
such as Peter Toth of the opposition daily
Sme, faced accusations of "slander" against
public officials. At year's end, the prosecutor
was still investigating the charges in this
and similar cases, which had not yet come
to trial.

The Slovak government now tolerates
foreign investment in the media. And several
independent media ventures began operation, although at least one so-called private
television channel, nationwide TV Koliba,
was said to be backed by people close to the
prime minister.

March 26

All Journalists, LEGAL ACTION

Prime Minister Vladimir Meciar's ruling party pushed an amendment to the Penal Code through Parliament that would punish those who "spread false information abroad damaging Slovakia's interests." The amendment also bans rallies organized to "subvert the country's constitutional system." Those convicted under the so-called anti-subversion law may be punished by a fine or up to two years in prison. On April 9, President Michal Kovac vetoed the bill after the European Union (EU) criticized the amendment for "affecting the freedom of expression." Slovakia is attempting to gain membership into NATO.

On Dec. 17, the Parliament passed a new law, which was essentially an amended form of the anti-subversion law. The clause that allowed for imprisonment of individuals who spread false information abroad was omitted from the new law. However, provisions in the law remained vague and opened the door for government suppression of opposition groups and their media outlets. Opposition members of Parliament walked out in protest during the vote.

On Dec. 31, President Kovac returned the law to the Parliament for further discussion. He objected to clauses that allowed imprisonment of those who "call for mass riots with the intention of subverting the country's constitutional system, territorial integrity, or defense capability." Kovac also said that the Parliament had violated procedure by drafting the new law before officially rejecting the earlier version.

November 20

Karol Lovas, Radio Twist, LEGAL ACTION

Dusan Velko, TV Markiza, LEGAL ACTION

Ales Kratky, *Novy Cas,* LEGAL ACTION

Martin Krno, *Pravda,* LEGAL ACTION

Reporters Lovas of the independent, privately owned Radio Twist; Velko of the privately owned television station TV Markiza; Kratky of the independent daily *Novy Cas*; and Krno of the independent daily *Pravda*, were stripped of their accreditation by the Slovak government. The only explanation offered for the move was that the government "did not have a good experience" with the journalists.

CPJ appealed to President Michal Kovac and Prime Minister Vladimir Meciar to ensure that the journalists' accreditations are reinstated. The government subsequently reversed its revocation of the credentials.

Tajikistan

Despite peace talks, civil war flared again in Tajikistan, and the forces opposing President Imomali Rakhmonov's autocratic rule seized control of several key provincial towns in clashes with Tajik government and Russian troops. Sporadic fighting in and around Dushanbe and other cities has created difficulties for both local and foreign (mainly Russian) journalists attempting to cover events. At times of particular intensity in the conflict, Tajik and Russian officials have discouraged or condemned the coverage by the foreign press corps. In August, for example, the Russian border guards' press service accused Radio Liberty's Dushanbe correspondents of "disinformation."

Journalists reported several incidents of censorship or confiscation of film to the Glasnost Defense Foundation in Moscow. On May 7, for example, the Tajik Minister of Culture and Information prohibited RTV (Russian State Television) correspondent Tatayana Logunova from filing a report about the murder of two professors in Dushanbe, explaining that the story could "hurt the republic's international image." Unidentified troops briefly detained a Western news crew traveling near a border zone, and questioned them at gunpoint. Later, equipment and notebooks were taken from the news crew's parked vehicle.

All Tajik media are state-controlled, and opposition newspapers published by Tajik

refugees in Moscow, such as *Charogi-ruz*, are banned by the Supreme Court and regularly confiscated from travelers. Several new literary and cultural newspapers have emerged, and have cautiously and indirectly raised some political points. As in the Soviet era, many Tajiks rely on Radio Liberty's Tajik-language broadcasts as an alternative source for domestic news. Against the odds, one commercial features service, Asia-Plus, began operation in Dushanbe this year, providing news on business, international aid organizations, and Tajiks' social ills—stories often neglected by the official press. But the agency's dispatch writers did not risk tackling controversial topics such as the civil war and refrained from criticizing the government. In December, the Tajik government passed a broadcasting law, the first in any Central Asian republic to regulate procedures for obtaining frequency licenses. The mere appearance of a law that explains how to get a license holds out some hope for prospective independent broadcasters.

Russian television—even channels heavily controlled by the Kremlin—provides a welcome supplement to the Tajik government's sparse and dull fare. Tajik viewers appreciate Russian television for its reporting from within Tajikistan and its neighbors that is unavailable on Tajik state television. But such reporting comes at a price: Russian journalists regard Dushanbe as one of the most dangerous assignments in the Commonwealth of Independent States. Viktor Nikulin, the Tajikistan bureau chief for ORT (Russian Public Television) was murdered in March—the 29th journalist documented by CPJ as killed in the line of duty in Tajikistan since 1992. Although there were no other reported killings of journalists this year, the Tajik government's failure to prosecute these 29 cases means that Tajikistan remains one of the most perilous countries in the world for journalists.

On Aug. 21, the Supreme Court in Dushanbe convicted and meted out death sentences to two men, Abdunabi Boronov and Nurali Janjolov, for the murder of Zayniddin Muhiddinov, a member of Parliament and editor of a local newspaper. According to the opposition Radio Voice of Free Tajikistan, Boronov and Janjolov were members of the People's Front, which had helped bring the present government to power. Muhiddinov, formerly a collective farm chairman, was not included in CPJ's list of journalists killed in the line of duty because his murder on March 13, 1995, shortly after his election to the Tajik Parliament, appeared to be related to his political rather than journalistic activity. The opposition radio claimed that the conviction, which it described as the first in four years for a journalist's murder, proved the fallacy of the government's position that the opposition is responsible for the murder of journalists.

March 28

Viktor Nikulin, ORT Television, KILLED
Nikulin, a correspondent for Russian state television (ORT), was shot and killed in his office in Dushanbe at 4:20 p.m. News accounts reported that he was shot twice when he answered knocks at his office door. A week before he was killed, he had received three threatening telephone calls. A colleague reported that, as a result, Nikulin put a heavy lock on his door. The Tajik government stated that his killing was a "terrorist act" by opposition forces.

CPJ wrote to Tajik President Imomali Rakhmonov and urged him to order a thorough investigation of Nikulin's murder and to ensure the safety of foreign correspondents in Tajikistan. In a letter to Russian President Boris Yeltsin, CPJ urged him to demand a full accounting from Tajik authorities of Nikulin's murder and to ask for assurances that the safety of foreign correspondents in Tajikistan be guaranteed.

On April 7, *Moskovskiye Novosti* reported that Gennady Blinov, first deputy interior minister of Tajikistan, announced that approximately 100 people had been detained in connection with the Nikulin case and that he was examining Nikulin's articles to determine possible motives for his murder.

CPJ received no response from the Tajik government to its letters about Nikulin's death and the unsolved murders of other journalists. In May, a CPJ representative met with R. Grant Smith, the U.S. ambassador to Tajikistan, to express concerns about lack of follow-up on this and other cases of journalists' murders and unsafe working conditions for reporters.

On Aug. 24, the Tajik president's press secretary hinted in an interview with the Russian radio station Mayak that "certain progress" was being made in the Nikulin murder investigation and would soon be publicized, but at year's end, no announcement had been made.

Turkmenistan

Wielding absolute power over the media, President Saparmurad Niyazov used them mainly to promote his cult of personality. He declared himself "founder" of all periodicals, which effectively gave him control over the country's newspapers and magazines. (To obtain a publishing license in post-Soviet states, a publication must have a "founder.") Some observers characterize Turkmenistan as the former Soviet republic with the least amount of press freedom, the result of the state's heavy hand and little initiative by local reporters.

The two state television channels specialize in footage of the president, known as "Turkmenbashi" ("the Father of Turkmen") and his meetings with foreign dignitaries. Turkmen television typically offers "endless [official] interviews, slow music, and pictures of horses and flags, with an occasional pirated Western movie dubbed into Russian thrown in for good measure," one knowledge-able Western observer noted. The only other option is ORT, Russia's public television station, which staunchly supports Russian President Boris Yeltsin. In recent years, the government has closed down even state-run regional broadcasters.

The Turkmen government refused to grant residence permits to opposition journalists in neighboring Tajikistan who had contemplated taking refuge in Turkmenistan from their country's civil wars. Foreign correspondents in Turkmenistan, including Russians, have deplored the lack of reporting freedom and access to information.

There do not appear to be any independent periodicals. The two leading government dailies, *Turkmenistan* (in the Turkmen language), and *Neitralniy Turkmenistan* (in Russian), have circulations of only 50,000 and 40,000, respectively, apparently because of high production costs. Government policies effectively keep foreign publications out of Turkmenistan: Border authorities confiscate periodicals, and visitors arriving by air must leave their newspapers on the plane.

October 25
Marat Durdiyev, Staff writer, IMPRISONED, HARASSED
Durdiyev, a leading journalist with government accreditation and an educator who had held a number of prestigious jobs, was fired from all of his posts after he published three articles in Russia's newspaper *Pravda-5* that were critical of Turkmenistan's president. Before being dismissed but after publication of the articles in *Pravda-5*, Durdiyev spent several weeks in a psychiatric facility in the capital of Ashgabat.

His colleagues were concerned that he may have been held against his will, but CPJ has been unable to confirm that the government intentionally used the psychiatric facility as a means to suppress Durdiyev. It is clear, however, that Durdiyev had been threatened by security police.

Durdiyev was released from the psychiatric ward in late November in poor condition, but he returned to giving history lectures at the Institute of Culture. At year's end, he had not been reinstated to positions he had held on the editorial boards of *Neitralniy Turkmenistan*, a major official newspaper, and *Turkmen Medeniyeti*, a government-sponsored monthly, or to other teaching positions. In addition, the Academy of Science reportedly revoked his membership.

Ukraine

The Ukrainian parliament passed a new constitution with formulations for press freedom and the forbidding of censorship borrowed from Article 19 of the Universal Declaration of Human Rights. Regrettably, lawmakers also copied the latter part of Article 10 of the European Convention for Human Rights that restricts expression in the interests of natural security, public order, and the protection of reputations, notions that are open to wide interpretation and abuse in Ukraine, where separation of powers is weak. In the countries of Western Europe, such constraints on speech are rarely used, overturned in constitutional courts, or ultimately appealed to the European Court of Human Rights, where a substantial body of case law has developed to protect journalists' rights to criticize the government. In Ukraine, such remedies are absent.

Violence against the media continued in Ukraine, with at least one killing attributed to a journalist's work and all suspicious deaths of journalists in past years still unsolved. Three television journalists from an independent production company, Lita-M, were declared missing in Chechnya. Reporters covering the conflict in Crimea—a region contested between Ukraine and Russia and the site of intense competition among ethnic and political groups—were particularly vulnerable to physical attack. The tension ran so high that in November, when Russia's ORT (Russian Public Television) began broadcasting weather forecasts about the Ukrainian cities of Sevastopol and Odessa along with those from Russian cities, the Ukrainian Foreign Ministry sent a diplomatic note of protest to the Russian government, claiming that the meteorologists were aggressively engaging in "information expansionism."

Both government and organized crime place pressure on news outlets, forcing some reporters to engage in self-censorship. Diatribes against critical independent journalists in the state-owned press contribute to the climate of intolerance. Law-enforcement officers are impervious to correspondents' pleas for protection from assailants, and themselves at times engage in beatings of those covering controversial public events.

The Ukrainian government maintains heavy control over radio and television broadcasting, although several independent stations survived a year of occasional censorship and threats. In January, for example, according to Moscow News, media officials told a Ukrainian company called Nova Mova, an affiliate of Russia's NTV (Independent Television) and producer of "Postscript," a popular news program, to cancel the program within an hour's notice one week after airing a segment on dissension within the ranks of the presidential administration. Although the administration denied responsibility for the crackdown, the pressure was believed to originate in the executive branch. In September, the prosecutor general filed a law suit against a radio station for "insulting" the president of neighboring Belarus. In December, the Parliament passed a law banning the privatization of satellite transmitters and broadcasting channels; independent companies must rent from the state.

According to the Open Media Research

Institute, in September, the government set up a committee to monitor the distribution of broadcast licenses after the parliament declared a moratorium on licensing by the National Broadcasting Council. The council's chair protested that the legislature and government were trying to wrest control of Ukraine's three national channels from his presidentially appointed body.

Ukrainian news kiosks were forced to discontinue carrying Russian-language publications vital to Ukraine's large Russian-language population when tariffs on imported newspapers and magazines grew prohibitively high. Ukrainian officials repeatedly complained about what they viewed as "inequality" in the information exchange between Russia and Ukraine.

The independent Ukrainian Media Club, the Odessa Journalists' Association, a support group of reporters in Crimea from NTV, Moscow News and other publications, as well as similar local organizations battled to preserve their colleagues' freedoms and protested numerous incidents of attacks against the press in Ukraine.

May 10
Igor Hrushetsky, Free-lancer KILLED
Hrushetsky, a free-lance journalist well-known for his articles on political corruption that were published in newspapers such as *Nezavisimost* and the now-defunct *Respublika*, was found dead near his home in Cherkassy. Police said he died from a blow to the head. According to press reports, Hrushetsky had recently testified in a criminal court case involving, among others, the son of a high-ranking police official in his region. Upon searching Hrushetsky's home after his murder, police reportedly found two files containing information about criminal cases from police archives. Colleagues believe he may have been targeted for his reporting on political corruption. On May 20, CPJ wrote to President Leonid Kuchma and Ukraine's minister of justice, calling for a prompt and thorough

investigation into Hrushetsky's murder.

May 11
Anna Konyukova, NTV, ATTACKED, THREATENED
Viktor Sosnovsky, NTV, ATTACKED, THREATENED
Unidentified assailants set fire to the home of Konyukova and her husband, Sosnovsky, in Simferopol, Crimea. Konyukova is the Crimean bureau correspondent for NTV, Russia's only independent TV station, and Sosnovsky is a cameraman for the station. Just after midnight, the couple noticed that their front door, which had been doused with a flammable liquid, was ablaze. They extinguished the fire and called the police. Konyukova and Sosnovsky detected and put out a second fire before the police arrived after 1:30 a.m. The couple had been subjected to a similar arson attempt a year earlier. Police found that the same flammable substance had been used in both incidents, but they have no suspects in either case.

On May 9, shortly before the latest arson attempt, Konyukova and Sosnovsky had filmed police in Simferopol blocking demonstrators from entering a Victory Day parade, in some cases by beating them to keep them back. Plainclothes security police warned the couple not to broadcast the incident. Konyukova and Sosnovsky later tried unsuccessfully to send their footage by relay to Moscow. They suspect their transmissions were intentionally blocked.

In March, Konyukova and Sosnovsky were told by the head of the Ukrainian Security Service in Crimea that "the CIA arranges car accidents for journalists who dig where they shouldn't." At the time, the pair had been investigating an alleged government conspiracy to blacklist certain Ukrainian organizations that were accused of harboring spies for Russia.

NTV in Moscow protested the arson attempts, but Ukrainian authorities claimed that NTV had staged the incidents to increase its ratings. CPJ urged the Ukrainian government to investigate the attacks and bring the perpetrators to justice.

June 14
Alexander Spakhov, *Express-Chronicle*,
   ATTACKED, HARASSED
According to a report in *Express-Chronicle*, an independent Moscow-based news agency and weekly newspaper, Spakhov, a local political activist working as a stringer for the agency, had been detained and abused by police. The newspaper said that Spakhov had tried to photograph a police barricade around Sevastopol's Nakhimov Square, which had been cordoned off two hours before ethnic Russians seeking autonomy in the Crimean region of Ukraine were scheduled to begin an unsanctioned rally. After Spakhov took some pictures of officers in the square, he was detained by members of a police squad known as the Berkut Unit.

Police reportedly refused to acknowledge Spakhov's credentials from *Express-Chronicle* or his Russian citizenship. They reportedly pushed him into a police car, where officers choked him and punched him in the face. He was then brought to the Lenin District of the Sevastopol Interior Ministry, detained for three hours, and released. In a letter to President Leonid Kuchma, CPJ expressed concern about the beating and detention of Spakhov and called for a stop to the harassment of journalists in Ukraine.

June 15
Vecherniy Sevastopol, HARASSED
The Sevastopol city administration issued a press release criticizing the local newspaper *Vecherniy Sevastopol* and warning that the authorities would seek the newspaper's closure for alleged violations of the press law. Editors of *Vecherniy Sevastopol*, which is known for its opposition to city authorities, believe the paper is being targeted for its critical coverage of social and political controversies.

July 25
Viktor Frelix, Publisher, INVESTIGATION OF
   DEATH CLOSED

After more than a year of investigation, the prosecutor of the Chernovets region closed the criminal case in the death of Frelix, who died on June 2, 1995, in Lvov, reportedly of poisoning. Frelix, a publisher and founder of the ecological group Green World of Ukraine, had been investigating the military's connection with an epidemic in the city of Chernovtsy, and had alleged that the illnesses were caused by the city's proximity to a military base. According to the hospital where Frelix spent his last days, he was poisoned "by substances with unknown qualities." But authorities investigating the case concluded from legal and medical expert evidence that there were no poisonous compounds found in his body.

Uzbekistan

Despite dramatic gestures by President Islam Karimov to create the impression that Uzbekistan has improved its human rights record, the government has not relinquished its tight grip on information flow in this most populous of the newly independent Central Asian nations. In fact, an October issue of a major state newspaper in Tashkent published a government report that concludes, "Given that the media is a powerful means of influencing the masses, it was deemed advisable to maintain state control over the work of the media in Uzbekistan."

Shortly before Karimov traveled to the United States in June in search of financial aid, he granted amnesty to 80 political prisoners, among them three activists from the banned opposition party Erk (Freedom). The three had been convicted of anti-government activities, including the distribution of the party's outlawed newspaper. But at year's end, at least four other activists involved in newspaper distribution remained imprisoned.

Some observers praised unprecedented conferences on human rights and media free-

dom, held in Tashkent by the Organization for Security and Cooperation in Europe but attended primarily by government officials who did not address deep-rooted obstacles to press freedom. On Sept. 12, Abdumannob Polat, a prominent exile permitted to return to Uzbekistan, declared on state radio that there was "no such thing" as freedom of the press or speech in Uzbekistan.

Several Uzbek journalists reported beatings and intimidation by authorities, but declined to go on the record for fear of retaliation. The violent death of Sergei Grebenyuk, a reporter for the Russian news agency Interfax whose body was found near a canal in Tashkent on Feb. 8, remains under investigation by CPJ. And several Russian correspondents returned to Russia in 1996 because of inhospitable working conditions and intimidation in Uzbekistan.

Uzbek officials allowed the British Broadcasting Corp. (BBC) to begin medium-wave broadcasting, and Radio Free Europe/Radio Liberty finally received permission to open a news bureau in Tashkent after a two-year delay in the implementation of an agreement with the government.

Thirty to forty small, nongovernmental Uzbek television and radio stations operated in Uzbekistan. But nationwide broadcasting by private Uzbek stations was forbidden. In May, Karimov exempted government-controlled Uzteleradio from paying taxes on advertising revenue until the year 2000. But to gain the same tax-free status, private companies will have to come back under the state's wing.

Print media is heavily controlled by the state, with prior censorship and bans. By their own admission, journalists at government-backed publications do not challenge government leaders in print. Subscriptions to all Uzbek newspapers and magazines as of January had fallen by 94 percent since 1992. Even the official Uzbek Journalists' Union attributed this drop to lack of variation in news reports, a sign of censorship.

February 8
Sergei Grebenyuk, Interfax, KILLED
Grebenyuk, a reporter for the independent Russian news agency Interfax, was found dead in a canal in the Uzbek capital of Tashkent. CPJ has received conflicting reports regarding the circumstances under which he died, and the Uzbek Interior Ministry said that the exact cause of death is unknown. Grebenyuk was last seen alive on Jan. 27 at his brother's home, near where his body was later found.

Both independent observers and government spokesmen said the murder was not politically motivated and was unrelated to Grebenyuk's journalistic activities, but Russian correspondents working in Tashkent who themselves had been the victims of anonymous threats claimed that Grebenyuk had received warnings and had been previously attacked. CPJ is continuing to look into the case and wrote to President Islam Karimov, urging him to order a thorough investigation into Grebenyuk's death.

Yugoslavia

Independent media in Yugoslavia, which now consists of the republics of Serbia and Montenegro, struggled with technical, legal and financial problems throughout the year. *Nasa Borba* (Our Struggle), the independent newspaper in Belgrade founded after the ruling Socialist Party took over the original *Borba* in 1995, for the most part maintained a circulation of under 30,000 because of high paper costs and distribution difficulties. Meanwhile, the pro-government daily *Politika* benefited from well-equipped offices and boasted a circulation of 300,000.

Late in the year, however, these figures changed dramatically, after demonstrations began against Serbian President Slobodan Milosevic and his Socialist Party. Opposition

Central Europe

supporters, at times numbering in the hundreds of thousands, took to the streets on Nov. 18, the day after Milosevic annulled opposition victories in municipal elections throughout Serbia. The demonstrations continued every day into the new year. The political unrest sent sales of independent tabloids soaring—*Nasa Borba*'s readership jumped 60 percent, while *Politika*'s circulation reportedly dropped to 45,000.

As sales of independent newspapers peaked during the demonstrations, so did government suppression of the media. Belgrade's only independent radio station, Radio B92, experienced constant interference with its transmissions as it reported on the demonstrations. State-run media almost completely ignored the political turmoil. The government eventually cut B92's broadcasts from the airwaves altogether, along with those of five radio stations in Cacak that were broadcasting B92 segments. Radio station Boom 93, in the town of Pozarevec, and Radio Index, a student-run Belgrade station, were also shut down. Radio B92, Radio Index, and only one of the Cacak stations were back on the air within 52 hours, after outcry from the international community.

CPJ Chair Kati Marton traveled to Belgrade as soon as the Committee learned that the government had attempted to silence B92. Marton met with Milosevic and, during a two-and-a-half-hour meeting, obtained his verbal assurance that he would not suppress B92. Marton presented the Serbian president with a handwritten document saying that he was committed to supporting "a free press and the right to publish and broadcast without censorship freely in the Federal Republic of Yugoslavia." Milosevic first ripped up the document. Marton quickly re-drafted a second version on a scrap of the original. Milosevic crossed out the words "without censorship" and signed the paper.

Although the demonstrations in Belgrade began very peacefully, by the 36th day violence broke out among opposition marchers, Milosevic supporters the government had bussed to the capital from outlying areas, and Serb police. During the next two days, journalists became frequent targets of physical attacks by police. CPJ documented 11 assaults by Serb police on camera crew members, photographers, and reporters. One protest marcher was killed on Dec. 24.

Meanwhile, there was no independent television coverage of the demonstrations, because the government in February had taken control of the only independent television news station, NTV Studio B, in a maneuver reminiscent of the 1995 *Borba* takeover.

Government harassment of the media reached outside the country's political centers as well. In the predominantly ethnic Albanian region of Kosovo, in southern Serbia, the prosecutor's office stopped the printing presses at the Albanian-language weekly *Koha* because the prosector was offended by a satirical composite photograph in the issue that depicted Milosevic alongside men in Nazi uniforms. In Podgorica, Montenegro, police brought managers of the independent radio station Antenna M to the local police station for "talks" after Antenna M aired a popular local singing group's live performance of a satirical political song. By year's end, the Montenegrin government had announced that it would auction the rights to Antenna M's frequency, a move that jeopardizes the station's future. Antenna M's editors doubt they would be able to buy back the frequency because other stations that enjoy more government support would likely offer higher bids.

February 15

NTV Studio B, HARASSED, CENSORED
Police from the ruling Socialist Party of Serbia (SPS) entered the offices of NTV Studio B, the only independent television news station in the Federal Republic of Yugoslavia, and shut down

its broadcast equipment. The Commercial Court annulled Studio B's registration as a joint stock company, allowing Belgrade's Municipal Assembly to gain control of the station. Most of Studio B's employees are being replaced by members of the Municipal Assembly or the SPS. CPJ urged President Slobodan Milosevic to allow Studio B to resume broadcasting without state interference.

March 9

B92 Radio, CENSORED

During a live broadcast of an opposition party rally, the transmission of B92, Belgrade's only independent radio station, was blocked. According to the station's political news editor, the transmission jammed 17 or 18 times while it was broadcasting the 35-minute speech of Serbian Renewal Movement leader Vuk Draskovic, and three to four times during the 20-minute speech of Zoran Djindjic, the Democratic Party leader. The editor said they believe the police caused the transmission problems since it is only possible to block transmissions from police stations. She said this happened every time the station covers an event about the opposition party. B92 Radio did not complain to the authorities this time because they have done so in the past and received no response.

April 7

Koha, CENSORED

Six policemen entered the printing offices of *Koha,* an Albanian-language weekly magazine in Pristina, and ordered that printing stop until they examined the issue's contents. The prosecutor's office apparently took offense at a satirical composite photograph that depicted President Slobodan Milosevic alongside men in Nazi uniforms. For two hours, police questioned the director of the printing office. By law, police can intervene only after printing. Officials from the general prosecutor's office later told employees at the printing offices not to print issues of *Koha* without prior consent. Editors at *Koha* decided not to provide their

materials to police before publication. On April 10, the manager at the printing press received informal permission from the prosecutor's office to proceed, and *Koha* was allowed to publish.

May 29

Radio Smederevo, HARASSED, LEGAL ACTION

The Municipality of Smederevo voted unanimously to increase its ownership of Radio Smederevo from 17 to 63 percent. With majority ownership, the Municipality immediately installed members of the ruling Socialist Party of Serbia (SPS) on the station's executive board, appointed a Party member station manager, and cut off electricity at the station's offices to ensure the success of the takeover. Radio Smederevo was the only independent broadcast outlet in the region; prior to the Municipality's vote, Radio Smederevo's employees owned 83 percent of the station. CPJ urged authorities to reinstate the station's original staff and board.

July 14

Slobodan Rackovic, Free-lancer, HARASSED

Rackovic, a free-lance journalist based in Petrovac, Montenegro, was arrested and detained for more than three hours at a police station in Petrovac. Police did not bring formal charges against him, but rather described the incident as an "informal talk." Rackovic's house was searched during his detention and the "talk" was continued the next day.

At an earlier press conference, Rackovic had called for the removal from office of Montenegro's public prosecutor, Vladimir Susovic, and others responsible for the arrest of Bosnian refugees in Montenegro. The refugees were extradited to the Republika Srpska (Serb Republic) in Bosnia and Herzegovina.

October 18

Milovan Brkic, *Srpska Rec,* ATTACKED

Brkic, an investigative journalist for the opposition-owned monthly journal *Srpska Rec* and a candidate for the city assembly, was escorted

Central Europe

from his office by two plainclothes state security policemen who presented their badges and asked to speak with him. Once outside, the two officers pushed Brkic into a car and drove him to an undetermined location outside Belgrade, where other state security policemen were waiting. The officers then undressed Brkic, beat him with sticks, and kicked him. Brkic was eventually released and taken to a hospital, where doctors determined he had suffered three broken ribs, a damaged spleen, and a concussion.

Before the attack, in the latest issue of *Srpska Rec*, Brkic had published an article on the links between state security and organized crime.

CPJ appealed to Serbian President Slobodan Milosevic to launch an immediate investigation into the attack and to ensure that any further intimidation of the press is immediately halted.

November 27
Blic, CENSORED
The state-owned Borba publishing house refused to print more than 70,000 copies of the independent daily *Blic*. The newspaper had started a press run of 250,000, with coverage of widespread demonstrations in Belgrade against Serbian President Slobodan Milosevic and his government. The entire editorial board of the newspaper resigned after it was told to stop reporting on the demonstrations.

November 29
Antenna M, THREATENED, HARASSED
Authorities threatened not to extend the frequency license of Antenna M, the only independent radio station in Podgorica, Montenegro. Antenna M had been broadcasting reports from Radio B92, the independent radio station in Belgrade that was later shut down by Serbian authorities for 52 hours. The harassment of the radio stations was related to widespread demonstrations that began in November in Belgrade against Serbian President Slobodan Milosevic and his government. Antenna M also broadcasts news reports from Voice of America and Radio Free Europe.

On Dec. 28 the station received a notice from the Ministry of Industry and Energy of Montenegro that its frequency, 87.6 MHz, would be auctioned off at an unspecified date after the new year. The notice informed Antenna M that it was welcome to "compete" for the highest bid. The editor in chief told CPJ that the station would not be able to bid as much as competing companies that are more supportive of the government. CPJ appealed to President Momir Bulatovic to ensure that the auction for Antenna M's frequency be canceled and that the station be permitted to continue broadcasting. At year's end the station's license was renewed.

November 29
Radio Ozon, CENSORED
Radio Soliter, CENSORED
Dzoker Radio, CENSORED
Radio 96, CENSORED
Star FM, CENSORED
The Yugoslav Federal Inspector for Traffic and Communications banned five independent radio stations in Cacak, one of the cities in Serbia where the opposition defeated supporters of Serbian President Slobodan Milosevic in the recent municipal elections. Milosevic annulled the election results. Some of the stations had been broadcasting news programs from Belgrade's independent station Radio B92. Serb authorities in December suspended B92 for 52 hours, amid widespread demonstrations against Milosevic and his government.

December 3
Radio B92, HARASSED, CENSORED
Radio B92, the only independent radio station in Belgrade, was taken off the air by order of the Federal Ministry for Transport and Communication of the Federal Republic of Yugoslavia. The Ministry claimed that B92 did not have a valid license to operate. The station had applied for a license repeatedly since 1991, but its petitions had been rejected or ignored.

B92 had experienced constant interference in its transmission since it began covering widespread demonstrations against Serbian President Slobodan Milosevic's annulment of Nov. 17 municipal elections. Opposition candidates in the elections, held throughout Serbia, had defeated Milosevic supporters. On Nov. 27, the station's signal was blocked four times during news broadcasts about the protest marches. On Nov. 28, other signals, most likely sent by the government to interfere with B92's transmission, began jamming B92's entire programming from 9 a.m. to 2 a.m. B92's staff, however, continued to gather the news and disseminate it by electronic mail, and their programs were broadcast on Voice of America, Radio Free Europe, and Radio Deutsche Welle. B92 was also able to post the latest news from Belgrade on its Internet site on the World Wide Web.

On Dec. 5, B92 was allowed back on the air as Serb authorities backed down under intense pressure from demonstrators and from the international community. CPJ Chair Kati Marton traveled to Belgrade on Dec. 6 and met with Milosevic to raise the radio station's plight. She obtained assurances it would be allowed to broadcast. Marton held two press conferences in Belgrade about the problems B92 and other media in Serbia are facing.

On Dec. 12, B92 obtained a 10-year contract with Radio and Television Serbia, allowing it to broadcast over a state-owned transmitter. In the meantime, the station will continue working to obtain its own frequency.

December 3
Radio Index, CENSORED
Radio Index, a student-run independent station in Belgrade that shared a transmitter with the independent station Radio B92, was taken off the air by Serbian authorities along with B92. The shutdowns occurred amid widespread demonstrations by students and others protesting Serbian President Slobodan Milosevic's decision to annul the recent opposition victories in municipal elections. Authorities claimed Radio Index had been cut off because of technical problems. The station was back on the air

48 hours later.

December 3
Boom 93, CENSORED
Authorities banned Boom 93, a private independent radio station in the town of Pozarevec, from broadcasting. The station owned its own transmitter and was operating under a temporary license. The ban occurred the same day the Belgrade independent station Radio B92 was taken off the air during widespread demonstrations against Serbian President Slobodan Milosevic and his government. While B92 regained the right to broadcast on Dec. 5, authorities continued to keep Boom 93 off the air.

December 3
Radio Ozon, CENSORED
Radio Soliter, CENSORED
Dzoker Radio, CENSORED
Radio 96, CENSORED
Star FM, CENSORED
Radio Ozon, Radio Soliter, Dzoker Radio, Radio 96, and Star FM, all independent radio stations in Cacak, were taken off the airwaves. The Belgrade independent station Radio B92 was also stopped from broadcasting. The actions occurred during widespread demonstrations against Serbian President Slobodan Milosevic and his regime that began after Milosevic annulled November municipal elections in Serbia. Opposition candidates had defeated Milosevic supporters in Cacak, Milosevic's birthplace, Belgrade, and other cities throughout Serbia. B92 was restored to the air Dec. 5, as was Radio Ozon. The other four stations remained off the air.

December 3
Pierre Peyrichout, Free-lancer, HARASSED
Peyrichout, a French citizen who is a Prague-based free-lance correspondent for Radio Canada in Montreal, was turned away at the Belgrade airport when authorities refused to grant him an entry visa. He had attempted for nearly a month to obtain a visa from the

Central Europe

253

Yugoslav Embassy in Prague. Peyrichout has covered events in Slovenia, Bosnia and Herzegovina, and Yugoslavia for many years.

Other journalists also reported delays in the processing of entry visas for Yugoslavia as widespread demonstrations against Serbian President Slobodan Milosevic continued throughout Belgrade. Peyrichout was issued a visa following CPJ's protest to authorities.

December 6
Independent Press Center, THREATENED, HARASSED

Wire services to the International Press Center in Belgrade, an equipped work space available to foreign correspondents, were cut off with no explanation. Authorities claimed the problem was due to technical failures. The incident occurred during widespread demonstrations in Belgrade against Serbian President Slobodan Milosevic and his regime.

Before the wire services were cut off, the press center's restaurant and coffee bar, where correspondents often met to discuss events, were closed. And on Dec. 12, drinking water to the center was cut off. One correspondent reported that the center has been threatened with closure for the three months since Milosevic appointed a new director to the state-run news agency Tanjug, which owns the center.

Late December
Ognjen Radosevic, *Dnevni Telegraf,* ATTACKED
Alexander Lamakin, Associated Press Television (AP-TV), ATTACKED
Alexander Mursa, Associated Press Television (AP-TV), ATTACKED
Ivan Milutanovic, Associated Press (AP), ATTACKED
Oleg Chupin, NTV, ATTACKED
Rade Radovanovic, *Nezavisnost,* ATTACKED
Momcilo Miloyevic, *Politika,* ATTACKED
Djordje Nikolic, ORF, ATTACKED
Nikola Majdak, Radio B92, ATTACKED
Branko Filipovic, Reuters TV, ATTACKED
Petar Kujundzic, Reuters, ATTACKED

During ongoing demonstrations that swept Belgrade after Serbian President Slobodan Milosevic annulled the victories of opposition candidates in Nov. 17 municipal elections, police attacked several camera crew members, photographers, and reporters.

On Dec. 24, Radosevic, a photographer for *Dnevni Telegraf,* was beaten. On Dec. 26, Lamakin and Mursa, Russian cameramen for AP-TV, and AP photographer Milutanovic were beaten; and Chupin, a cameraman for Russia's independent station NTV, was beaten and hospitalized and his camera destroyed. On Dec. 27, the camera crew for London's ITN station were attacked and their camera destroyed; Radovanovic, a reporter for the Serbian independent trade union newspaper *Nezavisnost,* who was recognized by plainclothes police as a journalist, was beaten on his legs and head; and Miloyevic, a correspondent for *Politika,* the official government newspaper, who was not covering the demonstration but was watching the attack on Radovanovic, was beaten and kicked severely, as was his wife. Also on Dec. 27, Nikolic, a cameraman with Austria's ORF station, was very seriously beaten and hospitalized and his camera destroyed; Majdak, a cameraman for Belgrade's Radio B92, was beaten and hospitalized; a cameraman for the Rome station TV-5 was beaten and hospitalized; Filipovic, a cameraman for Reuters TV, was beaten and his camera smashed; and Kujundzic, a photographer for Reuters, was beaten.

According to other reports, journalists from the daily newspapers *Blic* and *Nasa Borba* were also physically attacked. When the journalist from *Nasa Borba* hit the ground, he reportedly yelled to policemen that he was a member of the press, and they replied, "What press?" and continued to beat him.

CPJ appealed to President Milosevic on Dec. 28 to cease any further attacks on journalists during the demonstrations and to uphold the personal written commitment he had signed with CPJ Chair Kati Marton on Dec. 6 to ensure free broadcasting and reporting.

Media Freedom After Dayton

September 5, 1996

via fax:41-31-322-53-20
His Excellency Flavio Cotti
Chairman in Office of OSCE
Federal Department for Foreign Affairs
Bern, Switzerland

Your Excellency:

The Committee to Protect Journalists (CPJ), a nonpartisan, non-governmental organization based in the United States, is dedicated to defending journalists and press freedom around the world.

Since the signing of the Dayton Peace Accords on Dec. 14, 1995, the Committee has been particularly concerned about the dire state of press freedom in the Republic of Bosnia and Herzegovina. We are writing to express our great concern regarding both the constraints on press freedom and the free movement of journalists that we have observed in the period leading up to the Sept. 14 elections, and the future of independent local journalists and news media following the scheduled departure of international troops in December.

By definition, no election can be considered truly free and fair unless the news media is able and willing to report fairly and openly to the entire electorate on the campaigns of all major contending parties, and all reporters, local and foreign, are free to cover the news without restrictions on their movements or justified fears of reprisals.

With few exceptions, throughout Bosnia and Herzegovina, these standards have not been met in the weeks leading up to the Sept. 14 elections.

Despite guarantees of press freedom in the human rights annexes of the Dayton Accords, as well as separate agreements on accreditation procedures and the rights and duties of journalists, print and broadcast media are heavily restricted, particularly in Republika Srpska (Serb-controlled territory) and in Herzeg-Bosna (Croat-controlled territory) in the Federation of Bosnia and Herzegovina (the Muslim-Croat Federation, as distinct from the Sarajevo-based government of the Republic of Bosnia and Herzegovina).

As CPJ and other international groups have confirmed, despite IFOR (Peace Implementation Force) press passes theoretically allowing freedom of movement, the few local reporters brave enough to drive from one ethnic enclave to another are intercepted on the roads and sometimes beaten, their ethnic identity easily determined from the residence codes on their license plates. Correspondents' submissions are rejected for "harming the national interest." Journalists who cover the opposition are subjected to the same violence directed against rival political parties by those in power. Independent radio stations are drowned out by more powerful state-run programs and television screens go blank during critical debates. Air time reserved for opposition parties is either withheld in practice or used by the ruling parties to denounce their competitors.

CPJ has received many other credible reports from foreign and domestic journalists about serious restrictions on their ability to work and travel, although they are reluctant to put such complaints on the record for fear of compromising their access to sources or opening themselves up to further recriminatory measures.

The international community, charged with promoting and monitoring press freedom, has been slow to address these critical problems. Local and foreign journalists covering the election say the NATO alliance and the Organization for Security and Cooperation in Europe (OSCE), charged with implementing the Dayton Accords, have been seemingly unwilling or unable to enforce compliance from the signatories to the Dayton agreement. Local governments have instead been blatantly obstructionist, preventing opposition parties from access to the media and harassing independent or opposition publications and broadcasts. Serb authorities expel reporters covering controversial stories; the Bosnian government has withheld permission for international satellite television; and Croat authorities threaten outsiders attempting to scrutinize corrupt local government.

As an organization devoted exclusively to the defense of journalists and press freedom around the world, CPJ does not monitor the content or quality of local news coverage of election campaigns. In Bosnia, this important task has been undertaken by such respected organizations as the London-based International Crisis Group and the Institute for War and Peace Reporting, Media Plan, the Bosnian research institute, and the Swiss organization Medienhilfe Ex-Jugoslawien. Their findings about the discriminatory and obstructionist tactics of the ruling parties vis-a-vis media content dovetail with CPJ's findings about the mistreatment of journalists and the constraints upon the independent media.

The attached briefing paper contains 1) summaries of the obligations assumed by all parties in the region on media freedom; 2) examples of harassment and intimidation of the print and broadcast media; and 3) comments by Western correspondents and monitors as well as local journalists.

Monitors on the scene, as well as foreign and local reporters attempting to cover the news, quickly discovered months ago that there is no press freedom in Bosnia except for what is artificially created from the outside, and to some extent from the inside by the scarce number of independent journalists—all at considerable difficulty, risk, and expense. All the major television, radio, and large-distribution newspapers are state-controlled, essentially the mouthpieces of the ruling parties of the SDS (Serbian Democratic Party of Republika Srpska), the SDA (Party for Democratic Action of Bosnian President Alija Izetbegovic), and the HDZ, (the Croatian Democratic Union of Croatian President Franjo Tudjman). Efforts to inject alternatives into this extremely rigid situation have foundered.

CPJ and other press freedom organizations have received numerous reports of anonymous intimidation of news media; dismissals or censorship of reporters for ethnic or political reasons; "power outages" that seem timed to controversial radio and television broadcasts; beatings of outspoken journalists in retaliation for their reporting; and near total obstruction of freedom of movement. A symbol of the region is what reporters have dubbed the "ghost bus" of Mostar, running between the divided sides of the city, empty except for the driver, accompanied by an IFOR patrol car—and only once by a daring film crew. Most local reporters refuse to take advantage of even the rare escorted outings across ethnic borders organized by IFOR and OSCE. In most cases, both foreign and domestic correspondents do not want to publicize their difficulties, fearing reprisals.

INTV, known colloquially as "Carl Bildt's television" after the High Representative of the international community, an effort to patch together five local independent stations through satellite uplinks to provide unbiased campaign reporting for a majority of the population, is not scheduled to go on the air until Sept. 7—only a week before the elections. While the project has been plagued with financial and staffing difficulties, the Bosnian government has been the main obstacle, refusing to grant the necessary broadcast frequency, and using police force and threats of violence to pressure the station into compromise. In a conversation on Sept. 2 with CPJ chair Kati Marton, High Representative Bildt acknowledged the problem of reaching rural audiences and recognized that the station's impact would be limited to major cities. He expressed concern for the future of the station, and has urged that its structures be used as a foundation for a more far-reaching and independent news broadcasting operation in the months and years ahead.

The OSCE-sponsored FERN (Free Election Radio Network) radio station has persisted in broadcasting despite a recent ban from Republika Srpska authorities.

While enormous international effort has been devoted to persuading Radovan Karadzic to step down from political life, his daughter, Sonja Karadzic, head of the government-controlled International Press Center in Pale, notorious for its exorbitant fees for foreign press accreditation and the imposition of "bodyguards" on foreign journalists, has quietly proceeded to invest heavily in a powerful new radio station, Orthodox Radio St. John. Western monitors are concerned that another newly established independent station, Radio Drina, with less technical capability, will be drowned out. Meanwhile Radio Zid, a popular independent station based in Sarajevo, has discovered that Radio St. John is broadcasting on its frequency, so that it can no longer reach its listeners. Radio Zid's efforts to get a new frequency assigned by the Ministry of Culture and to obtain intervention by IFOR or OSCE have been fruitless to date.

A veteran foreign correspondent with international support and funding tried to help start an independent election daily in Banja Luka, the opposition base in Republika Srpska, but was unable to find independent editors or reporters willing to assume the risk.

In conversations with CPJ, correspondents and media monitors expressed a great sense of discouragement with the international community. The failure to guarantee freedom of movement and of communication for local news media before the election bodes ill, as

NATO forces are planning to withdraw by the end of the year and OSCE may not be financed for a continued presence after the elections. "You have to remember that we already went through a war. Our human and financial resources are exhausted, and we are on the edge of existence," commented one leading news executive, summarizing the sentiments of many. None of the local governments can be counted upon to enforce press freedom guarantees without constant outside pressure, experienced local journalists say.

The OSCE's Media Experts Commission and subcommissions in regional centers, charged with ensuring freedom of information and movement and the unhindered work of the media, as well as free and equal access to the media, have not been functioning effectively. They must greatly improve their record of staying informed and responding rapidly. The commission may require a different composition, since local journalists say they have been discouraged by the presence of Serb and Bosnian police chiefs in the commission. While Interior Ministers are supposed to use their clout to foster freedom of movement, they are helping to institutionalize the notion that permission must be granted for travel across ethnic borders.

As the international community assesses its response to the elections, we urge you to give serious consideration to the severe problems of journalists and press freedom in Bosnia. We urge that mechanisms be put in place to ensure that after the elections and after the withdrawal of IFOR troops, freedom to travel regardless of ethnic background will be enforced; the bias of state-controlled media will be monitored and exposed; forceful intervention will be made with regional authorities on behalf of struggling independent and opposition media; and rapid financial and technical assistance will be provided to private print and broadcast organizations. After the elections, the international community must continue to fund INTV and work to guarantee its autonomy and professionalism, while encouraging the emergence of other independent broadcast outlets as examples for the development of free media throughout the region.

Thank you for your attention and we await your comments.
Sincerely,
William A. Orme, Jr.
Executive Director

cc: High Rep. Carl Bildt
Hon. Herve de Charette
Hon. Warren Christopher
Amb. Robert Frowick
Hon. Richard Holbrooke
Gen. George Joulwan
Hon. Yevgeny Primakov
Hon. Chris Smith
Sec. Gen. Javier Solana

Berne, 12 September 1996

Dear Mr. Orme:

I thank you very much for your letter of 5 September 1996 concerning freedom of the press and the free movement of journalists in Bosnia and Herzegovina. When certifying the political conditions for the elections on 25 June 1996 in Vienna, I stated that the minimal prerequisites which must be met so that "free, fair and democratic elections" could take place had, at that time and in spite of some small progress, not been fulfilled. Thereby I was referring, among other things, to the poor state of freedom of expression and association and the hindrance of freedom of movement. For a number of other reasons and factors, for which I would like to refer you to the speech attached, I nevertheless fixed 14 September as election day. This decision was connected to the hope that conditions would improve in the months remaining till the elections. Unfortunately, I recently had to state, two months after certification of the election date, that political conditions for the elections had not essentially improved. In particular, I had to affirm that freedom of opinion and freedom of assembly were being encroached upon by acts of intimidation and that free access to media had been attained only on a very limited scale.

As concerns your queries regarding the freedom of the press after the 14 September elections, it has been agreed now that, as far as the OSCE is concerned, the Parties of the Agreement on Elections (Annex 3 of the General Framework Agreement) have agreed to an extension of the mandate of the OSCE concerning the elections until the end of 1996. This includes the mandate of the Provisional Election Commission which, through the Media Expert Commission, has been monitoring the press and media situation and which has taken actions in numerous cases of violations of the respective rules and regulations.

Sincerely yours,

Chairman-in-Office of the OSCE
Flavio Cotti, Federal Councillor
Head of the Federal Department of Foreign Affairs

Battling Seditious Libel in Croatia

Two journalists with the satirical newspaper Feral Tribune *were acquitted in September of charges that they defamed Croatian President Franjo Tudjman in an article critical of his decision to rebury the remains of World War II fascists alongside their victims. The defendants faced up to three years in prison if convicted.*

As part of the international campaign launched on behalf of editor in chief Viktor Ivancic and reporter Marinko Culic, CPJ board member James C. Goodale traveled to Zagreb in June to present a legal brief, reprinted below, on the opening day of the trial. The brief condemned the proceedings and the criminal libel statutes upon which they were based. The Feral Tribune *case was the first application of a law passed in March that makes it significantly easier to criminally prosecute journalists for critical reporting or satirical commentary on the president, the prime minister, and other high-level government officials.*

The victory for Ivancic and Culic may be a temporary one. On Oct. 10, the prosecutor filed an appeal against the acquittal. At year's end, the appeal was still pending.

June 14, 1996

TO THE MUNICIPAL JUDGE
COUNTY COURT IN ZAGREB
CROATIA
RE: INDICTMENT PROPOSAL NO. KT-8848/96

BRIEF OF THE COMMITTEE TO PROTECT
JOURNALISTS
IN SUPPORT OF DEFENDANTS
VIKTOR IVANCIC AND MARINKO CULIC

Preliminary Statement
The Committee to Protect Journalists (CPJ), represented by James C. Goodale, Esq., a member of the CPJ Board and its former Chairman, presents this brief in support of the defendants, Viktor Ivancic

and Marinko Culic of the weekly newspaper *Feral Tribune*. CPJ is a private, nonpartisan organization based in the United States and devoted to the defense of the professional rights of working journalists around the world.

All criminal libel statutes are pernicious, and CPJ condemns their use anywhere, at any time. Seditious libel statutes are especially pernicious, because they are used exclusively to silence dissent against the governing regime. Croatia's new amendments to its Penal Code, Articles 71 and 72, constitute seditious libel statutes because they shield only high government officials from criticism. Such laws have no place in any country, and are especially to be condemned in a self-proclaimed democracy such as Croatia.

Democratic societies do not criminalize critical reporting—they tolerate and protect it. The right to speak freely without fear of government reprisal is at the very heart of democracy. Freedom of speech rests upon political dialogue, not upon a monologue of orthodoxy.

Through this prosecution, Croatia—a country aspiring to join the community of Western democracies—flouts this tradition. No journalist in any Western democracy is in prison as a result of a conviction of seditious libel. The European Court of Human Rights and the United States Supreme Court have crowned freedom of the press regarding political officials as the most powerful of the rights of free expression.

First, we respectfully urge the court to dismiss the indictment proposals against Mr. Ivancic and Mr. Culic, because this prosecution represents a grave threat to freedom of the press in Croatia. Second, we appeal to the executive and legislative leaders of Croatia to repeal the statutes in question, as well as any other law that sanctions the use of seditious libel doctrine to muzzle free expression.

CPJ is gravely concerned about freedom of the press in Croatia. We repeatedly have expressed our concerns to President Franjo Tudjman and other officials regarding the Penal Code, the use of these statutes against *Feral Tribune*, and other harassment of the independent press. In a meeting last month with CPJ board chairman Kati Marton, President Tudjman himself raised *Feral Tribune's* coverage as an example of what, in his view, was a misuse of the rights of the press. President Tudjman showed Ms. Marton a copy of *Feral Tribune* with a cover featuring a caricature of himself, and asked: "Would any other world leaders put up with this?" Ms. Marton replied: "All leaders in democracies."

Statement of Facts

On April 29, 1996, *Feral Tribune* published an article titled "Bones in the Blender" and a photo montage, "Jasenovac—The Biggest Croatian Underground City." These pieces commented upon President Franjo Tudjman's plans to create a single monument in the former concentration camp of Jasenovac that would put the bones of Croatian Fascists alongside those of the Jews and Serbs they massacred during World War II. The montage depicted the Fascist dictator Ante Pavelic handing Tudjman a miniature version of the Jasenovac monument. An accompanying text titled the "Other Side of Satire" drew a satirical parallel between Tudjman and the late Generalissimo Francisco Franco of Spain.

The government now intends to prosecute Mr. Ivancic and Mr. Culic under its newly amended criminal libel statute, threatening them with a maximum penalty of three years in jail for allegedly injuring the President's honor and his personal integrity.

This prosecution is only the latest in a disturbing series of governmental attacks upon Croatia's free press. The government also has instigated civil libel suits, shut down newspaper offices, and levied punitive taxes against prominent independent newspapers critical of the Tudjman regime.

Argument

Croatia's attempt to impose criminal penalties directed against journalists who criticize political leaders is completely at odds with norms of democracy and Western practice. These prosecutions of Mr. Ivancic and Mr. Culic for their publication of satirical commentary on President Tudjman's controversial plan to commingle the remains of Croatian Fascists and World War II concentration camp victims represents an unacceptable intrusion into the freedom of expression that is guaranteed by international and European law.

The prosecution today of journalists for the dissemination of political views in Europe is a rare and startling event. No journalist is in prison today in any Western democratic nation as a result of a conviction on charges of seditious libel based on published criticism of a political figure. Croatia's law is particularly egregious because it targets only critics of five top government officials, and therefore has no legitimate basis in the protection of private reputations.

As the European Court of Human Rights has recognized, the press has a unique responsibility in democratic societies to impart information enabling the electorate to "discover and form an opinion of the ideas and attitudes of political leaders."[1] To enable the press to fulfill this critical responsibility, democratic nations afford especially stringent protection to speech concerning political issues and to the expression of value judgments and opinions. The Croatian law does not merely fail to respect democratic principles and international norms; it inverts them by threatening the unprecedented sanction of imprisonment as punishment for the exercise of the most important form of free speech: political opinion regarding a ruling official.

A. International, U.S., And European Law Recognize That Freedom Of Political Debate Lies At The Core Of Democracy

Freedom of expression and opinion are guaranteed under the U.N. Declaration of Human Rights,[2] the International Covenant on Civil and Political Rights,[3] to which Croatia has acceded, and the European Convention for the Protection of Human Rights and Fundamental Freedoms.[4] Moreover, these universal principles have passed into customary international law.[5] As the European Court of Human Rights has acknowledged, acceptance of these principles requires the toleration even of speech which is shocking or offensive.[6]

The Court has further indicated that the prosecution of journalists who criticize politicians or government officials is an interference with free expression that is never "justified in a democratic society."[7] The Court has held that "freedom of expression is an essential element for the formulation of political opinion."[8] For this reason, the Court has afforded a particularly high degree of protection to speech of a political character and has held that the appropriate response of the criticized government is to engage its opponent in further debate rather than to impose criminal sanctions.[9]

The United States Supreme Court similarly has acknowledged that political debate lies at the very heart of the protection of free speech. In the landmark case of *New York Times Co. v. Sullivan*, the Supreme Court reversed a jury finding that *The New York Times* had libeled a state official, holding that in order to obtain libel damages for publication of a defamatory falsehood, a public official must meet the heavy burden of proving that the defamatory statement was made with knowledge of its falsity or with reckless disregard of whether it was true or false.[10] The Court reiterated the words of James Madison: the power to prosecute libel of public officials "ought to produce universal alarm, because it is leveled against the right of freely examining public characters and measures, and of free communication of the people thereon, which has ever been justly deemed the only effectual guardian of every other right."[11] Later, in a case striking down a criminal libel statute, the Court stressed that speech concerning public affairs is "more than self-expression; it is the essence of self-government."[12]

Feral Tribune's satires fall squarely within the tradition of rigorous protection for political speech. The European Court of Human Rights has recognized that politicians—particularly those who are presently in office, as President Tudjman is—must tolerate more criticism than a private individual.[13] The President's Jasenovac proposal aroused national and international debate. By commenting on that proposal, *Feral Tribune* exercised "the very function of the press in a democratic society, to participate in the political process by checking on the development of the debate of public issues carried on by political office-holders."[14] Criminal prosecution of Mr. Ivancic and Mr. Culic for fulfilling this critical function violates international law and contravenes democratic principles.

B. Expressions of Opinion and Value Judgments Also Merit The Highest Legal Protections

Mr. Ivancic and Mr. Culic are facing prosecution for the expression of a value judgment regarding President Tudjman's proposal. The European Court of Human Rights has noted that "a careful distinction has to be made between facts and value judgments" and has prohibited a state from requiring a libel defendant to prove the truth of his opinions.[15] Such a requirement is impossible to meet, and therefore "infringes freedom of expression to a degree incompatible with the fundamental principles of a democratic society."[16] In a case closely analogous to this one, the Court held that the prosecution of a journalist who had drawn a parallel between the position of an Austrian Liberal Party official and the platform of the Nazi party violated the journalist's right to "express clear value judgments."[17] The Court of Human Rights has recognized that expressions of value judgments can never present legitimate grounds for a libel prosecution, because they cannot be either true or false: "the truth of value-judgments is not susceptible of proof."[18]

American constitutional law similarly embraces the principle that statements of opinion, having no provably false factual connotation, should be accorded the full protection of the law.[19] In the line of cases most relevant to the *Feral Tribune* trial, the U.S. Supreme Court has jealously guarded the right of a satirical publication to engage in political or social commentary of a biting or harsh nature. The Court has noted that public officials in a democracy must tolerate "vehement, caustic, and sometimes unpleasantly sharp attacks."[20] In various cases the U.S. Supreme Court has held that "rhetorical hyperbole," "vigorous epithet" or "lusty and imaginative expression[s] of contempt" used in a "loose, figurative sense" are not libelous because they can never be objectively false.[21] Protection of such speech "provides assurance that public debate will not suffer for lack of 'imaginative expression' or the 'rhetorical hyperbole' which has traditionally added much to the discourse of our nation."[22]

Likewise, the use of epithets in political debate enjoys strong protection because such language constitutes nothing more than strongly worded views that are neither provably true nor false. The U.S. Supreme Court has been especially vigilant in using constitutional law to shelter strong, even outrageous, political speech. Thus the Court has repeatedly found that the use of political labels (e.g., "blackmail," "traitor," "scab") during spirited debate is not actionable because the allegations are offered in the exchange of public discourse.[23] Recognizing political invective as part of the democratic process, the Court has afforded it strong protection. Public officials do not need the special protections of the libel laws, because they have "sufficient access to means of counter-argument to be able to expose through discussion the falsehood and fallacies of the defamatory statements."[24] As the U.S. Supreme Court has said, in a case that is particularly instructive on the plight of Messrs. Ivancic and Culic: "[T]o use loose language or undefined slogans that are part of the give-and-take in our economic and political controversies—like 'unfair' or 'Fascist'—is not to falsify facts."[25]

Mr. Ivancic and Mr. Culic have not told lies, they have expressed opinions. Whether one agrees or disagrees with their views—and CPJ does neither—their expression of political opinion, far from exposing them to criminal sanction, merits the fullest protection of the law.

Conclusion

The law under which Mr. Ivancic and Mr. Culic face prosecution is an intolerable interference with freedom of expression. It criminalizes exactly the type of political speech that international, European, and U.S. law have recognized to be essential to an informed democracy. Mr. Ivancic and Mr. Culic should not be put at risk of criminal prosecution by the very regime they seek to criticize, simply because they have exercised their responsibility to impart opinions and engage in debate. Under the European Convention, a nation may regulate free speech only to the extent necessary to a democratic society.[26] Croatia cannot possibly meet this standard if it insists on prosecuting these or any journalists for what they publish. Croatia's criminalization of libel based on political opinions is fundamentally antithetical to the values of a democratic society. Because these prosecutions of Mr. Ivancic and Mr. Culic are in flagrant violation of democratic principles, the Municipal Court should dismiss the indictment proposals.

Respectfully submitted,

COMMITTEE TO PROTECT JOURNALISTS

By: James C. Goodale, Esq.

330 Seventh Avenue
New York, New York 10001, USA
Telephone: (212) 465-1004/Fax: (212) 465-9658
E-Mail: info@cpj.org
Of Counsel:
DEBEVOISE & PLIMPTON
875 Third Avenue
New York, New York 10022 USA

---

1. Lingens v. Austria, Eur. Ct. H.R. (Ser. A., No. 103)(1986) ¶ 42.

2. G.A. Res. 217 (III 1948), art. 19.

3. 999 U.N.T.S. 171 (entered into force on March 23, 1976), art. 19.

4. 213 U.N.T.S. 221 (entered into force on September 3, 1953), art. 10(1).

5. Karel Vasak, The International Dimensions of Human Rights 106 (1982) (emphasizing the authoritative force of the Universal Declaration of Human Rights and stating that "no responsible member of the international community may disregard an appeal to the rights enshrined in it").

6. Handyside v. United Kingdom, Eur. Ct. H.R. (Ser. A, No. 24) (1976) ¶ 49.

7. Castells v. Spain, Eur. Ct. H.R. (Ser. A., No. 236) (1992) ¶ 72; Lingens ¶ 1(d).

8. Castells ¶ 68.

9. Id. ¶ 68, 72.

10. 376 U.S. 254 (1964)

11. Sullivan, 365 U.S. at 274, citing 4 Elliot's Debates.

12. Garrison v. Louisiana, 379 U.S. 64, 75 (1964).

13. Lingens ¶ 42, Castells ¶ 65.

14. Oberschlick v. Austria, Eur. Ct. H.R. (Ser. A., No. 204) (1995) ¶ 67.

15. Lingens ¶ 46.

16. Id. 2.

17. Oberschlick 70.

18. Id. ¶ 69.

19. Milkovich v. Lorain Journal Co., 497 U.S. 1 (1990).

20. Sullivan, 365 U.S. at 270.

21. Milkovich, citing Greenbelt Coop. Publishing Ass'n, Inc. v. Bresler, 398 U.S. 6 (1970) & Old Dominion Letter Carriers v. Austin, 418 U.S. 264 (1974).

22. Milkovich, 497 U.S. at 20.

23. Greenbelt, Letter Carriers, supra.

24. Curtis Publishing Co. v. Butts, 388 U.S. 130 (1967).

25. Cafeteria Employees Local 302 v. Angelos, 320 U.S. 293, 295 (1943).

26. The Sunday Times v. United Kingdom, Eur. Ct. H.R. (Ser. A., No. 30) (1979) ¶ 65.

Prepared with the assistance of Jeremy Feigelson, Shannon Conaty, Lorraine Ford, and Maura Monaghan of Debevoise & Plimpton; Catherine A. Fitzpatrick; and William A. Orme, Jr.

Russia's Harsh Press Climate

by Catherine A. Fitzpatrick

ALTHOUGH BORIS YELTSIN WON the presidential election, the Russian media, which unabashedly backed the president, lost. That's the view of most American journalists, and some liberals in Moscow. Is it just?

Once lauded as the most democratic institution in society, Russia's fourth estate is having to prove itself all over again amid charges of bias and lack of professionalism. The issues aren't just credibility or crying wolf about communism, but a chronic dependency on government handouts or private investment by business groups transparently close to power, and a more insidious tendency toward self-censorship to avoid trouble with anyone. In a year-end article in the weekly newspaper *Kommersant* (The Merchant), 16 journalists were interviewed about what they had been afraid to write in 1996. Some feared provoking libel suits, others avoided writing about the mafia or government leaders, and some refrained from criticizing their colleagues. One journalist said his worst fear was writing two words: his first name and his last name. Indeed, few detractors of the Russian press appreciate the difficult, and at times even frightening, climate for news-gatherers in the heart of the former Soviet Union.

Moscow's television and newspaper reporters have impressed the world with their hard-hitting coverage of controversial topics, but little is known about the incredible persistence they need to perform their jobs. While a new generation of inquisitive journalists has emerged since the 1991 failed coup that brought down the Communist system, the philosophy—and even the identity—of many of the people who control the media has not changed.

Throughout the Chechen conflict, Russian troops failed to honor press credentials and hindered journalists particularly during the worst battles, jamming satellite transmissions, exposing film, destroying equipment, and even firing on their cars from checkpoints or gunships. In a modern twist on the notion of "the pen is mightier than the sword," a soldier once seized a reporter's satellite phone, saying, "Those things are more dangerous than weapons." A correspondent from the independent NTV had to disguise herself as a Chechen peasant, hiding a video camera in the folds of her long garments, and even rode on horseback over the hills to foil numerous military barriers designed to keep out the press.

In 1995, the Yeltsin government first threatened to revoke NTV's license because of its unflinching coverage of the carnage, then tried to prosecute a journalist for interviewing a Chechen leader. NTV depends on the government for access to state-owned satellite transmitters, and originally shared the frequency for Channel 4 with state-owned television. NTV kept up its grim newscasts from Chechnya but seemed to soften at least the anti-Yeltsin rhetoric when its chairman, Igor Malashenko, joined the president's campaign as a media adviser. Many observers believed that Malashenko was rewarded for excellent service when, after his victory, Yeltsin decreed all of Channel 4 for NTV's use. Quipped *Moscow News*, "The most statist television company became the most independent in its judgments and the opposite, the station with no relationship to the government whatsoever, became the most tame."

Last year, the gas conglomerate Gazprom, once run by Prime Minister Viktor Chernomyrdin, bought 30 percent of NTV's shares, possibly giving the station more latitude through increased private investment, but creating other kinds of problems. Gazprom itself is still 40 percent state-owned, and run by Chernomyrdin's cronies. (Investment from Most-Bank financial group, close to the mayor of Moscow, could provide some counterweight in Moscow politics, so dependent on individual charismatic leaders. So far, however, all the investors back Yeltsin.)

Independent television, radio, and print media have generally thrived in Russia since 1991. But paradoxically, the press under Yeltsin's administration has suffered its most brutal attacks since the Stalin era. Despite the Yeltsin government's reliance on the media's support, and regardless of the media's proximity to power, the government has failed to properly investigate and prosecute the murders of journalists, let alone track down the sources of myriad threats against journalists from government offices and from the underworld.

The Committee to Protect Journalists has confirmed that since 1994, at least 13 journalists have been assassinated in the Russian Federation, and 8 are currently missing. Some of those who have disappeared are presumed dead, including American free-lance photojournalist Andrew Shumack, last seen in Grozny in July 1995. These numbers are comparable to the journalists' death toll under the world's worst regimes. It seems counterintuitive that the man whom the Russian press supported as the guardian of its freedoms could be in any way responsible for this phenomenon. Yet by his government's inaction in pursuing justice for the murders, and his failure to galvanize law-enforcement agencies to protect journalists from coercion, Yeltsin has effectively signaled that enemies of the press may act—even kill—with impunity.

Attacks on the press do not emanate from the president's office, although the Kremlin might occasionally prevent the peskier reporters from coming to official press conferences, or fire a state television executive like Russian State Television's Oleg Poptsov, who was dismissed in 1996 after publishing memoirs in which he was critical of the president. But violence against journalists *does* stem from Yeltsin's lack of control over the "power ministries" (defense, armed forces, police and internal troops, security, and counterintelligence) and from their failure, in turn, to control both their own rank-and-file and various violent groups in society.

After the elections, a much ballyhooed "clean sweep" of corrupt ministries by then-security chief Alexander Lebed—himself a general—was no substitute for the institutionalized civilian oversight of a free press. Nor were parliamentary hearings into military corruption—encouraged by Yeltsin's post-election effort to reform the military—a substitute for independent investigative journalism. Such efforts did nothing to address the inherent dangers faced by journalists whose probing of such sensitive topics as corruption in the military, law enforcement, or business has led to their colleagues' deaths in mafia-style contract killings. In 1996 alone, at least two journalists were murdered near their homes and four were assassinated in Chechnya (not accidentally killed in crossfire), apparently in connection with their work. Several more suffered brutal beatings and others narrowly escaped assaults or endured anonymous threats.

In 1995, Natalya Alyakina, a correspondent for the German news service RUFA, was shot dead after being waved through a checkpoint during the Chechen hostage-taking crisis in Budyonnovsk near the Chechen border. Following a bungled investigation, an Interior Ministry soldier was convicted in July 1996 on the lesser charge of "involuntary manslaughter through misuse of firearms," and given a suspended sentence of two and a half years. Yeltsin and other high officials failed to make good on their original, highly publicized promises to obtain justice in this case as a deterrent to military abuses.

In March 1996, Nadezhda Chaikova, a prominent war correspondent for the weekly *Obshchaya Gazeta* who was known for her exposés of Russian military atrocities and her close contacts with the Chechen resistance, was found murdered execution-style outside the Chechen village of Gekhi. Russian federal troops, angered at Chaikova's videotaping of Samashki, a village they had demolished, were suspects. Chechen leaders, acting on rumors spread by the KGB's successor, the Federal Security Service (FSB), that Chaikova was a spy, may have ordered the killing. The federal government never investigated the murder. An inquiry begun by Chechen prosecutors was transferred to the North Caucasus prosecutor's office, where it has stalled.

In August, in an incident eerily similar to Alyakina's killing, Ramzan Khadzhiev, ORT's North Caucasus bureau chief, said to be the subject of past threats from Chechen fighters, was shot dead after he had shown his journalist's credentials and had been waved through a checkpoint outside Grozny. The shots came from armored vehicles; Khadzhiev's wife and son, traveling with him, were unhurt. Another passenger gave testimony, aired on NTV, that Russian troops were responsible. No investigation has been launched, and ORT has not pursued any public inquiry. Clearly, the largely symbolic punishment of Alyakina's killer and his superiors sent a message to the armed forces that the government tolerates such actions.

The military is notorious for coercive treatment of journalists, and not only in war zones. *Izvestia* disclosed in May 1996 that military prosecutors and other authorities had forced its correspondents in Moscow and elsewhere to "share information." A *Moskovsky Komsomolets* journalist, Yulya Kalinina, suffered anonymous threats and a break-in at her apartment after publishing articles in the newsmagazine *Itogi* and in *Obshchaya Gazeta* on officers' abuses of power, such as the use of conscripts to build villas. The Minister of Construction subsequently filed a lawsuit against Kalinina over her exposé of misspent Chechen reconstruction funds, despite the fact that the Parliament used her signed articles as evidence in its inquiries on the subject. In November 1996, in two front-page stories, *Izvestiya* chronicled the Federal Security Service's efforts to infiltrate the press—compensation for what the secret police saw as their loss of the propaganda war to Chechen spokespersons.

Journalists also confirm the FSB's role in spreading rumors to discredit reporters who cover Chechnya or other security-related topics, setting them up as targets for violence from any quarter. Summonses for "chats" at the FSB and offers to collaborate—or face career difficulties–are still facts of life that journalists and their editors fear publicizing. In 1996, Yevgeniya Albats, an *Izvestiya* journalist who had published a book and a series of exposés about the security police, was fired from her job. An *Izvestiya* editor killed her critical piece on the FSB on Nov. 18 just as it was to go to the printer, and FSB, with copies of the galleys, called Albats the next day and warned her not to publish the article. It ran in *Nezouisimoya Gazeta* (Independent Newspaper) soon afterwards. In one follow-up investigation of a journalist's murder in 1996, CPJ discovered that callers using false names had threatened colleagues of the victim who had been conducting their own investigation of the killing, demanding that they cease their independent probe into the death if they valued their safety.

Even the boldest press freedom advocates in Russia are unable to sustain inquiries into assassinations. Doing so would mean bucking both silent, vindictive officials and a resistant public that questions why journalists should get special treatment over the thousands of other Russian murder victims whose cases remain unsolved. Thus, for example, editors at the muck-raking *Moskovsky Komsomolets* have yet to reveal their allegations about the death of Dmitry Kholodov, their reporter killed by an exploding briefcase in 1994 while following up on a tip about army corruption.(See David Satter's special report on Russia in CPJ's *Attacks on the Press in 1995*.)

In his short reign as head of the security council, Lebed managed to unseat Defense Minister Pavel Grachev, long suspected of corruption and possible complicity in the Kholodov murder. That didn't help to move the homicide investigation forward. Authorities have long claimed to be holding a soldier as a suspect, but have yet to explain his motivation. Lebed's purges of other officials in the power ministries, and his *ad hominem* attacks against Interior Minister Anatoly Kulikov that precipitated Lebed's dismissal, did not appear to diminish threats to journalists or remove the impediments to obtaining justice for their attackers.

Both the press and parliament were puzzled and even scandalized by the subsequent appointment of Boris Berezovsky, one of Russia's self-described "Big Seven" businessmen with holdings in media, automobiles, and oil, to the post of deputy chairman of the Security Council, largely responsible for political and commercial negotiations in Chechnya. (The position has traditionally been held by people with experience in government or security.) Berezovsky, who has interests in TV-6 and respected publications like the daily *Nezavisimaya Gazeta* and the weekly *Ogonyok*, is part-owner of Russian Public Television (ORT), having persuaded the government to sell off 49 percent of its shares. After he assumed his new post, Berezovsky revealed to the *Financial Times* that he and six others with media interests had bankrolled the Yeltsin campaign, raising the question of whether the election media campaign meant that Yeltsin had reinforced his grip on news organizations, or whether the shadowy business community with major media control had reinforced its hold on Yeltsin.

Berezovsky's position at ORT fueled rumors of his knowledge or even involvement in the murder of Vladimir Listyev, a popular talk show host and producer who was shot to death, gangland-style, in March 1995 after agreeing to head the then-newly established public television station. In an attempt to deal with rampant corruption in the station's advertising contracts, Listyev had frozen all accounts until new ethical standards could be devised. Berezovsky, originally deputy chairman of ORT, assumed the chair after Listyev's death. He resigned from the board in late 1996 after his appointment to the Security Council post, but kept his 8 percent of ORT's shares and his considerable influence over the station. His official calendar has been filled with meetings with Chechen and Transcaucasian leaders discussing the oil business. Although Berezovsky has declined to comment, his extensive negotiations in Grozny apparently included bargaining for the release of two ORT journalists who disappeared Jan. 19 and were eventually freed and allowed to return to Moscow on Feb. 18. It is not known if Berezovsky sparked any probes into other reporters' disappearances or killings, including the assassination of ORT's Khadzhiev.

In an article in the Dec. 30, 1996 issue, *Forbes* magazine claimed that Listyev got caught between "two ruthless characters"—Berezovsky and Sergei Lisovsky, head of Premier SV advertising. Lisovsky, an ORT board member who had also been involved in an alleged Yeltsin campaign-financing scandal, would have taken heavy financial losses because of Listyev's advertising moratorium. The *Forbes* account said that Listyev had wanted to transfer $100 million in damages to Lisovsky as compensation for future losses, and gave the money to Berezovsky, who stalled. After *Sovetskaya Rossiya*, a pro-Communist newspaper, ran an excerpt of the *Forbes* piece, NTV anchor Yevgeny Kiselyov asked Berezovsky point-blank on national television if he had killed Listyev. Berezovsky denied any involvement, claiming that it was the "work of the special services," the KGB's successors. Berezovsky himself was injured in an unsolved car bombing in 1994 that killed his driver.

Rather than telling more about what he knows, Berezovsky has sued *Forbes* for libel, claiming in a prepared statement that the "Capitalist Tool" had "become a mouthpiece of Communist and nationalist propaganda," and that the article was "a rare and regrettable example of the Western mass media falling victim to a disinformation campaign which is being carried out purposefully by Communist circles with the aim of discrediting the administration of President Yeltsin."

The Yeltsin administration has already reinforced its cadres in the public-relations wars. Just prior to the elections, Vitaly Ignatenko, general director of the wire service ITAR-TASS, the main government news agency, was appointed by Yeltsin as vice premier of the Russian government responsible for media and information policy. In Gorbachev's *glasnost* era, when Ignatenko worked in the Central Committee, journalists had looked to him as their defender, although he also served on a government humanitarian commission that often deflected foreign concern about human rights. Queried by *Moscow News* in January 1997 about his relationship with the "new information power personages" like Most-Bank's Pavel Gusinsky or Berezovsky, Ignatenko responded that "they all visit me, and I have talks and disputes with them, but for me it is very important that they correctly understand the press's responsibility to the state. Yes, it should be free from the government's *diktat*. But in the media's mood and...attitude to what is happening, the media should serve the state's interest in their choice of topics, the problems they address, their coverage of various situations—in all of these matters, the media must take into account the interests of society." Asked if the media moguls who visited him were "state-minded people," he replied in the affirmative.

Like other media officials, Ignatenko wrung his hands at the lack of protection for reporters and the numerous unsolved killings. They die, he explained, "not because we have so many flashpoints" like Chechnya, but "because our colleagues are easier to kill than convince." His suggestion? Form a more "militant" union of journalists to "raise the alarm, to speak to the public, the government, and the president in the highest tones." Ignatenko may have muted his own cries within the corridors of power.

In January, in an interview with Vsevolod Bogdanov, head of the Russian Journalists Union, a reporter from *Argumenty i Fakty* commented, "It is very easy to manipulate journalists. One can buy off those who are necessary and kill those who are not necessary." Bogdanov responded: "Yes, that's true....If a journalist receives $50 a month... and he is offered $1,000 for an article, then it is difficult to talk about moral choice. You have to create the conditions for such a choice, provide a decent living and protection for the journalist.... We are negotiating with the government and will arrive at a system of state protectionism for the mass media."

Meanwhile, skeptical of such "state protectionism" from journalists' unions based on the old Soviet-era organizations, some media organizations have advocated the formation of an Academy of the Free Press. In December, leading outlets such as *Izvestia*, *Argumenty i Fakty*, *Kommersant*, *Moscow News*, and *Interfax* appealed to Yeltsin—not to help investigate journalists' murders, but to establish presidential press awards for the academy. Yeltsin quickly complied, decreeing annual presidential stipends and a prize for young journalists in time for Russian Press Day, Jan. 13.

Rather than presidential prizes, personnel changes in the Kremlin, anti-crime raids, or law-and-order decrees, a true test of the Yeltsin administration's intentions to preserve the media's freedoms would be the removal of obstacles to the prosecution of the murderers of Kholodov, Listyev, and others who have attacked or threatened reporters. That means freeing journalists as well as prosecutors and judges from the fear of both big government and big business.

The Clinton administration and other Western governments that supported Yeltsin's re-election should urge the Yeltsin administration to demonstrate commitment to a free press by seeking justice for those who harm it. Russia's journalists need a pledge of safe working conditions—as well as a safe distance from the powers that be—if the press is to reclaim its reputation as Russia's freest institution.

An excerpt of this article appeared in Moscow Times *on Aug. 12, 1996.*

The Middle East
and North Africa

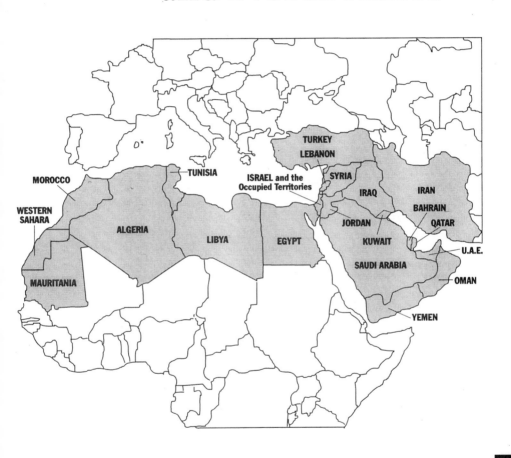

OVERVIEW
OF
The Middle East and North Africa

by Joel Campagna

P RESS FREEDOM REMAINS AN ELUSIVE GOAL for journalists in the Middle East. While governments continue to display remarkable resistance to local and international demands for greater political liberalization, journalists face familiar obstacles in their attempt to provide independent news coverage. Censorship, legal prosecution, and imprisonment endure as real threats for most journalists, serving as the primary means for state control over the flow of news and information.

Throughout the region, 110 journalists were in prison at year's end for non-violent offenses either directly or tangentially related to their reporting. A more ominous statistic, however, was the nine journalists who were murdered because of their profession. Seven of those deaths occurred in Algeria, where government censorship of the bloody four-year civil conflict has helped fuel a lethal campaign against the press by Islamic militants currently battling the state. Over the past three years, 59 journalists in Algeria have been killed as a result of assassination.

Across the Mediterranean in Turkey, the formation of a new Islamist-led government failed to alter the state's ongoing persecution of journalists who report critically on the Kurdish issue. Seventy-eight journalists now languish in jail—the largest number ever documented by CPJ in a single country. As in previous years, they were the victims of the authorities' indiscriminate use of sweeping provisions to the infamous Anti-Terror Law and Penal Code.

The Turkish government's repression of the independent press was largely symbolic of a growing trend in the Arab world toward applying the rule of law to punish dissenting journalists. In Jordan, the government went on the offensive

Joel Campagna *is program coordinator for the Middle East and North Africa. He has also worked as a consultant for Human Rights Watch/Middle East, conducting fact-finding missions to Egypt and Lebanon, and as a researcher for the Cairo-based Center for Human Rights Legal Aid (CHRLA). Campagna has a master's degree in international affairs from Columbia University.*

against what it termed "excesses" of the press, invoking the Press and Publications Law and Penal Code to arrest, fine, and prosecute outspoken journalists. Authorities in Iran, meanwhile, employed their country's press law to similar effect against those journalists critical of government officials and the Islamic Republic in general. And, in Lebanon–once a model to the Arab world with its lively broadcast media—government legislation authorized the official licensing of a handful of television and radio stations with close ties to government officials. Scores of independent stations were subsequently ordered to close.

Elsewhere in the region, abysmal press conditions remained the norm in countries such as Saudi Arabia, Syria, Iraq, and Tunisia, where the state either asserts direct control over the media or discourages independent journalism through intimidation and the threat of reprisal. The nascent Palestinian press increasingly resorted to self-censorship following the Palestinian National Authority's harsh crackdown on dissenting journalists during the initial two years of its rule.

All of these disturbing developments were offset, to a modest degree, by the Egyptian government's decision in June to amend a series of restrictive legal provisions governing the press. The move came in response to a sustained, one-year campaign by Egyptian journalists and human rights activists who voiced opposition to the draconian legislation. Although flaws remain in existing legislation, the Egyptian government's move underscored the potential for the press to affect change. Across the region, through greater mobilization within their profession and their participation in the burgeoning regional human rights movement, journalists are increasingly vigorous in opposing government attempts to silence them. Creative initiatives to utilize advances in technology such as the Internet promise to facilitate the free flow of information to all citizens in the region in the near future, thus rendering government censorship practices irrelevant. In many countries, however, the success of these efforts will depend largely on the willingness of governments to relinquish their control over the distribution of information services.

Middle East

Algeria

As the fourth year of brutal civil conflict came to an end, journalists continued to face great peril, and Algeria remained the most dangerous place in the world for journalists. Since the army canceled parliamentary elections in January 1992 to prevent victory by the Islamic Salvation Front (FIS), an estimated 60,000 people have died as a result of the ensuing violence. Meanwhile, both sides of the conflict continue to victimize the press.

Since May 1993, 59 journalists have been murdered—presumed to be the work of Islamist militants seeking to overthrow the current government. In 1996 alone, seven journalists were assassinated, while several other media employees met similar fates. Strict government censorship of independent reporting on "security matters" has helped to fuel the Islamists' campaign against the press. Factions such as the Armed Islamic Group (GIA)—which has claimed responsibility for nearly half the total number of journalists' murders in Algeria—indiscriminately kill journalists for what they view as the media's complicity with the Algerian government. The Islamists' perception of the press stems in part from official censorship of news relating to security forces' casualties or human rights abuses and the exclusion of Islamist viewpoints. Emergency law, for example, grants the state sweeping power to prosecute journalists whom it deems a threat to state security. Governmental decrees forbid newspapers to publish any stories on the conflict except those from the state-run Algerian Press Service (APS).

In February, the government further tightened its control over the press, establishing "reading committees" to ensure that stories on the civil strife conform with official accounts. The independent daily *La Tribune* summarized the overall effect of government restrictions, noting that "[p]ublications must stick to terse statements carried by the [official] Algerian Press Service (APS) which report the number of terrorists shot dead by the forces of order but ignore the death of tens of thousands of civilians and spectacular operations by armed gangs."

Independent newspapers are, in effect, forced to walk a tightrope. Either they censor their own news stories and face the wrath of Islamists (who use the assassination of journalists as a way of getting into the papers), or they expose themselves to legal prosecution from the state and their publications to lengthy suspensions. Either they reprint APS stories, or ignore security matters altogether. In 1996, authorities continued to confiscate newspapers at the state printing press for articles that failed to conform to state guidelines.

Journalists were also subject to punitive measures for publishing material beyond the scope of "internal security." In July, Chawki Amari, a cartoonist for the independent daily *La Tribune*, was charged with defaming the Algerian flag for a cartoon satirizing the political situation in Algeria. An appeals court, on Sept. 3, upheld a three-year suspended prison sentence against him. In addition to Amari, the paper's publisher and editor in chief also received suspended prison sentences and the paper was subsequently banned for six months. In another case, state prosecutors summoned Omar Belhouchet, editor in chief of the independent daily *Al-Watan*, for questioning in regard to a libel accusation by the brother of a former government official. Although the charges against Belhouchet were later dropped, he remained under judicial supervision for nearly a month.

In addition to the blanket censorship of security matters, the authorities use more subtle means to constrain political discourse in the press. The government controls the supply of newsprint and owns the printing presses and is thus able to put economic pressure on newspapers. The state also wields considerable authority over the distribution of advertising, giving preferential treatment to those newspapers whose editorial line on the conflict most closely matches the government's. When subtle means fail to restrain the press, the Interior Ministry suspends publications and summons reporters to court.

Foreign reporters traveling to Algeria continue to face restrictions on their freedom of movement. The government, citing security concerns, prevents foreign correspondents from moving around the country freely and meeting with opposition figures. This was the case for many foreign reporters trying to cover the country's Nov. 28 constitutional referendum.

As 1996 came to a close, at least one journalist, Abdelkader Hadj Benaamane, a correspondent for APS, remained in prison. A state military court sentenced him in July 1995 to three years in prison for "attacking the security of the state and national unity." The charges apparently stemmed from an internal APS news wire, which reported on the whereabouts of imprisoned FIS leaders Abassi Madani and Ali Belhadj. Another journalist, Djamel Fahassi, a reporter with the government-run French-language radio station Alger Chaine III and a former contributor to the now-banned *Al-Forqane*—a weekly organ of the FIS—was arrested by security forces in May 1995. Although witnesses and family members attest that security forces apprehended Fahassi, authorities continue to deny his arrest and his whereabouts remain unknown.

January 10
Mohamed Mekati, *El Moudjahid,* KILLED
Mekati, a correspondent for the government-owned newspaper *El Moudjahid*, died from gunshot wounds. He was shot the previous day, as

he was returning from work, by unidentified gunmen near his home in Ain Naadja, a southwestern suburb of Algiers. In a press release, CPJ condemned the murder.

January 14
Nourredine Guittoune, *L'Indépendant,* ATTACKED
Guittoune, owner and editor in chief of the daily *L'Indépendant*, was gravely wounded in an attack by unidentified gunmen in Algiers. Khaled Aboulkacem, a librarian at the newspaper, was shot and killed in the attack.

February 10
Abdallah Bouhachek, *Révolution et Travaille,* KILLED
Bouhachek, editor of *Révolution et Travaille*, the weekly organ of Algeria's largest workers union (UGTA), was shot and killed by unknown assailants near the town of Blida, south of Algiers, while on his way to work. CPJ condemned the murder in a press release and called on all parties to the conflict to respect the status of journalists as civilian noncombatants.

February 10
All journalists, CENSORED
The Ministry of Interior ordered newspaper editors to submit "unofficial" accounts of security incidents to a government censor. Newspapers are only allowed to carry stories about the country's security situation that have been supplied by the official Algerian Press Service. In a press release, CPJ condemned the policy, noting that the government was further endangering journalists by forcing them to print state propaganda.

February 11
Allaoua Ait M'barak, *Le Soir d'Algérie,* KILLED
Mohamed Dorbane, *Le Soir d'Algérie,* KILLED
Djamel Derraz, *Le Soir d'Algérie,* KILLED
Le Matin, ATTACKED
L'Opinion, ATTACKED
El Watan, ATTACKED
Ait M'barak, editor in chief of the independent

evening daily *Le Soir d'Algérie*; Dorbane, a columnist with the newspaper; and Derraz, a writer with the paper's leisure section, were killed when a car bomb exploded outside the newspaper's office, which is located in the Maison de la Presse Tahar Djaout building in Algiers. In a press release, CPJ condemned the killings.

The press building houses several independent newspapers. The offices of the dailies *Le Matin*, *L'Opinion*, and *El Watan* were damaged in the attack. No group claimed responsibility for the bombing, but Islamic fundamentalist rebels are presumed responsible. The Armed Islamic Group (GIA) has claimed responsibility for the bulk of journalists' slayings in Algeria.

March 3
La Nation, CENSORED
The March 6 issue of *La Nation* was banned by the Ministry of Interior. The issue featured a special report on human rights in Algeria that was co-published with the French monthly newspaper *Le Monde Diplomatique*.

March 12
Djilali Arabidou, *Algérie-Actualité*, KILLED
Arabidou, a reporter and photographer with the French-language pro-government weekly *Algérie-Actualité*, was shot and killed by unidentified gunmen in Ain Naadja, a southwestern suburb of Algiers. Arabdiou was considered by many to be the dean of Algerian photojournalists. In a press release, CPJ condemned the assassination.

March 18
La Nation, CENSORED
Authorities seized the March 19-25 edition of the French-language weekly *La Nation* at the state-run printing house Société d'Impression d'Alger (SIA). No explanation was given for the seizure.

March 24
Ferran Sales, *El País*, EXPELLED

Algerian authorities withdrew the press accreditation of Sales, an Algiers correspondent for the Spanish daily *El País*. He was given seven days to leave Algiers after having worked in Algeria as *El País's* correspondent for the past five years. Sales was not given an official explanation for the measure.

March 25
La Nation, CENSORED
The Interior Ministry seized the March 25-April 1 edition of the French-language independent weekly *La Nation* at the state-run printing house, Société d'Impression d'Alger (SIA). No explanation was given for the seizure.

April 7
Al-Hourria, CENSORED
The Arabic-language weekly *Al-Hourria* was seized by security forces at the state-run printing house where the newspaper is printed. There was no official explanation for the seizure. *Al-Hourria's* sister publication, the French-language *La Nation*, was banned three times in March.

April 14
Omar Belhouchet, *El Watan*, LEGAL ACTION
Belhouchet, the editor in chief of the independent daily *El Watan*, was summoned to the prosecutor's office and put under judicial supervision while being investigated on charges of libeling the brother of former prime minister Mokdad Sifi. For nearly a month, Belhouchet was forced to report to an examining magistrate once a week and was forbidden to leave the country. The charges against him cited an article published in *El Watan* on April 11, which alleged that Zoubir Sifi had been arrested for embezzling money from a state-owned company.

April 25
El Watan, CENSORED
The state-run printing press, Société d'Impression d'Alger (SIA), refused to print the April 24

edition of the French-language independent daily *El Watan*. SIA again refused to publish *El Watan* on May 7. No official explanations were given for SIA's actions. Journalists at the paper attributed the censorship to *El Watan's* coverage of government counterinsurgency operations.

July 3
Chawki Amari, *La Tribune,*
 IMPRISONED, LEGAL ACTION
Kheireddine Ameyar, *La Tribune,*
 LEGAL ACTION
Baya Gacemi, *La Tribune,* LEGAL ACTION
La Tribune, CENSORED

The offices of the independent French-language daily *La Tribune* were sealed because the paper published a political cartoon July 2 that depicted the Algerian flag in a satiric manner.

On July 4, Amari, the cartoonist, was arrested in the early morning at his home in Algiers and charged with desecrating a national emblem. He was held at Serkadji prison for nearly a month. Ameyar, the paper's publisher, and Gacemi, the editor in chief, were placed under judicial supervision and ordered to appear before the court twice a week.

In a July 11 letter to Algerian authorities, CPJ denounced Amari's arrest and the suspension of *La Tribune*, and called on the Algerian government to end press censorship.

The case went to trial on July 20. On July 31, Gacemi was acquitted, and *La Tribune* was allowed to resume publication. But Amari received a three-year suspended prison sentence, and Ameyar was given a one-year suspended sentence.

On Aug. 6, the public prosecutor of Algeria appealed the July 31 verdict that reopened the newspaper. On Sept. 3, the court ordered *La Tribune* closed for six months, upheld the suspended sentences of Amari and Ameyar, and convicted Gacemi, giving her a six-month suspended sentence.

August 12
Mohamed Guessab, Algerian Radio, KILLED

Guessab, host of "Radio Koran," a religious program on Algerian Radio, was murdered by gunmen while driving with his two brothers in the Algiers suburb of Beau Fraisier. One of Guessab's brothers was also killed and the other seriously wounded when the unidentified attackers sprayed their car with gunfire. Guessab was the seventh Algerian journalist murdered in 1996 and the 59th victim since 1993 of an ongoing campaign by extremists to assassinate journalists. No one has yet claimed responsibility for the attack, but Islamic fundamentalist rebels are presumed responsible. CPJ issued a press release condemning the murder.

December 16
Al-Hourria, CENSORED
Algerian authorities seized issues of the Arabic-language weekly *Al-Hourria* from the state-controlled printing press in Algiers. No official reason was given for the confiscation. Spokesmen from the newspaper suspect that an interview with an opposition figure and a review of a book on the human rights situation in Algeria prompted the move. The occasion marked the third time in 1996 that authorities confiscated *Al-Hourria*.

Egypt

The press is guardedly optimistic, following the government's modest revisions to a series of restrictive articles of the penal code—collectively known as Law 93 of 1995. The law, which opposition journalists dubbed the "Press Assassination Law," was the focus of a sustained, year-long campaign by Egyptian journalists and human rights activists, who lobbied strenuously against its draconian provisions. The bill imposed lengthy prison terms together with hefty fines for journalists convicted of libel and a host of other ill-defined publications crimes.

With the new amendments, the govern-

Middle East

ment repealed some of the more contentious articles of Law 93, including a provision granting authorities the right to detain journalists without charge. Cases involving libel of the president can still land journalists in preventive detention.

For the most part, however, the essence of Law 93 remains intact, and journalists continue to face imprisonment and heavy fines for their writing. In effect, the government's revisions merely lessen the severity of penalties. For example, individuals charged with libel offenses face a maximum prison sentence of one year under the new amendments–a slight improvement over the three-year sentences originally mandated under Law 93. In cases where journalists face accusations of libeling public officials, offenders may receive up to two years in prison. The revisions to the law lower the ceilings on monetary penalties in some cases, but they still range as high as £E20,000 (US$6,000) for each offense.

Journalists remain vulnerable to prosecution under a host of highly interpretive charges, including "inciting hatred," "violating public morality," and "harming the national economy"—charges that carry one-to-two-year prison sentences and heavy fines. Egyptian authorities continue to use such rubrics to prosecute journalists. For example, Mustafa Bakri, the former editor in chief of the Liberal Party organ, Al-Ahrar, was charged along with his brother Mahmoud with defamation in a suit brought by former Minister of Religious Endowments Muhammad Mahgoub. Both men were covicted in November and ordered to pay a fine of £E5,000 (US$1,500) and compensation of £E10,000 (US$3,000).

When not prosecuting journalists for their writing, authorities were active in censoring a variety of local publications. Ministry of Information officials continued their harassment of the English-language weekly Middle East Times. In October, the ministry banned one of the paper's editions because of an article that commented on President Hosni Mubarak's 15 years in power, and censors forced the paper's editors to remove or alter individual articles on at least eight occasions. Another favorite target of government censors was the Arabic weekly Al-Dustour. On at least two occasions, authorities prevented the paper's distribution, without giving a reason for their actions.

January 24
Essam Refa't, Al-Ahram Al-Iqtesadi,
LEGAL ACTION
Refa't, editor in chief of Al-Ahram Al-Iqtesadi, was sentenced to a fine of £E12,000 (US$ 3,500) and ordered to pay compensation to the chairman of the board of directors at the Ash-Shams for Housing company, a housing and construction enterprise. The chairman accused Refa't of abusing and insulting him and filed a lawsuit before the Cairo Felonies Court for an article that was published in August 1995 titled "Collapse of Share Value at Ash-Shams for Housing."

January 31
Magdi Hussein, Al-Shaab, HARASSED,
LEGAL ACTION
A Cairo court convicted Hussein, the editor in chief of Al-Shaab, the biweekly organ of the pro-Islamist Labor Party, of libel and sentenced him to serve one year in prison with hard labor and to pay a fine of £E15,000 (US$4,500) and £E501 (US$150) in compensatory damages. Hussein, who is appealing the decision, was tried under Law 93 of 1995, a controversial series of amendments to the penal code pertaining to crimes of publication. He was convicted on charges that the paper had libeled Alaa Hassan el-Alfi (the son of the interior minister, Gen. Hassan el-Alfi) by publishing an article that accused him of refusing to pay his bills at a Cairo hotel and trying to bully its managers when they demanded payment. CPJ urged President Muhammad Hosni Mubarak to order

the appropriate judicial authorities to overturn Hussein's conviction on appeal and cease the prosecution of other journalists who are being tried under Law 93. And CPJ called for the repeal of Law 93, arguing that it undermines Egyptian constitutional protections for press freedom. Hussein is free pending the outcome of his appeal.

On May 8, Hussein was jailed for two days for refusing to pay the fine, even though at the time his appeal was still pending. On May 28, the Cairo Appeal Court sentenced him to a one-year suspended prison term, and upheld the fine and the compensatory damages.

February 26
Mahmoud Al-Touhami, *Rose al-Youssef,*
LEGAL ACTION
Al-Touhami, editor in chief of the weekly *Rose Al-Youssef,* was convicted of libel and sentenced to a one-year suspended prison sentence and a £E1,000 (US$300) fine. He was tried under Law 93 of 1995, a controverial series of amendments to the penal code pertaining to crimes of publication.

April 4
Mahmoud al-Maraghy, *Al-Arabi,*
LEGAL ACTION
Gamal Fahmi, *Al-Arabi,* LEGAL ACTION
Al-Maraghy and Fahmi, the editor in chief and a columnist, respectively, for the opposition weekly paper *Al-Arabi,* were each sentenced to six months in prison for "slandering a member of Parliament," and fined £E650 (US$200). Both appealed the decision and remained free pending the outcome of their appeal. The conviction cited an editorial in *Al-Arabi* denouncing an article written by Tharwat Abadha, an Egyptian member of Parliament, which was critical of former Egyptian president Gamal Abdel Nasser.

August 27
Al-Tadamun, CENSORED
Ten thousand copies of the August edition of

Al-Tadamun, a monthly Arabic newspaper published in Cyprus, were confiscated by Egyptian authorities because of a front-page article, titled "A Chronic Mental Illness." The article questioned the mental health of Arab leaders who cooperate with the United States and Israel. Egypt's Ministry of Information said that the article was unfit for publication because it "arbitrarily soiled [the reputation of] Arab governments."

September 12
Middle East Times, CENSORED
The Ministry of Information prohibited the *Middle East Times,* a Cairo-based, English-language weekly, from publishing an interview with Saudi dissident Muhammad Maasari in its Sept. 15-21 issue. It was the second time in 1996 that the newspaper was ordered by ministry officials to remove an article deemed critical of Saudi Arabia. *Middle East Times* replaced the interview with another article and published the issue. CPJ urged President Hosni Mubarak to end the government's censorship of the *Middle East Times.*

Iran

In certain respects, the press in Iran is among the liveliest in the Middle East. Newspapers and magazines regularly engage in substantive discourse on a variety of political, social, and economic issues affecting the Islamic Republic of Iran. But certain topics—namely, criticism of public officials and the ideals of the Islamic Revolution—are strictly off limits to journalists. In May, spiritual guide Ayatollah Ali Khamenei alluded to these restrictions when he warned members of the press that the "principles of the revolution and the regime of the Islamic Republic is a red line that must be respected."

Those who dare to cross this so-called "red line" risk prosecution under the press

Middle East

law, which is frequently invoked to fine, censor, or imprison outspoken journalists. Iranian authorities—particularly the Ministry of Culture and Islamic Affairs—actively monitor newspapers in order to identify those who violate the law's many restrictive provisions, which include bans on the publication of false information and news that harms national interests.

In January, Abbas Maroufi, editor in chief of the monthly magazine *Gardoon*, received a six-month prison sentence and 35 lashes for "publishing lies"—the result of an article that described the 17-year-old Islamic Republic as a period of "depression" in the country's history. Maroufi, who was also slapped with a two-year ban on working as a journalist, eventually fled to Germany before the sentence could be enforced. Other notable incidents of state censorship in 1996 involved the radical daily *Salam* and the weekly newspaper *Bahar*. Both were temporarily suspended in March without explanation. Officials from the newspapers speculated that their criticisms of the government's handling of the March 8 parliamentary elections sparked the suspension.

January 27
Abbas Maroufi, *Gardoon*, LEGAL ACTION
A Tehran court sentenced Maroufi, editor in chief of the literary and cultural monthly *Gardoon*, to 35 lashes and six months in prison for "publishing lies" and insulting Iran's spiritual leader, Ayatollah Ali Khamenei. The court banned Maroufi from engaging in journalistic activities for two years. On July 10, it was reported that Maroufi, who was permitted to leave Iran without serving his sentence, is in Germany seeking political asylum.

March 6
Salam, CENSORED
An Iranian Special Clerical Court suspended the radical daily *Salam* for two days. The court gave no reason for the suspension, which came

just before parliamentary elections. Journalists with the paper speculated that its suspension was retaliation for an interview in *Salam* criticizing the Council of Guardians, a body of clerics that oversees elections.

March 12
Bahar, CENSORED
The weekly newspaper *Bahar* was suspended by an order of the Ministry of Culture and Islamic Guidance less than a month after it started its publication. The State Press Review Board, a special press screening committee, suspended the weekly until a "court hearing the case gives it verdict," for violating the country's press laws. No further reasons were given for this action. However, *Bahar* reportedly published articles implying that the spiritual guide of the Islamic Revolution, Ayatollah Ali Khamenei, interfered in the process of determining the eligibility of candidates for the parliamentary election of March 8. A week earlier, authorities suspended the daily *Salam* for publishing the same article.

November 2
Hesmatollah Tabarzadi, *Payam-e-Daneshjoue,*
IMPRISONED
Iranian authorities arrested Tabarzadi, the director of the radical weekly magazine *Payam-e-Daneshjoue*, for challenging a publication ban on the magazine. Tabarzadi was freed on bail Nov. 9. *Payam-e-Daneshjoue* is run by university students known for their tough criticism of President Mohamed Hashemi Rafsanjani and his government's controversial reform policies.

Iraq

Contrary to earlier international speculation that his hold on power was weakening, President Saddam Hussein appears to maintain unchallenged authority in Iraq. As a result, little has changed in the area of press freedom; the notoriously ruthless Ba'ath regime continues its stranglehold over the media. News outlets are under the full control of the Ministry of Information, where government officials are responsible for composing all "news." The pages of the country's daily newspapers differ little in content, which consists of endless articles extolling Hussein's virtues. Reporting on events outside Baghdad, the capital, is virtually nonexistent, and in cases where international stories make the newspapers, the content is highly resticted. Saddam's son Uday unofficially serves as the head of the Ministry of Information and appears to exercise increasing control over the country's media. He owns Iraq's only "private" newspaper (*Babil*) and television station (*Al-Shabab*).

Foreign journalists encountered unexpected difficulties when covering armed clashes between Kurdish factions in northern Iraq in September. Supporters of the government-backed Kurdistan Democratic Party (KDP) temporarily prohibited foreign correspondents from entering the Kurdish city of Irbil. In a separate incident, KDP insurgents detained and confiscated the passports of a group of Turkish journalists near the city of Dohuk. The journalists were eventually released and their passports returned.

Israel and the Occupied Territories

Despite the fact that "autonomy" is the regional catchword since Israel relinquished control of parts of the West Bank and Gaza Strip to the Palestinian National Authority in 1994, Israel continues to impose restrictions upon the Palestinian media. The May elec-

tion of Benjamin Netanyahu as prime minister has had little effect on these conditions. Palestinian journalists chafe under severe limitations on their freedom of movement. In the aftermath of a series of suicide bombings in Israel, the Israeli government closed access to Israel from the West Bank and Gaza and in the process, even prevented accredited Palestinian journalists from both the local and foreign press from entering the country. During that period, Israeli authorities also denied Palestinian journalists access to East Jerusalem, where many press offices are located.

Even when the Israelis partially lifted the closure, Palestinian journalists faced obstacles in gaining entrance into Israel. In May, members of the Association of Palestinian Broadcasting Journalists were denied permits to travel to Israel to report on the Israeli elections. Other Palestinian journalists, meanwhile, complain about the daily impediments they face entering and exiting Jerusalem. Those traveling by car must stop for routine security checks at checkpoints where vehicles are prohibited from crossing. As a result, journalists—especially camera crews—are burdened by having to carry their equipment to the other side.

In September, 13 journalists were severely wounded during armed clashes that erupted between Israeli and Palestinian forces following the Israeli government's decision to open a controversial archaeological tunnel in Jerusalem near the Temple Mount and the al-Aqsa Mosque. Among the victims were 10 Palestinian journalists who were wounded by Israeli gunfire in what observers described as inadvertent crossfire. Some of the wounded, however, accused Israeli forces of negligence for failing to notice the journalists who were conspicuously carrying camera equipment and were physically far removed from both sides of the conflict. Two Israeli journalists were also wounded during the conflict, shot by Pales-

Middle East

tinian police as they viewed the fighting from atop a tower in Gaza. It was unclear whether or not the police were aware that both men were journalists.

One of the Israeli government's most disturbing abridgments of press freedom took place in Lebanon, where on June 13, the army abducted the Lebanese journalist Ali Diya from its nine-mile occupation zone in south Lebanon. Diya, a stringer for Agence France-Presse and the Lebanese daily newspaper *Al-Safir*, was detained in Israel for over a month on suspicion of "aiding the Shi'ite militia Hezbollah (Party of God)." CPJ issued a letter of protest to Israeli Prime Minister Benjamin Netanyahu on June 19, calling for Diya's release. He was released on July 18.

June 13
Ali Diya, Agence France-Presse (AFP), *Al-Safir*,
Future Television, IMPRISONED
Diya, a Lebanese journalist and stringer for AFP, was summoned to the headquarters of the South Lebanon Army (SLA) in the Israeli-occupied town of Marjayoun, Lebanon. The SLA, a pro-Israel militia, handed Diya over to Israeli soldiers, who took him to Israel. On June 18, a spokesman for the Israeli army said that Diya was being held and interrogated in Israel on suspicion of "aiding the [Lebanese] Shi'ite militia Hezbollah, and [he] may be charged with serious crimes."

Diya, who is also a contributor to Beirut's *Al-Safir* newspaper and the Beirut-based Future Television, has reported on clashes between Israeli soldiers and Hezbollah guerrillas in southern Lebanon.

CPJ, in a letter to Israeli Prime Minister Benjamin Netanyahu, denounced the Israeli army's abduction of Diya in Lebanon, calling it a violation of international law, and demanded that Israel release Diya. Diya was released on July 18.

August 8
Naim Toubassi, Arab Journalists' Association,

HARASSED
Toubassi, head of the Arab Journalists' Association, was detained briefly by Israeli police during a protest at the Ram checkpoint, at the northern entrance to Jerusalem from the West Bank. He was taken into custody for "violating public order" but was released shortly thereafter without charge. Toubassi and other journalists were protesting the Israeli closure of the West Bank and Gaza Strip, which prevents journalists from entering Israel unless they have special permission from Israeli authorities.

September 6
Uri Avneri, *Maariv*, ATTACKED
Avneri, a columnist for the daily newspaper *Maariv*, was attacked by a crowd during a Likud National Committee meeting in Tel Aviv. Upon entering the meeting hall and presenting his press credentials, Avneri was greeted with shouts from angry participants who then punched him and forced him out of the meeting hall. The incident took place in the presence of Prime Minister Benjamin Netanyahu and Likud National Committee Chair and acting Minister of Justice Tsahi Hanegbi. Neither took action to restrain the crowd.

September 25
Abdel Karim Zeneid, Palestinian Broadcasting
Corp. (PBC), ATTACKED
Murad Siyyam, PBC, ATTACKED
Ali Shanaan, PBC, ATTACKED
Zeneid and Siyyam, PBC cameramen, and Shanaan, their driver, were struck in the head by rubber bullets fired randomly by Israeli forces during clashes with Palestinians on the West Bank, near Ramallah. They were treated for their injuries and released from the hospital the same day.

September 26
Muhammad Saadi, Palestinian Broadcasting
Corp. (PBC), ATTACKED
Ahmed Kaddoumi, PBC, ATTACKED
Abdel Nasser, PBC, ATTACKED

Khaled Abu Hattab, PBC, ATTACKED
Ghassan Kandah, PBC, ATTACKED

Saadi and Kaddoumi, reporters for the PBC; PBC cameramen Nasser and Abu Hattab; and driver Kandah were wounded by rubber bullets fired from Israeli positions during clashes between Israeli soldiers and Palestinians near the West Bank town of Ramallah. They were treated and released from the hospital the same day.

September 26
Issa Freij, CBS, ATTACKED

Freij, a cameraman for the U.S. television network CBS, was shot in the chest during armed clashes between Israelis and Palestinians in Ramallah in the West Bank. His injury appeared to be the result of random cross fire. Freij was taken to the hospital, and reportedly was in good condition.

September 26
Manoocher Deghati, Agence France-Presse (AFP), ATTACKED

Deghati, a photographer for AFP, was shot in the leg during gun battles between Israelis and Palestinians near Ramallah in the West Bank. Deghati suffered fractures to his right leg. He was taken to Ramallah Hospital and later transported to Hadassah Ein Kerem Hospital in West Jerusalem, where he underwent surgery.

September 26
Majdi al-Arabid, Worldwide Television News (WTN), ATTACKED

Al-Arabid, a cameraman for WTN, was wounded in both hands and one of his legs by random gunfire in Gaza, near the Erez checkpoint, during clashes between Israelis and Palestinians. Al-Arabid wanted his injuries treated in Israel, but both Palestinian and Israeli authorities denied him permission to leave Gaza and enter Israel. The next morning he was transported to Cairo to receive medical care.

September 30
Israeli Journalists, HARASSED

The Israeli army banned all Israeli journalists from traveling to areas under control of the Palestinian National Authority (PNA) in the West Bank and Gaza. The ban was imposed on the grounds that conditions in the PNA-controlled territories were too dangerous for journalists after three days of armed clashes between Israelis and Palestinians. In spite of the ban, Israeli journalists traveled freely throughout the West Bank and Gaza, and the ban was rescinded the following day, after protests from the Israeli media.

Areas Under the Palestinian National Authority

The Palestinian National Authority (PNA) under President Yasser Arafat appears to be easing its repression of the Palestinian media. There has been a notable decrease in the incidence of arrest and detention of outspoken journalists and the closure of independent newspapers—frequent occurrences during the initial two years of Palestinian self-rule in the West Bank and Gaza. Such promising indicators, however, don't tell the full story. "We aren't sending material to the Palestinian censor because we haven't such a thing," explained Maher al-Alami, editor of the Jerusalem daily *Al-Quds*, who was detained by Palestinian security forces in

Middle East

December 1995 for refusing to publish an article about Arafat on the front page of his newspaper. "But on the other hand, we have self-censorship."

Indeed, according to many Palestinian journalists, the PNA's harsh crackdown on dissenting journalists in the early months of its existence has instilled widespread fear among the press. Vigorous reporting or critical analysis of the PNA may lead to the closure of their newspapers, detention, or mistreatment. As a result, news stories pertaining to PNA policy matters tend to mirror the accounts of WAFA, the official Palestinian news agency. Whatever "critical" reporting exists is politically toothless, sidestepping truly sensitive issues.

Although the press rarely provokes the authorities, journalists still have to contend with the unpredictable behavior of the security forces. In May, security agents detained and beat Agence France-Presse photographer Fayez Noureddin for taking a photograph of a donkey near a beach in the Gaza Strip. They accused him of distorting "the image of the city and the Palestinian Authority." In another incident, Arafat's bodyguards physically assaulted three journalists in August who were attempting to cover a PNA cabinet meeting in Gaza.

While overall the outlook for press freedom gives little cause for optimism, one positive development was the PNA's approval of some 30 broadcast licenses for private radio and television stations—a clear indication of its desire to diversify the nascent Palestinian media. It remains to be seen, however, what degree of independence the PNA will allow these stations in their news coverage.

May 13
Fayez Noureddin, Agence France-Presse (AFP) ATTACKED, HARASSED
Plainclothes policemen detained Noureddin, a photographer for AFP, at the security forces' office in Gaza City. Noureddin was beaten and kicked repeatedly during his 10-hour incarceration. He was told that he had distorted the international image of the Palestinian National Authority with his photograph of some boys washing a donkey at the beach. The photo caption claimed that the picture showed Gaza to be backward. The picture had been published in a Palestinian newspaper based in East Jerusalem several days before Noureddin was detained. The AFP photographer said he did not write the caption.

August 24
Shamseddin Oudeh, Reuters, ATTACKED, HARASSED
Sawah Abu Seif, Reuters, ATTACKED, HARASSED
Muhammad al-Dahoudi, Free-lancer, ATTACKED, HARASSED
Oudeh, a Reuters cameraman; Abu Seif, a Reuters soundman; and al-Dahoudi, a free-lance cameraman, were assaulted by presidential guards outside a building in Gaza City, where a meeting of the Palestinian National Authority (PNA) cabinet was in progress.

The incident began when the journalists were prevented by a guard from entering the cabinet meeting, an event normally open to journalists. The officer, a member of the elite Force 17 unit of the president's guards, made the journalists wait for 30 minutes with no explanation. When Abu Seif demanded to know why they were being delayed, the guard began yelling at the journalists, calling them "traitors" and "collaborators." The guard then struck Abu Seif in the stomach. The other two journalists stepped in to help their colleague and were struck themselves by the guard. Police broke up the fight. No one was seriously injured, and no equipment was damaged.

The journalists reported the attack to the Arab Journalists Association (AJA), which called for an immediate boycott of the meeting. Several hours later, a representative from PNA President Yasser Arafat's cabinet promised the AJA that the guard who had attacked the journalists would be arrested, and that a room would be set aside for journalists to facilitate reporting on cabinet meetings and other activities of Arafat's administration. The association then called off the boycott.

September 26
Yossi Eindor, Second Channel, ATTACKED
Chaim Assias, Second Channel, ATTACKED
Eindor and Assias, a reporter and a cameraman, respectively, for Israel's Second Channel, were shot by Palestinian police after they climbed a tower to get a better view of clashes between Palestinians and Israelis in the Gaza Strip. Eindor sustained bullet wounds to his arm and leg. Assias suffered wounds to his stomach and arm. According to news reports, Palestinian police believed the television crew was an Israeli army patrol.

Jordan

Jordan displayed increasing intolerance for critical journalism, unleashing a long-antici-pated clampdown against the opposition press. In August, authorities arrested five journalists from the weekly *Al-Bilad* and charged them with "inciting sedition" for reporting on demonstrations near the south-ern city of al-Karak protesting a government decision to raise the price of bread. Several other opposition journalists were also arrest-ed following the events, and many still face the prospect of prosecution and prison. In November, King Hussein declared an amnesty for those individuals involved in the riots. But at the end of the year it was still unclear whether authorities would drop the charges against journalists.

The state has continued to prosecute outspoken journalists under the restrictive 1993 Press and Publications Law, which broadly criminalizes any news that "offends the King or the Royal Family," or that "dam-

ages national unity" and "foments hatred." State prosecutors, exploiting the law's vague language, targeted journalists across a broad political spectrum with libel suits, detaining, charging, and inflicting heavy monetary penalties on those who went too far in their criticism of the state.

In two instances, however, the govern-ment showed an inclination to curb its repressive policies. One positive develop-ment was the decision to forgo increasing the severity of the penalties under the Press and Publications Law. The government also put on hold proposed changes to the Journal-ists Association Law designed to stiffen pro-fessional requirements for journalists. Nevertheless, Jordanian journalists face an uncertain future. "It is still difficult to know what to expect from this government," said the editor in chief of a weekly newspaper. "Look at what happened in August."

April 20
Salameh Ne'mat, *Al-Hayat,* LEGAL ACTION
Jihad al-Khazen, *Al-Hayat,* LEGAL ACTION
Ne'mat, a correspondent for the London-based, Saudi-owned Arabic-language daily *Al-Hayat,* and al-Khazen, *Al-Hayat* editor in chief, were acquitted of charges of violating Jordan's Press and Publications Law by publishing an article "harmful to national unity." The two had been accused in October 1995 in connection with a story alleging that many Jordanian business-men, journalists, and officials were on the Iraqi government's payroll.

July 20
Nasir Khammash, *Sawt al-Mar'a,* IMPRISONED
Khammash, editor in chief of the weekly *Sawt al-Mar'a,* was ordered detained for two weeks in "preventative custody" after the Press and Pub-lications Department of the Information Min-istry filed a complaint against him. The authorities accused Khammash of "harming Jordan's image" in an article published in *Sawt al-Mar'a* about drug use in an Amman neigh-

Middle East

borhood. Khammash was released on July 24, after local and international press groups criticized his detention.

August 18
Nayef al-Tawarah, *Al-Bilad*, IMPRISONED, LEGAL ACTION
Khaled Kasasbeh, *Al-Bilad*, IMPRISONED, LEGAL ACTION
Taha Abu Ridan, *Al-Bilad*, IMPRISONED, LEGAL ACTION
Rakan Saideh, *Al-Bilad*, IMPRISONED, LEGAL ACTION
Malek Atamneh, *Al-Bilad*, IMPRISONED, LEGAL ACTION

Publisher al-Tawarah; editor in chief Kasasbeh; and reporters Abu Ridan, Saideh, and Atamneh of the weekly newspaper *Al-Bilad*, were arrested between Aug. 18 and Aug. 20 on charges of inciting sedition. The charge, filed under the Press and Publications Law of 1993, was in connection with an article published in the Aug. 21 edition of the weekly about protests in southern Jordan against the government increase in bread prices. The journalists were released after about a week in custody, pending trial. If convicted, the five face a penalty of six months to three years in prison. CPJ urged King Hussein to have the charges against the journalists dropped.

August 22
Usamah al-Rantisi, *Al-Ahali*, IMPRISONED, LEGAL ACTION

Al-Rantisi, a reporter for the weekly newspaper *Al-Ahali*, was arrested by Jordanian authorities for an article he wrote that was published in the newspaper's Aug. 21 edition. The article discussed public demonstrations that took place Aug. 16-17 in southern Jordan following a government decision to increase the price of bread. Al-Rantisi, who was released after 15 days in custody, is awaiting trial on the charge of "inciting sedition," which carries a possible six-month to three-year sentence under the Penal Code. CPJ wrote to King Hussein, urging him

to order all charges dropped against al-Rantisi and other journalists accused of violating the press law.

September 18
Hilmi Asmar, *Al-Sabil*, IMPRISONED

Asmar, the editor in chief of the Arabic weekly *Al-Sabil*, was arrested and detained by Jordanian authorities because of an article in which he described the alleged torture of an Islamic activist by Jordanian security officials. On Sept. 26, CPJ denounced Asmar's arrest in a letter to King Hussein. Asmar was released on Sept. 29 without charge.

October 3
Nahed Hattar, *Shihan*, IMPRISONED, LEGAL ACTION

Hattar, a journalist with the weekly newspaper *Shihan*, was taken into police custody after turning himself in to authorities who had been seeking his arrest for several weeks. The arrest was in connection with a series of articles in which Hattar described his support for unification of Jordan and Syria. He was charged with "harming national unity," "inciting the public," and "insulting the king," all vaguely worded offenses that are criminalized under Jordan's Penal Code. Hattar will be tried in a state security court and faces a possible sentence of one-and-a-half to three years in prison. In a letter to King Hussein, CPJ urged that the case against Hattar be dropped.

October 8
Ahmed Awaidi al-Abaddi, *Shihan*, LEGAL ACTION
Jihad al-Mo'mani, *Shihan*, LEGAL ACTION

Al-Abaddi, a prominent writer who contributes to the weekly *Shihan*, and al-Mo'mani, editor of *Shihan*, were charged under Jordan's Press and Publications Law with "harming national unity." The charge stemmed from a June interview in *Shihan* in which al-Abaddi expressed his view that Palestinian refugees in Jordan should relocate to areas in the West Bank and Gaza Strip now under the control of the Palestinian National Authority. If convicted, both journalists face heavy fines or prison. In a letter to Jordan's King Hussein on Oct. 9, CPJ expressed its alarm at the Jordanian government's ongoing legal harassment of journalists.

Lebanon

The free press in Lebanon suffered significant setbacks. In what was described by government officials as a fair attempt to regulate the country's broadcast media, a cabinet order granted licenses to four television and 11 radio stations, but ordered the closure of dozens of others it called "pirate" stations. Forty-seven stations, mainly from the opposition media, were denied licenses after submitting applications to the government. Companies in which government officials had financial interests received preferential treatment. Members of the government, including Prime Minister Rafiq Hariri, Interior Minister Michel al-Murr, and Speaker of Parliament Nabih Berri, owned or directly influenced three of the four newly licensed TV stations.

The government also imposed regulations on the newly approved stations that will affect the content of news and other broadcasts. Only the four licensed TV companies and three of the approved radio stations, including the Hariri-owned Radio Orient and Nabih Berri's yet-unformed National Broadcasting Network, may offer political programming. "The end result," noted one human rights activist, "is that now four or five politicians in the country monopolize the public and private sector [of the broadcast media]."

The print media were the target of harsh legal measures. In March, state prosecutors brought six libel suits against employees of the vocal daily opposition newspaper *Al-Diyar* for a series of articles and a cartoon that denounced the policies of President Elias Hrawi and Prime Minister Hariri. The suits charged editor in chief Charles Ayyoub, director Youssef al-Howeyyek, and cartoonist Elie Saliba with defamation. The defendants, who were awaiting trial at year's end, face up to two years in prison and fines of 100 million Lebanese lira (US$60,000) for each offense. Heavy monetary fines would likely force the paper out of business.

February 29
Ahmad Azakir, Associated Press (AP), HARASSED
Ali Hassan, *Al-Nahar*, HARASSED
Michel Barzagal, Free-lancer, HARASSED
Azakir, a photographer with AP, Hassan, a photographer with the daily *Al-Nahar*, and Barzagal, a free-lance photographer were detained and held for several hours by Lebanese soldiers. The photographers were accused of taking pictures of a military location during a curfew. Their film was confiscated.

March 5
Al-Diyar, LEGAL ACTION
Charles Ayyoub, *Al-Diyar*, LEGAL ACTION
Youssef Howeyyek, *Al-Diyar*, LEGAL ACTION
Elie Saliba, *Al-Diyar*, LEGAL ACTION
A Lebanese prosecutor charged the Beirut opposition newspaper *Al-Diyar* with libel in the first of six libel suits filed against the paper in March. The newspaper's editor in chief, Ayyoub; the director, Howeyyek; and a cartoonist, Saliba, were also charged in the case. The journalists were accused of "defaming and soiling the honor of the president of the republic and the government" in six articles and a cartoon that were critical of government officials.

One of the articles discussed the political relationship between President Elias Hrawi and Prime Minister Rafiq al-Hariri. The cartoon satirized current members of the government, including the president. All three men face up

Middle East

297

to two years in prison and fines of up to 100 million Lebanese lira (US$60,000) for each charge if convicted. CPJ wrote to Prime Minister Hariri on Oct. 17, the eve of his visit to Washington to meet with President Clinton, and urged Hariri to drop the charges. The trials are slated to begin on May 22, 1997.

March 9
Henri Sfeir, *Nida al-Watan,* LEGAL ACTION
Elias Shahine, *Nida al-Watan,* LEGAL ACTION
Ronnie Alfa, *Nida al-Watan,* LEGAL ACTION
Prosecutors charged Sfeir, owner of the daily *Nida al-Watan*; editor Shahine; and reporter Alfa with slandering Islam and fanning sectarian strife in Lebanon for publishing an article on Islamic sectarianism.

December 23
Pierre Atallah, *Al-Nahar,* IMPRISONED,
    LEGAL ACTION
Atallah, an editor of the daily *Al-Nahar*, was arrested without warrant at his Beirut home during a wave of arrests against suspected Christian opposition figures that began after a van carrying Syrian workers was attacked by gunfire just north of Beirut on Dec. 18. The Ministry of Defense held him incommunicado for seven days until transferring his case to a military court for investigation into possible security crimes against the state.

Lebanese government officials claimed that Atallah's arrest was not related to his journalistic work, but during the initial investigation, officials focused their questioning on a series of articles Atallah had written for *Al-Nahar*. These included two articles that contained interviews with former Christian militia leader Etienne Saqr, recently convicted by a Lebanese court of treason for his alleged collaboration with Israel's occupation army in south Lebanon. A third article reported on an incident in October 1996, during which the Lebanese army allegedly harassed a congregation of Christians and prevented them from entering a church in Beirut.

On Dec. 31, CPJ wrote to Prime Minister Rafiq al-Hariri, urging Atallah's release. He was released on Jan. 6, 1997, after posting bail of 7 million Lebanese lira (US$4,000). His case remains under investigation.

Mauritania

Authorities persist in their use of the infamous Article 11 of Mauritania's 1991 press ordinance to censor independent journalism. Under the ordinance, the interior minister has the power to ban the distribution and sale of any newspaper or periodical that is likely to harm Islamic principles, state authority, or that jeopardizes public order. In practice, authorities use these broad prescriptions to prevent the distribution of newspapers that touch on sensitive political issues, such as the practice of slavery in Mauritania and the country's October legislative elections.

In many cases, however, authorities do not go to the trouble of publicly invoking the vague language of the press ordinance, choosing instead to confiscate publications without official explanation. This was the case with several newspapers, including the weeklies *Teissir*, *La Tribune*, and *Al-Akhbar*. In contrast, the authorities were careful to spell out the alleged press offenses of the weekly *Mauritanie Nouvelles*, which was suspended for three months in May for "sow[ing] subversion and harm[ing] the interests of the country." In a separate case in November, authorities slapped a three-month ban on the weekly *Le Calme* for "harming state interests."

March 13
Mauritanie Nouvelles, CENSORED
The March 17 issue of the independent weekly *Mauritanie Nouvelles* was seized by order of the Ministry of the Interior. No official explanation

for the seizure was given to the paper. The Ministry of the Interior also ordered the weekly's March 24 issue seized, offering no explanation.

April 9
Mauritanie Nouvelles, CENSORED
The Ministry of the Interior ordered the independent weekly *Mauritanie Nouvelles* suspended for three months. The magazine was informed that it was suspended because it "sowed subversion and harmed the interests of the country."

September 16
Teissir, CENSORED
The Ministry of the Interior confiscated issues of the weekly *Teissir* in accordance with Article 11 of the press law. The authorities provided no official reason for the confiscation, but some Mauritanian journalists speculated that an article on political rivalries in the government was the cause.

October 26
Le Calme, CENSORED
The Ministry of the Interior banned the weekly *Le Calme* for three months under Article 11 of the press law. Authorities charged the paper with "harming state interests" but cited no specific reason for the ban. Observers in Mauritania suspect that the government's move might be connected to an article *Le Calme* published the previous week calling for the cancellation of recent legislative election results.

December 9
La Tribune, CENSORED
Authorities banned the Dec. 9 edition of the independent weekly *La Tribune,* invoking Article 11 of the press law. The government offered no official reason for its action, although the newspaper's editor believed that the paper was banned because of an article on slavery in Mauritania.

December 18
Al-Akhbar, CENSORED
Authorities confiscated issues of the Dec. 15 edition of the Arabic-language weekly *Al-Akhbar,* using Article 11 of the press law. No official reason was given for the confiscation, although journalists suspect that it was because of an article about prostitution in the capital, Nouakchott.

Morocco

Although in recent years the press has enjoyed expanded freedom, clear limits exist for journalists in Morocco. The press code, for example, prohibits any writing that the authorities deem insulting to Islam or calls into question Morocco's territorial integrity—specifically, its sovereignty over Western Sahara. Authorities also reserve the right to seize newspapers or other publications if they contain articles that are a "threat to public order." One of the more sensitive topics for the government, however, is the royal family. The publication of news on the king and his family is subject to prior authorization—a restriction which is, in effect, political censorship. Furthermore, Article 77 of the press code prohibits news reporting or opinion that insults the king or his relatives.

In October, authorities lifted an 11-month distribution ban on the Paris-based weekly magazine *Juene Afrique,* which had stemmed from an article that discussed King Hassan II's failing health. But the following month, officials placed an indefinite ban on the Arabic weekly *Al-Ousbou al-Sahafi.*

January 28
Anoual, CENSORED
The Jan. 28 edition of the daily *Anoual* was seized by the Interior Ministry without explanation. Officials from the newspaper, however, maintained that the reason for the confiscation

was the publication of excerpts from a book on the Moroccan monarchy.

November 20
Al-Ousbou al-Sahafi, CENSORED
The Interior Ministry imposed an indefinite ban on the weekly political newspaper *Al-Ousbou al-Sahafi*. Authorities provided no official reason for the ban.

Saudi Arabia
And Other Members Of the Gulf Cooperation Council

The countries of the Gulf Cooperation Council (GCC) include Saudi Arabia, Bahrain, Kuwait, Oman, Qatar, and the United Arab Emirates (UAE). The autocratic and largely undemocratic regimes that govern these countries have significantly hindered the development of a free press. While private ownership of the media exists, journalists operate under severe constraints in providing independent or critical reporting on the domestic affairs of their own country.

Saudi Arabia, the largest and most influential member of the GCC, has perhaps the most restricted press in the Middle East. King Fahd must approve the hiring of editors and may dismiss them at will. Journalists, as a result, keep to the unofficial boundaries of acceptable journalism and almost never challenge the policies of the royal family or report on sensitive domestic matters.

Beyond its borders, Saudi Arabia exercises tremendous leverage over the regional and international press. For example, the Arabic daily newspaper *Al-Hayat* and the magazine *Al-Wasat*, both based in London, are owned by Prince Khaled Bin Sultan, a nephew of King Fahd. Similarly, the London-based daily *Al-Sharq al-Awsat* and its sister publication, *Al-Majallah*, belong to Prince Ahmad Bin Salman. And the wire service United Press International (UPI), which is a subsidiary of the Middle East Broadcasting Corp. (MBC), is owned by the prominent Saudi businessman Sheikh Walid al-Ibrahim.

The type of indirect influence the kingdom employs over news content is perhaps best exhibited by the constraints faced by the respected daily *Al-Hayat*. On the one hand, the newspaper is able to maintain editorial autonomy over news content. On the other hand, due to its overwhelming dependency on advertising revenue from companies within Saudi Arabia, it carefully avoids sensitive news stories which might lead to its banning in the kingdom and the subsequent alienation of advertisers.

The Saudi government also exerts considerable influence over the local press in other Arab countries. According to Abdul Bari Atwan, editor of the independent London-based Arabic daily *Al-Quds al-Arabi*, the Saudi government has signed "media protocols" with the ministries of information in several Arab countries that, in effect, obligate them to censor any news that discusses internal Saudi politics or criticism of state officials. Government officials in Egypt appeared to operate under this pretext when the Ministry of Information prohibited the *Middle East Times*, a Cairo-based, English-language weekly, from publishing an interview with Saudi dissident Muhammad Maasari in its Sept. 15-21 issue. Elsewhere, government censors from five Gulf countries—Saudi Arabia, Oman, Qatar, Kuwait, and the UAE—banned the distribution of *Reader's Digest* magazine in July because of an article dealing with political instability in Saudi Arabia.

In Kuwait, the press ultimately remains loyal to the ruling Al-Sabah family, avoiding meaningful criticism of the government. At the close of 1996, 15 journalists remained in prison in Kuwait—the largest number of imprisoned journalists for any country in the Arab world. They were tried and convicted by state security courts for allegedly collaborating with the Iraqi occupiers by working for a newspaper published during the occupation.

In Qatar, the press witnessed at least one positive development in 1996. In February, the government of Sheikh Hamad Bin Khalifah al-Thani privatized the nation's existing radio and television stations. The move followed a previous effort toward liberalization when, in late 1995, the state formally abolished requirements for the screening of publications and media broadcasts. Although certain guidelines still exist for journalists, the media have clearly become more aggressive in its reporting in recent months.

Bahrain

February 24

Nabil Al-Hammar, *Al-Ayam*, ATTACKED

Al-Ayam, ATTACKED

A bomb exploded in Bahrain in front of the office of *Al-Ayam*, a privately owned, pro-government daily in Manama. The car belonging to *Al-Ayam's* editor in chief, Nabil al-Hammar, was destroyed by the explosion, but al-Hammar was not hurt. According to one report, an employee in the paper's library was slightly wounded by the explosion. The newspaper received an anonymous call after the attack, claiming responsibility and connecting the bomb with *Al-Ayam's* publication of the photos of four suspects arrested by police for the bombing of two hotels and a commercial center. Al-Hammar is a critic of the country's Shiite opposition.

Syria

The brutal regime of President Hafez al-Assad has all but eradicated professional journalism in Syria, once an intellectual and literary center of the Arab world. Newspapers and the broadcast media remain firmly under the control of the state, which discourages journalists from any reporting that might be interpreted as being critical of the regime. Arrest, torture, and long-term imprisonment have been very real threats to journalists during Assad's 26-year rule. Despite the country's relatively high literacy rate, newspapers have very low circulation figures because of the moribund state of the press. In the few outlets available for independent news, government censors stringently screen news content for material they deem inappropriate. Authorities prevented the London-based Arabic-language daily *Al-Hayat*, for example, from distributing issues on at least 20 occasions.

Despite the release in December 1995 of some 1,200 political prisoners as part of a general amnesty commemorating the 25th year of Assad's rule, six journalists remain in Syrian prisons. Between 1992 and 1994, the Supreme State Security Court sentenced the six to prison sentences ranging from three to 15 years for nonviolent activities that included their involvement in political organizations and their affiliation with the leading Syrian human rights group, the Committees for the Defense of Democratic Freedoms and Human Rights in Syria (CDF). Nizar Nayouf, an activist with the CDF who received a 10-year sentence in 1992, has remained in solitary confinement at Mezze military prison in Damascus since 1993.

Tunisia

The press in Tunisia continues to stagnate under the nine-year-old presidency of Zine Abdine Ben Ali. Despite the existence of privately owned newspapers, few journalists dare to report news that might antagonize the government, for fear of reprisal. By and large, the practice of self-censorship has become institutionalized within the journalistic profession. Over the past two years, local and foreign correspondents have learned that being critical of the government in their reporting could easily get them dismissed from their jobs or earn them a one-way ticket out of the country. The private press is further squeezed by its reliance on advertising revenue from state-owned companies.

Despite the passive nature of the media, the ministry of information reviews all newspapers, particularly foreign ones, in order to weed out undesirable news and ensure total compliance with the government mandate for acceptable journalism. Among the casualties of state censorship were the French-language newspapers *Le Monde* and *Liberacion*. Authorities banned more than 60 issues of *Le Monde* alone during the course of the year.

January 9

Kamel Labidi, United Press International (UPI), *La Croix-L'Evenement*, HARASSED

Sihem Bensedrine, *Al-Mawqif*, HARASSED

Labidi, Tunis correspondent of the French daily *La Croix-L'Evenement*, and Bensedrine, director of the weekly *Al-Mawqif*, were prevented from participating in the UNESCO/UN conference Promoting an Independent and Pluralistic Arab Press held in Sana'a, Yemen, from Jan. 7-11. Tunisian authorities had confiscated their passports earlier, and refused to return them. In a joint communiqué with other press freedom groups, CPJ called on the Tunisian government to immediately return the journalists' passports.

Turkey

Authorities have sustained their all-out assault on the press. Censorship, arbitrary detention, harassment, and imprisonment of journalists persists, as the state punishes independent reporting and commentary on the government's 11-year-old conflict with Kurdish rebels in the Southeast. Seventy-eight journalists remain in prison—the highest such total of any country in the world. Turkish courts sentenced the majority of these prisoners for violating the infamous Anti-Terror Law and the Penal Code. Both laws give courts considerable latitude in prosecuting journalists.

The most prominent case in 1996 was a state security court's March 7 conviction of noted author and journalist Yasar Kemal under Article 312 of the Penal Code. Kemal received a 20-month suspended sentence for "inciting hatred" in relation to two articles he had written for a book of essays titled *Turkey and Freedom of Expression*. In one of the articles, Kemal accused the Turkish government of waging a "campaign of lies" in its comprehensive censorship of reporting on the Kurds.

The state security courts have used the Anti-Terror Law and the Penal Code with equal severity to censor newspapers, frequently issuing closure orders. The leftist daily *Evrensel*, in particular, suffered a series of harsh measures in early 1996. On April 4, an Istanbul security court ordered the paper closed for one month for "inciting hatred" and "promoting racism." On April 9, April 19, and May 9, the paper was again ordered closed, for periods ranging from 10 to 30 days, for violating both the Anti-Terror Law and the Penal Code.

Beyond prosecution and censorship, journalists have increasingly been the targets of harassment and police violence. In 1996, CPJ was able to document 14 cases of arbitrary detention and 19 instances of police physically assaulting journalists doing their jobs. Most alarming was the Jan. 8 beating death of *Evrensel* journalist Metin Goktepe. Eleven police officers charged with Goktepe's murder went on trial in October. If convicted, they each face up to 16-and-a-half years in prison.

In the self-styled republic of Northern Cyprus, propped up by 35,000 Turkish troops, unknown assailants on July 6 gunned down Kutli Adali, a 61-year-old columnist for the daily *Yeni Duzen*, near his home. Adali was an outspoken critic of the Ankara-backed northern government's controversial population policies, which continue to facilitate the settlement of Turkish nationals in north Cyprus. Shortly before his murder, he had received anonymous threats spurred by an investigative report about the theft of antiquities from a Cypriot monastery, in which he had implicated a retired Turkish general. A little-known group, the Turkish Defense Brigades, claimed responsibility for Adali's murder, although no one has yet been charged in the crime. Government investigations into the murder have been described by many observers as inadequate.

The formation of the Islamist-led government of Prime Minister Necmettin Erbakan in June 1996 failed to result in any noticeable improvements in the realm of press freedom. But the international community's sustained scrutiny of the Turkish government's actions offers a modest degree of hope for the future. Efforts such as the European Parliament's decision in October to temporarily suspend hundreds of millions of dollars in economic aid to the government, because of its poor human rights record, may produce the necessary leverage to pressure Ankara for change.

January 1
Sedat Hayta, *Devrimci Emek,* IMPRISONED
A former editor for the leftist weekly *Devrimci*

Emek, Hayta was arrested and charged with aiding an outlawed organization under Article 169 of the Penal Code. He is currently in Bayrampaşa Prison in Istanbul.

January 8
Metin Goktepe, *Evrensel,* KILLED
Goktepe, a reporter for the left-wing daily *Evrensel*, was found beaten to death near a gymnasium in Istanbul. Earlier that same day Goktepe was covering a funeral for two leftist inmates killed during a prison riot. He had been stopped by police and taken to a nearby Istanbul gymnasium, where 1,053 mourners from the service were being detained. In the presence of hundreds of detainees, police officers ordered Goktepe to lie face down on the floor and began kicking him and beating him with their batons and fists. After losing consciousness, Goktepe was dragged out of the gym and left to die on a bench outside. An autopsy determined the cause of death was a brain hemorrhage brought on by severe blows to the head. In a letter to Turkish Prime Minister Tansu Çiller, CPJ urged the government to conduct an immediate and thorough investigation into the matter. *Evrensel* blames police for Goktepe's murder, but the police have denied responsibility. Although no one was formally arrested, 11 policemen are charged with Goktepe's murder. Their trial began in October, and, if convicted, they each face up to 16-and-a-half years in prison.

January 30
Erhan Il, *Devrimci Emek,* IMPRISONED
Il, a reporter for the leftist magazine *Devrimci Emek*, was arrested and charged with being a member of an outlawed organization under Article 168 of the Penal Code. He is being held in Bayrampaşa Prison.

February 19
Özgür Öktem, *Devrimci Emek,* IMPRISONED
Öktem, a reporter for the leftist magazine

Devrimci Emek, was arrested and charged with being a member of an outlawed organization under Article 168 of the Penal Code. He is being held in Bayrampaşa Prison in Istanbul.

March 7
Yasar Kemal, LEGAL ACTION
An Istanbul State Security Court convicted the prominent Turkish author and journalist Kemal of "inciting hatred" and imposed a 20-month suspended prison sentence on him. He was convicted of violating Article 312 of the Penal Code for two articles he published in a collection of essays called *Turkey and Freedom of Expression*. One of the articles was originally written for the German magazine *Der Spiegel*. In that article, he accused the Turkish government of waging a "campaign of lies" to hide its oppression of the Kurds. He was sentenced even though the prosecutor recommended that Kemal be acquitted and despite the fact that in December 1995 he had been found innocent of similar charges regarding the same article's publication in *Der Spiegel*. Kemal's publisher was also convicted on the same charge but had his sentence converted to a suspended fine. Kemal is planning to appeal the suspended sentence, stating that accepting it would be tantamount to admitting guilt for writing about the Kurdish insurgency.

March 13
Hamza Yalcin, *Odak*, IMPRISONED
Yalcin, a reporter with the left-wing monthly *Odak*, was detained during a police raid on *Odak's* office in Istanbul. Five other journalists with *Odak* who were detained with Yalcin were released on March 21. Yalcin was formally arrested and charged with belonging to an illegal organization. He is being held in Bayrampaşa Prison in Istanbul.

March 15
Aslihan Yucesan, *Atilim*, IMPRISONED
Ibrahim Çiçek, *Atilim*, IMPRISONED

Haci Orman, *Atilim*, IMPRISONED
Aysel Çiçek, *Atilim*, IMPRISONED
Sabahat Karahan, *Atilim*, IMPRISONED
Zeynel Yesil, *Atilim*, IMPRISONED
Dogan Sahin, *Atilim*, IMPRISONED

Yucesan, owner of the weekly *Atilim*, and at least six reporters and editors from the weekly were taken into police custody. Among the detained journalists were Çiçek, Orman, Çiçek, Karahan, Yesil, and Sahin. Police initially denied that they had detained the journalists; then, after three days, acknowledged the fact. Atilla Cinar, chief of the counter-terrorism department of the Istanbul police, accused the journalists of membership in the Marxist Leninist Communist Party, an urban guerrilla organization thought to be responsible for several bombings and robberies in Istanbul. On March 29, Ibrahim Çiçek, Sahin and Orman were transferred to Bayrampaşa Prison. They have been charged with membership in an illegal organization, a violation of Article 168 of the Penal Code. The reporter Karahan and *Atilim's* owner, Yucesan, were released.

March 16
Ibrahim Çiçek, *Atilim*, IMPRISONED
Çiçek, a former editor in chief of the leftist weekly *Atilim*, was detained during a police raid on the paper's headquarters in Istanbul. He has been charged with being a member of an outlawed organization under Article 168 of the Penal Code and is being held in Bayrampaşa Prison.

March 18
Hatice Onaran, *Devrimci Çözüm*, IMPRISONED
Onaran, formerly the editor legally responsible for the left-wing monthly *Devrimci Çözüm*, was arrested and detained after her sentence to six years and ten months in prison was upheld. She was convicted of publishing terrorist propaganda under Article 7 of the Anti-Terror Law. The charges cited six articles published in *Devrimci Çözüm*. She is currently being held in Gebze Prison, outside Istanbul.

March 19
Atilim, LEGAL ACTION, CENSORED
Ismail Akkin, *Atilim,* LEGAL ACTION
Ozgür Genclik, LEGAL ACTION

Istanbul's State Security Court ordered the weekly paper *Atilim* closed for one month for allegedly disseminating "separatist propaganda." The court also sentenced Akkin, the weekly's editor, to six months in prison on the same charge. Akkin is free pending an appeal. The order also suspended *Ozgür Genclik,* a magazine for young people published by *Atilim.* CPJ urged the Turkish government to reverse the closure of *Atilim* and the sentencing of Akkin.

March 21
Serpil Korkmaz, *Demokrasi,* IMPRISONED

Korkmaz, a reporter with the pro-Kurdish daily *Demokrasi,* was detained by police in Istanbul. She was released on April 2 without charge.

March 23
Burhan Ozbilici, Associated Press (AP), ATTACKED
Kemal Gokcanli, Channel 6, ATTACKED
Serkan Cinier, Interstar, ATTACKED

Police officers beat photographers and cameramen who were covering a police raid on an Ankara University building that had been taken over by students protesting tuition increases. Among those assaulted were Ozbilici, a photographer with the AP; Gokcanli, a cameraman for the privately owned Channel 6 television station; and Cinier, a cameraman with the privately owned Interstar television station. The two cameramen were hospitalized after the attack. Ozbilici's account of the incident indicated that police intentionally targeted the journalists. CPJ called on the Turkish government to discipline the police officers who brutalized the journalists.

April 9
Evrensel, CENSORED
Ali Erol, *Evrensel,* LEGAL ACTION

An Istanbul State Security Court ordered the leftist daily *Evrensel* shut down for one month for charges relating to two articles it published on Aug. 30, 1995. The first article, titled "Special Forces Execution in Midyat," was ruled to have incited racism, which is in violation of Article 312 of the Penal Code. The second, "Efforts To Mediate Between Iraqi Kurdish Groups," was deemed a violation of Article 6 of the Anti-Terror Law banning the publication of "statements by terror organizations." Earlier, on April 4, *Evrensel* was ordered shut down for one month for "inciting hatred" and "promoting racism" in a September 1995 column about World Peace Day. The column called for an end to the fighting between the Turkish army and Kurdish rebels. The daily continued publishing pending an appeal. Also on April 9, Erol, the editor legally responsible for *Evrensel,* was sentenced to two years in prison and fined US$1,050 on the same charges as those made against the newspaper. On April 4, a previous two-year prison sentence against Erol was commuted to a US$60 fine. Erol remains free and the paper continues publishing pending appeals of these convictions.

April 18
Evrensel, LEGAL ACTION

An Istanbul State Security Court ordered the leftist daily *Evrensel* closed for 10 days for publishing the statement of a terrorist organization, a violation of Article 7 of the Anti-Terror Law. The charge cited an article about the Revolutionary Front of the People's Liberation Party, published in the paper on Oct. 29, 1995.

April 18
Hürriyet, ATTACKED

Gunmen raked the Istanbul headquarters of *Hürriyet,* one of Turkey's leading dailies, with automatic gunfire as they sped past in a car. No injuries were reported, but bullets shattered the windows. No one claimed responsibility for the attack.

Middle East

May 3
Veli Aydin, *Özgür Gelecek,* IMPRISONED

Aydin, a reporter for the leftist magazine *Özgür Gelecek,* was arrested and has been charged with membership in an illegal organization under Article 168 of the Penal Code. He is currently in Sağmalcilar Prison.

May 7
Emin Konar, *Özgür Halk,* IMPRISONED

A reporter for the pro-Kurdish monthly magazine *Özgür Halk,* Konar was detained during a police raid on the magazine's office in Elazig and later arrested and charged under Article 169 of the Penal Code (aiding an outlawed organization). He was sentenced to three years and six months in prison and is currently in Elbistan Hapas Prison.

May 9
Evrensel, LEGAL ACTION
Ali Erol, *Evrensel,* LEGAL ACTION
Haluk Gerger, *Evrensel,* LEGAL ACTION

An Istanbul State Security Court ordered the leftist daily *Evrensel* closed for 20 days for publishing an article titled "Confessions of a Military Officer," which allegedly incited racism, a violation of Article 312 of the Penal Code. Erol, the editor legally responsible for *Evrensel,* received a two-year prison sentence, which was commuted to a US$50 fine.

Earlier in May, in a separate case, Gerger, a free-lance writer and contributor to the newspaper, was convicted of inciting racial hatred and was sentenced to 20 months in prison for an article published in *Evrensel* in June 1995. He remains free pending appeal.

In a letter to Prime Minister Mesut Yilmaz, CPJ expressed its fear that the paper was being targeted for demanding that policemen who beat an *Evrensel* reporter to death in January be brought to justice.

May 12
Mustafa Demirdağ, *Özgür Gelecek,* IMPRISONED

Demirdağ, an editor for the leftist magazine *Özgür Gelecek,* was arrested and later tried and convicted under the Anti-Terror Law. He is serving a three-year and five-month sentence in Sakarya prison.

May 13
Bülent Balci, *Kurtulus,* IMPRISONED

A former editor of the leftist weekly *Kurtulus,* Balci was sentenced to 12 years and six months in prison under Article 168 of the Penal Code (being a member of an outlawed organization). He is in Umraniye Prison.

May 21
Aydinlik, CENSORED

A court ordered the leftist weekly *Aydinlik* to cancel an article it planned to publish in its May 25 issue. The article contained allegations by a leader of Turkey's criminal underworld that Minister of Justice Mehmet Agar, formerly the national police chief, had ties to organized crime. *Aydinlik* complied with the court order to remove the story, but on May 24 the issue was seized at the printer anyway, on charges that it was pornographic.

On May 31, police confiscated the June 1 issue of *Aydinlik* after a judge ruled that one of its articles insulted the judiciary. The piece, titled "Are the Judges Mehmet Agar's Personal Bodyguards?," criticized the May 24 seizure of the weekly. CPJ wrote to Turkey's Prime Minister Mesut Yilmaz and condemned the ongoing government campaign against the newspaper.

May 29
Radio Aktif, ATTACKED

Radio Aktif, a local radio station in the Mediterranean coastal town of Mersin in southern Turkey, was set on fire by unidentified assailants. The fire destroyed all the station's equipment, tapes, and documents. No one was injured in the blaze.

June 8
Mehmet Guc, ATV, HARASSED

Sevil Erdogan, *Siyah Beyaz*, HARASSED
Sukran Can, *Demokrasi*, HARASSED
Nadire Mater, IPS, HARASSED
***Atilim* reporter,** HARASSED
***Devrimci Emek* reporter,** HARASSED
Mete Cubukcu, ATV, ATTACKED
Musa Agacik, *Milliyet*, ATTACKED
Other journalists, ATTACKED

Six reporters—Guc of the privately owned ATV; Erdogan of the mainstream daily *Siyah Beyaz*; Can of the pro-Kurdish newspaper *Demokrasi*; Mater of IPS; and two unidentified journalists, one with the leftist *Atilim* and the other with *Devrimci Emek*—were detained by police while covering a demonstration in Istanbul against poor working conditions for civil servants. Two other reporters, Cubukcu of ATV and Agacik of the mainstream daily *Milliyet*, were kicked and punched by police. Other journalists were also assaulted. Police dispersed the demonstrators, who had not obtained permission for the rally, and detained more than 250 people.

June 17
Interstar, CENSORED
Channel D, CENSORED
ATV, CENSORED
Show TV, CENSORED
Channel 7, CENSORED
Can TV, CENSORED
Mega Radio, CENSORED

The Radio and Television High Board (RTUK) ordered blackouts of four television stations and issued warnings against six stations for a wide range of coverage that they deemed unacceptable. RTUK ordered Interstar Television of Istanbul to stop broadcasting for three days (June 27-29) and three other television stations — Channel D, ATV, and Show TV, all in Istanbul — to shut down for a day. RTUK also warned Interstar, Channel D, and Show TV that they could face another blackout for further transgressions. The RTUK also issued warnings against Channel 7 of Istanbul, Can TV of Diyarbakir, and Mega Radio of Ada-

pazari. A warning is the first step toward a blackout.

Interstar was accused of "going overboard" in its criticism of a public figure, aired during a news bulletin on April 25. ATV was reprimanded for a May 29 newscast that reported on a controversial trial. The board said that ATV had violated a court order not to report the proceedings. Channel D and Show TV were accused of violating an article of the radio and television law banning programs that "could harm the psychological development of children and youth." Channel D had aired a magazine show about ghosts and spirits, and Show TV had aired a program about genies.

June 25
Yildiz Gemicioglu, *Kurtulus*, IMPRISONED
Gemicioglu, a former Adana bureau chief of the leftist weekly *Kurtulus*, was arrested by authorities and remains in Konya Prison without charge.

June 25
Altan Koman, *Atilim*, IMPRISONED
Koman, a reporter for the Iskenderun bureau of *Atilim*, was arrested and charged with being a member of an outlawed organization under Article 168 of the Penal Code. He is currently in Malatya Prison.

June 28
Nurcan Turgut, *Demokrasi*, IMPRISONED
Turgut, a reporter for the pro-Kurdish daily *Demokrasi*, was detained by police during a raid on the newspaper's office in Elazig. She was sentenced to three years and nine months in prison under Article 169 of the Penal Code (aiding an outlawed organization). Turgut is serving her sentence in Nevsehir Prison.

Early July
Fehmi Calmuk, *Aksam*, HARASSED
Ahmet Hamdi Takan, Interstar Television, HARASSED
Noyan Unal, Interstar Television, HARASSED

Middle East

307

Calmuk, a political reporter for the mainstream daily *Aksam*; Takan, a political reporter for Interstar Television; and Unal, an Interstar cameraman, were covering parliamentary coalition negotiations when they were harassed by police. The police had been called by politicians from the Welfare and True Path parties, who were participating in the negotiations and knew that the journalists were waiting to interview them as they emerged from the talks. When the journalists showed the police their government-issued press cards, the police reportedly told them they could not tell whether their identification cards were authentic. The three were taken into custody around midnight and released a few hours later.

July 6
Kutlu Adali, *Yeni Duzen*, KILLED
Adali, a political columnist with the leftist daily newspaper *Yeni Duzen*, was shot and killed near his home in Lefkosa, the Turkish sector of Nicosia in north Cyprus. The Turkish Revenge Brigade, a little-known, extreme right-wing group, claimed responsibility for the murder. The Turkish Revenge Brigade first came to public attention several months ago when it circulated pamphlets in Northern Cyprus warning that it would punish those who oppose the cause of the Turks in Cyprus.

Yeni Duzen is an organ of the leftist Republican Turkish Party (CTP). Adali was an outspoken critic of policies of the Northern Cypriot government and had criticized many politicians in his newspaper column. He was known as an advocate of peaceful cooperation with the Greek-dominated state of Cyprus. CPJ wrote to the Northern Cypriot authorities and urged them to conduct a thorough investigation into Adali's murder.

July 15
Hatice Tuncer, *Cumhuriyet*, ATTACKED
Kaan Saganak, *Cumhuriyet*, ATTACKED
Irfan Kurt, *Evrensel*, ATTACKED
Muhittin Erdogan, *Kurtulus*, ATTACKED

Aysun Gunduz, *Atilim*, ATTACKED
Sevil Erdogan, *Siyah Beyaz*, ATTACKED
Alper Turgut, *Cumhuriyet*, ATTACKED
Efe Erdem, *Milliyet*, ATTACKED
Yuksel Koc, *Global Daily*, ATTACKED
Saban Dayanan, Mavi Radio, ATTACKED

Tuncer, a reporter for the daily newspaper *Cumhuriyet*; Saganak, a photographer with *Cumhuriyet*; Kurt, a journalist with *Evrensel*; Erdogan, a reporter for *Kurtulus*; and Gunduz, a reporter with *Atilim*, were beaten and detained by police while trying to cover a demonstration against police brutality in front of the office of the governor of Istanbul. Police dragged several of the journalists away by their hair, broke cameras, and confiscated film. The journalists were later released. Police also beat five other photographers and reporters. According to eyewitness accounts, police intentionally targeted journalists.

Several reporters who were attacked fled to the office of the Turkish Journalists Association. They were chased by three police officers, who forced their way into the association's office. The secretary general of the association, Leyla Tavsanoglu, objected to the police raid, telling the police that they were pursuing legitimate journalists. The police countered by claiming the journalists were terrorists. CPJ wrote a letter to Turkish Prime Minister Necmettin Erbakan expressing fear that unchecked police brutality against journalists will have a chilling effect on press freedom in Turkey. CPJ urged the Turkish government to bring to justice those officers responsible for the attacks and to issue clear directives to the police aimed at preventing the abuse of journalists.

July 19
Can TV, CENSORED
Diyarbakir-based Can TV was warned by the Radio and Television High Board (RTUK) not to use the Kurdish language in news broadcasts. A Can TV official said that Kurdish was used only when local interviewees were responding to questions. A second warning from the

RTUK could result in a one-day blackout of the station.

August
Fatih Yeşilbag, *Özgür Gündem*, IMPRISONED
A former editor in chief of the pro-Kurdish daily *Özgür Gündem*, Yeşilbag was arrested and charged under numerous articles of the penal code and Anti-Terror Law. He is currently being held in Bursa-Keles Prison.

August
Gennue Kiliç, *Özgür Ülke*, IMPRISONED
Kiliç, a former editor of the now-defunct pro-Kurdish daily *Özgür Ülke*, was charged and convicted under Article 169 of the penal code (aiding an outlawed organization). She also faces additional charges under the penal code and the Anti-Terror Law for articles published in the newspaper during her tenure.

November
Beyazit Ekiz, *Kizilbayrak*, IMPRISONED
Duygu Tuna, *Kizilbayrak*, IMPRISONED
Ekiz and Tuna, reporters for the Gebze bureau of the leftist weekly *Kizilbayrak*, were detained during a police raid on the magazine's office. Both women were formally arrested and charged with being members of an outlawed organization under Article 168 of the penal code. They are being held in Gebze Prison.

November
Esra Yildirim, *Kurtulus*, IMPRISONED
Yildirim, a Trabzon correspondent for the leftist weekly *Kurtulus*, was charged with aiding an outlawed organization under Article 169 of the penal code and is currently being held in Ankara Prison.

November 17
Cuma Akin, *Özgür Halk*, IMPRISONED
Akin, the Batman bureau chief for the pro-Kurdish monthly magazine *Özgür Halk*, was detained after a police raid on the magazine's Diyarbakir office. He is being held in

Diyarbakir Prison, awaiting official charge.

November 17
Özgür Çavusoglu, *Atilim*, IMPRISONED
A reporter working at the Izmir bureau of *Atilim*, Çavusoglu was arrested at his home and charged with being a member of an outlawed organization under Article 168 of the penal code. He is being held in Buca Prison.

November 19
Muteber Yildirim, *Özgür Ülke*, IMPRISONED
Yildirim, a reporter for the now-defunct pro-Kurdish daily *Özgür Ülke*, was convicted under Article 312 of the penal code for an article he wrote for the newspaper. He is currently being held in Bayrampaşa Prison.

November 20
Adil Harmanci, *Demokrasi*, IMPRISONED
Harmanci, a reporter for the pro-Kurdish daily *Demokrasi*, was detained at his home in Van by police along with his wife. Although his wife was released, Harmanci remains in Van Prison without charge.

1996
Tekin Aygün, *Kurtulus*, IMPRISONED
Aygün, a reporter for the leftist weekly *Kurtulus*, was arrested and remains in Umraniye Prison. The circumstances of his arrest are unclear.

1996
Songül Çinar, *Kurtulus*, IMPRISONED
Çinar, a reporter for the leftist weekly *Kurtulus*, was arrested and charged with being a member of an outlawed organization under Article 168 of the penal code. She is currently in Ankara Prison.

1996
Adil Kurt, *Newroz*, IMPRISONED
Kurt, a reporter for the pro-Kurdish magazine *Newroz*, was arrested in early 1996 and remains incarcerated in Gaziantep Prison. The circumstances of his imprisonment are not clear.

Middle East

1996
Özden Özbay, *Özgür Ülke*, IMPRISONED

Özbay, the former editor of the now-defunct pro-Kurdish *Özgür Ülke*, was arrested and charged with violating Article 312 of the Penal Code and Articles 6,7, and 8 of the Anti-Terror Law. He has yet to be sentenced and is currently in Gebze Prison.

1996
Hafize Sayran, *Kurtulus*, IMPRISONED

Sayran, the Zonguldak bureau chief for the leftist weekly *Kurtulus*, was arrested and is being held in Ankara Prison. It is unclear what charges, if any, were filed.

Yemen

"The press is 100 percent free," declared Yemeni Information Minister Abdel Rahman al-Akwaa in January. Indeed, Yemenis have enjoyed a notable degree of press freedom since the unification in 1990 of the Yemen Arab Republic (north Yemen) and the People's Democratic Republic of Yemen (south Yemen), which ushered in multi-party politics and the creation of liberal press laws designed to protect the press. Nevertheless, few Yemeni journalists would agree that the press functions without restrictions.

Although a number of independent newspapers have started up during the past five years, the state still controls the country's three dailies, as well as all broadcast media. And while opposition newspapers have a certain amount of freedom to criticize the government, authorities frequently seek to silence outspoken journalists. Police and agents from the Political Security Office continue to employ extra-legal means such as physical attacks and confiscation of newspapers to harass journalists.

The state's intolerance for the press was manifest in a July 7 speech by President Ali Abdullah Saleh, who cautioned two independent newspapers—the English-language weekly *Yemen Times* and the Arabic-language biweekly *Al-Ayyam*—to restrain their "dubious" reporting on the government. "I am directing an early warning to them, because I know that the Minister of Information or the Ministry of Information is hesitant to take legal measures against the papers," he said. "But I shall take the appropriate measures at the appropriate time."

Such threats, coupled with the restrictive practices of security forces over the past few years, have had a chilling effect on Yemeni journalists, who increasingly practice self-censorship. "We still criticize the government," noted the editor in chief of an independent opposition newspaper. "But we use restraint and self-censorship on sensitive issues that we feel will backfire."

June 17
Al-Tagammu, CENSORED

Al-Tagammu, the weekly newspaper of the opposition Unionist Rally Party, was forced to interrupt publication when its printer, the government-owned 14th of October Printing House, refused to print the newspaper, apparently on orders from the Ministry of Information. The suspension came after *Al-Tagammu* reported on public demonstrations in Mukalla, the capital of the southern Hadramout region. Demonstrators were protesting remarks made by the Hadramout prosecutor that were insulting to Hadramout's women. CPJ urged the Yemeni government to end the suspension of the paper. *Al-Tagammu* resumed publication in late July.

July 11
Arafat Mudabish, *Al-Thawri*, ATTACKED

Mudabish, the parliamentary correspondent for the weekly *Al-Thawri*, an organ of the opposition Yemeni Socialist Party, was attacked by security guards inside the Parliament building. His colleagues reported that he was beaten with rifle butts and dragged outside. The guards, calling him a secessionist, confiscated his parliamentary press accreditation. The attack ended only when a member of Parliament offered Mudabish safe haven in his car and drove him away from the scene. CPJ wrote a letter to President Ali Abdallah Saleh to express concern about the assault on Mudabish.

September 28
Abdel Rahman Khobara, *Al-Ayyam*, HARASSED
Plainclothes Yemeni police officers entered the Aden office of the independent biweekly *Al-Ayyam* and attempted to arrest Khobara, a columnist, even though they had no warrant. Khobara's colleagues argued with the police, telling them that Khobara could not lawfully be taken into custody without official court orders. The police eventually left the building, but they waited outside until early the next morning in an apparent attempt to detain Khobara as he exited. Khobara was forced to remain inside the office to avoid being arrested.

Khobara, an outspoken critic of Yemeni government policy, had broadcast a report on Radio Kuwait about public demonstrations in the town of Mukallah on Sept. 25. In 1995, Khobara was detained for four days by political security officials in connection with another Radio Kuwait story, about explosions at a government ammunition depot in Aden. On Oct. 2, 1996, CPJ called on Yemen's President Ali Abdullah Saleh to instruct security authorities to stop harassing Khobara.

September 30
Muhammad al-Saqqaf, HARASSED,
LEGAL ACTION
Al-Saqqaf, a writer and former university professor who occasionally contributes articles to the Yemeni press, was summoned by officials from the attorney general's office in Sanaa. He was interrogated for one-and-a-half hours about two articles he wrote for *Al-Wahdawi*, a weekly newspaper that is Nasserite in ideology, after the former Egyptian President Gamal

Abdel Nasser. He was charged with "publishing false information with malicious intent," a violation of Yemen's press law. In both articles, which were published separately in August and September, al-Saqqaf spoke critically of the High Elections Committee, the government-run body preparing for Yemen's 1997 elections. CPJ wrote to President Ali Abdullah Saleh urging that all charges against al-Saqqaf be dropped.

CPJ's Campaign for the Release of Ocak Işik Yurtçu

ON NOV. 26, CPJ HONORED imprisoned Turkish editor Ocak Işik Yurtçu with one of its 1996 International Press Freedom Awards during ceremonies at New York's Waldorf-Astoria Hotel. The event marked the beginning of a long-term campaign to free Yurtçu, who in December 1994 was sentenced to nearly 16 years in prison for articles his newspaper, *Özgür Gündem*, had published on the Turkish government's ongoing conflict with Kurdish insurgents.

Writing from his cell in Turkey's Sakarya Prison, Yurtçu sent the following letter, which Terry Anderson read at the awards dinner:

Dear Colleagues at the Committee to Protect Journalists,
I've been in jail for two years just because I tried to learn the truth and relay this truth to inform the public—in other words, to do my job with the belief that it is impossible to have other freedoms in a country where there is no freedom of the press.

When I learned about CPJ's award from newspapers that are allowed in my prison ward daily and the details of it from my lawyer who came to visit, I felt joy but also sadness. I was happy because you had honored me with such an award, but sad because I could not be there with you to share my joy.

This award has special meaning for me because of the message it will carry for my colleagues in Turkey. We're living through tough times when the powers that be have increased their terrorizing pressure around the nation, especially in the region where Kurdish people live, when journalists are killed, lost, put in prison, beaten up, when newspaper offices are burned and bombed, when publications with unorthodox views or news are censored or confiscated. As my colleagues struggle against all this pressure justified by the excuse of "defending the state" and continue in a relentless effort to carry out their journalistic duties, this award has special meaning because it shows that they are not alone, will not be alone as they strive to report the truth, that the global support, in contrast to the lack of national support, is great and sincere.

What a pleasure to be able to dream about the day when peace, democracy, human rights, and freedom of expression and of the press will become a reality in my country. What a pleasure to see a light of hope despite the surrounding prison walls and the deep darkness here. I especially thank CPJ for giving me an opportunity to feel this pleasure. I also congratulate my other colleagues honored with the award: Mr. Jesús Blancornelas, Mr. Yusuf Jameel, and Mr. Daoud Kuttab. And I send my hearty greetings, filled with love and respect, from Sakarya Prison, to you and all your guests who will be there at the award ceremony.

Ocak Işik Yurtçu
November 10, 1996
Sakarya Prison, Turkey

MORE THAN 300 JOURNALISTS, media executives, and human rights activists who attended the awards ceremonies in New York signed individual appeals to Turkish Prime Minister Necmettin Erbakan, urging his government to grant Yurtçu's freedom. On Jan. 23, 1997, CPJ Chair Kati Marton, Executive Director William A. Orme, Jr., and Middle East program coordinator Joel Campagna hand-delivered the appeals to Ambassador Nuzhet Kandemir in Washington, D.C., during a one-hour meeting devoted to the plight of Yurtçu and the 77 other journalists currently imprisoned in Turkey.

CPJ intends to keep the issue of Yurtçu's imprisonment at the forefront of its advocacy efforts on Turkey and looks to sustain international attention to his plight, which is emblematic of the obstacles facing independent journalists in many parts of the world. Already, members of the Turkish press have responded by publicizing Yurtçu's case in the Turkish press and calling on the government to release him.

Journalists in Jail: a Year-End Account
A Record 185 Cases of Reporters Imprisoned in the Line of Duty

A T THE END OF EVERY YEAR, The Committee to Protect Journalists surveys the world's prisons to document cases of journalists who have been jailed simply because of their profession. On Dec. 31, 1996, there were at least 185 reporters, editors, and broadcasters in prison in 24 countries—the largest number CPJ has yet recorded. Most of their names appeared on the December 1995 list as well, as most are serving long terms of five years or more.

Countries that routinely imprison journalists are a diverse lot, ranging from staunch U.S. allies to near-pariah states.

Turkey is once again the single most egregious example of a government that criminalizes independent reporting. We confirmed a startling 78 cases of journalists held in Turkish jails at the end of 1996—more than in the next five worst offenders combined. The majority of the imprisoned Turkish journalists were guilty only of reporting openly and often critically about issues of concern to the Kurdish minority and details of military campaigns against Kurdish rebels.

Ethiopia, with 18 prisoners, is for the third straight year the largest jailer of journalists in Africa—despite a reduction in the prison population from last year's record of 31, prompted in part by CPJ's close scrutiny of Ethiopia's press freedom problems. China, despite some carefully timed releases, continues to hold 17 journalists, most of whom have been in custody for seven years or more. In Kuwait, 15 journalists—most of them ethnically Palestinian—are still serving sentences of 10 years to life for alleged collaboration (which they attribute to coercion) with Iraqi occupation forces before the Gulf War. Burma and Nigeria each hold eight journalists in prison, most for openly critical political commentary and analysis.

In almost every instance, the jailers concede that these imprisonments were intended as censorship—reprisals for what governments considered excessively critical or candid reporting. We are respectfully petitioning each of the 24 governments on this list for the immediate release of these journalists, on the grounds that their continued imprisonment constitutes an illegal infringement of their right "to seek, receive and impart information and ideas through any media and regardless of frontiers," as guaranteed to them by Article 19 of the Universal Declaration of Human Rights.

Imprisoned Journalists

Countries Holding Journalists in Prison

Algeria (2)

Abdelkader Hadj Benaamane,
Algerian Press Service (APS)
Imprisoned: February 28, 1995

Security forces arrested Benaamane, a correspondent for the official Algerian Press Service (APS) in the southern town of Tamanrasset. The reasons for Benaamane's imprisonment are unclear, but reports indicate that he was charged with "attacking the security of the state and national unity" in connection with an internal APS news wire report he filed on the whereabouts of Abassi Madani and Ali Belhadj, leaders of the Islamic Salvation Front (FIS) who had recently been transferred from Janan al-Mufti prison to a detention center in the desert. Benaamane appeared before a Tamanrasset military court on July 10, 1995. He was convicted and sentenced to three years in prison.

Djamel Fahassi, Alger Chaîne III
Arrested: May 7, 1995

State security officials arrested Fahassi, a reporter for the government-run French-language radio station Alger Chaîne III and formerly a contributor to *Al-Forqane*, a weekly organ of the Islamic Salvation Front (FIS) that was banned in March 1992. Officials have refused to acknowledge his arrest. His family believes he is in a secret detention center and fears for his life.

APPEALS TO:
His Excellency Liamine Zeroual
President
The Presidential Palace
El Mouradia
Algiers, Algeria
Fax: 213-2-590-407

Burundi (1)

Michel Nziguheba, *L'Eclaireur*
Imprisoned: March 19, 1996

Nziguheba, editor of *L'Eclaireur*, was arrested on a warrant issued by the federal public prosecutor. *L'Eclaireur* was suspended on March 18 for "inciting ethnic hatred." After several postponements, Nziguheba's trial opened on Oct. 3, and the journalist appeared before a court of high instance. His lawyer, Fabien Segatwa, an ex-minister and member of the Constitutional Commission, requested bail for his client. The court granted Nziguheba bail, but the prosecutor opposed the decision and Nziguheba was not released.

APPEALS TO:
His Excellency Sylvestre Ntibantunganya
President of the Republic of Burundi
Bujumbura, Burundi
Fax: 257 22 66 13/257 22 60 63

Central African Republic (1)

Mathias Goneyo Reapago,
Le Rassemblement
Imprisoned: July 19, 1995

Reapago, editor of the opposition newspaper *Le Rassemblement*, was arrested on July 19 and on Aug. 21 he was convicted on criminal charges of attacking "the dignity and honor of the president of the republic." He was sentenced to a two-year prison term and fined 500,000 CFA (US$1,000).

APPEALS TO:
His Excellency Ange-Felix Patasse
President of the Central African Republic
Bangui, Central African Republic

China (17)

Fan Jianping, *Beijing Ribao*
Imprisoned: 1989

Fan, an editor at *Beijing Ribao* (Beijing Daily), was arrested sometime after the Tiananmen Square crackdown on June 4, 1989.

Ji Kunxing, *Pioneers*
Tried: September 1989

Ji was tried in Kunming on charges of "fomenting a counter-revolutionary plot." He and three others had published an underground magazine called *Pioneers*, circulated anti-government leaflets, and put up anti-government posters.

Jin Naiyi, *Beijing Ribao*
Imprisoned: 1989

Jin, a journalist with *Beijing Ribao* (Beijing Daily), was arrested sometime after the Tiananmen Square crackdown on June 4, 1989.

Li Jian, *Wenyi Bao*
Imprisoned: July 1989

Li, a journalist with *Wenyi Bao* (Literature and Arts News), was arrested.

Shang Jingzhong, *Pioneers*
Tried: September 1989

Shang was tried in Kunming on charges of "fomenting a counterrevolutionary plot." He and three others had published an underground magazine called *Pioneers*, circulated anti-government leaflets, and put up anti-government posters.

Shi Qing, *Pioneers*
Tried: September 1989

Shi was tried in Kunming on charges of "fomenting a counterrevolutionary plot." He and three others had published an underground magazine called Pioneers, circulated anti-government leaflets, and put up anti-government posters.

Yang Hong, *Zhongguo Qingnian Bao*
Imprisoned: June 13, 1989

Yang, a reporter for *Zhongguo Qingnian Bao* (China Youth News), was arrested in Kunming and charged with circulating "rumormongering leaflets" and protesting against corruption.

Yu Anmin, *Pioneers*
Tried: September 1989

Yu was tried in Kunming on charges of "fomenting a counterrevolutionary plot." He and three others had published an underground magazine called *Pioneers*, circulated anti-government leaflets, and put up anti-government posters.

Yu Zhongmin, *Fazhi Yuekan*
Imprisoned: 1989

Yu, a journalist with *Fazhi Yuekan* (Law Monthly) in Shanghai, was arrested sometime after the Tiananmen Square crackdown on June 4, 1989. He was later described in an article in Wenhui Daily as an "agitator" of the Shanghai student demonstrations.

Chen Yanbin, *Tielu*
Imprisoned: Late 1990

Chen, a former Qinghua University student, was arrested in late 1990 and sentenced to 15 years in prison and four years without political rights after his release. Together with Zhang Yafei, he had produced an unofficial magazine called Tielu (Iron Currents) about the 1989 crackdown at Tiananmen Square. Several hundred mimeographed copies of the magazine were distributed. The government termed the publication "reactionary" and charged Chen with dissemination of counterrevolutionary propaganda and incitement.

Zhang Yafei, *Tielu*
Imprisoned: September 1990

Zhang, a former student at Beifang Communications University, was arrested and charged with dissemination of counterrevolutionary propaganda and incitement. In March 1991, he was sentenced to 11 years in prison and two years without political rights after his release. Zhang edited an unofficial magazine called *Tielu* (Iron Currents) about the 1989 crackdown at Tiananmen Square.

Wu Shishen, Xinhua News Agency
Imprisoned: October or November 1992

Arrested in the fall of 1992, Wu, a Xinhua News Agency reporter, received a life sentence in August 1993 for allegedly providing a Hong Kong journalist with a "state-classified" advance copy of President Jiang Zemin's 14th Party Congress address.

Gao Yu, Free-lancer
Imprisoned: October 2, 1993

Gao was detained two days before she was to depart for the United States to start a one-year research fellowship at

Columbia University's Graduate School of Journalism. On Nov. 10, 1994, she was tried without counsel and sentenced to six years in prison for "leaking state secrets" about China's structural reforms in articles for the pro-Beijing Hong Kong magazine *Mirror Monthly*. Gao had previously been jailed for 14 months following the June 1989 Tiananmen Square demonstrations and released in August 1990 after showing symptoms of a heart condition.

Ma Tao,
China Health Education News
Sentenced: August 1993

Ma, editor of *China Health Education News*, received a six-year prison term for allegedly helping Xinhua News Agency reporter Wu Shishen provide a Hong Kong journalist with President Jiang Zemin's "state-classified" 14th Party Congress address. According to the Associated Press, Ma is believed to be Wu's wife.

Xi Yang, *Ming Pao*
Imprisoned: September 27, 1993

Xi, Beijing correspondent for the Hong Kong daily *Ming Pao*, was arrested on Sept. 27, 1993, and on March 28, 1994, was sentenced to 12 years in prison for stealing and publishing state secrets. The secrets in question included unpublished interest rate changes on savings and loans at the People's Bank of China, as well as information on the bank's international gold transaction plans, both of which were provided to Xi by a bank official named Tian Ye. Xi was released on parole on Jan. 25, 1997, following widespread appeals for his release in Hong Kong and abroad. Under the terms of his release, Xi is free to travel between Hong Kong and China, but may not work as a journalist for the duration of his parole period.

Wei Jingsheng
Imprisoned: April 1, 1994

Police detained Wei, one of the most prominent dissidents in China and former co-editor of the pro-democracy journal *Tansuo* (Explorations), shortly after he met with then-U.S. Assistant Secretary of State John Shattuck. He was not formally arrested and charged until Nov. 21, 1995. On Dec. 13 of that year, the Beijing Intermediate People's Court convicted him of "conspiring to subvert the government" and sentenced him to 14 years in prison. Foreign reporters were barred from attending the trial. The dissident's sentence was upheld on Dec. 28, after a closed appeal hearing. Wei had already served 14 years of a 15-year sentence for "counterrevolutionary" activities that included writing essays strongly criticizing the government and calling for democratic rule. After he was released on parole from that prison term, on Sept. 14, 1993, he wrote several op-ed pieces for publications abroad and concluded a deal with a Hong Kong magazine for the publication of his prison memoirs—actions that prompted an official warning that he

Imprisoned Journalists

was violating the terms of his parole.

Wang Dan
Imprisoned: May 21, 1995

Wang, a former student leader, pro-democracy activist, and frequent contributor to overseas publications was detained at an undisclosed location. On Oct. 30, 1996, he was sentenced to 11 years in prison for conspiring to subvert the government. Wang's offenses consisted of publishing articles in the overseas press that were deemed objectionable by Beijing and receiving donations from overseas human rights groups. Foreign reporters were barred from the courtroom during his trial, and the domestic press was prohibited from reporting on the trial. Following the denial of his appeal on Nov. 10, Wang was sent to a prison in remote Jinnzhou, in Liaoning province, 500 kilometers northeast of Beijing. Wang had previously been jailed for three-and-a-half years after he led pro-democracy protests in Tiananmen Square in 1989.

APPEALS TO:
His Excellency Tao Siju
Minister of Public Security
Gong'anbu
14 Dongchang'anlu
Beijing 100741
People's Republic of China
Fax: 86-1-524-1596

Ivory Coast (3)

Abou Drahamane Sangaré,
Nouvel Horizon Group
Emmanuel Koré, *La Voie*
Imprisoned: December 21, 1995

Sangaré, director of publications for the Nouvel Horizon Group, which owns the opposition daily *La Voie*, and Koré, a reporter for *La Voie*, were arrested in connection with a Dec. 18 satirical *La Voie* article that suggested that President Henri Konan Bédié's attendance at the African Champions Cup final brought bad luck to Ivory Coast's national soccer team, causing its loss to South Africa. On Dec. 28, Sangaré and Koré each received a two-year prison term for "offending the chief of state" and a 3 million CFA (US$6,000) fine. They were released on Jan. 1, 1997.

Freedom Neruda, *La Voie*
Imprisoned: January 2, 1996

Deputy editor Neruda was taken into custody, and on Jan. 3, he was charged with insulting the head of state in connection with a satirical article published in *La Voie* suggesting that President Henri Konan Bédié's presence at the African Champions Cup final brought bad luck to the Ivorian soccer team, which lost to South Africa. On Jan. 11, Neruda was sentenced to two years in prison and fined 6 million CFA

320

(US$12,000). CPJ wrote to President Bédié on two occasions: first, to denounce Neruda's arrest, and second, to condemn the court's action and urge the president to revoke Neruda's sentence along with the two-year prison sentences handed down to journalists Sangaré and Koré for "offending the chief of state." [See above] He was released on Jan. 1, 1997.

APPEALS TO:
His Excellency Henri Konan Bédié
President of the Republic of Ivory Coast
La Présidence
Boulevard Clozel
Abidjan, Ivory Coast
Fax: 225-21-14-25 or 225-33-14-25

Ethiopia (18)

Andargue Mesfin, *Tenager*
Tekle Yishal, *Tenager*
Imprisoned: March 24, 1995

Ethiopia's Central High Court sentenced Andargue and Teklel, reporters for the weekly *Tenager*, to 18 months and 12 months in prison, respectively, for publishing an Oromo Liberation Front communiqué about the group's armed struggle and for publishing three other political articles, including a story about the arbitrary murder of civilians by soldiers of the Woyane ethnic group.

Solomon Gebre Amlak, *Mogad*
Dereje Birru, *Tekwami*
Girmayeneh Mammo, *Tomar*
Abinet Tamirat, *Dagmawi*
Imprisoned: June 21, 1995

Government agents arrested the four journalists for stories published in their newspapers about the armed conflict between the government and opposition groups. The charges were "warmongering, incitement of the public, and discrediting the government."

Solomon Lemma, *Wolafen*
Imprisoned: March 7, 1996

Solomon, editor of the independent Amharic-language weekly newspaper *Wolafen*, was sentenced to an 18-month prison term for "publishing false reports in order to incite war and unrest." The reports in question, a series of articles published in 1995, were about an insurgency group fighting in three provinces in western Ethiopia. Solomon had just completed a one-year sentence when he received the new prison sentence.

Terefe Mengesha, *Roha*
Imprisoned: Early February 1996

The Central High Court sentenced Terefe, the former editor in chief of the Amharic-language weekly *Roha*, to an additional one-year prison term just as completed a one-year sentence for "publishing and distributing false information" and for "inciting the public to anxiety and insecurity." Terefe was leaving the prison grounds when policemen rearrested him and

321

transported him to Ma'ekelawi Central Prison in Addis Ababa. Terefe's original conviction cited two articles, published in the October and December 1994 issues of *Roha*, titled "Colonel Mengistu on the Offensive in Gambella" and "Woyane Combatants Suffered Heavy Defeats in South, West, and East Ethiopia."

Tesfaye Tegen, *Beza*
Imprisoned: March 25, 1996

Authorities summoned Tesfaye, the editor in chief of the Amharic weekly *Beza*, to appear at Ma'ekelawi Central Prison in Addis Ababa, where he was asked to present a personal guarantor for 10,000 birr (US$2,000). When Tesfaye failed to do so, he was transported to Central State Prison, where he is currently being held incommunicado. The summons cited a cartoon, published in *Beza* in late 1995, portraying Prime Minister Meles Zenawi and other government officials as members of a soccer team. Meles was depicted as much larger than his colleagues.

Taye Belachew, *Tobia*
Imprisoned: November 22, 1996

Taye, editor in chief of the privately owned weekly magazine *Tobia* and the monthly magazine of the same name, was arrested without charge and detained at Ma'ekelawi Central Criminal Investigation Office. Police interrogated Taye about an article published in the November issue of *Tobia* titled "A Strategy to Reunite Eritrea With Ethiopia." A Dec. 9 proceeding in the Addis Ababa District Court extended Taye's detention by 14 days.

Anteneh Merid, *Tobia*
Imprisoned: November 25, 1996

Police arrested Anteneh, the deputy editor in chief of the weekly and monthly magazines *Tobia*, without charge and detained him at Ma'ekelawi Central Criminal Investigation Office. His interrogators focused on an article in the November issue titled "A Strategy to Reunite Eritrea With Ethiopia." At Anteneh's appearance before the Addis Ababa District Court on Dec. 9, authorities ordered a 14-day extension of his detention.

Sintayehu Abate, *Remet*
Imprisoned: December 5, 1996

Sintayehu, editor in chief of the privately owned Amharic weekly magazine *Remet*, was rearrested on the day he should have been released for completing a one-year sentence. The new arrest came after his magazine published articles and a photograph that the public prosecutor deemed pornographic. Sintayehu remains in Addis Ababa Central Prison.

Tefera Kitila, *Tikuret*
Imprisoned: Early December 1996

During the week of Dec. 8, Tefera, editor in chief of the privately owned Ahmaric weekly *Tikuret*, was arrested and detained without charge. Authorities have not provided any

322

reasons for his detention.

Dawit Kebede, *Fyameta*
Imprisoned: December 11, 1996

Dawit, publisher of the Amharic weekly *Fyameta*, was arrested and detained in the Woreta Ten police station, in the district of Woreta. Observers believe his arrest is in connection with *Fyameta's* Dec. 4 story titled "Police College Has Trained a Thief."

Daniel Dershe, *Kitab*
Imprisoned: December 11, 1996

The High Court found Daniel, editor in chief of the now-defunct Amharic-language weekly *Kitab*, guilty of an unspeci-fied charge and immediately remanded him into police custody. Officials have not released information about the length of his sentence.

Aklilu Tadesse, *Ma'ebel*
Imprisoned: December 11, 1996

Security officers arrested and detained Aklilu, editor in chief of the Amharic weekly *Ma'ebel*, without charge at Ma'ekelawi Central Criminal Investigation Office.

Wesson Seged Mersha, *Kitab*
Imprisoned: December 12, 1996

Wesson, publisher of the Amharic weekly *Kitab*, was sentenced to a six-month prison term and immediately jailed. Officials have provided no reasons for his incarceration.

Goshu Moges, *AKPAC*
Imprisoned: December 12, 1996

Security officers arrested Goshu, acting manager of AKPAC, which publishes the weekly and monthly magazines *Tobia*, without charge in connection with the publication of an article about the November 1996 hijacking of Ethiopian Airlines Flight 961. Goshu is being held at Ma'ekelawi Central Crimi-nal Investigation Office.

Tilahun Bekele, *Ruhama*
Imprisoned: December 18, 1996

Authorities arrested and detained Tilahun, editor in chief of the privately owned Amharic weekly *Ruhama*, without charge, refusing to provide reasons for his detention.

APPEALS TO:
His Excellency Prime Minister Meles Zenawi
Office of the Prime Minister
Addis Ababa, Ethiopia
Fax: 251-1-514-300 (c/o Ministry of Foreign Affairs)

Indonesia (4)

Adnan Beuransyah,
Serambi Indonesia
Imprisoned: August 16, 1990

Beuransyah, a journalist with the newspaper *Serambi Indonesia*, was arrested. He was tried in March 1991 in Banda Aceh on charges of subversion and sentenced to eight years in prison.

Maryadi, a member of the Alliance of Independent Journalists

Imprisoned Journalists

Eko Maryadi, Alliance of
Independent Journalists (AJI)
Imprisoned: March 16, 1995

(AJI), was arrested along with several others at an AJI gathering. He was convicted on Sept. 1 of violating Article 19 of the press law, which prohibits the publication of an unlicensed newspaper or magazine, and Article 154 of the Criminal Code, which bars the expression of "feelings of hostility, hatred, or contempt toward the government." The charges stemmed from articles in AJI's unlicensed newsmagazine Independen that dealt with topics such as the succession to President Suharto and the personal wealth of the country's leaders. Maryadi's 32-month sentence was increased on Oct. 11, 1995, to 36 months in prison, following a closed appeal hearing. On Aug. 15, 1996, he was shifted from Jakarta's Cipinang prison to a less accessible facility in Cirebon, 200 kilometers east of the capital. The move was in apparent retaliation for the publication in *Suara Independen*—the successor to *Independen*—of an exclusive interview with José Alexandre ("Xanana") Gusmaõ, the jailed leader of the East Timorese independence group Fretelin and an inmate at Cipinang.

Tri Agus Susanto Siswowihardjo,
Kabar Dari Pijar
Imprisoned: March 9, 1995

Siswowihardjo, editor of *Kabar dari Pijar*, a bulletin published by the Jakarta-based nongovernmental organization Pijar, was arrested during a police raid on the organization's offices. He was convicted on Sept. 11 of "intentionally insulting" President Suharto, in violation of Articles 55(1) and 134 of the Criminal Code, and sentenced to two years in prison. The case against Siswowihardjo was based on the publication of an article in the bulletin's June 1994 issue, titled "This Country Has Been Messed Up by a Man Called Suharto." On Aug. 15, 1996, he was shifted from Jakarta's Cipinang prison to a less accessible facility in Cirebon, 200 kilometers east of the capital, in apparent retaliation for the publication in the underground magazine *Suara Independen* of an exclusive interview with José Alexandre ("Xanana") Gusmaõ, the jailed leader of the East Timorese independence group Fretelin and an inmate at Cipinang.

Ahmad Taufik, Alliance of
Independent Journalists (AJI)
Imprisoned: March 16, 1995

Taufik, president of the Alliance of Independent Journalists (AJI) was arrested along with several others at an AJI gathering. He was convicted on Sept. 1 of violating Article 19 of the press law, which prohibits the publication of an unlicensed newspaper or magazine, and Article 154 of the Criminal Code, which bars the expression of "feelings of hostility, hatred, or contempt toward the government." The charges stemmed from articles in AJI's unlicensed newsmagazine Independen that dealt with topics such as the succession to

President Suharto and the personal wealth of the country's leaders. Taufik's 32-month prison sentence was increased on Oct. 11 to 36 months, following a closed appeal hearing. CPJ honored Taufik with its annual International Press Freedom Award on Dec. 6. On Aug. 15, 1996, Taufik was shifted from Jakarta's Cipinang prison to a less accessible facility in Cirebon, 200 kilometers east of the capital, in apparent retaliation for the publication in *Suara Independen*—the successor to *Independen*—of an exclusive interview with José Alexandre ("Xanana") Gusmaõ, the jailed leader of the East Timorese independence group Fretelin and an inmate at Cipinang.

APPEALS TO:
His Excellency Suharto
Office of the President
Istana Merdeka
Jakarta, Indonesia
Fax: 62-21-778-182

Iran (2)

Salman Heidari, *Salam*
Imprisoned: June 1992

Heidari, a reporter for the Tehran daily *Salam*, was arrested and accused of espionage. It is unclear whether he has been formally charged and tried.

Manouchehr Karimzadeh,
Free-lancer
Imprisoned: April 11, 1992

Karimzadeh, a cartoonist, was arrested after one of his cartoons appeared in the science magazine *Farad*. It depicted a turban-wearing soccer player with an amputated arm. The image was interpreted by the authorities to be a caricature of the late Ayatollah Khomeini. An Islamic Revolutionary Court originally sentenced him to one year in prison, but he was retried in 1993 by order of the Supreme Court and sentenced to 10 years in prison.

APPEALS TO:
His Excellency Ali Akbar Hashemi Rafsanjani
President of the Islamic Republic of Iran
The Presidency
Palestine Avenue
Azerbaijan Intersection
Tehran, Islamic Republic of Iran
Telex: 214231 MITI IR or 213113 PRIM IR

Imprisoned Journalists

325

Iraq (1)

Aziz al-Syed Jasim, *Al-Ghad*
Imprisoned: April 18, 1991

Jasim, editor of *Al-Ghad* magazine and former editor of the official daily *Al-Thawra*, was taken into custody at a secret police station in Baghdad and has not been heard from since. Government officials deny that he is under arrest. During a previous term of imprisonment that began in 1989, Jasim was forced to write a number of books in support of Iraqi President Saddam Hussein.

APPEALS TO:
His Excellency President Saddam Hussein
c/o Iraqi Mission to the United Nations
14 East 79th Street
New York, NY 10021
United States

Kuwait (15)

Fawwaz Muhammad al-Awadi
Bessisso
Ibtisam Berto Sulaiman al-Dakhil
Usamah Suhail Abdallah Hussein
Abd al-Rahman Muhammad
Asad al-Husseini
Ahmad Abd Mustafa
Sentenced: June 26, 1991

A Kuwaiti court sentenced the five journalists to life in prison, after first commuting the death sentences imposed on them 10 days earlier under martial law. The journalists were accused of working for the Iraqi occupation newspaper *Al-Nida*. They were taken into custody after Kuwait's liberation and charged with collaboration. Their trials, which began on May 19, failed to comply with international standards of justice and the defendants reportedly were tortured during their interrogations. Their defense—that they were forced to work for the Iraqi newspaper—was not rebutted by prosecutors, but on June 16, 1991, they were sentenced to death. The death sentences were commuted after strong condemnation by the international community.

Walid Hassan Muhammad Karaka
Rahim Muhammad Najem
Ghazi Mahmoud al-Sayyed
Sentenced: June 1991

A martial law tribunal sentenced the three men to 10 years in prison with hard labor for their "supporting role...in helping to publish the [Iraqi occupation] paper [*Al-Nida*]." The defendants reportedly were tortured during interrogation. The prosecution did not offer direct evidence to rebut their defense that they had had been coerced into working for the paper. Four staff members—Riyadh Fouad Shaker Ali, Ahmad Muhammad Hannoun, Zuhra Muhammad Adel Abd al-Khaleq, and Lefta Abdallah Menahi—were also sentenced to 10 years in prison for allegedly working for *Al-Nida*, though it appears that they did not work as journalists.

Daoud Suleiman al-Qarneh
Hassan al-Khalili
Muhammad Zahran
Nawwaf Izzedin al-Khatib
Sentenced: June 20, 1992

The State Security Court convicted the four Palestinian journalists on charges of having worked for the Iraqi occupation newspaper *Al-Nida* and sentenced them to 10 years in prison. The court also fined them 2,000 dinars (US$6,700) each and ordered them expelled from the country when their sentences were completed. Al-Qarneh is a former deputy chief editor for the Kuwait News Agency (KUNA), and al-Khalili is a former editor for KUNA.

Bassam Fouad Abiad
Mufid Mustafa Abd al-Rahim
Ghazi Alam al-Dine
Sentenced: July 28, 1992

The State Security Court convicted Abiad, Abd al-Rahim, and Alam al-Dine of working for the Iraqi occupation newspaper *Al-Nida*. Abiad, a Lebanese citizen, was sentenced to 15 years in prison. Abd al-Rahim, a Palestinian, and Alam al-Dine, a Jordanian citizen and former editor at the Kuwait News Agency, were each sentenced to 10 years in prison. Alam al-Dine had worked a total of only 12 hours for *Al-Nida*. The court also fined each of the three men 2,000 dinars (US$6,700) and ordered that they be expelled from Kuwait when their sentences were completed.

APPEALS TO:
His Highness Shaikh Sa'ad al-'Abdallah al-Sabah,
    Crown Prince and Prime Minister
Al-Diwan al-Amiri
Al-Safat
Kuwait City, Kuwait
Telegrams to: His Highness Shaikh Sa'ad al-'Abdallah al-Sabah, Kuwait City, Kuwait
Fax: 965-243-0121

Lebanon (1)

Pierre Atallah, *Al-Nahar*
Imprisoned: December 23, 1996

Atallah, an editor of the daily *Al-Nahar*, was arrested without warrant at his Beirut home during a wave of arrests against suspected Christian opposition figures that began after a van carrying Syrian workers was attacked by gunfire near the northern city of Tripoli on Dec. 18. The Ministry of Defense held him incommunicado for seven days until transferring his case to a military court for investigation into possible security crimes against the state. Lebanese government officials claimed that Atallah's arrest was not related to his journalistic work, but during the initial investigation, officials focused their questioning on a series of articles Atallah had written for *Al-Nahar*. On Dec. 31, CPJ wrote to Prime Minister Rafiq al-Hariri, urging Atallah's release. He was released on Jan. 6, 1997, after posting bail of 7 million Lebanese lira (US$4,000).

His case remains under investigation.

APPEALS TO:
His Excellency Rafiq al-Hariri
Prime Minister
Office of the Prime Minister
Grand Serail
Rue des Arts et Metiers
Sanayeh, Beirut
Republic of Lebanon
Fax: 961 1 200 469 / 354 318 / 862 001

Libya (1)

Abdallah Ali al-Sanussi al-Darrat
Imprisoned: 1974 or 1975

Al-Darrat, a journalist and writer from Benghazi, was arrested in 1974 or 1975 and has been held since then without trial.

APPEALS TO:
Revolutionary Leader
Col. Muammar al-Qadhafi
c/o Libyan Mission to the United Nations
309-315 East 48th St.
New York, NY 10017
United States

Malaysia (1)

Nasiruddin Ali, Karya One
Imprisoned: May 6, 1996

Nasiruddin, a director of the publishing firm Karya One, which published four magazines linked to the banned Islamic movement al-Arqam—*Tatib*, *O.K!*, *Ayu*, and *Dunia Baru* — was arrested and imprisoned, at the Kemunting Detention Center in Perak. The magazines were suspended on June 4. Authorities detained Ali for the 60-day period allowed under section 73(1) of the Internal Security Act (ISA), then on July 7 invoked section 8 of the ISA, which allows up to two years' imprisonment without trial. The charges against Nasiruddin have not been made public. However, the pro-government daily New Straits Times reported in May that Nasiruddin had been arrested along with three other Al-Arqam members for attempting to revive the activities of the sect, which the government banned in 1994 for allegedly deviating from true Islamic teachings.

APPEALS TO:
His Excellency Dato' Seri Dr. Mahathir Mohamad

Prime Minister and Minister of Home Affairs
Jabatan Perdana Menteri
Jalan Dato' Onn
Kuala Lumpur 50502
Malaysia
Fax: 60-3-2383784

Myanmar (Burma) (8)

U Nay Min, British Broadcasting Corp. (BBC)
Imprisoned: 1988

U Nay Min, a lawyer and BBC correspondent, was arrested in 1988 and sentenced in October 1989 to 14 years' hard labor.

U Win Tin
Imprisoned: July 4, 1989

U Win Tin, former editor of two daily newspapers and vice-chair of Burma's Writers Association, was arrested and sentenced to three years' hard labor—a sentence that was subsequently extended. U Win Tin was active in establishing independent publications during the 1988 student democracy movement, and he also worked closely with imprisoned National League for Democracy leader Daw Aung San Suu Kyi. U Win Tin is reported to be gravely ill; during a February 1994 visit to Myanmar, then-U.S. Congressman Bill Richardson saw him wearing a neck brace. Authorities extended U Win Tin's sentence by five more years on March 28, 1996, after they convicted him of smuggling letters describing conditions at Insein prison to Professor Yozo Yokota, the U. N. Special Rapporteur for human rights in Myanmar.

U Maung Maung Lay Ngwe
Imprisoned: September 1990

U Maung Maung Lay Ngwe was arrested and charged with writing and distributing publications that "make people lose respect for the government." The publications were titled, collectively, *Pe-Tin-Tan.*

U Myo Myint Nyein,
What's Happening
Imprisoned: September 1990

U Myo Myint Nyein was arrested for contributing to the satirical newsmagazine *What's Happening.* He was sentenced to seven years in prison. On March 28, 1996, another seven years were added to his sentence after authorities convicted him of smuggling letters describing conditions at Insein prison to Professor Yozo Yokota, the U. N. Special Rapporteur for human rights in Myanmar.

U Sein Hlaing, *What's Happening*
Imprisoned: September 1990

U Sein Hlaing, publisher of the satirical newsmagazine *What's Happening,* was arrested and sentenced to seven years in prison under the 1950 Emergency Provisions Act.

Imprisoned Journalists

Daw San San Nwe
U Sein Hla Oo
Imprisoned: August 5, 1994

Dissident writer Daw San San Nwe and journalist U Sein Hla Oo were arrested on charges of spreading information damaging to the state and contacting anti-government groups. On Oct. 6, Daw San San Nwe was sentenced to 10 years in prison and U Sein Hla Oo was sentenced to seven years. Officials said they had "fabricated and sent anti-government reports to some diplomats in foreign embassies, foreign radio stations, and visiting foreign journalists." Both men were previously imprisoned for their involvement with the National League for Democracy (NLD), Burma's main pro-democracy party.

Ye Htut
Imprisoned: September 27, 1995

Ye Htut was arrested on charges of sending fabricated news abroad to Burmese dissidents and opposition media. Among the organizations to which Ye Htut allegedly confessed sending reports was the Thailand-based Burma Information Group (BIG), which publishes the human rights newsletter *The Irawaddy*. Myanmar's official media claimed that BIG had presented a false picture of the country to foreign governments and human rights organizations. Ye Htut was sentenced to seven years in prison.

> APPEALS TO:
> His Excellency General Than Shwe
> Prime Minister and Minister of Defense
> Chairman of the State Law and Order Restoration
> Council
> Ministry of Defense
> Signal Pagoda Road
> Yangon, Myanmar
> Telex: 21316

Nigeria (8)

Kunle Ajibade, *TheNEWS*
Imprisoned: May 5, 1995

Police arrested Ajibade, an editor of the daily *TheNEWS*, and demanded to know the source of the article "No One Guilty: The Commission of Inquiry Presents an Empty File Regarding Suspects in the Coup d'Etat." They held him because he refused to divulge the whereabouts of his colleague Dapo Olorunyomi, who went underground. In July, a special military tribunal held a secret trial for Ajibade and George Mbah of *Tell* magazine, charging them as accessories to treasonable felony and sentencing them to prison terms of undisclosed length. On Oct. 1, Nigeria's Independence Day, the Provisional Ruling Council amended their sentences to 15 years in prison.

Christine Anyanwu, *The Sunday Magazine*
Imprisoned: May 1995

Anyanwu, publisher and editor in chief of *The Sunday Magazine*, was arrested for her reports on an alleged coup plot in March. In July, a special military tribunal secretly tried Anyanwu, along with Ben Charles Obi, editor of *Weekend Classique*. [See below] Both got life sentences. On Oct. 1, Nigeria's Independence Day, the Provisional Ruling Council commuted their sentences to 15 years in prison.

George Mbah, *Tell*
Imprisoned: May 5, 1995

Soldiers arrested Mbah, assistant editor of *Tell* magazine, for contributing to a report about a military officer who died during interrogation about his involvement in an alleged coup plot. In July, a special military tribunal secretly tried Mbah and Kunle Ajibade of *TheNEWS*, charging them with being accessories to treasonable felony. They were sentenced to life in prison. On Oct. 1, Nigeria's Independence Day, the Provisional Ruling Council amended their sentences to 15 years in prison.

Ben Charles Obi, *Weekend Classique*
Imprisoned: May 1, 1995

Obi, the editor of the weekly newsmagazine *Weekend Classique*, was arrested for his reports on an alleged coup plot in March. In July, a special military tribunal tried Obi and Christine Anyanwu of *The Sunday Magazine*. [See above] Both received life sentences. On Oct. 1, Nigeria's Independence Day, the Provisional Ruling Council commuted their sentences to 15 years in prison.

Jude Sinnee
Imprisoned: Early March 1996

Armed agents of the Rivers State Internal Security Task Force arrested Sinnee, a newspaper vendor in Bori, an Ogoni settlement in Rivers State, at his newsstand. The agents also seized 500 copies of various publications and the vendor's accumulated sales for the day. They then transported Sinnee to the Internal Security Task Force's office at Kpor, near Bori, where he is being held incommunicado. Sinnee, a disabled person, went on a hunger strike to protest his detention.

George Onah, *Vanguard*
Imprisoned: May 15, 1996

Onah, defense correspondent for the independent newspaper *Vanguard*, was arrested without charge and held in incommunicado detention. Authorities pressured Onah to reveal his sources for an article he wrote about promotions and other changes in rank among Nigerian military officers. On Dec. 31, Chief of Defense Staff Maj. Gen. Abdul Salaam Abubakar told reporters that he would look into Onah's case, but to date, officials have not released any information on Onah's status or location.

Imprisoned Journalists

Okina Deesor, Radio Rivers
Imprisoned: July 31, 1996

Deesor, a producer with Radio Rivers in the state of Rivers, was arrested and detained at the Government House Cell prison, reportedly without food or water. On Aug. 3, he was transferred to the Mobile Police Headquarters in Port Harcourt. According to Maj. Obi Umabi, Deesor's detention was in connection with the July 18 Radio Rivers broadcast of the national anthem of the Ogoni people. In a letter to President Sani Abacha, CPJ denounced Deesor's continued detention and asked for his immediate and unconditional release.

Godwin Agbroko,
The Week
Imprisoned: December 18, 1996

Three men who said they were security agents arrested Agbroko, editor in chief of the privately owned weekly magazine *The Week*. The arrest is believed to be in connection with an article published in the Dec. 16-23 edition of *The Week* titled "A Deadly Power Play," which reported on a dispute between Army Chief of Staff Ishaya Bamaiyi and Guard Brigade Commander Yakubu Mu'azu.

APPEALS TO:
Gen. Sani Abacha
Chairman of the Provisional Ruling Council
   and Commander in Chief of the Armed Forces
State House
Abuja
Federal Capital Territory, Nigeria
Fax: 234-95-232-138

Pakistan (2)

Farhan Effandi, *Parcham*
Imprisoned: September 14, 1995

Effandi, Hyderabad correspondent for the Karachi-based Urdu-language daily *Parcham*, was seized in Hyderabad by government paramilitary rangers. Effandi told colleagues that he was blindfolded, kicked, and beaten. On Sept. 16, 1995, he was charged with illegally possessing a Kalashnikov automatic rifle, which rangers claimed to have found during a raid on his office the day before, and with involvement in terrorist activities. Effandi's bail application has been denied twice by a judge of the Suppression of Terrorist Activities (STA) court in Hyderabad, and his trial proceeded through 1996. His newspaper is widely seen as an organ of the Mohajir Qaumi Movement (MQM), an armed opposition party of Muslim immigrants from India and their descendants. Effandi was released on a 30-day medical parole on Jan. 25, 1997, upon the order of the Chief Minister of Sindh, Mumtaz Ali Bhutto.

Zahid Ali Qaimkhani,
Pakistan Press International
(PPI), *Sindh Sujhag, Barsat*
Imprisoned: July 23, 1996

Qaimkhani, a correspondent for the private news agency PPI as well as the Sindhi-language dailies *Sindh Sujhag* and *Barsat,* was sentenced to five years in prison after being convicted of an arson attack on the telephone exchange in Kandiaro, in Sindh province. He was jailed immediately. In reaching the verdict, the court disregarded a note written by the magistrate of the Naushehro Feroze district to the public prosecutor saying that he had found no evidence linking Qaimkhani to the arson attack. Qaimkhani had been arrested for the attack on Jan. 22, after the official in charge of the Kandiaro telephone exchange filed a complaint against him. At that time, he was held for five days and then released on bail. Before his arrest, Qaimkhani had written articles alleging that certain local officials were corrupt. Qaimkhani was released from Sukkur jail on Jan. 21, 1997, after the Sindh High Court overturned the judgment of the lower court on appeal.

APPEALS TO:
His Excellency Farooq Ahmad Khan Leghari
President
Office of the President
Constitution Avenue
Islamabad, Pakistan
Fax: 92-51-811390

Peru (4)

Javier Tuanama Valera, *Hechos*
Imprisoned: October 16, 1990

Tuanama, editor in chief of the magazine *Hechos,* was arrested on charges of terrorism. He was sentenced on Nov. 7, 1994, to 10 years in prison for alleged links with the terrorist group Revolutionary Movement Tupac Amaru. He is currently being held at the Picsi Prison near Chiclayo.

Hermes Rivera Guerrero,
Radio Oriental
Imprisoned: May 8, 1992

First arrested in May 1992, Rivera, a reporter for Radio Oriental, was sentenced to 20 years in prison in February 1994 for alleged terrorist activity. He is currently being held in the Picsi Prison near Chiclayo.

Pedro Carranza Ugaz,
Radio Oriental
Imprisoned: November 29, 1993

Carranza, a journalist with Radio Oriental, was detained in November 1993 and sentenced on Nov. 7, 1994, to 20 years in prison on charges of being a member of the Revolutionary Movement Tupac Amaru terrorist group. He is being held in the Picsi Prison near Chiclayo.

Augusto Ernesto Llosa Giraldo,
El Casmeno, Radio Casma

Llosa, editor in chief of the newspaper *El Casmeno* and a reporter with Radio Casma, was arrested in Casma and

Imprisoned: February 14, 1995

charged with involvement in a 1986 terrorist incident in Cuzco. A secret tribunal of the Superior Court of Cuzco convicted and sentenced him on Aug. 10 to six years in prison. Llosa is being held in the maximum security Yanamayo prison.

> APPEALS TO:
> Su Excelencia Alberto Fujimori
> Presidente de la República del Perú
> Palacio de Gobierno
> Lima 1, Perú
> Fax: 51-14-326-535

Sudan (2)

Osama Ghandi,
  Sudanese Television
Hassan Saleh,
  Sudanese Television
Imprisoned: February 1996

Television cameraman Osama Ghandi and technician Hassan Saleh of the state-owned Sudanese Television were arrested and accused of being involved in an alleged coup attempt. They were among 10 civilians who went on trial in late August in an *in camera* military-court trial, in which most of the defendants were military officers. Ghandi told the court on Sept. 18 that military intelligence agents had coerced his confession by torturing him.

> APPEALS TO:
> His Excellency Lt. General Omar Hassan al-Bashir
> c/o His Excellency Ambassador Mahdi Ibrahim Muhammad
> Embassy of Sudan
> 2210 Massachusetts Ave., N.W.
> Washington, D.C. 20008

Syria (6)

Faisal Allush
Imprisoned: 1985

Allush, a journalist and political writer who has been in jail since 1985, was sentenced in June 1993 to 15 years' imprisonment for membership in the banned Party for Communist Action.

Anwar Bader, Syrian Radio and
  Television
Imprisoned: December 1986

Bader, a reporter for Syrian Radio and Television, who has been in jail since his arrest by the Military Interrogation Branch in December 1986, was convicted in March 1994 of being a member in the Party for Communist Action. He was sentenced to 12 years in prison.

Samir al-Hassan, *Fatah al-Intifada*
Imprisoned: April 1986

Al-Hassan, Palestinian editor of *Fatah al-Intifada*, who has been in jail since his arrest in April 1986, was convicted in June 1994 of being a member of the Party for Communist Action. He was sentenced to 15 years in prison.

Jadi Nawfal, Free-lancer
Imprisoned: December 18, 1991

Nawfal, a free-lance journalist, was arrested on Dec. 18, 1991, and sentenced the following March to five years in prison for belonging to The Committees for the Defense of Democratic Freedoms and Human Rights in Syria.

Salama George Kila
Imprisoned: March 1992

Political Security officers arrested Kila, a Palestinian writer and journalist, in Damascus. His trial began in the summer of 1993. The court ruled that he was guilty of a misdemeanor rather than a felony. Since the maximum sentence for a misdemeanor is three years, his release was expected in March 1995. But he remains in prison.

Nizar Nayouf, Free-lancer
Imprisoned: January 1992

Nayouf, a free-lance journalist who has contributed to Al-*Huriyya* and *Al-Thaqafa al-Ma'arifa*, was arrested in Damascus with several human rights activists from The Committees for the Defense of Democratic Freedoms and Human Rights in Syria. In March, he was sentenced by the State Security Court to 10 years in prison for "disseminating false information and receiving money from abroad." He was severely tortured during his interrogation. He now remains in solitary confinement in Mezze military prison.

APPEALS TO:
His Excellency Hafez al-Assad
President of the Syrian Arab Republic
Presidential Palace
Damascus, Syria
Telex: 419160 munjed sy

Tunisia (2)

Hamadi Jebali, *Al-Fajr*
Imprisoned: January 1991

Jebali, editor of *Al-Fajr*, the weekly newspaper of the banned Islamist Al-Nahda party, has been in jail since January 1991, when he was sentenced to one year in prison after *Al-Fajr* published an article calling for the abolition of military courts in Tunisia. On Aug. 28, 1992, he was sentenced to 16 years in prison by the military court in Bouchoucha. He was tried along with 170 others accused of belonging to Al-Nahda. Jebali was convicted of "aggression with the intention of changing the nature of the state" and "membership in an ille-

Imprisoned Journalists

gal organization." During his testimony, Jebali denied the charges against him and displayed evidence that he had been tortured while in custody. International human rights groups monitoring the mass trial concluded that it fell far below international standards of justice.

Abdellah Zouari, *Al-Fajr*
Imprisoned: February 1991

Zouari, a contributor to *Al-Fajr*, the weekly newspaper of the banned Islamist Al-Nahda party, has been in jail since February 1991, when he was charged with "association with an unrecognized organization." On Aug. 28, 1992, he was sentenced to 11 years in prison by the military court in Bouchoucha. He was tried along with 170 others accused of belonging to Al-Nahda. International human rights groups monitoring the trial concluded that it fell far short of international standards of justice

APPEALS TO:
His Excellency Zine El Abidine Ben Ali
President of the Republic
Palais Presidentiel
Tunis, Tunisia
Fax: 216-1-744-721

Turkey (78)
Imprisoned before 1994 (8)

Naile Tuncer, *Devrimci Proletarya*
Imprisoned: May 1992

Tuncer, formerly an editor for the left-wing magazine *Devrimci Proletarya*, was charged under Article 8 of the Anti-Terror Law. She remains in Canakkale Prison.

Ismail Beşikçi
Imprisoned: November 12, 1993

Beşikçi, a prominent writer and journalist, was arrested and sentenced to one year in prison for an article he wrote in the now-defunct *Yeni Ülke* daily. Since then, he has been convicted in other cases for articles he published on the Kurdish question in the now-defunct *Özgür Gündem* and for books he has written on the matter. By the end of 1996, the prison sentences he had received totaled more than 100 years. More cases against him are pending.

Bektaş Cansever, *Devrimci Çözüm*
Imprisoned: January 7, 1993

Cansever, a reporter for the left-wing magazine *Devrimci Çözüm*, was taken into custody during a police raid on the magazine's headquarters in Istanbul. He was subsequently charged with being a member of an outlawed organization and sentenced to 12 years and six months in prison. He is in Gebze Prison.

Ismail Günes, *Özgür Gündem*
Imprisoned: December 11, 1993

Günes, a correspondent for the pro-Kurdish daily *Özgür Gündem*, was taken into custody during a police raid on the Agri bureau of the newspaper. He was subsequently charged under Article 168 of the Penal Code with being a member of the outlawed Kurdistan Workers' Party and arrested. He was sentenced to 12 years and six months in prison. He is serving his sentence in Çankiri Prison.

Hasan Özgün, *Özgür Gündem*
Imprisoned: December 9, 1993

Özgün, Diyarbakir correspondent for *Özgür Gündem*, was taken into custody during a police raid on the paper's bureau in Diyarbakir. He was charged under Article 168 of the Penal Code with being a member of an outlawed organization and was sentenced to 12 years and 5 months in prison. He is serving his sentence in Aydin Prison.

Hüseyin Solak, *Mücadele*
Imprisoned: September 1993

Solak, Gaziantep bureau chief of the now-defunct weekly magazine *Mücadele*, was arrested in September 1993 and later sentenced to 12 years and six months in prison under Article 168 of the Penal Code. He is serving his sentence in Çankiri Prison.

Kemal Topalak, *Devrimci Çözüm*
Imprisoned: January 7, 1993

Topalak, a reporter for *Devrimci Çözüm*, was taken into custody during a police raid on the magazine's headquarters in Istanbul. He was subsequently charged with being a member of an outlawed organization and sentenced to 12 years and six months in prison. He is in Gebze Prison.

Sinan Yavuz, *Yoksul Halkin Gücü*
Imprisoned: 1993

Yavuz, formerly the editor of the left-wing weekly *Yoksul Halkin Gücü*, was arrested in 1993 for articles published in the magazine. He remains in Ankara Prison.

Imprisoned in 1994 (13)

Mehmet Akdemir, *Isçi Hareketi*
Imprisoned: November 24, 1994

Akdemir, a reporter for the left-wing magazine *Isçi Hareketi*, was taken into custody during a police raid on the magazine's main offices in Istanbul. He was subsequently arrested and is being held in Sağmalcilar Prison

Metin Alhas, *Mücadele*
Imprisoned: October 23, 1994

Alhas, one of the Antakya correspondents for the weekly magazine *Mücadele*, was detained during a police raid on the magazine's Antakya bureau. He was charged with violating Article 168 of the Penal Code and remains in Antakya Prison.

Aysel Bölücek, *Mücadele*
Imprisoned: October 11, 1994

Bölücek, one of *Mücadele's* Ankara correspondents, was picked up by the police at her home and detained. She was later sentenced under Article 168 of the Penal Code to 12 years and six

Imprisoned Journalists

months in prison. She is being held in Canakkale Prison.

Ali Sinan Çaglar, *Mücadele*
Imprisoned: August 6, 1994

Çaglar, *Mücadele's* Ankara correspondent, was arrested and charged with membership in an illegal organization. On Jan. 23, 1995, he was sentenced to 12 years in prison. His articles in *Mücadele* and his status as a staff correspondent were used as evidence that he belonged to an outlawed left-wing organization. He is serving his sentence in Konya Prison.

Burhan Gardaş, *Mücadele*
Imprisoned: January 26, 1994

Gardas, a former Ankara bureau chief for the weekly *Mücadele*, was the target of several legal cases in 1994 relating to articles published in the magazine. He was sentenced to a total of 15 years in prison and is currently being held in Aydin Prison.

Serdar Gelir, *Mücadele*
Imprisoned: April 16, 1994

Gelir, one of *Mücadele's* Ankara correspondents, was detained on April 16, 1994, and arrested 10 days later. A security court sentenced him to 12 years and six months in prison for being a member of an illegal organization. He is serving his sentence in Yozgat Prison.

Nuray Gezici, *Yoksul Halkin Gücü*
Imprisoned: April 1994

Gezici, a reporter for *Yoksul Halkin Gücü*, was arrested in April 1994 and is currently serving a 15-year prison term in Canakkale Prison.

Teoman Gül, *Newroz*
Imprisoned: November 1994

Gül, a reporter for *Newroz* magazine, was arrested in November 1994. He is being held in Malatya Prison, although it is unclear under what circumstances.

Ibrahim Özen, *Devrimci Çözüm*
Imprisoned: April 1994

Özen, a former owner of the magazine *Devrimci Çözüm*, was taken into custody during a police raid on the magazine's headquarters in Istanbul. He was charged with being a member of an outlawed organization and sentenced to 12 years and six months in prison. He is being held in Gebze Prison in Istanbul.

Gülcan Sarioğlu, *Mücadele*
Imprisoned: October 23, 1994

Sarioğlu, one of the Antakya correspondents for the weekly magazine *Mücadele*, was detained during a police raid on the magazine's Antakya bureau. He was charged with aiding an illegal organization and sentenced to three years and nine months in prison. He is serving his term in Nevsehir Prison.

Utku Deniz Sirkeci, *Tavir*
Imprisoned: August 1994

Sirkeci, the Ankara bureau chief of the leftist magazine *Tavir*, was charged under Article 168 of the Penal Code and sentenced to 12 years and six months in prison. He is serving his sentence in Aydin Prison.

Ocak Işik Yurtçu, *Özgür Gündem*
Imprisoned: December 28, 1994

Yurtçu, a prominent writer and journalist who served as the editor of the pro-Kurdish daily *Özgür Gündem* in 1991 and 1992, was arrested and sent to prison when an appeals court upheld a 15-year and 10 month sentence against him. Charged under the Anti-Terror Law, he was convicted of publishing "separatist propaganda" in various articles that appeared in the daily while he was the editor. He is being held in Sakarya Prison.

Ali Yolcu, *Mücadele*
Imprisoned: November 1994

Antakya bureau chief of the weekly *Mücadele*, Yolcu was charged under Article 169 of the Penal Code and sentenced to three years and nine months in prison. He is being held in Antakya Prison.

Imprisoned in 1995 (30)

Hasan Abali, *Atilim*
Imprisoned: June 15, 1995

Abali, a reporter for the leftist weekly newspaper *Atilim*, was taken into custody during a police raid on the newspaper's Mersin bureau. He was later charged with being a member of an outlawed organization and sentenced to 12 years and six months in prison. He is in Silifke-Mersin Prison.

Salih Bal, *Medya Gunesi*
Imprisoned: June 2, 1995

Bal, former editor in chief of the now-defunct Kurdish-language periodical *Medya Gunesi*, was arrested along with his wife when their home was raided by police. He and his wife, who was eight months pregnant at the time, were held at the anti-terror branch of Istanbul Police Headquarters. Bal's wife was released after 10 days but Bal was accused of disseminating separatist propaganda under the Anti-Terror Law, among other charges, and sentenced to 12 years and six months in prison. He is being held in Istanbul's Bayrampaşa Prison.

Fatma Bilgin, *Kurtulus*
Imprisoned: December 12, 1995

Bilgin, an Antakya reporter for the leftist weekly *Kurtulus*, was convicted under Article 168 of the Penal Code and sentenced to 12 years and six months in prison. She is serving her sentence in Malatya Prison.

Mesut Bozkurt, *Atilim*
Imprisoned: June 15, 1995

Bozkurt, bureau chief of the Iskenderun office of *Atilim*, was charged with being a member of an outlawed organization and sentenced to 12 years and six months in prison.

Mehmet Çakar, *Partizan Sesi*
Imprisoned: February 13, 1995

Çakar, the bureau chief in Izmir for the leftist monthly *Partizan Sesi*, was arrested and charged with being a member of an outlawed organization. He is being held in Izmir-Buca Prison.

Necla Can, *Kurtulus*
Imprisoned: April 20, 1995

Can, a reporter for the leftist weekly *Kurtulus*, was charged with aiding an outlawed organization. She is currently in Umraniye Prison in Istanbul.

Sadik Çelik, *Kurtulus*
Imprisoned: May 8, 1995

Çelik, an Ankara-based reporter for the leftist weekly Kurtulus, was sentenced under Article 168 of the Penal Code and is presently serving a 12-year and 6 month sentence in Ankara Prison.

Musafa Çoskun, *Partizan Sesi*
Imprisoned: May 8, 1995

Çoskun, Elazig bureau chief of the leftist monthly *Partizan Sesi*, was charged and sentenced to prison for being a member of an outlawed organization. He is in Bursa Prison.

Erdal Dogan, *Alinteri*
Imprisoned: July 14, 1995

Dogan, a reporter for the Ankara office of the leftist weekly *Alinteri*, was arrested and later charged under Article 168 of the Penal Code. He was sentenced to 12 years and six months in prison. He is being held in Bursa Prison.

Ufuk Doğubay, *Kurtulus*
Imprisoned: July 26, 1995
Özgür Güdenoğlu, *Mücadele*
Imprisoned: May 24, 1995

Doğubay, a former editor of the leftist weekly *Kurtulus*, was convicted under Article 168 of the Penal Code. He is serving a 12-year and six-month sentence in Sağmalcilar Prison. Güdenoğlu, *Mücadele's* Konya bureau chief, was arrested. He remains in Konya Prison.

Fatma Harman, *Atilim*
Imprisoned: June 15, 1995

Harman, a reporter for the leftist weekly newspaper *Atilim*, was taken into custody during a police raid on the newspaper's Mersin bureau. She was later charged and sentenced under Article 168 of the Penal Code to 12 years and six months in prison. She is currently in Sakarya Prison.

Hanim Harman, *Mücadele*
Imprisoned: February 4, 1995

Harman, one of *Mücadele's* Malatya correspondents, was sentenced to 12 years and six months in prison under Article 168 of the Penal Code. She is serving her sentence in Sakarya Prison.

Kamber Inan, *Kurtulus*
Imprisoned: July 26, 1995

Inan, a reporter for the leftist weekly *Kurtulus*, was arrested and charged with being a member of an outlawed organization. He is currently in Sağmalcilar Prison in Istanbul.

Mustafa Kiliç, *Newroz*
Imprisoned: 1995

Kiliç, a reporter with the pro-Kurdish weekly *Newroz*, was arrested sometime in 1995 and remains in Malatya Prison.

Murat Kirsay, *Kurtulus*
Imprisoned: November 22, 1995

Kirsay, Adana bureau chief of the leftist weekly *Kurtulus*, was arrested on Nov. 22, 1995, and is being held in Sayaimbeyil Prison in Adana.

Bülent Öner, *Atilim*
Imprisoned: June 15, 1995

Öner, a reporter for the leftist weekly newspaper *Atilim*, was taken into custody during a police raid on the newspaper's Mersin bureau. He was later charged with being a member of an outlawed organization and sentenced to 12 years and 6 months in prison. He is currently being held in Iskenderun Prison.

Kemal Şahin, *Özgür Gündem*
Imprisoned: November 1995

Şahin, the former editor in chief of the now-defunct pro-Kurdish daily *Özgür Gündem*, was arrested and accused of being a member of an outlawed organization. There are also several cases pending against him stemming from his days as the daily's editor. He is being held in Umraniye Prison in Istanbul.

Bülent Sümbül, *Özgür Halk*
Imprisoned: April 1995

Sümbül, a reporter working in the Diyarbakir bureau of the pro-Kurdish monthly magazine *Özgür Halk*, was arrested during a police raid on the Diyarbakir office. Tried and convicted under Article 168 of the Penal Code, he was sentenced to three years and six months in prison. He is being held in Diyarbakir Prison.

Nuray Tekdağ, *Özgür Halk*
Imprisoned: October 31, 1995

Tekdağ, a correspondent in Diyarbakir for the pro-Kurdish monthly magazine *Özgür Halk*, was arrested and charged with aiding an outlawed organization. She was convicted and sentenced to three years and six months in Batman Prison.

Bülent Ecevit Özdemir, *Kurtulus*
Imprisoned: December 7, 1995

Özdemir, a reporter for the leftist weekly *Kurtulus*, was arrested and charged under Article 168 of the Penal Code. He is currently in Konya Prison.

Asaf Şah, *Kurtulus*
Imprisoned: 1995

An Antakya reporter for the leftist weekly *Kurtulus*, Şah was convicted under Article 169 of the Penal Code and is serving a three-year and nine-month sentence in Nevsehir Prison.

Semiha Topal, *Kurtulus*
Imprisoned: December 12, 1995

Topal, a reporter for the Antakya bureau of *Kurtulus*, was arrested and later sentenced to 12 years and six months in prison under Article 168 of the Penal Code. She is serving her term in Malatya Prison.

Sakine Topoglu, *Özgür Gündem*
Imprisoned: April 11, 1995

Topoglu, a former editor for the pro-Kurdish daily *Özgür Gündem*, was sentenced under Article 168 of the Penal Code for articles published in the paper during her tenure. Several other cases are pending against her. She is presently being held in Malatya Prison.

Ali Toprak, *Atilim*
Imprisoned: October 20, 1995

Toprak, Mersin bureau chief of the leftist weekly newspaper *Atilim*, was detained during a police raid on the paper's office.

Imprisoned Journalists

He was charged under Article 168 of the Penal Code and awaits a court decision on his case.

Özlem Türk, *Mücadele*
Imprisoned: 1995

Türk, a reporter for the leftist magazine *Mücadele,* was sentenced to 12 years and six months under Article 168 of the Penal Code. She is in Canakkale Prison.

Güray Ülkü, *Kizilbayrak*
Imprisoned: October 3, 1995

Ülkü, a former editor of the leftist weekly *Kizilbayrak,* has been charged under various articles of the Penal Code and Anti-Terror Law. He is in Bayrampaşa Prison.

Suleyman Yaman, *Newroz*
Imprisoned: 1995

Yaman, a reporter for *Newroz,* was arrested sometime in 1995 and remains incarcerated in Malatya Prison.

Bariş Yildirim, *Tavir*
Imprisoned: March 1995

Yildirim, a columnist for the leftist magazine *Tavir,* was convicted under Article 168 of the Penal Code and sentenced to 12 years and six months in prison. He is currently in Buca Prison in Izmir.

Ali Yilmaz, *Atilim*
Imprisoned: March 16, 1995

A reporter for *Atilim's* Ankara bureau, Yilmaz was charged and sentenced to three years and nine months in prison for helping and providing shelter to an outlawed organization. He is being held in Ankara Prison.

Imprisoned in 1996 (27)

Cuma Akin, *Özgür Halk*
Imprisoned: November 17, 1996

Akin, the Batman bureau chief for the pro-Kurdish monthly magazine *Özgür Halk,* was detained after a police raid on the magazine's Diyarbakir office. He is being held in Diyarbakir Prison, awaiting official charge.

Veli Aydin, *Özgür Gelecek*
Imprisoned: May 3, 1996

Aydin, a reporter for the leftist magazine *Özgür Gelecek,* was arrested and has been charged with membership in an illegal organization under Article 168-2 of the Penal Code. He is currently in Sağmalcilar Prison.

Tekin Aygün, *Kurtulus*
Imprisoned: 1996

Aygün, a reporter for the leftist weekly *Kurtulus,* was arrested and remains in Umraniye Prison.

Bülent Balci, *Kurtulus*
Imprisoned: May 13, 1996

A former editor of the leftist weekly *Kurtulus,* Balci was sentenced to 12 years and six months in prison under Article 168 of the Penal Code. He is in Umraniye Prison.

Özgür Çavusoglu, *Atilim*
Imprisoned: November 17, 1996

A reporter working at the Izmir bureau of *Atilim,* Çavusoglu was arrested at his home and charged under Article 168 of the Penal Code. He is being held in Buca Prison.

Ibrahim Çiçek, *Atilim*
Imprisoned: March 16, 1996

Çiçek, a former editor in chief of the leftist weekly *Atilim*, was detained during a police raid on the paper's headquarters in Istanbul. He has been charged under Article 168 of the Penal Code and is being held in Bayrampaşa Prison.

Songül Çinar, *Kurtulus*
Imprisoned: 1996

Çinar, a reporter for the leftist weekly *Kurtulus*, was arrested and charged under Article 168 of the Penal Code. She is currently in Ankara Prison.

Mustafa Demirdağ, *Özgür Gelecek*
Imprisoned: May 12, 1996

Demirdağ, an editor for the leftist magazine *Özgür Gelecek*, was arrested and later tried and convicted under the Anti-Terror Law. He is serving a three-year and five-month sentence in Sakarya Prison.

Beyazit Ekiz, *Kizilbayrak*
Duygu Tuna, *Kizilbayrak*
Imprisoned: November 1996

Ekiz and Tuna, reporters for the Gebze bureau of the leftist weekly *Kizilbayrak*, were detained during a police raid on the magazine's office. Both women were formally arrested and charged under Article 168 of the Penal Code. They are being held in Gebze Prison.

Yildiz Gemicioglu, *Kurtulus*
Imprisoned: June 25, 1996

Gemicioglu, a former Adana bureau chief of the leftist weekly *Kurtulus*, was arrested and remains in Konya Prison without charge.

Adil Harmanci, *Demokrasi*
Imprisoned: November 20, 1996

Harmanci, a reporter for the pro-Kurdish daily *Demokrasi*, was detained at his home in Van by police along with his wife. Although his wife was released, Harmanci remains in Van Prison without charge.

Sedat Hayta, *Devrimci Emek*
Imprisoned: January 1, 1996

A former editor for the leftist weekly *Devrimci Emek*, Hayta was arrested and charged under Article 169 of the Penal Code. He is currently in Bayrampaşa Prison in Istanbul.

Erhan Il, *Devrimci Emek*
Imprisoned: January 30, 1996

Il, a reporter for the leftist magazine *Devrimci Emek*, was arrested and charged under Article 168 of the Penal Code. He is being held in Bayrampaşa Prison.

Gennue Kiliç, *Özgür Ülke*
Imprisoned: August 1996

Kiliç, a former editor of the now-defunct pro-Kurdish daily *Özgür Ülke*, was charged and convicted under Article 169 of the Penal Code. She also faces additional charges under the Penal Code and the Anti-Terror Law for articles published in the newspaper during her tenure.

Altan Koman, *Atilim*
Imprisoned: June 25, 1996

Koman, a reporter for the Iskenderun bureau of *Atilim*, was arrested and charged with violating Article 168 of the Penal Code. He is currently in Malatya Prison.

Emin Konar, *Özgür Halk*
Imprisoned: May 7, 1996

A reporter for the pro-Kurdish monthly magazine *Özgür Halk*, Konar was detained during a police raid on the magazine's office in Elazig and later arrested and charged under Article 169 of the Penal Code. He was sentenced to three years and six months in prison and is currently in Elbistan Hapas Prison.

Adil Kurt, *Newroz*
Imprisoned: 1996

Kurt, a reporter for the pro-Kurdish magazine *Newroz*, was arrested in early 1996 and remains incarcerated in Gaziantep Prison. The circumstances of his imprisonment are not clear.

Özgür Öktem, *Devrimci Emek*
Imprisoned: February 19, 1996

Öktem, a reporter for the leftist magazine *Devrimci Emek*, was arrested and charged under Article 168 of the Penal Code. He is being held in Bayrampaşa Prison in Istanbul.

Hatice Onaran, *Devrimci Çözüm*
Imprisoned: March 19, 1996

Onaran, a former editor for the left-wing magazine *Devrimci Çözüm*, was sentenced to six years and 10 months in prison under the Anti-Terror Law and the Penal Code for articles published in the magazine during her tenure. She is being held in Gebze Prison.

Özden Özbay, *Özgür Ülke*
Imprisoned: November 1996

Özbay, the former editor of the now-defunct pro-Kurdish *Özgür Ülke*, was arrested and charged with violating Article 312 of the Penal Code and Articles 6, 7, and 8 of the Anti-Terror Law. He has yet to be sentenced and is currently in Gebze Prison.

Yazgül Güder Öztürk, *Kurtulus*
Imprisoned: April 10, 1996

Öztürk, a reporter for the leftist weekly *Kurtulus*, has been charged with being a member of an outlawed organization under Article 168 of the Penal Code. She remains in Sağmalcilar Prison.

Hafize Sayran, *Kurtulus*
Imprisoned: 1996

Sayran, the Zonguldak bureau chief for the leftist weekly *Kurtulus*, was arrested and is being held in Ankara Prison.

Nurcan Turgut, *Demokrasi*
Imprisoned: June 28, 1996

Turgut, a reporter for the pro-Kurdish daily *Demokrasi*, was detained by police during a raid on the newspaper's office in Elazig. She was sentenced to three years and nine months in prison under Article 169 of the Penal Code. Turgut is serving her sentence in Nevsehir Prison.

Fatih Yeşilbag, *Özgür Gündem*
Imprisoned: August 1996

A former editor in chief of the pro-Kurdish daily *Özgür Gündem*, Yeşilbag was arrested and charged under numerous articles of the Penal Code and Anti-Terror Law. He is currently being held in Bursa-Keles Prison.

Esra Yildirim, *Kurtulus*
Imprisoned: November 1996

Yildirim, a Trabzon correspondent for the leftist weekly *Kurtulus*, was charged under Article 169 of the Penal Code and is currently being held in Ankara Prison.

Muteber Yildirim, *Özgür Ülke*
Imprisoned: November 19, 1996

Yildirim, a reporter for the now-defunct pro-Kurdish daily *Özgür Ülke*, was convicted under Article 312 of the Penal Code for an article he wrote for the newspaper. He is currently being held in Bayrampaşa Prison.

APPEALS TO:
His Excellency Necmettin Erbakan
Prime Minister
Basbakanlik
06573 Ankara, Turkey
Fax: 90-312-417-04-76

Vietnam (5)

Doan Viet Hoat,
Dien Dan Tu Do
Imprisoned: November 17, 1990

Public security police arrested Hoat, editor and publisher of the pro-democracy newsletter *Dien Dan Tu Do* (Freedom Forum). The Ho Chi Minh City People's Court sentenced him in late March 1993 to 20 years of hard labor for his involvement with the newsletter. He is currently serving out his sentence, commuted to 15 years on appeal, in Thanh Cam prison. Located in northern Vietnam, near the Laotian border, Thanh Cam is normally reserved for serious criminal offenders. Hoat suffers from kidney stones, a condition that developed during his previous 12-year incarceration by the Hanoi regime.

Pham Duc Kham, *Dien Dan Tu Do*
Imprisoned: Late 1990

Public security police arrested Kham in the fall of 1990. In March 1993, he was sentenced to 16 years in prison for his involvement with the pro-democracy newsletter *Dien Dan Tu Do* (Freedom Forum). His sentence was reduced on appeal to 12 years. Kham is presently incarcerated at Xuan Phuoc labor camp.

Nguyen Van Thuan (Chau Son),
Dien Dan Tu Do
Imprisoned: Late 1990

Thuan, whose pen name is Chau Son, was arrested in the fall of 1990 and in March 1993 was sentenced to 12 years in prison for his involvement with the pro-democracy newsletter *Dien Dan Tu Do* (Freedom Forum). His sentence was reduced on appeal to eight years. Thuan suffered a stroke on Feb. 25, 1994, that left him partially paralyzed. Authorities ordered him to return to Ham Tan prison camp after 30 days in the hospital.

Imprisoned Journalists

Le Duc Vuong, *Dien Dan Tu Do*
Imprisoned: Late 1990

Vuong was arrested in the fall of 1990 and sentenced in late March 1993 to seven years in prison for his involvement with the pro-democracy newsletter *Dien Dan Tu Do* (Freedom Forum). Vuong is presently incarcerated at Xuan Phuoc labor camp.

Nguyen Dan Que
Sentenced: November 1991

Que was convicted of compiling and distributing subversive literature and sentenced to 20 years in prison. Before he was imprisoned, he had distributed political handbills and sent documents abroad. Que, who suffers from hypertension and a bleeding gastric ulcer, is imprisoned at the Xuyen Moc labor camp in Dong Nai province.

APPEALS TO:
His Excellency Do Muoi
General Secretary of the Central Committee
Communist Party of Vietnam
1 Hoang Van Thu
Hanoi, Socialist Republic of Vietnam
Fax: 84-4-259-205 or 84-4-459-205

Zaire (2)

Mukalayi Mulongo, OZRT-Shaba
Kabemba wa Yulu, OZRT-Shaba
Imprisoned: May 19, 1995

Lubumbashi Security Service officers arrested Mulongo, the program director of the state-owned radio station OZRT-Shaba, and wa Yulu, a journalist with the station. Mulongo was arrested for granting the president of the Shaba province branch of the Union of Independent Republicans Party (UFERI) the right to respond to statements made by the national UFERI president.

APPEALS TO
His Excellency Leon Kengo wa Dondo
Prime Minister of the Republic of Zaire
Kinshasa, Zaire
Fax: c/o Embassy of Zaire
202-686-3631

Zambia (1)

Gerard Gatare, Rwandan National Television
Imprisoned: October 10, 1995

Gatare, a former editor at Rwandan National Television, was arrested and later imprisoned in Kabwata Central Prison in Lusaka. Early in 1995, Gatare, fearing for his life, had fled to Zambia from a refugee camp outside Rwanda. No charges have been brought against him. His arrest came after a Rwandan government minister visited Zambia, reportedly bringing a list of "wanted" Rwandan intellectuals with him. Gatare, a recipient of the 1994-95 Fulbright Hubert Humphrey Fellowship for International Journalists, is one of at least 16 Rwandan refugees currently imprisoned in Zambia.

APPEALS TO
His Excellency Frederick Chiluba
President of the Republic of Zambia
State House
Independent Avenue
Lusaka, Zambia
Fax: 260-1-221-939

Journalists Killed In 1996
27 Cases of Journalists Who Died in the Line of Duty

JOURNALISM, ESPECIALLY WHEN PRACTICED without the protective shield afforded in the United States by the First Amendment, is all too often hazardous work. The founding principle behind the creation of the Committee to Protect Journalists 15 years ago was a sense of moral obligation to defend colleagues abroad whose lives were threatened because they reported events accurately or gave voice to opposing points of view.

In 1996, CPJ confirmed 26 cases of journalists who were murdered because of their work, and one accidental death in a plane crash of journalists assigned to travel on military aircraft with U.S. officials in the former Yugoslavia. This number, while still intolerably high, represents a stark drop from the figures of recent years. In 1995, at least 57 journalists were killed in the line of duty, including six cases not confirmed by CPJ until 1996: a murdered Hutu Burundian radio news director; a Bosnian Serb cameraman murdered, allegedly by Bosnian government troops; and three Russian newspaper reporters and one American free-lancer who were killed while on assignment in Chechnya.

Algeria remains the most dangerous country for journalists, with seven assassinations in 1996, bringing the toll since 1993 to 59. There were six journalists murdered in Russia, four while covering the war in Chechnya. One of the most shocking deaths of the year was the June murder of Irish crime reporter Veronica Guerin: It was the first such murder in Western Europe in many years. Guerin was a recipient of CPJ's International Press Freedom Award in 1995. In sharp contrast to most of the 1996 murder cases on the following list, her accused killers were apprehended and are facing trial.

CPJ's mission to monitor and protest attacks on journalists and news organizations around the world depends upon the research staff's careful documentation of journalists killed each year because of their profession. CPJ defines "journalists" as persons who cover news or write commentary on a regular basis, or work as editors, publishers, and directors of news organizations. Photojournalists and members of radio, television, and cable news teams are included, as are the staffs of online news publications that have proliferated on the Internet.

When a journalist is killed, CPJ's researchers investigate the circumstances of the death. As far as can possibly be ascertained, they differentiate between those journalists who have died because of the perilous nature of their work and those who have died in circumstances unrelated to their jobs. Each account is corroborated by at least two independent sources for accuracy and, if murder is involved, for confirmation that the motive was to silence the journalist. If the researchers conclude that the killing was intentional and stemmed from the journalist's work, CPJ strongly protests the murder and presses the local authorities to investigate and prosecute the perpetrators of the crime.

But not all job-related killings of journalists are deliberate assassinations. CPJ also counts those who die on dangerous assignments. For example, journalists covering wars can become casualties in the crossfire, or they can be targeted by the combatants. And there are some deaths that can only be described as accidents. One overriding criterion determines which accidental deaths belong on the list: whether the nature of the assignment placed the journalist in harm's way. Of course, journalists, like other travelers, die in car wrecks and plane crashes. But when, to cite this year's example, a journalist dies because he has to fly on a inadequately equipped aircraft attempting an ill-advised landing in low-visibility conditions at a badly lit airstrip in mountainous terrain to get the story, CPJ deems his death an accident in the line of duty.

CPJ's classification of "unconfirmed killings" also bears explanation. Frequently, given the social and political turmoil or geographical remoteness of the regions in which many journalists' murders occur, it is not possible, no matter how good our sources, to know immediately if the killing was an act of retribution for news coverage or commentary. When the motives for a journalist's murder are unclear, but there are sound reasons to suspect that it was related to the journalist's profession, CPJ classifies that death as "unconfirmed." These unconfirmed killings remain active cases for CPJ, which continues its research to identify the motives for the crimes and perseveres in its efforts to persuade the appropriate authorities to fully investigate the killings and apprehend and punish the culprits.

Countries Where Journalists Were Killed in 1996

Deaths by Assassination: 26

Algeria: (7)

Mohamed Mekati, *El Moudjahid*
Date of Death: Jan. 10, 1996
Place of Death: Ain Naadja

Mekati, a correspondent for the government-owned newspaper *El Moudjahid*, was shot near his home in Ain Naadja southwest of Algiers Jan. 9 and died Jan. 10. He was the first of seven journalists killed in Algeria in 1996 and the 53rd murdered since Islamic rebels began targeting journalists in 1993. The Armed Islamic Group (GIA) has claimed responsibility for the bulk of the murders. As of the end of 1996, 59 journalists had been killed in the civil strife that began after the Algerian government canceled a 1992 general election in which radical Islamists were leading.

Abdallah Bouhachek, *Révolution et Travail*
Date of Death: Feb. 10, 1996
Place of Death: Blida

Bouhachek was editor of the weekly *Révolution et Travail*, the publication of Algeria's largest workers union. He was fatally shot Feb. 10 near the town of Blida, south of Algiers, on his way to work. Islamic militants are presumed responsible.

Allaoua Ait M'barak, *Le Soir d'Algérie*
Mohamed Dorbane, *Le Soir d'Algérie*
Djamel Derraz, *Le Soir d'Algérie*
Date of Death: Feb. 11, 1996
Place of Death: Algiers

M'barak, Dorbane, and Derraz all were journalists with the independent evening daily *Le Soir d'Algérie*. They were killed Feb. 11 while at work in the Maison de la Presse in Algiers when a car bomb exploded outside the building. Three other daily newspapers whose offices are also in the building were damaged in the attack, and at least 15 other persons were killed. Islamic militants are presumed responsible.

Djilali Arabidou, *Algérie-Actualité*
Date of Death: March 12, 1996
Place of Death: Ain Naadja

Arabidou, the acknowledged dean of Algerian photojournalists, worked for the pro-government weekly *Algérie-Actualité*. He was fatally shot March 12 in a suburb of Algiers, Ain Naadja. Islamic militants are presumed responsible.

Mohamed Guessab, Algerian Radio
Date of Death: Aug. 12, 1996
Place of Death: Algiers

Guessab was the host of "Radio Koran," a religious program on state-run Algerian Radio. He was fatally shot Aug. 12 while driving with his two brothers, one of whom was killed and the other seriously wounded, in the Algiers suburb of Beau Fraisier. Islamic militants are presumed responsible.

Angola: (1)

Antonio Casemero, Televisao
Popular de Angola
Date of Death: Oct. 30, 1996
Place of Death: Cabinda

Casemero was a correspondent in Cabinda for Televisao Popular de Angola, the state-owned television station. He was fatally shot Oct. 30 at his home in Cabinda, reportedly by police. Colleagues say he was harassed several weeks earlier by a regional official in Cabinda.

Bangladesh: (1)

Mohammad Quamruzzaman,
Neel Sagar
Date of Death: Feb. 19, 1996
Place of Death: Nilphamari

Quamruzzaman was a reporter for the weekly newspaper *Neel Sagar*. He was fatally shot Feb. 19 by police while covering their crackdown on a violent protest against election results in the northern town of Nilphamari.

Cambodia: (1)

Thun Bun Ly, *Odom K'tek Khmer*
Date of Death: May 18, 1996
Place of Death: Phnom Penh

Bun Ly was a writer and former editor of the opposition newspaper *Odom K'tek Khmer*, ordered closed by the government. He was appealing two convictions carrying penalties of fines or imprisonment on charges of defamation and disinformation for criticizing the government in articles and cartoons. He was fatally shot May 18 while riding a motorcycle in central Phnom Penh.

Colombia: (1)

Norvey Díaz, Radio Colina
Date of Death: Oct. 18, 1996
Place of Death: Girardot

Díaz was director and editor of "Rondando los Barrios" on Radio Colina. He was found murdered, a gunshot wound in his neck, Oct. 18 in the resort town of Girardot. He had received death threats because of his reporting on alleged police involvement in the murder of street people and on investments in local resorts by drug traffickers.

Cyprus: (1)

Kutlu Adali, *Yeni Duzen*
Date of Death: July 6, 1996
Place of Death: Lefkosa

Adali was a political columnist with the leftist newspaper *Yeni Duzen* in Turkish-occupied Northern Cyprus. He was fatally shot July 6 in front of his home. He had written critically about the Northern Cypriot government's immigration policies enabling Turkish nationals to live and work in Cyprus. a little-known group called the Turkish Revenge Brigade claimed responsibility for his assassination, but he had also received threats for a recent investigative report on an antiquities heist said to involve a Turkish general.

India: (2)

Ghulam Rasool Sheikh,
Rehnuma-e-Kashmir and *Saffron Times*
Date of Death: April 10, 1996
Place of Death: Kashmir

Sheikh was editor of the Urdu-language daily *Rehnuma-e-Kashmir* and English-language weekly *Saffron Times*. He was found dead April 10 floating in Kashmir's Jhelum River. He had written about an increase in killings and arson incidents in the area of his hometown, Pampur. Family members say he was kidnapped in March by a militia group backed by Indian state security forces. He was the sixth journalist to be murdered in Kashmir since the onset of armed conflict between separatist militants and Indian government forces in late 1990.

Parag Kumar Das, *Asomiya Pratidin*
Date of Death: May 17, 1996
Place of Death: Assam

Das was editor in chief of the largest circulation daily in Assam, *Asomiya Pratidin*. He was fatally shot May 17 in the state capital, Guwahati, as he was picking up his 7-year-old son from school. He was the leading journalistic voice for self-rule for Assam and had continued his coverage of separatist perspectives despite arrests in 1992 and 1993. A monitor of human rights, he also published a newsletter that reported on army and counter-insurgency abuses against the Assamese. His recent interview with the leader of the separatist United Liberation Front of Assam is believed by colleagues to have triggered his assassination by a splinter group.

Indonesia: (1)

Fuad Muhammad Syafruddin,
Bernas
Date of Death: Aug. 16, 1996
Place of Death: Yogyakarta

Syafruddin was a correspondent for the Yogyakarta daily *Bernas*. He was beaten into unconsciousness in his home Aug. 13 by two assailants and died Aug. 16. Colleagues believe his killing was in reprisal for reports on local land disputes.

Ireland: (1)

Veronica Guerin, *Sunday Independent*
Date of Death: June 26, 1996
Place of Death: Dublin

Guerin was a crime reporter for the *Sunday Independent*. She was shot dead June 26 by assailants on motorcycle as she was stopped in her car at a traffic light in Dublin. She had been the target of repeated physical attacks, a shooting, and death threats for her incisive, continuing investigation into Ireland's criminal underworld that had garnered CPJ's 1995 International Press Freedom Award. A known Dublin drug trafficker has been charged with her murder.

Philippines: (1)

Ferdinand Reyes, *Press Freedom*
Date of Death: Feb. 13, 1996

Reyes was editor in chief of the weekly newspaper *Press Freedom*. He was fatally shot Feb. 13 while at his desk in his office

Journalists Killed in 1996

Place of Death: Dipolog

in Dipolog, some 400 miles south of Manila. He had received death threats in the past for his frequent writings about official corruption and human rights abuses and criticism of government policies.

Russia: (6)

Felix Solovyov, Free-lancer
Date of Death: Feb. 26, 1996
Place of Death: Moscow

Solovyov was a free-lance photojournalist and a contributor to the German newspaper *Bild am Sonntag.* He was fatally shot Feb. 26 in central Moscow. Two years earlier he had published a portfolio on Moscow mafia groups in three German newspapers. He was in Germany discussing story ideas two weeks before his death. Since 1994 at least 13 journalists have been assassinated in Russia, where probes into corrupt practices in government and business have resulted in mafia-style contract killings, and reports on atrocities in the armed rebellion in Chechnya have endangered journalists' lives.

Viktor Pimenov, Vaynakh
Television
Date of Death: March 11, 1996
Place of Death: Chechnya

Pimenov was a cameraman for Vaynakh, a Chechen television station supported by Moscow-backed forces. He was fatally shot in the back March 11 by a sniper positioned on the roof of a 16-story building in Grozny. Pimenov had been filming the devastation caused by the March 6-9 raid on the Chechen capital.

Nadezhda Chaikova, *Obshchaya*
Gazeta
Date of Death: March 30, 1996
Place of Death: Chechnya

Chaikova was a correspondent for the Russian weekly *Obshchaya Gazeta* who was known for her exposés of Russian military atrocities and close contacts with the Chechen resistance. She was fatally shot, execution-style, and her body was discovered March 30 outside the Chechen village of Gehki. Chaikova was known to have filmed the destroyed village of Samashki, leveled in an attack by Russian federal troops. While Russian federal troops are suspected in her death, the killing may have been ordered by Chechen fighters acting on rumors spread by Russian secret police that she was a spy.

Nina Yefimova, *Vozrozhdeniye*
Date of Death: May 9, 1996
Place of Death: Chechnya

Yefimova was a reporter for *Vozrozhdeniye,* a local Russian-language newspaper in Grozny. She was abducted with her mother from their apartment May 8. Both were found dead from bullet wounds May 9 in different parts of the city. Yefimova had written stories about crime in Chechnya.

Viktor Mikhailov, *Zabaikalsky*
Rabochy
Date of Death: May 12, 1996
Place of Death: Chita

Mikhailov was a crime reporter for the daily *Zabaikalsky Rabochy* in southeastern Siberia. He was beaten to death in broad daylight in the city center of Chita May 12. He had been working on a series of articles about crime and the work of law enforcement agencies.

Ramzan Khadzhiev,
Russian Public TV (ORT)
Date of Death: Aug. 11,1996
Place of Death: Chechnya

Khadzhiev was chief of the Northern Caucasus bureau of Russian Public Television (ORT). He was fatally shot Aug. 11 while attempting to leave Grozny by car with his wife and young son. ORT reported that Khadzhiev, an ethnic Chechen, was targeted by Chechen rebels because of his support of the Moscow-installed government. But an unidentified passenger in their car said on NTV, Russia's only independent television station, that Russian armored vehicles had opened fire on them.

Tajikistan: (1)

Viktor Nikulin,
Russian Public TV (ORT)
Date of Death: March 28, 1996
Place of Death: Dushanbe

Nikulin was a correspondent for Russian Public Television (ORT) in Dushanbe. He was fatally shot March 28 at the door to his office. He had received three threatening telephone calls a week before he was killed. Nikulin became the 29th journalist to be killed in Tajikistan since 1992 in a systematic suppression of press freedom that carries the signature of both government loyalists and armed opposition groups.

Turkey: (1)

Metin Goktepe, *Evrensel*
Date of Death: Jan. 8, 1996
Place of Death: Istanbul

Goktepe was a columnist for the left-leaning daily *Evrensel*. He was beaten to death by police Jan. 8. He had been covering the funeral in Istanbul of two leftist inmates killed during a prison riot. His death prompted a public outcry among journalists. Eleven policemen have been charged with his murder and 37 other police with "dereliction of duty." Their trial, which began in October in Istanbul, has been delayed—some say deliberately—by repeated moves to outlying provinces "for security reasons." The trial resumed Feb. 7.

Ukraine: (1)

Igor Hrushetsky, Free-lancer
Date of Death: May 10, 1996
Place of Death: Cherkassy

Hrushetsky was a free-lance journalist. He was found dead May 10 near his home in Cherkassy, killed by a blow to the head. He was known for his reports on political corruption published in *Nezavisimost* and *Respublika* and had testified recently in a criminal case involving the son of a high-ranking police official.

Journalists Killed in 1996

Deaths by Accident: 1

Croatia: (1)

Nathaniel Nash, *The New York Times*
Date of Death: April 3, 1996
Place of Death: Dubrovnik

Nash was Frankfurt bureau chief for *The New York Times*. He was killed April 3 when a U.S. Air Force plane carrying a U.S. trade mission to the former Yugoslavia crashed into a mountain as it was attempting to land at the Dubrovnik airport. All 35 persons aboard were killed, including U.S. Commerce Secretary Ron Brown. The Air Force flight on a stormy, low-visibility night disregarded previous advice from the Air Force Air Mobility Command to U.S.-based pilots to avoid landing at Dubrovnik except in clear weather. An Air Force investigation concluded that the crash was due to "failure of command, aircrew error, and an improperly designed instrument approach procedure."

Unconfirmed Cases: 8

Bangladesh: (1)

S.M. Alauddin, *Ogrodoot*
Date of Death: June 19, 1996
Place of Death: Satkhira

Alauddin was editor of the weekly *Ogrodoot* and a former member of Parliament for the governing Awami League in Satkhira. He was fatally shot June 19 while in his office. Police attribute the murder to a political feud, but have failed to provide details.

Guatemala: (2)

Juan José Yantuche, "TV Noticias"
Date of Death: April 11, 1996
Place of Death: Mixco

Yantuche was a reporter with the cable television news program "TV Noticias." He lay in a coma for a week in a Mixco hospital with injuries inflicted by gunshots and died April 11. A week after his assassination the director of "TV Noticias," Oscar Mazaya, reported receiving anonymous death threats.

Israel Hernández Marroquín,
Infopress Centroamericano
Date of Death: Dec. 10, 1996
Place of Death: Guatemala City

Hernández Marroquín was editor of the weekly newsletter *Infopress Centroamericano*. He was fatally shot Dec. 10 and found dead on the outskirts of Guatemala City.

Nigeria: (2)

Baguda Kaltho, *TheNEWS*
Date of Death: March 1996
Place of Death: Nigeria

Kaltho was the Kaduna-based senior correspondent for *TheNEWS*. He has been missing since early March and was last seen leaving the newspaper's office alone one evening. *TheNEWS's* management and his family have been unable to ascertain his whereabouts and he is presumed dead.

Chinedu Offoaro, *The Guardian*
Date of Death: May 1996
Place of Death: Nigeria

Offoaro was a reporter for *The Guardian*. He has been missing since the third week in May. He failed to return to the newspaper's offices on May 26 from a reporting assignment in Owerri, in Imo State. His family have been unsuccessful in their attempts to locate him and fear he is dead. State Security Service officials have refused to cooperate with the family or answer questions about whether they detained Offoaro.

Philippines: (1)

Alberto Berbon, DZMM Radio
Date of Death: Dec. 15, 1996
Place of Death: Manila

Berbon was senior editor for the radio station DZMM, which is owned by the Philippines' largest broadcast network, ABS-CBN. He was fatally shot Dec. 15 outside his home in the Manila suburb in an attack that also injured his wife. He headed a local journalists association and was a prominent anti-crime activist. As of February, a prosecutor had filed charges against four suspects.

Russia: (1)

Oleg Slabynko, Russian Television Channel 2
Date of Death: Jan. 25, 1996
Place of Death: Moscow

Slabynko was producer of the news programs "Moment Istiny" ("Moment of Truth") and "Zabytyye Imena" ("Forgotten Names") on Russian Television Channel 2. He was also general manager of an advertising agency. He was fatally shot Jan. 25 in the doorway of his Moscow apartment.

Uzbekistan: (1)

Sergei Grebenyuk, Interfax
Date of Death: Feb. 8, 1996
Place of Death: Tashkent

Grebenyuk was a reporter for the independent Russian news agency Interfax. He was found dead Feb. 8 in a canal in the Uzbek capital of Tashkent, the cause of death unknown. He was last seen Jan. 27. Russian correspondents working in Tashkent have been the victims of anonymous threats, and Grebenyuk had received similar warnings and had previously been attacked.

CPJ Confirms: 474 Journalists Killed* in Past 10 Years

Between 1987 and 1996, the most dangerous countries for journalists were: Algeria, Bosnia and Herzegovina, Colombia, Croatia, the Philippines, Russia, and Tajikistan.

116 in the AMERICAS
Colombia: 41
Peru: 19
Mexico: 10
Brazil: 9
El Salvador: 10
United States: 7
Haiti: 5
Chile: 1
Guatemala: 3
Canada: 1
Honduras: 2
Venezuela: 2
Argentina: 1
Dominican Republic: 1
Ecuador: 1
Nicaragua: 1
Panama: 1
Paraguay: 1

128 in EUROPE & THE REPUBLICS OF THE FORMER SOVIET UNION
Tajikistan: 29
Croatia: 26
Bosnia and Herzegovina: 21
Russia: 29**
Soviet Union: 8**
Georgia: 3
Azerbaijan: 2
Romania: 2
Ukraine: 2
Slovenia: 2
Belgium: 1
Ireland: 1
Lithuania: 1
United Kingdom: 1

94 in the MIDDLE EAST & NORTH AFRICA
Algeria: 60
Turkey: 20
Lebanon: 6
Iraq: 5
Egypt: 2
Cyprus: 1

85 in ASIA
Philippines: 30
India: 17
Sri Lanka: 9
Afghanistan: 8
Pakistan: 8
Cambodia: 4
Indonesia: 3
Bangladesh: 1
China: 1
Japan: 1
Papua New Guinea: 1
Thailand: 1
Vietnam: 1

51 in AFRICA
Rwanda: 15
Somalia: 9
Angola: 6
South Africa: 4
Chad: 4
Ethiopia: 3
Burundi: 3
Liberia: 2
Zaire: 2
Sudan: 1
Uganda: 1
Zambia: 1

**Between 1987 and 1991, eight journalists were killed in what was then the Soviet Union: three in Azerbaijan, three in Russia, and two in Latvia.*

*All figures above reflect the number of journalists killed in the line of duty.

Facts About the Organization and Its Activities

The Committee to Protect Journalists is a nonpartisan, nonprofit organization founded in 1981 to monitor abuses against the press and promote press freedom around the world.

How did CPJ get started?
A group of U.S. foreign correspondents created CPJ in response to the often brutal treatment of their foreign colleagues by authoritarian governments and other enemies of independent journalism.

Who runs CPJ?
CPJ has a full-time staff of 14 and five part-time research and editorial staffers at its New York headquarters, including an area specialist for each major world region. The committee's activities are directed by a 31-member board of prominent U.S. journalists.

How is CPJ funded?
CPJ depends on private donations from journalists, news organizations and independent foundations. CPJ accepts no government funding.

The press is powerful; why does it need protection?
The press in the United States does have great power and enjoys legal protection. But that is not the case in most countries. Scores of journalists are imprisoned every year because of what they have reported. Hundreds more are routinely subjected to physical attack, illegal detention, spurious legal action and threats against themselves or their families. And, on average, at least one journalist is killed every week somewhere in the world. Even in the United States, journalists have been murdered—in New York; California; Florida; Virginia; Washington, D.C.; Colorado and Arizona.

How does CPJ "protect" journalists?
By publicly revealing abuses against the press and by acting on behalf of imprisoned and threatened journalists, CPJ effectively warns journalists and news organizations where attacks on press freedom are likely to occur. CPJ organizes vigorous protest at all levels—ranging from local governments to the United Nations—and, when necessary, works behind the scenes through other diplomatic channels to effect change. CPJ also publishes articles and news releases, special reports, a quarterly newsletter and the most comprehensive annual report on attacks against the press around the world.

Where does CPJ get its information?
Through its own reporting. CPJ has full-time program coordinators monitoring the press in the Americas, Asia, the Middle East, Africa and Europe. They track developments through their own independent research, fact-finding missions and firsthand contacts in the field, including reports from other journalists. CPJ shares information on breaking cases with other press freedom organizations worldwide through the International Freedom of Expression Exchange

(IFEX), a global e-mail network.

When would a journalist call upon CPJ?

• **In an emergency.** Using local contacts, CPJ can intervene whenever foreign correspondents are in trouble. CPJ is also prepared to immediately notify news organizations, government officials and human rights organizations of press freedom violations.

• **When traveling on assignment.** CPJ maintains a database of local journalist contacts around the world. CPJ also publishes practical "safety guides" that offer advice to journalists covering dangerous assignments.

• **When covering the news.** Attacks against the press are news, and they often serve as the first signal of a crackdown on all freedoms. CPJ is uniquely situated to provide journalists with information and insight into press conditions around the world.

• **When becoming a member.** A basic membership costs only $35, and each donation helps assure that CPJ will be there to defend you or a colleague if the need arises. Members receive CPJ's quarterly newsletter, *Dangerous Assignments*, and a discount on other publications.

CPJ Publications

To order any titles listed below, please call (212) 465-9344 x350. All members receive a 50-percent discount on the cost of publications. We accept Visa, MasterCard, American Express, checks, or money orders. Please make checks and money orders payable to CPJ in U.S. funds drawn on a U.S. bank or U.S. resident branch. Several of the publications can also be found on-line at CPJ's Web site (http://www.cpj.org).

Attacks on the Press   **$30**

A comprehensive annual survey of attacks against journalists and news organizations around the world.

1996 Edition, Preface by Kati Marton
1995 Edition, Preface by Roger Rosenblatt
1994 Edition, Preface by John Seigenthaler
1993 Edition, Preface by Charlayne Hunter-Gault
1992 Edition, Preface by Terry Anderson

Dangerous Assignments Quarterly $35/year

CPJ's newsletter reports on international press conditions and attacks on the press. Free to members.

Clampdown in Addis:
Ethiopia's Journalists at Risk $10

Based on a fact-finding mission to Ethiopia, this comprehensive report documents how the Ethiopian government uses provisions of a restrictive press law to limit the news the independent press may report and to silence opposing viewpoints. OCTOBER 1996

Briefing on Press Freedom in Bosnia and Herzegovina Before the September 14 Elections $10

A comprehensive review of press freedom violations in Bosnia and Herzegovina in the run-up to the Sept. 14 national elections. The report also cites all clauses in the 1995 Dayton Peace Accords that specifically seek to protect the freedom of the press. SEPTEMBER 1996

Briefing on Press Freedom in Russia Before the Presidential Elections $10

This report details the numerous murders, attacks, and other difficulties Russian journalists have endured under President Boris Yeltsin's rule; highlights potential threats to a free press; and offers background on the economic hardships of the Russian media that foster a continued dependence on the government. JUNE 1996

Double Jeopardy: Homophobic Attacks on the Press, 1990-1995 $10

A sampling of 21 cases from 14 countries, this report demonstrates that in nations as politically and culturally disparate as Canada, Russia, and Zimbabwe, censorship is imposed selectively against gay journalists and news outlets covering gay issues. OCTOBER 1995

On a Razor's Edge: Local Journalists Targeted by Warring Parties in Kashmir $10

Based on a fact-finding mission to Kashmir, this report documents how local journalists are attacked by Indian armed forces and militant separatists for their reporting on the battle for control of the Indian-held state. JULY 1995

Silenced: The Unsolved Murders of Immigrant Journalists in the United States, (1976-1993) $10

This study of journalists killed in the United States reveals that when foreign-born journalists are murdered, their cases are rarely solved. DECEMBER 1994 [sold out but available at CPJ's Web site]

Journalists' Survivial Guide:
The Former Yugoslavia $10

This essential booklet provides advice from journalists for journalists on everything from where to get flak jackets, insurance, and rental cars to tips on avoiding sniper fire in Sarajevo.

It includes a list of phone numbers for U.N. and other relief agencies in the area, as well as organizations to call when making travel plans or in case of emergency. NOVEMBER 1994 [*sold out but available at CPJ's Web site*]

Don't Force Us to Lie $20
The Struggle of Chinese Journalists in the Reform Era
A detailed study of the determined efforts of Chinese journalists to speak and write freely throughout the 1980s and early 1990s, this book is one of the most comprehensive accounts available of how journalism works in the world's most populous country. With a foreword by Dan Rather and contributions by China scholar Anne Thurston. JANUARY 1993

In the Censor's Shadow $10
Journalism in Suharto's Indonesia
A comprehensive account of media repression in Indonesia, this report includes eyewitness accounts by two American reporters of the army massacre in Dili, East Timor. NOVEMBER 1991

The Soviet Media's Year of Decision $10
Pulitzer Prize-winning journalist Hedrick Smith analyzes the press in Gorbachev's Soviet Union and events leading up to the attempted coup of August 1991. This report includes a comprehensive guide to media organizations, primarily in Russia. SEPTEMBER 1991

How to Report an Attack on the Press

CPJ needs accurate, detailed information in order to document abuses of press freedom and effectively help journalists in trouble. CPJ corroborates the information and takes appropriate action on behalf of the journalists and news organizations involved.

What to report:

Journalists who are:
- Missing
- Killed
- Arrested or kidnapped
- Wounded
- Assaulted
- Threatened
- Harassed
- Wrongfully expelled
- Wrongfully sued for libel or defamation
- Denied credentials
- Censored

News organizations that have been:
- Attacked, raided or illegally searched
- Closed by force
- Wrongfully sued for libel or defamation
- Censored
- Materials confiscated or damaged
- Editions confiscated or transmissions jammed

Information Needed:

CPJ needs accurate, detailed information about:
- Journalists and news organizations involved
- Date and circumstances of incident
- Background information

Who to call:
Anyone with information about an attack on the press should call CPJ:

Call collect if necessary.
(212) 465-1004

Or send us a fax at:
(212) 465-9568

Africa:
(212) 465-9344, x103
E-Mail: africa@cpj.org

Americas:
(212) 465-9344, x104
E-Mail: americas@cpj.org

Asia:
(212) 465-9344, x109
E-Mail: asia@cpj.org

Central Europe (including the republics of the former Soviet Union):
(212) 465-9344, x106
E-Mail: europe@cpj.org

Middle East and North Africa:
(212) 465-9344, x105
E-Mail: mideast@cpj.org

What happens next:

Depending on the case, CPJ will:
- Confirm the report.
- Pressure authorities to respond.
- Notify human rights groups and press organizations around the world, including IFEX, Article 19, Amnesty International, Reporters Sans Frontières, PEN, International Federation of Journalists and Human Rights Watch.
- Increase public awareness through the press.
- Publish advisories to warn other journalists about potential dangers.
- Send a fact-finding mission to investigate.

Ways to Participate in CPJ

•Become a Member (membership form, p. 367)
Individual Members: Whether you're a journalist, media executive, or a member of the general public, you can show your support for freedom of the press and stay informed about press conditions by becoming a member of CPJ. Gift memberships are also available. All membership levels include a subscription to CPJ's quarterly newsletter, *Dangerous Assignments*. Levels of $100 and higher also include a complimentary copy of *Attacks on the Press*.
Corporate Members ($1,000 and above): **News Organizations:** CPJ works on behalf of journalists everywhere. Your organization's membership sends a powerful message that journalists across the globe are looking out for the rights of their colleagues. Demonstrate your organization's commitment to the profession and to your colleagues' safety by joining CPJ. **Corporations:** Every private-sector institution has a stake in furthering press freedom—the free flow of information is vitally important to business in the global marketplace. Show your company's support for CPJ's critical analyses and actions by becoming a corporate member.

•Support our Membership and Fundraising Campaigns
Encourage your colleagues to become members of CPJ by distributing our membership materials at your office. Contact your public/corporate affairs office and find out if your company will match your contribution to CPJ.

In-kind donations and services can make a significant difference to CPJ. Consider donating a broad range of products and services, including research; technology; advertising; publicity; printing; graphic design; photography; video; office space; furniture; and equipment.

•Match CPJ's Challenge Grant (matching-grant form, p. 369)
The Committee to Protect Journalists has been awarded a three-year, $300,000, challenge grant from the John S. and James L. Knight Foundation to help establish the Emergency Response Fund. The Knight Foundation will match every new contribution and every increase over your last contribution on a dollar-for-dollar basis. We urge you to respond at this critical time in CPJ's history and support us now.

The creation of the Emergency Response Fund makes it possible on an around-the-clock basis for CPJ staff to respond to attacks against journalists everywhere in the world. CPJ is the only organization in the United States devoted solely to reporting and intervening whenever and wherever press freedom violations occur.

• Support the Seventh International Press Freedom Awards Dinner, Fall 1997, New York City
Individuals: Purchase Tickets and Tables for the Seventh International Press Freedom Awards Dinner, Fall 1997, New York City
The International Press Freedom Awards Dinner honors the struggle of journalists who risk their lives to report the news. The annual gala is a major media-industry gathering of journalists, publishers, and producers—a must on the New York benefit circuit. It raises more than half of CPJ's operating funds. Show your support for freedom of the press by attending the key media event of the year.
Corporations: Sponsor the Seventh Annual International Press Freedom Awards Dinner and the Awardees' U.S. Tour

News Organizations: The gala, the major annual gathering of media, publishing, entertainment, and financial companies, garners more than half of CPJ's annual operating funds. Show your company's commitment to CPJ's work by sponsoring select aspects of the International Press Freedom Awards Dinner and related program.

Corporations: Show your company's commitment to CPJ's work by becoming a corporate sponsor, not only of the gala program, but also the awardees' tour of major U.S. cities.

•Buy CPJ's Publications (Members receive a 50% discount)

Individuals: For journalists and media executives, CPJ's reports on press conditions and safety manuals for journalists are invaluable tools. Buy them for your newsroom and help defray the cost of this important service. The general public can follow emerging global developments through CPJ's reports on press conditions around the world. They are essential reading for anyone interested in freedom of expression or human rights.

Corporations: CPJ's reports on press conditions around the world shed light on emerging political developments. This information can be extremely useful for international businesses.

•Provide Information on Cases and Support CPJ's Efforts to Release Victims and Prisoners

Journalists and Media Executives: Whenever a colleague or news organization is threatened, harassed, or attacked anywhere, CPJ needs accurate and reliable information immediately. Letters and communiques from journalists in support of colleagues under attack or in prison do make a difference. (See p. 363 for telephone and e-mail information.) Stay on top of late-breaking developments by visiting CPJ's Web site at http://www.cpj.org

General Public: We need information from as many sources as possible. If you have a report about a journalist or news organization being threatened, harassed, or attacked anywhere in the world, please contact CPJ at once. (See p. 363 for telephone and e-mail information.) Access CPJ's Web site at http://www.cpj.org.

Becoming a Member of CPJ

I wish to join as an individual member:

[ ] Participant $35
[ ] Contributor $100
[ ] Supporter..............................$500
[ ] Benefactor........................$1,000 and above
[ ] Student...................................$15
   (must submit identification)

My company is subscribing to a corporate membership:

[ ] Activist $1,000
[ ] Champion $2,500
[ ] Advocate $5,000
[ ] Catalyst $10,000
[ ] Corporate Supporter........$15,000
[ ] Corporate Leader $20,000

Contingent on the level of support, CPJ offers a range of services to our corporate members. Among these are an annual by-invitation-only forum with key CPJ board members; availability of select news reports; special consultation with CPJ staff about specific areas; as well as advertising opportunities in the CPJ newsletter *Dangerous Assignments*.

Member Name Mr./Miss/Mrs./Ms. (as you wish to be listed for acknowledgement)
_____

Corporation
_____

(Please indicate preferred mailing address)   [ ] Home [ ] Business

Title
_____

Company
_____

Street
_____

City   State   Zip
_____

Home Phone   Business Phone
_____

Fax   E-Mail

PAYMENT INFORMATION

Enclosed please find my check in the amount of $_____, or charge my credit card

$_____, as tax-deductible payment for my membership in CPJ.

[ ] Visa   [ ] MasterCard   [ ] American Express   [ ] Check Enclosed

Card Number   Expiration Date
_____

Name On Card
_____

Signature

Please write checks or money orders to Committee to Protect Journalists (funds must be drawn on a U.S. bank or U.S. resident branch), or indicate charge information, and send to:

Director of Development • CPJ • 330 Seventh Avenue, 12th Floor, New York, NY 10001, USA
(212) 465-1004 • Fax: (212) 465-9568 • E-Mail: lharrop@cpj.org
For further information about joining CPJ, please contact the Development Office at the
Committee to Protect Journalists at 212-465-9344, ext. 113.

Contribution in Support of the Challenge Grant from the John S. and James L. Knight Foundation

All donors supporting CPJ's Challenge Grant at these levels will be given permanent recognition on a plaque at CPJ headquarters, and will also be listed in the annual report, *Attacks on the Press*, as well as in other CPJ literature

[ ] Sponsor..........................$100,000 and above
[ ] Leader.............................$50,000 and above
[ ] Philanthropist..................$25,000 and above
[ ] Guarantor ....$20,000 and above
[ ] Guardian.........................$10,000 and above
[ ] Grantor............................$5,000 and above
[ ] Provider ....$1,000 and above

Donor Name Mr./Miss/Mrs./Ms. (as you wish to be listed for acknowledgement)

(Please indicate preferred mailing address)   [ ] Home   [ ] Business

Corporation

Title

Company

Street

City   State   Zip

Home Phone   Business Phone

Fax   E-Mail

PAYMENT INFORMATION

My corporation will match my gift to CPJ: [ ] Yes [ ] No (Enclosed is the relevant matching gift form.)

Enclosed please find my tax-deductible contribution of $_____, or charge my gift of

$_____, in new or increased support of CPJ's challenge grant.

[ ] Visa   [ ] MasterCard   [ ] American Express   [ ] Check Enclosed

Card Number   Expiration Date

Name On Card

Signature

Please write checks or money orders to Committee to Protect Journalists, (funds must be drawn on a U.S. bank or U.S. resident branch), or indicate charge information, and send to:

Director of Development • CPJ • 330 Seventh Avenue, 12th Floor, New York, NY 10001, USA
(212) 465-1004 • Fax: (212) 465-9568 • E-Mail: lharrop@cpj.org
For further information about supporting CPJ, please contact the Development Office at the
Committee to Protect Journalists at 212-465-9344, ext. 113.

Donors

The Committee to Protect Journalists is proud to recognize the following foundations, corporations, and individuals for their major support during 1996:

Executive Leadership
$100,000 and above
The Ford Foundation
The Freedom Forum
John S. and James L. Knight Foundation

Leadership
$50,000 to $99,999
Bloomberg News
Joyce Mertz-Gilmore Foundation
Robert R. McCormick Tribune Foundation

Underwriters
$25,000 to $49,999
Tom Brokaw
CBS Inc.
Phil Donahue and Marlo Thomas
Martin Geller
Katharine Graham
The John D. and Catherine T. MacArthur
  Foundation
The Menemsha Fund
Merrill Lynch & Co., Inc.
National Broadcasting Company, Inc.
The New York Times Company
Dan Rather
The Star-Ledger
Stone & McCarthy
Time Warner Inc
Willkie Farr & Gallagher

Donors
$10,000 to $24,999
ABC News
The Abernathy-MacGregor Group, Inc.
CBS News
The Coca-Cola Company
CS First Boston
Data General Corporation
Dow Jones & Company, Inc.
Fannie Mae Foundation

Ford Motor Company
James and Toni Goodale
Harper's magazine
The Hearst Corporation
Independent Newspapers, plc
Johnson & Johnson
Lazard Frères & Co. LLC
John R. MacArthur
Kati Marton and Richard Holbrooke
Microsoft Corporation
The New Yorker
Open Society Institute
Reader's Digest
Rockefeller Family Fund
The Scherman Foundation, Inc.
Simpson Thacher & Bartlett
Triarc Companies, Inc.
Viacom Inc.
The Washington Post Company

Patrons
$5,000 to $9,999
Adtran
Franz and Marcia Allina
American Lawyer Media, L.P.
Bozell, Jacobs, Kenyon & Eckhardt
BT Wolfensohn
CBS Foundation
CNN
Maureen and Marshall Cogan
Daedalus Foundation
Debevoise & Plimpton
Dow Jones News Services
Fox News Channel
GTE Corporation
Hachette Filipacchi Magazines
Drue Heinz
J.P. Morgan & Co. Incorporated
K-III Communications Corporation
Lockheed Martin
Los Angeles Times

Newsday
Newsweek
New York magazine
The New York Times Company Foundation
NYNEX
Offitbank
Philip Morris International, Inc.
Powell Tate New York
Random House, Inc.
The Reebok Foundation
Reuters America Inc.
Gene Roberts
Starr & Company, P.C.
Mr. and Mrs. A. Robert Towbin
Weil, Gotshal & Manges LLP
Worldwide Television News

Benefactors
$1,000 to $4,999
Allen & Company, Inc.
Terry Anderson
Giorgio Alpi
Ken Auletta and Amanda Urban
Mary Billard
Boston Globe
Mr. and Mrs. James E. Burke
Chase Manhattan Bank
Children's Television Workshop
The Christian Science Monitor
Mrs. Helen K. Copley
Cox Newspapers
Cypress Group
The Dallas Morning News
The Dilenschneider Group
Daniel Doctoroff
Donaldson Lufkin & Jenrette
Christine Doudna and Richard Grand-Jean
Edelman Public Relations Worldwide
Osborn Elliott and Inger McCabe Elliott
Estée Lauder Companies Inc.
Geraldine Fabrikant
Simone and Tom Fenton
Samuel N. Friedman
Mrs. R.J. Fuller
Global Technologies
Henry A. Grunwald

Gale Hayman-Haseltine
HKH Foundation
Alberto Ibargüen
Morton and Linda Janklow
Gilbert Kaplan
Kaufmann, Feiner, Yamin, Gildin & Robbins
Junji Kitadai
Knight-Ridder, Inc.
Steve Kroft and Jennet Conant
Elizabeth Larson
Felix and Elizabeth Rohatyn
Ruth Ann Leach
Richard A. Leibner
Lexis.Nexis
Kenneth and Evelyn Lipper Foundation
Vincent Mai
David Marash
Donald B. Marron
MCA, Inc.
Cynthia McFadden
Judith and Harry Moses
Nashville Scene
Anne and Victor Navasky
Samuel I. Newhouse Foundation, Inc.
Newspaper Association of America
The Newspaper Guild
Susan and Stephen Orlins
Alan and Hannah Pakula
Park Tower Group
Peter G. Peterson and Joan Ganz Cooney
Philadelphia Inquirer
Playboy Enterprises Inc.
Public Concern Foundation
Bonnie and Richard Reiss
Colette Rhoney
Andrew A. Rooney
Howard J. Rubenstein
Lewis Rudin
SBC Warburg Inc.
Star Tribune/Cowles Media Company
John Seigenthaler
Ben Shao
Bernard Shaw
Irby C. Simpkins, Jr.
Joan and Rollin Sontag
Martha Stewart

St. Petersburg Times
Straus Newspapers, Inc.
Televisa
The Salomon Foundation
Francesca Stanfill and Peter Tufo
Univisa
USA Today
Lally Weymouth
Marion and Elie Wiesel

We also extend our deepest gratitude to the many individuals and organizations who support the Committee to Protect Journalists with gifts below $1,000, and who cannot be recognized in this list, due to space limitations.

The Committee to Protect Journalists gives special thanks to Lexis•Nexis for its ongoing in-kind donation of research services.

CPJ is most grateful to the following organizations and individuals who have given in-kind services and contributions during the past year.

ABC News
Agence France-Presse
ARTE (Germany)
Associated Press
CBS
CNN
Columbia Journalism Review
GlobalVision
IDT
Independent Newspapers, plc
Lexis•Nexis
NBC News
Noticieros Sintesis
Reuters America Inc.
"Charlie Rose"
Tamouz Media
Television Azteca, SA
Univision (Mexico)
Worldwide Television News (London)

The Committee to Protect Journalists has created the following funds in memory of three journalists whose work exemplified the highest ideals of our profession:

Chris Gehring Memorial Fund
Joel Abrams
Roger Bahre
Ellen Carl
Jim Dexter
Jon Fullerton
David Goodnow
John B. Gray
Caleb H. Hellerman
Roderick E. Jussim
Garth Kant
Kristin E. Lawson
Lenora Anne Lindsey
Jerry Mihoch
Richard D. Perera
Kristine K. Petersen
Chuck Roberts
Henry Schuster
Elizabeth L. Shannon
Marc Silverberg
Shoshona Taylor
Inci D. Ulgur
Jack Womack
Nancy Zuckerbrod

Lee Lescaze Memorial Fund
Allen J. Bernstein
Karen Blumenthal
Benjamin C. Bradlee
Marcus W. Brauchli
Barney Calame
Amy Dockser Marcus
Daniel Hinson
David Ignatius
Joseph Kahn
Peter Kann
Melanie Kirkpatrick
Glynn Mapes
Jonathan Randal
Roger U. Ricklefs
John Shattuck
Terri Shaw
Cornelius M. Ulman

James L. Yuenger Memorial Fund

Jon S. Anderson
Terry Atlas
Joan B. Bromley
Jack W. Fuller
Paul Galloway
Marianne E. Goss
Margaret C. Holt
Richard C. Longworth
John W. Madigan
Gary Marx
Robert R. McCormick Tribune Foundation
John T. McCutcheon, Jr.
Carl J. Panek
Judy Peres
Karen Rew
Thom Shanker
Liz Sly
Patricia H. Widder

Staff

EXECUTIVE DIRECTOR
William A. Orme, Jr.
(212) 465-9344 x102
orme@cpj.org

DIRECTOR OF DEVELOPMENT
Lucy Mayer Harrop
(212) 465-9344 x113
lharrop@cpj.org

DIRECTOR OF PUBLICATIONS
Alice Chasan
(212) 465-9344 x108
achasan@cpj.org

**DIRECTOR OF MEDIA
RELATIONS**
Judith Leynse
(212) 465-9344 x105
media@cpj.org

REGIONAL PROGRAMS
Africa
Kakuna Kerina
Program Coordinator
(212) 465-9344 x103
africa@cpj.org

Selam Demeke
Research Assistant
(212) 465-9344 x118
sdemeke@cpj.org

The Americas
Suzanne Bilello
Program Coordinator
(212) 465-9344 x104
americas@cpj.org

Asia
Vikram Parekh
Program Coordinator
(212) 465-9344 x109
asia@cpj.org

James Bucknell
Research Associate
(212) 465-9344 x112
jbucknell@cpj.org

**Central Europe
and the Republics
of the former Soviet Union**
Catherine A. Fitzpatrick
Program Coordinator
(212) 465-9344 x101
europe@cpj.org

**Middle East
and North Africa**
Joel Campagna
Program Coordinator
(212) 465-9344 x120
mideast@cpj.org

ADMINISTRATION
Scott Bramlett
Administrative Assistant
(212) 465-9344 x100
sbramlett@cpj.org

Fiona Dunne
Communications Coordinator
(212) 465-9344 x119
fdunne@cpj.org

Kate Houghton
*Board Liaison and Assistant to
Executive Director*
(212) 465-9344 x106
khoughton@cpj.org

Business Office
Sunsh Stein
Business Manager
(212) 465-9344 x116
sstein@cpj.org

WEB EDITOR
Julianne Slovak
(212) 465-9344 x115
jslovak@cpj.org

Index of Countries